Bucking Conservatism

B~~#~~cking Conser-vatism

ALTERNATIVE STORIES OF ALBERTA FROM THE 1960s AND 1970s

EDITED BY LEON CRANE BEAR
LARRY HANNANT
KARISSA ROBYN PATTON

◊ AU PRESS

Copyright © 2021 Leon Crane Bear, Larry Hannant, and Karissa Robyn Patton
Published by AU Press, Athabasca University
1200, 10011 – 109 Street, Edmonton, AB T5J 3S8

https://doi.org/10.15215/aupress/9781771992572.01

Cover design by Natalie Olsen, kisscutdesign.com
Interior design by Sergiy Kozakov
Printed and bound in Canada

Title: Bucking conservatism : alternative stories of Alberta from the 1960s and
    1970s / edited by Leon Crane Bear, Larry Hannant, Karissa Robyn Patton.
Other titles: B#!king conservatism
Names: Crane Bear, Leon, editor. | Hannant, Larry, 1950– editor. | Patton,
    Karissa Robyn, editor.
Description: The word "Bucking" appears with a number sign and an
    exclamation mark over the letters "u" and "c" on source of information.
Identifiers: Canadiana (print) 20210315237 | Canadiana (ebook) 20210315318 |
    ISBN 9781771992572 (softcover) | ISBN 9781771992589 (PDF) |
    ISBN 9781771992596 (EPUB)
Subjects: LCSH: Political activists—Alberta—History—20th century. |
    LCSH: Political participation—Alberta—History—20th century. |
    LCSH: Alberta—Politics and government—1935–1971. | LCSH:
    Conservatism—Alberta—History—20th century. | CSH: Alberta—Social
    conditions—1945–1991. | CSH: Alberta—History—1945–
Classification: LCC Purchase on request / Achat sur demande | LCC JL336 .B83
    2021 | DDC 322.4097123/09046—dc23

We acknowledge the financial support of the Government of Canada through the
Canada Book Fund (CBF) for our publishing activities and the assistance provided
by the Government of Alberta through the Alberta Media Fund.

Canadä   Albertan
        Government

To all the buckers out there

Contents

PART I

Indigenous Activism and Resistance

PART II

Defying Heteropatriarchy

PART III **Doing Politics in a New Way**

PART IV **Countercultural and Environmental Radicalism**

Young protestors march on 8th Avenue in Calgary, April 1971, calling for an end to the U.S. war on Vietnam. Courtesy of Calgary Herald Photographs Collection, Glenbow Archives, Calgary, NA-2864-19095.

Preface

It would be only a slight exaggeration to say that it took more than three lifetimes for this book to emerge. The collaboration among the three of us to edit a collection that seeks to reconfigure the image of Alberta could come about only because of our deep roots in the province. That long history has, in turn, been tempered by skepticism about stereotypical views of Alberta and nurtured by a committed search for alternative stories. Understandably, such a reassessment of what has been done in and said about the province would materialize only with time and experience.

We are quintessential "Other Albertans," at once in the province but not blindly of it. For his part, Leon brings to the project the history of countless generations of the original people on the land, the Niitsitapi, or "real people"—the four tribes collectively known as the Blackfoot. The Niitsitapi call the place they live *kitáwahsinnooni*, which means "our land." As a child growing up in the 1960s and 1970s in Alberta, Leon saw virtually nothing in school textbooks about the Niitsitapi or about their close relationship to *kitáwahsinnooni*. It was not until he took up post-secondary schooling that his knowledge about *kitáwahsinnooni* and its intricate connection to treaties negotiated with incoming settlers began to resonate politically. Today, he continues to advocate about the treaties to his community of Siksika and to those who want to learn about the treaties from Niitsitapi themselves.

Karissa recalls that it was, ironically, former premier Ralph Klein who sparked her political consciousness. Her mother was a teacher who, in the mid-1990s, faced the brunt of the "Klein Revolution"—a term used to describe an austerity regime that slashed government spending by well over 20 percent, left roughly one in four public servants out of work, and undercut the foundation of public services in the province. Her parents, people who normally saw eye to eye with the Progressive Conservatives, never again felt quite the same about the party. Neither did Karissa. As a maturing feminist, socialist, and environmentalist, she not only questioned where she fit into the province but also set out to learn the stories of other outliers.

Larry had the good fortune to come of age in the 1960s, when young people worldwide struggled to demolish antiquated customs, institutions, and governments. In that context, Alberta's hidebound conservatism looked like easy pickings. While that optimism has faded somewhat over the decades, his determination to pursue an unconventional path in life and work has not.

Given our backgrounds, it is no surprise that when we set out on our academic lives, we sought out contrarian approaches to the prevailing view of Alberta as a monolithic conservative bastion. In 2016, our perspectives converged during a session at the annual meeting of the Canadian Historical Association, in Calgary, where we presented papers that laid out some alternative visions. Responding to a suggestion that we bring together other examples of progressive countercurrents in an otherwise right-leaning province, we leaped at the opportunity to seek out fellow "Other Albertans." We are gratified to have found an impressive array of authors who share our enthusiasm to describe the many disparate threads in the fabric of Alberta.

Acknowledgements

Compiling such a wide-ranging collection of articles about a vibrant time in the history of Alberta has brought us into contact with an impressive group of historians, archivists, and others, without whom we could not have hoped to succeed. Our profound thanks go out to the authors of the chapters in *Bucking Conservatism*, whose stories have taken us from the province's southwestern foothills to the Peace-Athabasca Delta, in the northeast corner, and to many fascinating places in between.

We thank archivists at the Glenbow Archives, especially Doug Cass; at the University of Alberta Archives, particularly Jim Franks; at the Provincial Archives of Alberta; and Elizabeth Kundert-Cameron at the Whyte Museum of the Canadian Rockies—all gave friendly and thoughtful assistance. Daryl Betenia, Manager of Collections at Glenbow Museum, arranged permission to reproduce Marion Nicoll's *Prophet*.

Thanks to Erika Dyck and the Department of History at the University of Victoria, who have generously provided financial assistance to allow us to include essential images.

Thank you to the staff at Athabasca University Press, especially senior editor Pamela Holway, who has been singularly enthusiastic and thoughtful in helping us bring together many disparate threads into a coherent whole. We are also thankful for the thought-provoking and enthusiastic feedback provided by the anonymous reviewers of this collection.

Specifically, Larry acknowledges the involvement of Leon Crane Bear and Karissa Robyn Patton and particularly thanks the nine contributors who worked directly with him; they have shown great patience and cooperative enthusiasm. PearlAnn and Baldwin Reichwein stand out for their unvarying dedication. Kurt Moench, Jane Reid, and Leslie Miller generously provided accommodation in Calgary, as did PearlAnn Reichwein in Edmonton. They, along with Jim Hamm, have contributed helpful insights. Alvin Finkel's suggestions about ways to approach a complex issue were much appreciated. Laura Sacilotto has listened to far more than her quota of accounts of Alberta history and politics over the course of this book's life.

Leon would like to thank Karissa and Larry for the opportunity to take part in the Bucking Conservatism panel presentation at the University of Calgary in 2016, which started the ball rolling. I also wish to thank my family, Eldon and Eldene, for their continued support. Finally, thank you to my mentor and former supervisor, Carol Williams, from the University of Lethbridge, without whom I would not have made it this far in my journey.

Karissa is thankful to her co-editors and the contributors for their hard work, patience, and perseverance throughout this project. Leon, your continued friendship and collegiality got me to the end of this project. And thanks, in particular, to the contributors in graduate school or outside of academia. The community we built and the solidarity you all offered throughout this endeavour made a world of difference. Thank you to my family, friends, and amazing mentors. To my spouse, Todd, as well as my good friends Candice, Kiera, Letitia, Laura, Anastasia, Erin, and Tyrel, your encouragement has been invaluable throughout this project. Thanks to my parents, Debbie and Kevin, and siblings, Breanna and Kaitlyn, who have always supported me no matter what I have bucked over the years. I also owe a special thank you to them, along with my Auntie Sherry and my friend Michelle Helstein, who housed me in Calgary, Edmonton, and Lethbridge (respectively) during many research trips to Alberta. Moreover, I am especially grateful to the support, advice, and mentorship of Erika Dyck, Carol Williams, and Katie Labelle in this project and many others.

Introduction

Larry Hannant

For thirty-five years after its creation as a province in 1905, Alberta held pride of place among the provinces for its political innovation and radicalism. Some of the notable steps in its line dance on the political edge are well known, others unjustly overlooked. Among the former is its 1921 rejection of the pattern of two-party control of provincial politics that prevailed in many other provinces—a dramatic dismissal of convention that came with the election of the upstart United Farmers of Alberta.[1] (Only later would that leap into the arms of a third party be revealed as a descent into a pattern of one-party rule.) Also recounted frequently in Alberta's history is the fact that the socialist Co-operative Commonwealth Federation got its start in 1932 in the Depression-racked city of Calgary. Another sign of political radicalism was the left-wing muscle evident in the coal-mining communities of the Crowsnest Pass district, which, as Tom Langford and Chris Frazer show, kept a "socialist workers' movement" in control of the region for the quarter century from World War I to the end of World War II.[2] Up to the late 1930s, the province also saw abundant radical activism among farmers, women, and Indigenous peoples.[3] And an innovative aspect of Alberta's political history that is not commonly remembered is its "remarkable period of electoral experimentation" from 1926 to 1956, when it used a proportional representation system rather than the "winner takes all" first-past-the-post method of electing members to the legislature.[4]

The election of Social Credit in August 1935 was another departure from the norm, even though it, too, would descend into stolid conformity. For evidence of how potentially destabilizing it was seen to be, it is worth casting an eye back to the well-nigh universal shock at news that a pack of political neophytes with an alarmingly disruptive economic agenda had taken power. Worse still, the havoc was the work of a political outsider, whose popular appeal was based partly on a masterful use of a new social medium, inflammatory radio broadcasts, and partly on his vitriolic contempt for political and economic insiders and their lackeys, who were determined to thwart the people's bid to overturn the failed status quo. The *New York Times* was aghast when the zealots around William Aberhart ridiculed newspaper "propaganda," which was said by Social Credit to be "poisoning" the minds of Albertans.[5] The *Washington Post* scoffed that his elected supporters would face a crisis when it came time to "legislate their constituents into the Garden of Eden."[6] The *Toronto Globe* wrote about the baffling stream of "contradictions" issuing from his mouth. Another Toronto journalist dismissed the new leader as a demagogue parading as "De Lawd of Alberta Green Pastures."[7]

Although the derisive references to Aberhart would persist, the Social Credit economic experiment quickly withered in the brutal Depression heat, and the provincial government descended into business-as-usual, cost-cutting orthodoxy.[8] Aberhart's protégé and successor, the ever-so-earnest Manning, took up Aberhart's pragmatic conservatism and forged it into principle. Manning's regular denunciations of federal government initiatives such as social housing and medicare had by 1967 made him "Canada's most identifiable enemy of the political left," in Max Foran's assessment.[9] His political intransigence was made possible by his supervision of rising prosperity in the province, owing initially to wartime demand for the province's agricultural output and, after 1947, to the addition of oil revenues to existing royalties from traditional energy sources such as coal and natural gas. Already by 1951, Albertans were showing themselves fully prepared to bask in the new wealth. In that year, over 250,000 of them registered cars—double the number on the road in 1945.[10] Albertans' worship of asphalt on and below ground was just beginning. By 1967, they enjoyed a disposable income more than double the Canadian average, thanks to low personal taxation and good salaries.[11]

James H. Marsh has designated the political shift of 1971, which replaced Social Credit with Progressive Conservatives, as the launch of "Alberta's Quiet Revolution," evoking the transformation in Québec of the previous decade.[12] But confined as it was to a reconfiguration in the makeup of the legislature, and lacking the wide-ranging social upheaval that dramatically remade Québec, developments in Alberta might be better described as a

"Palace Revolution." Over the course of the next decade, writes Alvin Finkel, "there was no indication of any revival" of Social Credit.[13] Partly because of that, the Conservatives went from strength to strength, extending their rule to a forty-four-year reign. Marsh lays it out bluntly in saying that aside from the Conservatives, "there was nowhere for formal political dissent to go."[14]

That lack of formal political options, already present by the 1940s, has devolved into a stereotype of Alberta being unvaryingly conservative. This label was given an academic stamp of approval in 1953 when the University of Toronto political philosopher C. B. Macpherson published *Democracy in Alberta*, a thought-provoking, if too rigid, assessment of fifty years of the province's political life.[15] Subtitled *The Theory and Practice of a Quasi-Party System*, the book adopted a quasi-Marxist methodology that offered what appeared to be an irrefutable explanation for why the province had charted its apparently-fixed political path.[16] Macpherson argued that Alberta was politically homogeneous because it was homogenous in its class composition. Independent commodity producers—primarily farmers—were the most numerous and politically influential class. Through economically good times (from the province's founding in 1905 to 1930, then again after 1940) and bad ones (between 1930 and 1940), that class sought to avoid dramatic political extremes, preferring reformism to revolution. Even what appeared to be striking shifts from one political administration to another yielded in fact only nominal change. Once in power, the political parties conceived in that cautious womb persisted on a conservative track because their class supporters had numerical ascendancy and resisted political change.

The merit of Macpherson's argument lay in its economic explanation for Alberta's tendency to elect governments of a single party for long periods. Only in the 1970s did there begin to emerge a challenge to the notion that Alberta was a quasi-democracy because the province lacked the multi-class social spectrum that sustained political diversity. As political economists John Richards and Larry Pratt put it in their groundbreaking 1979 study, *Prairie Capitalism*, "Alberta was not a classless society, but through Macpherson's eyes it approximated a one-class society."[17] Perceiving the election of the Progressive Conservative Party in 1971 as a sign of the coming to power of a new capitalist class, Richards and Pratt's work constituted one of the early efforts to rethink the prevailing view that small-scale capitalists ruled Alberta and to identify the driving force of its conservatism as large-scale petroleum-based capitalists. Other authors would challenge the Macpherson thesis by examining Social Credit history, observing that homogeneity did not in fact prevail in the province, neither in class terms nor in voting patterns. Macpherson's single-class depiction of Alberta was demographically and politically simplistic.[18] But the undermining of Macpherson's thesis about Alberta's lack of alternative voices came too late to prevent the notion from becoming rote, both in Canada and in the province itself.

Alberta's political leanings were long the object of derision by politicians and pundits in central Canada. The verdict about the 1935 election of "the funny money boys out West" became standard.[19] In 1969, the unthinking conservativism that allegedly permeated the province provoked *Globe and Mail* columnist George Bain to sneer that "Canada has its own deep South. . . . Alberta is our approximate Mississippi. Just as the folks in the land of cotton (where dear old hatreds ain't soon forgotten), the folks in the oil-rig and moo-cow country don't put a whole lot of stock in legislatin' things. No, sir. Keep government out of it."[20]

Under such caustic criticism, Albertans began to accept and even cherish a conviction that the province was of one conservative mind. So persuasive was the notion that an early twenty-first-century history promoting the idea of Albertans being mavericks locked itself into that ramshackle corral. Ironically, the prevailing storyline in Aritha van Herk's *Mavericks: An Incorrigible History of Alberta* is conformism.[21] Her mavericks are distressingly conventional. Reading it, you would never know, for instance, that Blairmore in the 1930s taunted the Conservative government in Ottawa by renaming its main street Tim Buck Boulevard, after the jailed leader of the Communist Party of Canada. That at the same time, Métis activists in northern Alberta would join the Communist Party as part of their campaign for justice and economic security. In particular, her account of the period taken up in *Bucking Conservatism*—the 1960s and 1970s—is shocking in how completely it ignores real troublemakers. In van Herk's hands, that moment of vibrant political, cultural, environmental, Aboriginal, and youthful experimentation and rebellion is so staid it's laughable. In a chapter titled "Crazy Politicians," she trots out the tired story of the replacement of the Socreds by the Conservatives. Harry Strom and Peter Lougheed as "crazy politicians." She does offer us a fleeting reference to Indian Association of Alberta president Harold Cardinal (although mistaken for the architect Douglas Cardinal), but there's nothing of Andy Russell's environmental advocacy, no Students for a Democratic University protests, no students at all.

The "Klein Revolution" of the 1990s, which saw Premier Ralph Klein impose deep cuts in public spending and massive job losses in the public sector, lit a fire under many Albertans. Yet the resulting eruption of popular, journalistic, and academic criticism of the government tended to focus specifically on an especially reactionary, foul-mouthed, and ill-tempered premier. One of those commentators, at least, did take on the broader misconception that Alberta was a province without unconventional thinkers or actors. *Edmonton Journal* writer Linda Goyette's 1998 collection of her columns, *Second Opinion*, confronts "the myth that Alberta, unlike Canada's other provinces, is homogenous in its outlook, uniformly behind the ruling party, and intolerant of anyone who challenges the right-wing orthodoxies of the provincial government."[22] Valuable as it was in dispelling the common notions of the 1990s, however, Goyette's work did not look beyond that painful historical moment.

Early in the twenty-first century, more profound challenges to the Macpherson thesis that Alberta is marked by single-minded adherence to conservatism began to appear. In 2006, Doreen Barrie, in *The Other Alberta*, set out to dismantle some of the most persistent political truisms about the province, casting a skeptical eye on, for instance, voting patterns. As she points out, since 1905, the average percentage of the vote received by the winning political party has been 50 percent, "not exactly a stampede towards a single party."[23] However, her work focuses almost exclusively on politics, so the vibrant alternative social and cultural threads woven into the Alberta fabric are not in evidence.

Perhaps Lois Harder is the author who most closely agrees with the argument of this book that resistance in Alberta has never ceased to flicker. Her book *State of Struggle: Feminism and Politics in Alberta* affirms that "feminist efforts to secure resources and recognition for women, as well as for racial and ethnic minorities, the poor, and the disabled, demonstrate that things are not entirely what they seem. Opposition [to the conservative paradigm] did and does exist." Where her project deviates from this one is evident in the book's opening phrase: "Since the 1970s." Her work, in other words, takes up where we leave off.[24]

In addition to Harder, other historians have delved into women's undermining of conservatism in the province, and we have benefited from them. Much has been written, for example, about progressive Alberta at the beginning of the twentieth century. Mainly focusing on the Famous Five, the

United Farmers of Alberta and the United Farm Women, the Co-operative Commonwealth Federation, and labour movements, this literature provides early examples of progressive tendencies in Alberta.[25]

Curiously, it is a journalistic work that seems to come closest to appreciating the rich diversity of ideas and initiatives in the province during the period we examine. That book is volume ten of a twelve-part survey, *Alberta in the 20th Century: A Journalistic History of the Province*. The volume, titled *The Sixties Revolution and the Fall of Social Credit*, swings through the depths of Manning's reign into the election of 1971 that brought the curtain down on Social Credit. Using little-seen photographs and sprightly journalistic prose, the book ranges widely over the province's cultural, social, gender, and racial landscape. It keeps a keen eye out for acts of resistance such as the protest by Lillian Piché Shirt, who, in 1969, set up a tipi in Sir Winston Churchill Square, across from Edmonton City Hall, after she and her four children were evicted from their apartment and prevented by racial bias from finding new rental accommodation.[26] The surprise is that the book is part of a multi-volume project launched by Ted Byfield, whose *Alberta Report* (and its predecessor) was for thirty years the Bible of the cantankerous right in western Canada. Given the book's origins, it is refreshing to see that unexpected attention to protest and countercultural trends in *The Sixties Revolution and the Fall of Social Credit*. A journalistic assessment of the sixties simply could not ignore the anti-conservative upsurge in the province.

In short, grassroots opposition to conservatism in the province does and has consistently existed. What is lacking is any deep awareness of it, both among the people of Alberta and Canada and among writers and historians. Our purpose is to begin to redress that narrow reading of the province's history. We look particularly at the undercurrents of opposition that welled up in the era from the mid-1960s to the late 1970s, a period described by some historians as the Long Sixties.[27] Worldwide, it was a moment when dissident voices—which had always been present but which in the twenty years after World War II had been hushed—again began to shout, sing, and clamour. It was an era when revolutions were on the agenda in countless ways and locations, stimulated in part by the coming to adulthood of the baby-boom generation. Despite the determined repression of them, revolutions succeeded here and there, in sometimes unexpected forms. In Alberta, the men in power regarded those bids for dramatic change as something like the rats that infested the rest of the world but that had been successfully purged from

Wild Rose Country. Yet they would learn that popular upheaval could not be halted at the province's boundaries. Albertans proved themselves equal to the inspired actions of their international counterparts. Indigenous dissenters, cultural mavericks, women challenging the status quo, pioneering environmentalists, leftist students, revolutionary artists, and determined gay liberation activists—all stood up to contradict what was claimed to be a province-wide conservative homogeneity.

Although Alberta was the setting, and social attitudes or political forces specific to the province often the targets of resistance, many of the initiatives documented here are part of a much wider pattern of rebellion that can be characterized—despite its pop-cultural description as the Age of Aquarius—as the Age of Activism. Although not yet widely used, the phrase "think globally, act locally" was on the minds of more than a few of the Albertans featured here. Local irritants there were, but broader national and world causes also animated opposition, and Albertans used methods they saw applied elsewhere. Conflicts in the neighbouring United States were particularly influential within the oppositional movement in Canada. Indeed, so noticeable was the friction in the US that Canadian left nationalists such as Robin Matthews and Jim Laxer worried about what they considered to be the colonization of not just Canada in general but even the emerging New Left.[28] They thought Canadian dissidents were too ready to emulate their American counterparts. Looking beyond their southern neighbor Albertans turned their critical attention to injustice further afield, which can be seen in the 1976 arrest in Edmonton of sixty-one people opposed to Canadian collaboration with South Africa's system of racial segregation, apartheid.[29]

Study of the 1960s and 1970s is growing, leading to a spate of new books about that time in Canada. Although most tend to overlook Alberta, a few works embrace the province. Kathryn Magee and Laurie Meijer Drees have been prominent in elaborating on Indigenous activism in Alberta.[30] Articles by Beth Palmer and Erika Dyck reveal the strategic and passionate engagement of Albertan women in the fight for reproductive rights.[31] Valerie Korinek's *Prairie Fairies: A History of Queer Communities and People in Western Canada, 1930–1985* illuminates the history of gay and lesbian communities and their activism on the Prairies, including in Calgary and Edmonton.[32] Although they address different eras and areas than this work, new books have successfully inserted into the picture some intriguing historical actors and issues, all of it complicating the standard perceptions of the

Canadian West and western identity. Among them are *The West and Beyond: New Perspectives on an Imagined Past* and *Unsettled Pasts: Reconceiving the West Through Women's History.*[33]

The chapters in *Bucking Conservatism* are organized into four sections, corresponding to themes that share common features—Indigenous people, gender and sexuality, politics, and counterculture and environment. (In creating these categories we acknowledge that they do not have sealed boundaries.[34] Indeed, it is difficult to find a "single-issue activist" within this collection or in Alberta during these decades.) Opening each section is a photograph that we see as representative of the issue and time. We also provide a brief primary source, a teaser that captures the conservatism of the day. Just as it was no small task to winnow down these expressions of conservatism, it was also difficult to limit the number of accounts of "bucking conservatism." So many buckers, so little space! Indeed, we are confident that, comprehensive as this volume is, ours is just a preliminary sketch in the process of redrawing the conceptual map of this diverse province.

Several articles within this collection rethink the way activism is discussed and defined. Erin Gallagher-Cohoon's "'Ultra Activists' in a 'Very Closeted Place': The Early Years of Edmonton's Gay Alliance Toward Equality, 1972–77" and Tom Langford's "Fed Up with the Status Quo: Alberta Women's Groups Challenge Maternalist Ideology and Secure Provincial Funding for Daycare, 1964–71" query who and what are considered activists. Is activism only present at confrontations and marches? What about the on-the-ground work done to address oppressive circumstances? By broadening the definition of activism, each of these chapters reveals important moments and forms of resistance.

Other chapters in this collection bring to light activism in unsuspecting places, as seen in Baldwin Reichwein and PearlAnn Reichwein's "Drop In, Hang Out, and Crash: Outreach Programs for Transient Youth and War Resisters in Edmonton." Their discussion of humanitarian programs in Edmonton uncovers a coming together of the Garneau United Church congregation and transient "hippies" and war resisters from the US, the latter of whom were perceived to be lazy and foolish youth running away from responsibility. The chapter shows the importance of looking for activism beyond the confines of demonstrations and disruptions.

Jennifer Salahub's essay on Calgary abstract artist Marion Nicoll illuminates two important considerations about the history of activism. First, age is not a limit to activism. Indeed, during a time when the phrase "don't trust anyone over 30" was common among youthful dissidents, Nicoll was in her fifties and bucking conservatism just as energetically as young people. Second, even conservative places can spawn resistance. Salahub observes that while Calgary is often seen as a conservative stronghold within the province (especially compared with its rival sibling, Redmonton) Nicoll prevailed against both conservatism in the city and patriarchy within her workplace. Beyond the account of Nicoll, the chapters in *Bucking Conservatism* demonstrate an essential fact about resistance in Alberta: although it looked to the world beyond for inspiration, it was not carried into the province by outsiders. In that regard, Van Herk, for all her obedience to stereotype, gets one thing right about Alberta: "we grow our own dissent."[35]

To supplement a diverse array of chapters by both young and established academics that casts new light on some of the many forms that resistance took, we have reached out to non-academics with a depth of experience in dissent. Still a student in 1971, Tom Radford took his activism in defence of Indigenous peoples and their land rights into what was then a new endeavour for him—filmmaking. "Death of a Delta" documents the people and landscape he came to embrace in producing a pioneering documentary film. Louise Swift embarked on her long engagement with grassroots organizing as a young mother in the early 1960s in Edmonton and found there a community that has sustained her throughout her life. Ken Novakowski grew up in one of the cradles of dissent in the province, the left-wing Ukrainian community of central Alberta. Once in university, he moved to the forefront of leftist student provincial politics, then graduated to become a long-time teacher and labour union leader in British Columbia. The loss to Alberta's left wing was BC's gain.

What did it mean to buck conservatism in a province known for the deep blue hue of both its sky and its politics? Bucking begins with rejection but takes the matter further. To buck is to resist, to shake off, to kick. As seen in these cases, bucking conservatism means both refusing to conform to and actively challenging the prevailing political, social, and cultural order. This does not mean that Alberta in the 1960s and 1970s saw mass uprisings like what shook elites and their governments in Paris, Prague, Mexico City, and Chicago in 1968. The most surprising shock to Alberta's status quo was the replacement in 1971 of one conservative government with a pro-business agenda by another with a slightly different pro-business agenda. What is indisputable about Alberta is that its electoral history—although nowhere nearly so homogenous as suggested by its string of nine consecutive Social Credit Party governments followed by twelve consecutive Progressive Conservative governments—is a story of uniformity. This volume takes no issue with that.

Little surprise, then, that with one exception, these chapters do not venture into the study of Albertans trying to effect change within formal politics.[36] Given the narrow range of political possibility in the province, activists at the time mostly avoided wasting energy on trying to effect change in that way. In any case, scorn for what was often called "big-people's politics" was commonplace among the New Left, which concentrated instead on extra-parliamentary political, social, and cultural initiatives. Even the one outlier in this collection, Novakowski's recollection of organizing the New Democratic Youth in Edmonton, includes elements of New Left–style activism such as the campaign to end the US war on Vietnam. So, almost without exception the stories in this collection are initiatives beyond the realm of formal politics. Their focus instead is social, cultural, environmental, and oppositional politics.

Yet, marginal as they might appear to be, these acts of resistance were not insignificant. For example, in unsanctioned demonstrations in the heart of the city in 1968 and 1970, students at the University of Calgary reasserted a right to public assembly in the streets that had not just been neglected for more than two decades but that Alberta Supreme Court Chief Justice J. V. H. Milvain told Albertans they had a *duty* to avoid.[37] Acts of defiance also included First Nations communities in the area of Saddle Lake occupying Blue Quills residential school; gay activists taking their challenge to Anita Bryant's anti-gay vitriol right inside an arena full of her devotees; and women and children facing down a Caterpillar D8 bulldozer at the Mill Creek Ravine in Edmonton. These initiatives often passed with little attention at the time, and they have largely been overlooked by historians since. Yet they constitute indelible threads in a web of determination to make change that would improve life for those folk and others like them.

Bucking Conservatism features people who insisted on both conceiving and realizing alternatives to the status quo. They are the human equivalent of the Okotoks Erratic on an Alberta field. Given the uniform political landscape of the province, these outcroppings of resistance were monuments to the considerable courage of the nonconformists. In the absence of a sizable community of fellow rebels, challenging conventions demanded real pluck. In their *joie de guerre*, many of the mavericks featured here acted consistently with the memorable words of US journalist I. F. Stone, who advised that country's subversives not to take on the air of martyrs but to fight "for the sheer fun and joy of it," even knowing that they would lose.[38] Probably without ever having heard of Stone, Métis trapper Frank Ladouceur—spinning tall tales on his boat on Lake Mamawi, which, as Radford explains in his chapter, was even then rapidly draining away because of a megaproject 700 kilometres distant—exhibited that indomitable spirit.

Did the cases of bucking conservatism we highlight here fundamentally refashion the conservative wardrobe of Alberta? Despite the best efforts of the stalwarts at the heart of this book, Alberta did not in fact see a profound change in the 1960s. Nor in the 1970s. Come to think of it, not in the 1980s, 1990s, or 2000s, either. In any case, expecting that a few dozen activists in the 1960s and 1970s would revolutionize the province is farfetched. Neither they nor the editors of this volume can change Alberta's past. We acknowledge that conservatism dominated Alberta through even this tumultuous moment, holding sway from the high-rise executive suites to the province's farms and grasslands. But the province was also home to defiant radicals, rabble-rousers, and heretics who dared to assert a contrary trend. Like many activists worldwide at that time, the Albertans who bucked conservatism understood that they were not the majority. But neither were they intimidated by the majority, and they courageously insisted that their experience be recognized as an integral part of the Alberta story. *Bucking Conservatism* salutes these nonconformists and, for the first time in a single volume, gives their voices an opportunity to be heard. More than just amplifying the shouts of these progressive Albertans, it presents them as historically relevant actors. By weaving a brilliant thread through Alberta's fabric, they have stitched themselves indelibly into the warp and woof of the province's history.

Larry Hannant

NOTES

1. The classic account of the farmers' movement's involvement in politics is W. K. Rolph, *Henry Wise Wood of Alberta* (Toronto: University of Toronto Press, 1950). The fact that Wood, a moderate progressive, was of American

origin illustrates that American influence in Alberta has not in fact been uniformly conservative. The radical influence of "Ambertans"—both right-wing and left-wing radicals—marked the province for a century. While right wing in the 1950s, the province shifted politically in the 1960s and early 1970s toward the left, in part because of the arrival of an untold number of US draft dodgers and deserters fleeing war, racism, and state repression. More recent works on the United Farmers of Alberta in government bring out some of its lesser-known innovations, including the appointment of Irene Parlby to cabinet, just the second case of a woman in cabinet in the British Empire. Parlby was responsible for groundbreaking, although controversial, legislation in 1923 establishing that fathers of children considered illegitimate should pay child support. See Bradford J. Rennie, "From Idealism to Pragmatism: 1923 in Alberta," in *Alberta Formed, Alberta Transformed,* ed. Michael Payne, Donald Wetherell, and Catherine Cavanaugh (Edmonton: University of Alberta Press; Calgary: University of Calgary Press, 2006), 448–49.

2. Tom Langford and Chris Frazer, "The Cold War and Working-Class Politics in the Coal Mining Communities of the Crowsnest Pass, 1945–1958," *Labour/Le Travail* 49 (Spring 2002): 43.

3. The histories of Alberta's early radicalism are too numerous to document here, but perhaps the least known is that of the Métis organizing efforts led by the leftist mixed-bloods Jim Brady and Malcolm Norris, which is set out in Murray Dobbin, *The One-and-a-Half Men: The Story of Jim Brady and Malcolm Norris, Métis Patriots of the Twentieth Century* (Vancouver: New Star, 1981). A self-published memoir by former Communist Party activist Ben Swankey includes an engaging account of the intense upsurge of farmer-worker resistance in the early 1930s, which culminated in the 12,000-strong Edmonton Hunger March in 1932. Swankey, *What's New: Memoirs of a Socialist Idealist* (Victoria, BC: Trafford Publishing, 2008).

4. Harold John Jansen, "The Single Transferable Vote in Alberta and Manitoba" (PhD diss., University of Alberta, 1998), 237, https://www.collectionscanada.gc.ca/obj/s4/f2/dsk2/tape15/PQDD_0004/NQ29051.pdf. Social Credit dismantled the system after the 1955 election, which saw its fifty-two seats in the legislature (out of a total of sixty-one) reduced to thirty-seven. As Jansen points out, "Social Credit was quite clearly trying to enhance its electoral chances through changing the electoral system" (235; see also 224–25).

5. John MacCormack, "Social Credit Prophet Will Rule a Province," *New York Times*, 1 September 1935, E12.

6. Osgood Nichols, "Alberta Citizens Seek Gold Bounty in Empty Treasury," *Washington Post*, 2 February 1936, B9.

7. Harold Dingman, "Alberta Government Depends on Aberhart," *Toronto Globe*, 25 July 1936, 1; William Marchington, "Canada Follows Path of Peace," *Globe and Mail*, 9 January 1937, 9.

8. Alvin Finkel, "1935: The Social Credit Revolution," in Payne, Wetherell, and Cavanaugh, *Alberta Formed, Alberta Transformed*, 507.

9. Max Foran, "1967: Embracing the Future . . . at Arm's Length," in Payne, Wetherell, and Cavanaugh, *Alberta Formed, Alberta Transformed*, 622.

10. Doug Owram, "1951: Oil's Magic Wand," in Payne, Wetherell, and Cavanaugh, *Alberta Formed, Alberta Transformed*, 575.

11. Foran, "1967," 634.

12. James H. Marsh, "Alberta's Quiet Revolution: 1973 and the Early Lougheed Years," in Payne, Wetherell, and Cavanaugh, *Alberta Formed, Alberta Transformed*, 643.

13. Alvin Finkel, *The Social Credit Phenomenon in Alberta* (Toronto: University of Toronto Press, 1989), 198.

14. Marsh, "Alberta's Quiet Revolution," 666.

15. C. B. Macpherson, *Democracy in Alberta: The Theory and Practice of a Quasi-Party System* (Toronto: University of Toronto Press, 1953).

16. Ian McKay has pointed out that although Macpherson was regarded as having been influenced by Marxism, he "was clear about who he was and what he was about, i.e., a humanist radical liberal democrat." McKay, "Challenging the Common Sense of Neoliberalism: Gramsci, Macpherson, and the Next Left," *Socialist Register* 54 (2018): 10. I thank Mack Penner for alerting me to McKay's reassessment.

17. John Richards and Larry Pratt, *Prairie Capitalism: Power and Influence in the New West* (Toronto: McClelland and Stewart, 1979), 148–50. It is significant that the 1970s saw an intellectual challenge to the notion of Alberta as a one-class province, since by that decade a full-spectrum class configuration had clearly emerged. Agriculture was declining in importance economically, and the small farmer was disappearing. Meanwhile, the burgeoning oil industry that had thrived for twenty-five years had helped to generate a large working class, with industrial workers having some considerable presence.

18. Larry Hannant, "The Calgary Working Class and the Social Credit Movement in Alberta, 1932–1935," *Labour/Le Travail* 16 (Fall 1985): 97–116; Edward Bell, "Class Voting in the First Alberta Social Credit Election," *Canadian Journal of Political Science* 23, no. 3 (1990): 519–30; Edward Bell, "The Rise of the Lougheed Conservatives and the Demise of Social Credit in Alberta: A Reconsideration," *Canadian Journal of Political Science* 26, no. 3 (1993): 455–75.

19. William Stevenson, "The Roots of Social Credit—1: Prosperity and One Party Rule for Alberta," *Globe and Mail*, 30 April 1962, 7.

20. George Bain, "Canada's Deep West," *Globe and Mail*, 7 February 1969, 6.

21. Aritha van Herk, *Mavericks: An Incorrigible History of Alberta* (Toronto: Viking, 2001).

22. Linda Goyette, *Second Opinion: The Best of Linda Goyette* (Edmonton: Rowan Books, 1998), vii.

23. Doreen Barrie, *The Other Alberta: Decoding a Political Enigma* (Regina: Canadian Plains Research Center, 2006), 57.

24. Lois Harder, *State of Struggle: Feminism and Politics in Alberta* (Edmonton: University of Alberta Press, 2003), x, 1.

25. To name a few examples: Bradford James Rennie, *The Rise of Agrarian Democracy: The United Farmers and Farm Women of Alberta, 1909–1921* (Toronto: University of Toronto Press, 2000); William C. Pratt, "Politics in Alberta and Saskatchewan in the 1930s," *Journal of the West* 41, no. 4 (2002): 51–56; Alvin Finkel, "Populism and Gender: The UFA and Social Credit Experiences," *Journal of Canadian Studies* 27, no. 4 (1992/93): 76–98; Carl Betke, "The UFA: Visions of a Cooperative Commonwealth," *Alberta History* 27, no. 3 (1979): 7–14; Veronica Strong-Boag, "Canadian Feminism in the 1920s: The Case of Nellie L. McClung," *Journal of Canadian Studies* 12, no. 4 (1977): 58–68; Robert J. Sharpe and Patrician I. McMahon, *The Persons Case: The Origins and Legacy of the Fight for Legal Personhood* (Toronto: University of Toronto Press, 2007); Vivien Hughes, "Women in Public Life: The Canadian Persons Case of 1929," *British Journal of Canadian Studies* 19, no. 2 (2006): 257–70; Anne White, "The Persons Case: A Struggle for Legal Definition and Personhood," *Alberta History* 47, no. 3 (1999): 2–9; Alvin Finkel, *Working People in Alberta: A History* (Edmonton: Athabasca University Press, 2011); C. A. Cavanaugh and R. R. Warne, eds., *Standing on New Ground: Women in Alberta* (Edmonton: University of Alberta Press, 1993).

26. Colby Cosh, "The First Shots Are Fired in the Modern Indian Wars," in *Alberta in the 20th Century: A Journalistic History of the Province*, ed. Ted Byfield, vol. 10, *The Sixties Revolution and the Fall of Social Credit, ed. Paul Bunner* (Edmonton: United Western Communications, 2002), 122.

27. Exactly what period constitutes the Long Sixties varies according to author. Arthur Marwick, who has devoted considerable attention to the history of the second half of the twentieth century, describes it as spanning the years from about 1958 to about 1974. Marwick, *The Sixties: Cultural Revolution in Britain, France, Italy, and the United States, c. 1958–c. 1974* (New York: Oxford University Press, 1998). Activist, politician, and writer Tom Hayden

includes the decades from 1960 to the presidency of Barack Obama, who was first elected in 2008. Hayden, *The Long Sixties: From 1960 to Barack Obama* (Boulder, CO: Paradigm, 2009).

28. David S. Churchill, "Draft Resisters, Left Nationalism, and the Politics of Anti-Imperialism," *Canadian Historical Review* 93, no. 2 (2012): 238–41, 256–57.

29. See Hannant, "Solidarity on the Cricket Pitch: Confronting South African Apartheid in Edmonton," in this volume.

30. Kathryn Magee, "'For Home and Country': Education, Activism, and Agency in Alberta Native Homemakers' Clubs, 1942–1970," *Native Studies Review* 18, no. 2 (2009): 27–49; Laurie Meijer Drees, *The Indian Association of Alberta: A History of Political Action* (Vancouver: University of British Columbia Press, 2002).

31. Beth Palmer, "'Lonely, tragic, but legally necessary pilgrimages': Transnational Abortion Travel in the 1970s," *Canadian Historical Review* 92, no. 4 (2011): 637–64; Erika Dyck, "Sterilization and Birth Control in the Shadow of Eugenics: Married, Middle-Class Women in Alberta, 1930s–1960s," *Canadian Bulletin for Medical History* 31, no. 1 (2014): 165–88. I thank Karissa Robyn Patton for alerting me to these sources and others focused on women's history, and for placing them historiographically.

32. Valerie Korinek, *Prairie Fairies: A History of Queer Communities and People in Western Canada, 1930–1985* (Toronto: University of Toronto Press, 2018).

33. Alvin Finkel, Sarah Carter, and Peter Fortna, eds., *The West and Beyond: New Perspectives on an Imagined Past* (Edmonton: Athabasca University Press, 2010); Sarah Carter, Lesley Erickson, Patricia Roome, and Char Smith, eds., *Unsettled Pasts: Reconceiving the West Through Women's History* (Calgary: University of Calgary Press, 2005).

34. The idea that activist identities ebbed and flowed around several issues is pointed out by Shannon Stettner in "'We Are Forced to Declare War': Linkages Between the 1970 Abortion Caravan and Women's Anti-Vietnam War Activism," *Social History/Histoire Sociale* 46, no. 92 (2013): 423–41.

35. Van Herk, *Mavericks*, 260.

36. The number of histories of provincial politics in the 1960s and 1970s alone is impressive, and it would be impossible to refer to them all here. But most of them address the transformation of 1971, documenting on the one hand the end of the Social Credit era and, on the other, the emergence of the Progressive Conservatives. Included in the former group are accounts such as A. J. Hooke, *30+5: I Know, I Was There* (Edmonton: Institute of Applied Art, 1971) and John Barr, *The Dynasty: The Rise and Fall of Social Credit in Alberta* (Toronto: McClelland and Stewart, 1974), each informed by personal

experience, although taking different perspectives stemming from being written by distinct generations of Social Credit insiders. Finkel's *The Social Credit Phenomenon in Alberta* is far and away the most comprehensive and enduring chronicle of the fifty-year life of the party. Among the histories of Peter Lougheed's personal bid to resurrect a business-friendly conservative alternative to Social Credit, perhaps the best is Alan Hustak, *Peter Lougheed* (Toronto: McClelland and Stewart, 1979). A new arrival on the scene from the perspective of the Liberal Party, which rode Pierre Trudeau's coattails to limited success, is Darryl Raymaker, *Trudeau's Tango: Alberta Meets Pierre Elliott Trudeau, 1968–1972* (Edmonton: University of Alberta Press, 2017).

37. See "The Real Threat to Order," *Globe and Mail*, 10 April 1969, 6.

38. I. F. Stone, AZQuotes.com, https://www.azquotes.com/quote/373884.

PART I

Indigenous Activism and Resistance

Calgary Urban Treaty Indian Alliance members occupy the Calgary office of the Department of Indian Affairs, 20 August 1974, demanding assistance for a self-help agency in the city. Courtesy of Calgary Herald Photograph Collection, Glenbow Archives, Calgary, NA-2864-25985-15

"His station did not run any FOREIGN language broadcasts"

A group of chiefs, meeting in the city, was addressed by a provincial government official. [...]

[One chief] explained the difficulty encountered in attempting to communicate with the white man.

He said he and another Indian approached the operators of a radio station in the province with the view of having a 15-minute radio program in CREE broadcast every week.

The radio station official, he said, was very kind but explained that his station did not run any FOREIGN language broadcasts.

Later they went back, explained the proposition to a HIGHER official of the station. Now the Cree program is on the air.

"Frank Hutton's Notebook," *Edmonton Journal*, 12 January 1967, p. 3

Introduction

On 30 May 1969, Lillian Piché—a member of the Saddle Lake Cree Nation—set up a tipi in downtown Edmonton, directly across from City Hall, to protest the lack of available housing for Indigenous people in the city. Some two months earlier, Piché had been evicted from her apartment, along with her four young children, when its ownership changed hands, and she had been unable to find another place to live. Landlords simply would not rent to her.[1] Her protest, which was covered in the national news, shed a clear light on the discrimination that Indigenous people face on a day-to-day basis, particularly in urban areas. Her action also provoked a promise from the provincial government to develop plans for welfare housing.[2] But Piché was concerned about more than just housing. As she explained, she was also protesting about the child welfare system and about the fact that Indigenous children were forced to attend public schools in which they were taught nothing about their own history.[3]

Lillian Piché was not alone in her outrage. The 1960s and 1970s witnessed a groundswell of activism among Indigenous groups throughout Canada. Locally and nationally, Indigenous people rose up against the injustices they continued to suffer at the hands of the state and demanded sovereignty over their affairs, including the right to self-government, control over land and resources, educational autonomy, and respect for their cultural and spiritual traditions. As the following chapters attest, and as many people may not realize, Indigenous activists in Alberta stood at the forefront of this struggle.

The injustices that provoked this activism have a long history, of course, but they are not injustices of the past, as Canadians are often encouraged to believe. They were very much alive in the 1960s and 1970s, and they continue down to the present day. In one way or another, the chapters that follow bear on an issue that has yet to be resolved: the relationship of Indigenous peoples to the nation-state of Canada. At least since 1830, when officials of the British Indian Department embarked on a policy of "civilization," Canada has steadfastly sought to "get rid of the Indian problem," as Duncan Campbell Scott so famously put it. The state's preferred solution has been the eventual assimilation of Indigenous peoples into the dominant society—to pursue its goal "until there is not a single Indian in Canada that has not been absorbed into the body politic."[4] This overarching objective has, over the years, given rise to policies designed to promote enfranchisement, to laws curtailing the rights of Indigenous peoples to practice their cultures, to residential schooling and subsequent educational policy, to a child welfare system designed to separate Indigenous children from their families, and, in 1969, to the Canadian government's White Paper on Indian policy, the release of which coincidentally overlapped with Piché's protest.

As the ultimate fate of the White Paper illustrates, Indigenous people have long resisted these tactics of assimilation and have repeatedly asserted their right to self-determination. For many First Nations, including those in Alberta, the struggle for sovereignty is inextricably bound up with treaties. Together, three of the eleven numbered treaties comprise most of the territory that is today Alberta: Treaty 6 (negotiated in 1876) extends across the central portion of the province, Treaty 7 (1877) spans southern Alberta, and Treaty 8 (1899) covers the northern half of the province. These agreements remain centrally important to treaty Indians, but their interpretation is a matter of contention. The federal government regards the written text of these documents as authoritative. The assumptions are that these versions represent an accurate transcription of what was agreed upon during negotiations, that the meaning of the words is perfectly clear, and that both parties must therefore have understood these words in precisely the same way. In contrast, in interpreting the meaning and intent of the treaties, Indigenous knowledge holders rely on oral histories of the negotiations, from which it is clear that the government's assumptions are unwarranted.[5]

In these treaties, the federal government made certain promises, which it has persistently shown itself reluctant to honour.[6] In the understanding of First Nations, a treaty is an inviolable trust, one that confers continuing obligations on both parties, and the government's failure to respect the spirit on which treaties are founded has long provoked frustration and a sense of betrayal. Another major thorn in the side of First Nations has been the

Indian Act. First passed in 1876, the act is still in existence, although it has undergone numerous amendments. Although in recent decades a number of its more blatantly discriminatory provisions have been repealed, over the course of its history amendments to the act have (like the act itself) served to restrict the rights of individual Indians, to curtail the power of band councils, to limit the number of those legally recognized as Indians, to mandate enfranchisement under certain circumstances, to appropriate additional land and resources from reserves, and to tighten the control of the state over decisions affecting the lives of First Nations.[7]

By way of an example, in 1920, an amendment to the Indian Act made it easier for the government to enfranchise, on its own initiative, Indians it found "fit" to become British citizens. Once enfranchised, Indians were required to relinquish their Indian status and hence their rights under treaty.[8] The same amendment made it compulsory for Indian children aged seven to fifteen to attend school. Although the amendment did not specify a particular kind of school, very often a residential school was the only one available, given that the government had gradually withdrawn financial support for on-reserve day schools.[9] When the Indian Act was revised seven years later, in 1927, it became illegal for anyone to accept payments from Indians in return for helping them pursue legal claims or raise money to do so—a provision that effectively barred Indians from hiring a lawyer.[10] But this is but a tiny sample of a list that seems endless.

Like government arrogance, Indigenous political action is nothing new. It dates back at least to the time of the Red River Resistance, in 1869–70, when the Métis fought against Ottawa's plans to annex the territory in which they lived. First Nations engaged in localized political agitation as well, sending petitions and/or representatives to Ottawa, usually in response to violations of treaty rights or government efforts to encroach on reserve lands. The first effort to form a nationwide organization came in 1919, with the founding of the League of Indians. Although it ultimately failed to coalesce at the national level, it had an active presence in both Alberta and Saskatchewan in the form of the League of Indians of Western Canada.[11] During the 1920s and into the 1930s, the league fought for improvements to education and living conditions, as well as for the protection of reserve lands and in defence of treaty rights. The 1930s also saw the founding of the Metis Association of Alberta. Under the leadership of Joe Dion, Malcolm Norris, and Jim Brady, L'association des Métis d'Alberta et des Territoires du Nord Ouest (as it was then known) advocated on behalf of the desperately impoverished Métis community, pressing for better education and health care and for the Métis right to self-determination—efforts that culminated in the Metis Betterment Act of 1938 and the subsequent establishment of Métis colonies.

Malcolm Norris was acquainted with John Callihoo, who lived on the Michel reserve, in the Edmonton area. A descendant of nineteenth-century Iroquois voyageurs from Québec, in 1937 Callihoo became president of the Alberta branch of the League of Indians and was also a strong supporter of Métis activism.[12] In 1939, the two jointly founded the Indian Association of Alberta (IAA), an organization that went on to become politically influential. The immediate purpose of the IAA paralleled that of the Metis Association of Alberta: to advocate for improvements to the living conditions afflicting the many impoverished First Nations communities in Alberta. But social and economic uplift was not the IAA's only objective. As historian Laurie Meijer Drees points out, the organization "was concerned, on an everyday level, with treaty rights."[13] Firmly rooted in day-to-day life on local reserves, the IAA understood the practical implications of unfulfilled treaty promises and of the government's refusal to allow Indian bands to manage their own affairs. By 1944, the association was already advocating with Indian Affairs officials in Ottawa on behalf of treaty Indians in Alberta.

Two and a half decades later, the IAA's strong emphasis on treaty rights would resurface in a new context, in which its views would prove decisive. In June 1969, the government of Pierre Elliott Trudeau released a document titled *Statement of the Government of Canada on Indian Policy, 1969,* better known as the White Paper. The White Paper proposed to eliminate Indian status altogether, thus bringing a swift end to Canada's treaty relationship with status Indians. The proposal provoked outrage among First Nations, who were prepared to do battle with the federal government. In 1970, the IAA issued a response to the White Paper, under the title *Citizens Plus,* in which it outlined a counterproposal. Central to the Red Paper, as it came to be called, was the forceful assertion of treaty rights and a demand for their full implementation. In chapter 1, "Indian Status as the Foundation of Justice," I examine the strategy used by Harold Cardinal and the IAA to resist the imposition of liberal democratic values, which, in the White Paper, became a political tool used to undermine the special status accorded to Indians—to "get rid of the Indian problem" by legislating Indians out of existence. The Red Paper had a galvanizing impact of First

Nations communities throughout Canada, encouraging them to insist on the right to control their destiny and to engage in organized political action in order to effect change,

The White Paper was not the only cause of the upsurge of activism that began in the 1960s—nor, of course, was it the sole manifestation of the government's aggressive pursuit of assimilation. As is now widely recognized, the destruction of Indigenous cultures was the principal objective of the residential school system, which saw its formal inception in the 1880s and was in place for roughly a century, with the last of the residential schools closing only in 1996. By the early 1940s, however, the Department of Indian Affairs had come to question the effectiveness of residential schooling and began instead to favour a new policy of "integration."[14] This meant educating Indigenous children together with non-Indigenous children in provincial public schools and, correspondingly, the eventual elimination of separate residential schooling. Despite the shift in rhetoric, however, the goal remained the assimilation of Indigenous children into the dominant culture. Moreover, as John Milloy observes with regard to the gradual abandonment of the residential school system, "The pattern of neglect and abuse rooted in the very bones of the system and the dynamics that animated it, as well as the dearth of financial and moral resources, did not change."[15]

One of the many residential schools was Blue Quills, located near St. Paul, Alberta, not far from the Saddle Lake reserve. In the fall of 1969, the local community learned of the government's plan to close the school, at which point its former students would be expected to attend classes in St. Paul. Although there had been complaints about the school, neither parents nor the district school committee found the alternative acceptable, and so the community decided to take action. In "Setting a Precedent: The Power of Public Protest at Blue Quills Residential School," Tarisa Dawn Little chronicles the events that culminated in the 1970 occupation of Blue Quills by local First Nations activists and their allies, who demanded that Indigenous peoples be given sovereignty over their own education. As a result of this mobilization, Blue Quills was transformed into the first community-controlled Indigenous school in the country. Today, University nuhelot'įne thaiyots'į nistameyimâkanak Blue Quills offers instruction to both Indigenous and non-Indigenous students that is grounded in traditional values and pedagogical principles rooted in Indigenous ways of being and knowing.

In "We are on the outside looking in . . . But we are still Indians," Corinne George highlights the groundbreaking work of the women who created the Voice of Alberta Native Women's Society and Indian Rights for Indian Women, a national organization with roots in Alberta. In the face of blatantly sexist clauses in the Indian Act, these women fought for their right to retain their Indian status and band membership regardless of whom they married.

As George's chapter suggests, much of the activism in the province focused on building strong alliances and supportive communities. For Indigenous people in the 1960s and 1970s, "conservatism" was less a position on the political spectrum than a set of social attitudes shared by a great many Canadians, including some who, like Pierre Trudeau, subscribed to liberal values. This form of conservatism survives despite changes in government: it cannot be uprooted merely by an election. Although social attitudes today seem softer, the issues to which Indigenous activists were responding half a century ago suggest that much remains for the future.

Leon Crane Bear

NOTES

1. Lillian Shirt, Corinne George, and Sarah Carter, "Lillian Piché Shirt, John Lennon and a Cree Grandmother's Inspiration for the Song 'Imagine,'" *Active History*, 5 December 2016, http://activehistory.ca/2016/12/lillian-piche-shirt-john-lennon-and-a-cree-grandmothers-inspiration-for-the-song-imagine/, para. 1.

2. Ibid., para. 10. See also Corinne George, "'If I Didn't Do Something, My Spirit Would Die . . .': Grassroots Activism of Aboriginal Women in Calgary and Edmonton, 1951–1985" (MA thesis, Department of History, University of Calgary, 2007), 76. As George points out, despite government assurances, little actually changed for Indigenous people. In 1976, Métis activist Muriel Stanley Venne—one of the driving forces behind the creation of Edmonton's Native Outreach Program, who would go on to found the Institute for the Advancement of Aboriginal Women—met with city officials to register her concern over ongoing housing discrimination, "explaining that Aboriginal people were obliged to live in slum-like conditions because many were unable to secure adequate housing elsewhere" (80).

3. Shirt, George, and Carter, George, Lillian Piché Shirt, para. 2. See also George, "'If I Didn't Do Something,'" 74–75.

4. Duncan Campbell Scott, the deputy superintendent general of the Department of Indian Affairs from 1913 to 1932, was commenting on a bill to amend the Indian Act, including its provisions regarding education and enfranchisement. "I want to get rid of the Indian problem," he said in 1920, addressing the special committee of the House of Commons convened to consider the bill. He went on to say: "Our objective is to continue until there is not a single Indian in Canada that has not been absorbed into the body politic and there is no Indian question, and no Indian Department." Library and Archives Canada, RG 10, vol. 6810, file 470-2-3, vol. 7, pp. 55 (L-3) and 63 (N-3). For an accurate description of the context, see John Leslie, *The Historical Development of the Indian Act* [Ottawa: Treaties and Historical Research Centre, P.R.E Group, Indian and Northern Affairs, 1978], http://publications.gc.ca/collections/collection_2017/aanc-inac/R32-313-1978-eng.pdf, 114. As John Leslie points out, Scott was of the opinion that "more Indians would become citizens under Canadian law if they were offered guidance through schooling and a more direct means of becoming enfranchised." Scott's comment is usually linked to residential schools but rarely to enfranchisement.

5. During the 1970s, researchers with the Indian Association of Alberta's Treaty and Aboriginal Rights Research (TARR) program conducted interviews with Elders throughout the province in order to collect oral histories relating to the three Alberta treaties and to determine how these treaties have been interpreted by local Indigenous communities. For the results of this research, see Richard T. Price, ed., *The Spirit of the Alberta Indian Treaties* (Edmonton: Pica Pica Press, 1987). See also Treaty 7 Elders and Tribal Council with Walter Hildebrandt, Sarah Carter, and Dorothy First Rider, *The True Spirit and Original Intent of Treaty 7* (Montréal and Kingston: McGill-Queen's University Press, 1997), which provides a First Nations perspective on Treaty 7, including a detailed account of the events surrounding the negotiations. Treaty 7 Elders argue, for example, that the treaty envisaged a "sharing of the land," not a land surrender. One cannot "cede, release, surrender and yield up" something that one does not possess, and the land is not a possession.

6. On the government's almost immediate reluctance to make good on its promises, see Truth and Reconciliation Commission of Canada (hereafter TRC), *Canada's Residential Schools*, vol. 1, pt. 1, *The History: Origins to 1939* (Montréal and Kingston: McGill-Queen's University Press, 2015), 122–24. The government's preference for a very literal reading of the treaties was also visible early on. In 1882, the deputy minister of Indian Affairs, Lawrence Vankoughnet, argued that, while the government had promised in treaties to

"maintain" schools on reserves, it was not obligated to construct them—nor should maintenance be understood to include salaries for teachers or funds for school supplies (152).

7. For a useful overview of the Indian Act, see TRC, *Canada's Residential Schools*, vol. 1, pt. 1, *The History: Origins to 1939*, 106–10.

8. In the words of the 1920 amendment, "every such Indian and child and wife shall thereafter have, possess and enjoy all the legal powers, rights and privileges of His Majesty's other subjects, and shall no longer be deemed to be Indian within the meaning of any laws relating to Indians." SC, 1919–20, c. 50, s. 3; Hinge, *Consolidation of Indian Legislation*, vol. 2, *Indian Acts and Amendments, 1868–1975*, 213. That enfranchisement meant lost of Indian status was not something new: this had been spelled out in the original Indian Act (SC, 39 Vict. [1876], c. 18, s. 88). The 1920 amendment merely expanded the circumstances under which the government could impose enfranchisement. In response to protest, the 1920 clause was greeted with protest was repealed in 1922 (SC, 1922, c. 26, s. 1), only to be reintroduced a decade later (SC, 1932–33, c. 42, s. 7). For a useful overview, see Tansi Nîtôtemtik, "Restrictions on Rights: Compulsory Enfranchisement," *Faculty Blog*, University of Alberta, Faculty of Law, 3 October 2018, https://ualbertalaw.typepad.com/faculty/2018/10/restrictions-on-rights-compulsory-enfranchisement.html.

9. SC, 1919–20, c. 50, s. 1; Hinge, *Consolidation of Indian Legislation*, vol. 2, *Indian Acts and Amendments, 1868–1975*, 178. The same amendment went on to allow the Superintendent General of Indian Affairs to appoint truant officers, who were granted police powers. They could arrest children (without need for a warrant) and physically take them to school, and they were also permitted to enter homes to search for children who should be in school, to issue warnings to parents, and to give them written notice that they must send their child to school. Parents who failed to comply with such a notice could be prosecuted.

10. RSC, 1927, c. 98, s. 141. For the original text, see Gail Hinge for the Department of Indian and Northern Affairs, *Consolidation of Indian Legislation*, vol. 2, *Indian Acts and Amendments, 1868–1975* (Ottawa: Department of Indian and Northern Affairs, c. 1978), 301. (The volume is available at http://publications.gc.ca/site/eng/9.835895/publication.html.)

11. Laurie Meijer Drees, *The Indian Association of Alberta: A History of Political Action* (Vancouver: University of British Columbia Press, 2002), 17–18.

12. Ibid., 23.

13. Ibid., xiv.

14. On the government's newfound preference for "integration," see J. R. Miller, *Shingwauk's Vision: A History of Native Residential Schools* (Toronto: University of Toronto Press, 1997), 382–83.

15. John S. Milloy, *A National Crime: The Canadian Government and the Residential School System, 1879 to 1986* (Winnipeg: University of Manitoba Press, 1999), 186.

1 Indian Status as the Foundation of Justice

Leon Crane Bear

Indigenous peoples were not included in the decision making that led to the 1867 creation of the country that settlers named Canada. In the decades following Confederation, "Indians" and "half-breeds" were systematically relegated to the margins of Canadian society through a combination of legislation and policy. Of particular concern to the government was the relationship of Indians, as a legally defined category, to the Canadian state, along with the Crown's potentially costly obligations under the numerous treaties that it had signed with Indian bands in order to appropriate their lands. These concerns were reflected in many of the provisions of the Indian Act—a document used chiefly to curtail the right of Indians to practice their traditional cultures, to deny them control over their own affairs, and to encroach on their reserves. From 1867 onward, the policies pursued by the Canadian government were driven by the desire to assimilate Indians into mainstream Canadian society through the process of enfranchisement and thereby to relieve itself of its responsibilities—which, in the meanwhile, it endeavoured to discharge in cheapest way possible.

By the early 1960s, the deplorable conditions in which most First Nations (then still known as "Indians") were obliged to live had become embarrassingly obvious even to the federal government. Its first step was, of course, to commission a report, for which it turned in 1963 to anthropologist Harry B. Hawthorn.[1] The resulting report—*A Survey of the Contemporary Indians of Canada,* otherwise known as the Hawthorn Report—was submitted in two volumes, in 1966 and 1967. As the authors made a point of stating "clearly and simply" at the outset, they did *not* think "that the Indian should be required to assimilate, neither in order to receive what he now needs nor at any future time." Their recommendations therefore took account of the possibility "that many Indians should reject some values or institutions held dear by the Canadian majority."[2] Indians were, at present, "citizens minus," the authors noted. Instead, they "should be regarded as 'citizens plus,'" given that "in addition to the normal rights and duties of citizenship, Indians possess certain additional rights as charter members of the Canadian community."[3] These were not ambiguous statements.

With the recommendations of the Hawthorn Report in hand, the federal government drafted its new Indian policy, which was announced in June 1969. *Statement of the Government of Canada on Indian Policy, 1969*, commonly known as the White Paper, offered a novel solution to the problems besetting the Indian population: it proposed to make Indians "equal" to other Canadians by abolishing Indian status altogether. "Special status," it declared in its opening statement, "has made of the Indians a community disadvantaged and apart." If Indians were now disaffected and disempowered—lacking in education, employment opportunities, and self-esteem—it was because they had become accustomed to "special treatment."[4] Obviously, then, the remedy was to eliminate that special status and assimilate Indians into the Canadian body politic.

The White Paper sent a wave of anger surging through First Nations communities from coast to coast. Outraged protests immediately ensued. In an impassioned response titled *The Unjust Society*, Harold Cardinal, then president of the Indian Association of Alberta, argued that what the government had set out was "a thinly disguised programme of extermination through assimilation."[5] In the end, the government felt obliged to withdraw the White Paper, a decision prompted in no small measure by an incisive and outspoken rebuttal issued in 1970 by the Indian Chiefs of Alberta, which swiftly became known as the Red Paper.[6] Central to the impact of the Red Paper was its thoroughgoing rejection of the White liberal universe. As I hope to make clear in what follows, the Red Paper's forceful affirmation of the right of Indians to a separate identity infused First Nations communities with a fiery, and enduring, spirit of rebellion.

The Assault on First Peoples

The government's White Paper on Indian policy reflected Prime Minister Trudeau's broader plan to create a "just society," a vision that formed the centerpiece of his 1968 campaign. Trudeau's "just society" was founded on the liberal principles of human equality and support for individual rights, foremost among them the right of individuals to pursue their own interests, provided that, in so doing, they do not violate the rights of others. In particular, Trudeau placed a strong emphasis on minority rights and on equality of opportunity, so that disadvantaged individuals and groups would have equal access to education and to participation in the market economy.[7] In an official statement made on 10 June 1968, roughly a year before the White Paper appeared, Trudeau declared that the "Just Society will be one in which our Indian and Inuit populations will be encouraged to assume the full rights of citizenship through policies which will give them both greater responsibility for their own future and more meaningful equality of opportunity."[8]

The meaning of these lofty-sounding words became clear a year later, when, on the afternoon of 25 June 1969, Jean Chrétien, Trudeau's minister of Indian Affairs, formally introduced the White Paper in the House of Commons. In the words of historian James Frideres, the White Paper "outlined a plan by which First Nations would be legally eliminated through the repeal of their special status and the end of their unique relationship with the federal government, and the treaties would cease to be living documents."[9] To this end, the government proposed repealing the Indian Act, abolishing the "Indian Affairs" branch of the Department of Indian Affairs and Northern Development, and transferring responsibility for the provision of services to First Nations from the federal to provincial and local governments, on the grounds that such services should be available to all Canadians on an "equitable basis."[10] It further announced its intention to grant Indians full title to their reserve lands, with a view to facilitating economic development. Noting that "full ownership" brings with it "an obligation to pay for certain services," the government recognized that "it may not be acceptable to put all lands into the provincial systems immediately and make them subject to taxes." However, it confidently predicted, "when the Indian people see that the only way they can own and fully control land is to accept taxation the way other Canadians do, they will make that decision."[11]

With regard to treaties, the White Paper adopted a somewhat weary tone. "The terms and effects of the treaties," it explained, have been "widely misunderstood"—evidently by the many Indians who "believe that lands have been taken from them in an improper manner, or without adequate compensation, that their funds have been improperly administered, that their treaty rights have been breached."[12] And yet "a plain reading of the words used in the treaties reveals the limited and minimal promises which were included in them." After defending the government's track record with regard to meeting these promises, the White Paper went on to declare that "the significance of the treaties in meeting the economic, educational, health and welfare needs of the Indian people has always been limited and will continue to decline."[13] Eventually, once Indians were securely in control of their lands, the treaties would need to be reviewed with a view to determining how they can be "equitably ended."[14] In the meanwhile, rather than pursue the idea of creating a Claims Commission, the government would appoint a single commissioner "to consult with the Indians and to study and recommend acceptable procedures for the adjudication of claims."[15]

Especially in view of the paternalism on display throughout the White Paper, that it provoked such outrage should have come as no surprise to either Chrétien or Trudeau. The anger it generated stemmed, in part, from a sense of betrayal. For over a year, the government had been making a show of engaging in community consultations, initially by distributing a pamphlet titled "Choosing a Path" to reserves all across the country, apparently with the intention of soliciting grassroots input regarding the future of Indian policy.[16] Once installed as Trudeau's minister of Indian Affairs and Northern Development, Jean Chrétien had resolved to amend the Indian Act. In July 1968, officials from the Indian Affairs branch of the department had accordingly embarked on a series of meetings with representatives from local First Nations communities. These meetings ran through the end of January 1969, but no concrete results had emerged from them. Then, in April 1969, shortly before the White Paper was released, the government had brought representatives from First Nations communities to Ottawa for a nationwide meeting. Throughout these consultations, Indian leaders had repeatedly expressed their concerns about Indian rights and treaty rights, about land title, about unresolved claims, about living conditions on reserves, and about the need to give Indians a voice in policy making.

When, barely two months later, the White Paper described itself as "a response to things said by the Indian people at the consultation meetings," Indian leaders were astonished.[17] They thought they had been participating in a process to amend the Indian Act, not to eliminate it, much less to abolish Indian status altogether and transform Indigenous people into just another minority group. Their reaction was both swift and critical. On 26 June, the day after the White Paper was unveiled, Indian leaders—who had been flown to Ottawa for the announcement of the new policy—issued a press release under the banner of the National Indian Brotherhood, firmly rejecting the policy on a number of grounds. The government, they argued, had failed to take into account the views expressed by Indian leaders during the consultation process. Moreover, the resulting policy refused to recognize not only that Indians had special rights but also that any new relationship between Indians and the government presupposed the resolution of existing grievances.[18] That same day, Dave Courchene, president of the Manitoba Indian Brotherhood, released a similar but more strongly worded statement in which he noted that, yet again, "the future of Indian people has been dealt with in a high-handed and arbitrary manner."[19]

In the weeks that followed, anger was quickly translated into plans for resistance. The Union of Nova Scotia Indians, which held its first meeting in July 1969, was founded expressly to provide a unified political voice for the province's Mi'kmaq people in the face of the threat posed by the White Paper, and the Union of New Brunswick Indians formed at roughly the same time.[20] On the opposite side of the country, in British Columbia, representatives from 140 different bands convened in Kamloops in November 1969 to draft a collective response to the White Paper and to map out the next steps in their fight for the recognition of land title and Indian rights.[21] Ultimately, however, it was the response of the Indian Association of Alberta—an organization with roughly a thirty-year history of political activism—that would have the greatest impact on the future direction of Indian policy.

The Indian Association of Alberta and the Arrival of Harold Cardinal

The Indian Association of Alberta (IAA) was founded in 1939 by John Callihoo, a Haudenosaunee-Cree from the Michel reserve, northwest of Edmonton, and Métis advocate Malcolm Norris, one of the leading members of the Metis Association of Alberta. Initially, the IAA's focus fell on efforts to improve the living conditions on reserves, where poverty, unemployment, poor access to education, and inadequate health care were part of everyday life. The link between these local problems and federal Indian policy was plain to see, and the IAA soon established a relationship with officials in Indian Affairs (then a branch of the Department of Mines and Resources). In 1944 and 1945, it submitted two "Memorials," or briefs, to Indian Affairs that addressed the social, educational, and economic needs of Indian communities in Alberta, the first within the context of federal Indian policy and the second in relation to the government's plans for postwar reconstruction. In its early dealings with Indian Affairs, the IAA generally adopted a non-confrontational approach, making an effort to operate within existing administrative and legislative structures.[22] It also gained valuable experience in working with government.

By the mid-1940s, in the face of growing discontent among First Nations communities, coupled with widespread criticism of the Department of Indian Affairs, the government had recognized that some sort of response was necessary. The result was the creation, in May 1946, of a special joint committee of the House of Commons and Senate, which met from 1946 to 1948 to review the policies of Indian Affairs and to consider possible amendments to the Indian Act. Members of the IAA were invited to make presentations to the committee. One of the many issues on the table was the situation of Indians with respect to citizenship rights—a timely topic, in view of the passage, in June 1946, of the Canadian Citizenship Act.[23] The committee held to the established view that, in order to be eligible for full citizenship rights, Indians first had to be educated in their civic duties and be fully able to contribute to the economy—that, under the terms of the Indian Act, they would remain wards of the Crown until they proved themselves worthy of citizenship.[24] But the IAA refused to accept this argument. In their view, the treaties already conferred the full rights of citizenship on Indian peoples. It was the intention of the treaties, they argued, to grant equal status to Indians and to enable them to be "self-sustaining, loyal citizens of the Crown" by providing them with education and the means to earn a livelihood.[25] It was a provocative position—although, not very surprisingly, it failed to convince the committee. All the same, a strong emphasis on treaty rights would continue to inform the IAA's thinking over the next two decades.

The dramatic challenge represented by the White Paper came at a moment of transition for the IAA, with the arrival of a dynamic leader in the person of Harold Cardinal. Born in 1945, Cardinal was the son of Frank Cardinal—an active member of the IAA who, in 1947, travelled to Ottawa as part of the delegation that presented the IAA's views to the special joint committee.[26] Harold grew up on the Sucker Creek Cree reserve, roughly 350 kilometres northwest of Edmonton, on the southwestern shore of Lesser Slave Lake. In 1968, at the age of only twenty-four, he was elected president of the IAA, the youngest person ever to serve in that role. Two years earlier, while he was still a student at St. Patrick's College in Ottawa, Cardinal had been elected president of the Canadian Indian Youth Council, an event that marked the beginning of a lifetime's involvement in political activism.[27]

From the start, Cardinal was confident and forthright in speaking about issues of concern to the Indian community. As president of the Indian youth council, for example, in 1967 he attended a conference at the University of Alberta, hosted by the Canadian Union of Students, to celebrate the country's centennial. There, he told the conference delegates, "We are tired and fed up with paternal futility. What have we got to celebrate during this centennial year?" He went on to question what was too often described as the "Indian problem": "Is there an Indian problem or just a White manufactured problem?"[28] If Indians were angry and dissatisfied, this was the result of colonialism, which had created a system to marginalize and subdue them. Cardinal carried this uncompromising, outspoken attitude with him into the presidency of the IAA, imbuing the organization with a newly activist spirit.

Faced with the government's sudden announcement of a plan to terminate its long-standing contract with Indian peoples, Cardinal reacted with an outraged expression of anger and disgust. "Instead of acknowledging its legal and moral responsibilities to the Indians of Canada and honouring the treaties that the Indians signed in good faith," he wrote on the opening page of *The Unjust Society*, the government "now proposes to wash its hands of Indians entirely." As he went on to point out, later in the book, "As far as we are concerned our treaty rights represent a sacred, honourable agreement between ourselves and the Canadian government that cannot be unilaterally abrogated by the government at the whim of one of its leaders unless that government is prepared to give us back title to our country."[29] In light of the overall policy direction laid out in the White Paper, Cardinal was also reminded of Chrétien's announcement, early the previous fall, of the impending reorganization of his department. Under the new structure, the existing branches were to be replaced by three program areas, under which Indian Affairs would then be subsumed.[30] Cardinal concluded that the government had known its intentions "long before any results could be expected from the phoney consultation meetings"—which were, he said, "the purest hypocrisy."[31]

By the time *The Unjust Society* appeared late in November 1969, it was already a bestseller.[32] Although the book was written as Cardinal's personal response to the White Paper, his views and sentiments were widely shared, and they would form the moral backbone of the Red Paper.

The Red Paper

Although Cardinal clearly exerted a strong influence over the content of the Red Paper, the document was the result of a collaborative effort and is formally credited to the Indian Chiefs of Alberta.[33] Preparation of the Red Paper began in early fall of 1969, with a series of discussions with reserve communities in Alberta.[34] On 22 January 1970, at a meeting in Calgary, the chiefs wrote to Prime Minister Trudeau to alert him to the impending submission of a "Counter Policy." In their letter, they stated, "This assembly of all the Indian Chiefs of Alberta reaffirms its position of unity and recognizes the Indian Association of Alberta as the voice of all the Treaty Indian people of this province." The letter, which was subsequently included in the preamble to the Red Paper, ended: "We request that no further process of implementation takes place and that action already taken be reviewed to minimize suspicions and to make possible a positive and constructive dialogue between your government and our people."[35] Trudeau had been put on notice.

When, in June, the Red Paper was released, it proved to contain a detailed assault on the White Paper's program of assimilation, one that repeatedly emphasized the government's obligation to respect the treaties as the foundation of its relationship to Indian peoples. In the argument of the Red Paper, treaties between Indians and the Crown signed in the latter half of the nineteenth century could not be extinguished in the name of equality and, in fact, needed to be honoured. "The Government has never bothered to learn what the treaties are and has a distorted picture of them," it declared. Instead, it must "recognize that treaties are historic, moral and legal obligations."[36] Moreover, if the government feels that "there should be positive recognition by everyone of the unique contribution of Indian culture to Canadian life," then it needs to understand that "the only way to maintain our culture is for us to remain as Indians. To preserve our culture it is necessary to preserve our status, rights, lands and traditions. Our treaties are the bases of our rights."[37]

The hundred-page text of the Red Paper consists of two main parts. The first part is devoted to a rebuttal of the White Paper's policy proposals, which are taken up one by one. This is followed by a consideration of the steps that need to be taken with respect to the Indian Act, the proposed transfer of responsibilities to the provinces, funding for economic development, the future of Indian Affairs, and the notion that a single commissioner be appointed to adjudicate claims.[38] The second part lays out detailed plans for both economic development and education that would put the Indians of Alberta in charge of their own future. While these plans are elaborated specifically within the context of Alberta, they provide a template that could easily be adapted for somewhere else.

Not surprisingly, the Red Paper unequivocally rejects the abolition of Indian status, the repeal of the Indian Act, and the dissolution of Indian Affairs, all three of which it regards as essential components of the special relationship between Indian peoples and the Canadian state. Under the heading "Immediate Requirements," it insists, first, that before any further policy discussions can take place (for example, about possible revisions to the Indian Act), the government must first accept the treaties as binding contracts and, second, that the government must appoint a minister responsible solely for Indian Affairs. Moreover, the Indian Affairs branch "needs to change its outlook"—it should "stop being authoritarian" and instead "start to serve people," functioning "mainly as the keeper of the Queen's promises, the treaties and the lands."[39] With respect to the devolution of responsibility for education onto the provinces, the Red Paper refuses to accept any arrangement under which decisions can be made without the direct participation of Indian tribal councils. "Our education is not a welfare system," it points out. "We have free education as a treaty right because we have paid in advance for our education by surrendering our lands."[40]

The Red Paper is impressive in part for its thoroughness: in repudiating the White Paper, it leaves few stones unturned. But it is also remarkable for its strong thematic unity. No government official reading the document could possibly miss its central message, which is summed up in the opening sentence of the preamble: "To us who are treaty Indians there is nothing more important than our Treaties, our lands, and the well being of our future generation."[41] These treaties recognize Indians as the original holders of title to the lands now called Canada and thus acknowledge the special status of Indian peoples. The government cannot simply decide to extinguish these agreements in the name of "equality." Equality will be achieved when, in the words of Harold Cardinal, "the buckskin curtain of indifference, ignorance and, all too often, plain bigotry" ceases to exist. But once it has been torn down, Indians will not become "good little brown white men": they will remain Indians.[42]

The Sound of Thunder

On 4 June 1970, the IAA presented its Red Paper on Parliament Hill at a meeting with Prime Minister Trudeau and his cabinet members, including Jean Chrétien. Also in attendance were representatives of the National Indian Brotherhood, who had convened in Ottawa a few days earlier. As a national organization, the brotherhood represented a large number of non-treaty Indians—that is, those who have Indian status under the terms of the Indian Act but whose bands never concluded treaties with the federal government. For non-treaty Indians, the Red Paper's emphasis on treaty rights clearly posed a stumbling block. After some debate among its members, the National Indian Brotherhood had agreed, just the day before, to endorse the Red Paper as its official response to the White Paper, but only after revisions were made to incorporate the concept of Indian rights into the Red Paper's discussion of treaties.[43]

At the meeting itself, two members of the IAA delegation—Adam Solway, chief of the Siksika Nation, and John Snow, chief of the Wesley band of the Stoney-Nakoda Nation—created a dramatic back-and-forth exchange between the White Paper and Red Paper by reading passages from each in turn. At the conclusion of their presentation, the chiefs placed the White Paper on the table in front of Chrétien, to signal its rejection, and then handed a copy of the Red Paper to the prime minister.[44] In his own statement, Cardinal stressed that the government's formal recognition of both Indian rights and treaty rights was fundamental to any new relationship between Indians and the Canadian state and proposed the creation of a

Claims Commission to resolve existing complaints about violations of these rights. After summarizing the main points in the Red Paper's position and reiterating the need for economic development and education, he called for the immediate cessation of efforts to implement the White Paper's proposals, followed by the development of consultative procedures that Indians would find acceptable.[45]

What followed would be a defining moment for everyone in attendance, but particularly for the IAA. In his response to the presentation, Trudeau sounded a note of contrition:

> I'm sure that we were very naive in some of the statements we made in the paper. We had perhaps the prejudices of small "l" liberals and white men at that who thought that equality meant the same law for everybody, and that's why as a result of this we said, "well let's abolish the Indian Act and make Indians citizens of Canada like everyone else. And let's let Indians dispose of their lands just like every other Canadian. And let's make sure that Indians can get their rights, education, health and so on, from the governments like every other Canadian." But we have learnt in the process that perhaps we were a bit too theoretical, we were a bit too abstract, we were not, as Mr. Cardinal suggests, perhaps pragmatic enough or understanding enough, and that's fine. We are here to discuss this.[46]

Here was the grand architect of the White Paper, acknowledging the "prejudices" of liberalism. Although Trudeau's statement stopped well short of an apology, and although he defended his position on special rights, he assured those in attendance that his government was prepared to reconsider its position in light of their response. "We won't force any solution on you," he said in closing, "because we are not looking for any particular solution."[47] In other words, the White Paper had been put on hold.

This victory was like a jolt of lightning, followed by a resounding thunderclap. From coast to coast, First Nations collectively flexed their muscles, recognizing that resistance could succeed. Although the battle was clearly just beginning, Indian communities were infused with an understanding of their own power and dignity, as well as with a sense of possibility. In the face of escalating protests, Trudeau's government soon began to back away from the White Paper. Finally, in a speech delivered in March 1971, Chrétien announced that the ideas put forward in the White Paper were "no longer a factor" in the continuing debate over the future of Indian policy. "The Government," he stated, "does not intend to force progress along the directions set out in the policy proposals of June 1969."[48] The White Paper was officially dead.

Conclusion

Fifty years later, Indigenous people grapple with many of the same problems that sparked protests in the 1960s and 1970s. However, the Red Paper represented a watershed moment in Indigenous activism. Indigenous people were now in the public eye and they were organized and ready to resist any threats to assimilation, or their "special status" as Indians. Although the Indian Association of Alberta spearheaded the resistance, they had support from other Indigenous organizations from across the country and it was with new-found resolve and confidence that Indigenous communities continued in their fight to have their rights recognized.

In the 1980s, Indigenous people had an impact on the repatriation of the Canadian constitution when Indigenous leaders advocated for the constitutional protection of Aboriginal and Treaty rights. Following the statements laid out in the Red Paper, the IAA advocated for the inclusion of treaties in any future amendments in the constitution. As a result, when the First Ministers' Conferences were convened between 1983 and 1987 to address the issue of self-government, among other topics, the IAA was an important participant.[49] These constitutional conferences offered an opportunity to the IAA to restate their position on the rights of Indigenous people to govern themselves.[50]

In 1991, when a Royal Commission on Aboriginal People (RCAP) was initiated by then Prime Minister Brian Mulroney, it came nearly fifty years after it had been first called for by the IAA.[51] The five-volume final report, completed in 1996, investigated the relationship between Aboriginal people in relation to non-Aboriginal people and society.[52] The report, noteworthy for its depth and breath of Indigenous content, included a series of recommendations, most of which were never implemented.

By the late 1990s, the IAA no longer played a major role on the national stage, in part due to cuts made to the federal and provincial funding programs that had sustained the organization for three decades. As a result, the IAA was forced to return to the work of collecting private donations, a practice that had funded the organization prior to 1968.

Harold Cardinal, a prominent IAA figure of the time, left the organization in the late 1970s to pursue other interests, but not before a brief time in the position of regional director general of Indian Affairs in Alberta. Although his term lasted only seven months, his appointment marked the first time that an Indigenous person had ever held the position. In 1999, Cardinal was awarded an honorary doctorate from the University of Alberta, before passing away in 2005. He will be remembered for his tenacity—when he spoke, his audience listened—and for his tireless efforts to implement the treaties. His work in the 1960s and 1970s empowered Indigenous people and continues to inspire activism efforts today.

NOTES

1. On the early development of the report and the choice of Hawthorn as lead author, see Dennis Magill, *Study on the Hawthorn Report* (Ottawa: Treaties and Historical Research Centre, Department of Indian Affairs and Northern Development, 1976).
2. H. B. Hawthorn, ed., *A Survey of the Contemporary Indians of Canada: A Report on Economic, Politicial, Educational Needs and Policies*, vol. 1 (Ottawa: Indian Affairs Branch, Department of Indian Affairs and Northern Development, 1966), 6. The generic use of the male pronoun was, of course, typical of the period.
3. Ibid., 6, 13. On the development and subsequent influence of the Hawthorn Report, see Sally M. Weaver, "The Hawthorn Report: Its Use in the Making of Canadian Indian Policy," in *Anthropology, Public Policy, and Native Peoples in Canada*, ed. Noel Dyck and James B. Waldram (Montréal and Kingston: McGill-Queen's University Press, 1993), 75–97.
4. *Statement of the Government of Canada on Indian Policy, 1969*, presented to the first session of the Twenty-Eighth Parliament by the Honourable Jean Chrétien, Minister of Indian Affairs and Northern Development (Ottawa: Department of Indian Affairs and Northern Development, 1969), http://publications.gc.ca/collections/collection_2014/aadnc-aandc/R32-2469-eng.pdf, 2. Note that, because this document is not paginated, page numbers refer to the page in the PDF.
5. Harold Cardinal, *The Unjust Society*, 2nd ed. (Vancouver: Douglas and McIntyre; Seattle: University of Washington Press, 1999), 1. First published 1969 by M. G. Hurtig (Edmonton).

6. Although Cardinal is usually credited as the principal author of the Red Paper, an unlikely source may have had a hand in it. According to historian Laurie Meijer Drees, "The IAA and Cardinal spent the winter of 1969/70 using government funds to pay for the writing of a response paper. To such ends they employed M and M Systems Research, a research firm established by the former Social Credit Premier of Alberta and his son, Preston Manning, for a reputed fee of $25,000. The resulting document, entitled 'Citizens Plus,' was ready for public consumption in the spring of 1970." Laurie Meijer Drees, *The Indian Association of Alberta: A History of Political Action* (Vancouver: University of British Columbia Press, 2002), 169.

7. On Trudeau's understanding of liberalism see, Thomas S. Axworthy and Pierre Elliot Trudeau, *Towards a Just Society* (Ontario, Canada: Penguin Books, 1990), 263.

8. "The Just Society," Official Statement by the Prime Minister, 10 June 1968, in Pierre Elliott Trudeau, *The Essential Trudeau*, ed. Ron Graham (Toronto: McClelland and Stewart, 1998), 19.

9. James S. Frideres, *First Nations in the Twenty-First Century* (Don Mills, ON: Oxford University Press, 2011), 15.

10. *Statement of the Government of Canada on Indian Policy, 1969*, 15. With regard to the transfer of federal funds to provincial governments, the White Paper noted: "Subject to negotiations with the provinces, such provisions would as a matter of principle eventually decline, the provinces ultimately assuming the same responsibility for services to Indian residents as they do for services to others" (15). In other words, the cost of these services would ultimately be borne by the provinces.

11. Ibid., 22.

12. Ibid., 19, 18.

13. Ibid., 19. The implication was, of course, that if First Nations now found themselves living in destitution, it was not because the government had failed to make good on its promises.

14. Ibid., 20. In the government's view, the treaties were in many ways relics of the past. Regarding the need for the government and First Nations to arrive at an agreement about the future role of the treaties, the White Paper commented: "Many of the provisions and practices of another century may be considered irrelevant the light of a rapidly changing society" (20).

15. Ibid., 8.

16. On "Choosing a Path," see Cardinal, *Unjust Society*, 101–2. According to Mark Anderson and Carmen Robertson, a number of prominent First Nations leaders (including Harold Cardinal) suspected that the pamphlet— soon dubbed "Down the Garden Path"—was "a moot exercise, the real

intention of which was to effectively disguise a hidden government agenda that had already been decided upon." Mark Cronlund Anderson and Carmen L. Robertson, *Seeing Red: A History of Natives in Canadian Newspapers* (Winnipeg: University of Manitoba Press, 2011), 159.

17. *Statement of the Government of Canada on Indian Policy, 1969,* 6.

18. See Sally M. Weaver, *Making Canadian Indian Policy: The Hidden Agenda, 1968–1970* (Toronto: University of Toronto Press, 1981), 173–74. As Weaver notes, the Indian leaders present in Ottawa held an "emergency session" on 26 June (173).

19. On Courchene's statement, see ibid., 174–75; the quotation from his press release appears on p. 174.

20. On its "About" page (http://www.unsi.ns.ca/about/), the Union of Nova Scotia Indians explicitly states that the organization came into existence "in the face of a proposed federal government policy to assimilate Canada's First Nations people into mainstream society."

21. See "The White Paper 1969," *Indigenous Foundations,* 2009, https://indigenousfoundations.arts.ubc.ca/the_white_paper_1969/, paras. 11–12. The Kamloops meeting led to the formation of the Union of British Columbia Indian Chiefs. Its response, *A Declaration of Indian Rights: The BC Indian Position Paper,* was released in November 1970.

22. Meijer Drees, *Indian Association of Alberta,* 73–74 .

23. Under the Canadian Citizenship Act, which went into effect at the start of 1947, British subjects living in Canada automatically became citizens of Canada. The act made no specific mention of Indians—but, at the time, only enfranchised Indians were British subjects, and such Indians were very few in number, given that enfranchisement meant loss of Indian status. The option of enfranchisement—first made available to Indians in 1857, with the passage of the Gradual Civilization Act—had long been recognized by Indians as a tactic of assimilation, and it had proved to be exceedingly unpopular.

24. Laurie Meijer Drees, "Citizenship and Treaty Rights: The Indian Association of Alberta and the Canadian Indian Act, 1946–48," *Great Plains Quarterly* 20, no. 2 (2000): 142.

25. Ibid., 151; the quotation is from the brief that the IAA presented to the special joint committee.

26. Ibid., 153. Also see, Laurie Meijer Drees' dissertation on which her book is based, http://www.collectionscanada.gc.ca/obj/s4/f2/dsk3/ftp04/nq24550.pdf, 209.

27. "Council President Says Indian Youth Refuses Passive Role," *Leader Post,* 13 October 1966, 5.

28. Cardinal's remarks are quoted in "Indians Not Celebrating Says Chief of Council," *The Gateway*, 9 March 1967, 1.

29. Cardinal, *Unjust Society*, 1, 25.

30. More specifically, under the new structure, the activities of the four existing branches—Indian Affairs, Northern Development, the Parks Service, and the Wildlife Service—were to be variously assigned to one of three programs: social affairs, economic development, and conservation. The ostensible goal was to cut costs and improve efficiency by eliminating redundancy. See Jean Chrétien, "Indian Affairs: Statement on Reorganization of Department," 2 October 1968, https://www.lipad.ca/full/1968/10/02/1/.

31. Cardinal, *Unjust Society*, 104. See also Anderson and Robertson, *Seeing Red*, 158–59. There, they quote remarks that Chrétien made in a September 1968 speech to the Indian-Eskimo Association, nine months prior to the appearance of the White Paper. "It is possible," Chrétien said, "that the Indian people will decide that there should not be an Indian Act at all. They might decide they do not want special legislation. There would then be required some transitional legislation which would transfer federal responsibility for the land to the Bands and individuals. On completion of the process, the Act would pass out of existence." As the authors point out, the parallel to the policy laid out in the White Paper is unmistakable. Cited in Peter McFarlane and Doreen Manuel, *Brotherhood to Nationhood: George Manuel and the Making of the Modern Indian Movement* (Toronto: Between The Lines, 1993), 108.

32. According to a profile of Cardinal that appeared in *Maclean's* at the time the book was released, the publisher received more than sixteen thousand advance orders. Jon Ruddy, "What the Canadian Indian Wants from You," *Maclean's*, 1 December 1969, https://archive.macleans.ca/article/1969/12/1/what-the-canadian-indian-wants-from-you, 20.

33. Meijer Drees, *Indian Association of Alberta*, 169.

34. Ibid., 166.

35. Indian Chiefs of Alberta, *Citizens Plus* (Edmonton: Indian Association of Alberta, 1970), reprinted as a Foundational Document in *Aboriginal Policy Studies* 1, no. 2 (2011): 191, 192. The reprint is available at https://journals.library.ualberta.ca/aps/index.php/aps/article/view/11690. To read a copy of the Red Paper, see http://caid.ca/RedPaper1970.pdf.

36. Ibid., 196.

37. Ibid., 194. The first quotation reproduces the words of the White Paper itself.

38. In the Red Paper, the first part comprises sections B (section A is the preamble) through E ("Conclusion"). The second part, which is substantially longer, is made up a series of "F" sections.

39. Ibid., 206.

40. Ibid., 202.

41. Ibid., 189.

42. Cardinal, *Unjust Society*, 1.

43. Weaver, *Making Canadian Indian Policy*, 183. Thus, for example, after proposing that the government entrench the treaties in the Constitution, the Red Paper states: "Only by this entrenching will Indian rights be assured as long as the sun rises and the river runs." Indian Chiefs of Alberta, *Citizens Plus*, 199.

44. Ibid., 183–84. Note that Weaver refers to Adam Soloway, but the name is more commonly spelled Solway.

45. Ibid., 184.

46. "Statement by the Prime Minister at a Meeting with the Indian Association of Alberta and the National Indian Brotherhood, Ottawa, June 4, 1970," typescript, http://publications.gc.ca/collections/collection_2018/aanc-inac/R5-598-1970-eng.pdf, 2–3.

47. Ibid., 7.

48. Jean Chrétien, "The Unfinished Tapestry: Indian Policy in Canada," speech delivered on 17 March 1971, Queen's University, Kingston, Ontario, quoted in Weaver, *Making Canadian Indian Policy*, 187. In the original typescript, the sentence quoted was underlined.

49. Colin H. Scott, "Custom, Tradition, and the Politics of Culture: Aboriginal Self-Government in Canada," in *Anthropology, Public Policy and Native Peoples in Canada*, ed. Noel Dyck and James B. Waldram (Montréal and Kingston: McGill-Queen's University Press, 1993), 311–33. Scott explained that this series of conferences between Indigenous leaders and the two levels of governments (federal and provincial) was to determine the nature of self-government. However, the federal and provincial governments had "limited" their understanding of self-government to two areas: "cultural survival and the resolution of socio-economic problems besetting aboriginal people" (316). While Indigenous leaders thought of self-government as "cultural rights to the historical priority of aboriginal peoples, and to an institutionally comprehensive definition of cultural survival" (317).

50. The Indian Association of Alberta, *Citizens Plus: the Red Paper*, 191. Note that, because this document is not paginated, page numbers refer to the page in the PDF.

51. The 1991 Royal Commission occurred in the wake of the Oka crises and was called as a result of the failed Meech Lake Accord, a process that excluded First Nations. The IAA had been informing the federal government of the concerns of Indigenous communities in Alberta for nearly fifty years when the commission was finally called. As early as the mid-1940s, the

IAA had submitted "Memorials" to Indian Affairs which addressed the social, education, and economic issues in their communities. Drees, *Indian Association of Alberta*, 97.

52. See the five volumes of the Royal Commission on Aboriginal Peoples here, https://www.bac-lac.gc.ca/eng/discover/aboriginal-heritage/royal-commission-aboriginal-peoples/Pages/final-report.aspx.

2 Teaching It Our Way

Blue Quills and the Demand for Indigenous Educational Autonomy

Tarisa Dawn Little

What was once Blue Quills Indian Residential School sits 190 kilometres northeast of Edmonton, not far from the western outskirts of the town of St. Paul. Constructed in 1931, the building looks like other colonial institutional facilities of the period: red brick façade accented by tall, narrow windows. But the history of Blue Quills begins much earlier than 1931. In the late 1890s, a Cree chief named Blue Quill (Sîpihtakanep) agreed to allow Oblate missionaries to build a school on the recently surveyed reserve lands at Saddle Lake, to replace an existing industrial school located further north, at Lac La Biche. As one of his descendants remembers, the chief responded to the request of the Oblate fathers by saying, "Yes, put it on my land. I'm thinking of the future of my grandchildren and the orphans." But if Chief Blue Quill was contemplating the educational needs of future generations, his son-in-law William Delver was apparently wary of that future. In the years to come, Delver predicted, "kipimâcihonâwâw ka-wehcasin; kinehi-yâwiwinâwâw wiî-âyiman ka-miciminamihk"—"Earning a living will be easy; being Cree will be hard to hold."[1]

From the time of its founding, in 1898, Blue Quills Indian Residential School—originally known as Saddle Lake Boarding School—was administered by the Catholic Church on behalf of the federal government, which owned the school and funded its operations. In 1931, the school moved from Saddle Lake to its St. Paul location, roughly 30 kilometres due east. Run by priests of the Oblate Order of Mary Immaculate, with classes taught mostly by Grey Nuns, the school was intended to serve children from reserves in northeastern Alberta whose families professed the Roman Catholic faith.[2] This arrangement remained in place until April 1969, when the federal government cancelled its contracts with churches and assumed direct control of residential schools, as part of its larger plan to close these schools entirely and integrate Indigenous students into provincial public schools.

Today, however, Blue Quills operates as an independent Indigenous postsecondary institution—University nuhelot'įne thaiyots'į nistameyimâkanak Blue Quills. Adopting a holistic approach to education grounded in the inherited world view and values of the Cree peoples, the university offers an array of programs to Indigenous and non-Indigenous students alike. This transformation—from residential school to self-governing Indigenous institution—came about as a direct result of activism on the part of Saddle Lake community members, who were determined to refuse the colonial state the right to dictate how, where, and by whom their children would be educated. Their efforts culminated in the summer of 1970, when activists occupied Blue Quills, demanding that the federal government allow the local community to operate the school. As a result, Blue Quills became the first fully Indigenous-controlled educational institution in Canada, as well as the first concrete success in the long-standing quest of First Nations for educational autonomy.[3] Not only did Saddle Lake community members refuse to see residential schooling continue, but they also firmly rejected the federal government's proposed alternative.

From Residential Schooling to Integration

Many Indigenous communities across Canada sought treaties in Canada in part due to their interest in western-style education. Although residential schooling had been unpopular among Indigenous communities virtually from the time the system was first put in place, during the 1880s, Indian Affairs officials continued their approval to dissolve day schools into residential schools. In the department's 1880 annual report, written by then superintendent general of Indian affairs at the time, E. Dewdney noted the department's preference for boarding schools and how such schools can effectively remove an Indigenous child from their "deleterious home influences to which he would be otherwise subjected."[4] Dewdney went on to write that when a child returns to their home, they are reclaimed into an "uncivilized state."[5] Similarly, the department's 1932 annual report describes day schools as "centres of Indian Educational activity" and thus a less desirable solution.[6]

Rather than equipping students with useful knowledge and skills, in a manner respectful of Indigenous traditions and values, residential schools focused on Christian conversion and subjected their pupils to multiple forms of mental and physical abuse. After graduating, students typically returned to their home communities not only unprepared to function successfully within mainstream society but also deeply alienated from their cultural roots. This was certainly not the vision of education that, in the eyes of Indigenous communities, was implied by treaty promises of education. In the words of Sheila Carr-Stewart, "The chiefs and headmen who signed the numbered treaties negotiated an educational right complementary to their own Aboriginal teachings"—not one that would attempt to eradicate the very cultures that gave rise to these teachings.[7] As historian J. R. Miller argues, residential schools were "the vehicle of the newcomers' attempts to refashion and culturally eliminate the first inhabitants' way of life and identity."[8]

Indigenous families and communities knew what was at stake. The ban on Indigenous languages and ceremonies at school were a significant cause of parental and student discontent, as was the unfair and abusive treatment of Indigenous students. Residential schools required that students speak English at all times even though many students had little to no exposure to the languages—if the children did not comply with the rules, the punishment was often severe.[9] At the residential school in Cardston, Alberta, Andrew Bull Calf recalls being abused by the instructors: "I didn't know English, you know, and the only language we spoke was Blackfoot in our community and so I got strapped a lot for that."[10] As historian Mary-Ellen Kelm explains, "the struggle between the schools' commitment to cultural imperialism and Indigenous peoples' ability to mediate the forces of that imperialism [was] inscribed on the bodies of the children who experienced residential schooling."[11] Following the dispossession of land and resources and the introduction of disease and alcohol, Indigenous children were subjected to physical and emotional abuse at residential school, the impact of which would be felt for generations.

Ironically, residential schools were no more a success in the eyes of the state. As John Milloy points out, a system designed to promote assimilation had in fact failed to produce "a generation of well-educated, re-socialized children" who would integrate into modern society, prepared to "lead their communities into a new Canadian future."[12] As early as the 1930s, the government had recognized this failure, which raised the question of what to do about the situation. One option—put forward in 1936 by D. A. Hoey, recently appointed superintendent of welfare and training at Indian Affairs—was to shift to a system of on-reserve day schools that would provide both academic instruction and vocational training at a greatly reduced cost. This proposal met with vigorous opposition from the churches that ran residential schools. In the view of church officials, if residential schools had thus far failed to meet the goal of assimilation, the solution "lay in the intensification of the system."[13] Conflicts between the government and the churches would not soon be resolved.

Discontent with residential schools was but one facet of a broader dissatisfaction with federal Indian policy that, by the time of World War II, was shared by government officials, church authorities, and Indigenous leaders alike.[14] In response to growing criticism, in 1946 the government convened a special joint committee of the Senate and the House of Commons, which was tasked with proposing possible amendments to the Indian Act. The committee held hearings for two years. In the end, however, the federal government ignored most of its recommendations, with the notable exception of those regarding education. The committee had proposed that the Indian Act be revised "to prepare Indian children to take their place as citizens" and that "wherever and whenever possible, Indian children should be educated in association with other children."[15] In accordance with these recommendations, Indian Affairs officials began pursuing a policy of integration. Residential schools would be gradually phased out, and Indigenous children would instead attend ordinary public schools.

Many Indigenous communities expressed concerns about the way Indigenous students were treated at non-Indigenous schools.[16] But the government favored integration for a number of reasons, including the "supposed benefits of schooling children of different backgrounds in common classrooms." As an added benefit, it was thought that integration would help Indian Affairs "economize" education. The government moved to implement integration, placing Indigenous children is provincial schools, without acknowledging the needs and concerns of the students and their families.

Historically, the provinces had not been involved in the provision of education to First Nations. Even though the 1867 Constitution Act made education a provincial responsibility, matters relating to "Indians" fell under federal jurisdiction—and the federal government was also obligated by treaty promises to provide education to reserve communities. When, however, the Indian Act was revised in 1951, an amendment was added that enabled the federal government to enter into agreements with provincial and territorial governments and with school boards for the purpose of providing education to First Nations children (much as it had already entered into such agreements with churches).[17] This amendment paved the way for the new policy of integration, which began to be implemented in the 1950s. The Catholic Church was staunchly opposed to these new provisions, however, on the grounds that they contravened the Indian Act's promise that "no child whose parent is a Roman Catholic shall be assigned to a school conducted under Protestant auspices."[18]

The shift to an integration model would take more than three decades to complete, during which residential schools continued to operate, if in gradually decreasing number. From the time of their inception, the education provided at these schools had been marginal, at best. Only half of the school day was devoted to academic subjects, and seldom would instructors have been qualified to teach in public schools.[19] In a review of the education offered at residential schools in the period up to 1950, R. F. Davey, director of educational services at Indian Affairs, quoted from a department study according to which, as late as 1950, more than 40 percent of residential school teachers still lacked professional training—while some had not even finished high school.[20] In 1951, the half-day system was officially terminated, and, over the following two decades, Indian Affairs made a concerted effort to improve both the credentials and salaries of residential school teachers. During the same period, the number of students who remained in school beyond grade 8 steadily increased.[21] Indeed, speaking at a Parents' Day meeting held at Blue Quills in 1956, former student Rosanne Houle noted that the quality of education was better than it had been twenty-five years earlier, when she attended the school, and that students now seemed to have a greater desire to learn.[22]

Yet, even at the end of the 1960s, a "fundamental impediment" remained at residential schools: "Both the curriculum and the pedagogy, which were not in any way appropriate to the culture of the students, made it difficult for the children to learn."[23] The same could be said of public schools. At that time, school curricula barely acknowledged the existence of Indigenous peoples and cultures, and what little students were taught typically reflected negative colonial stereotypes rooted in racist attitudes. Moreover, as a report on research conducted in 1966 for the Alberta government indicated, teachers lacked an adequate understanding of the problems facing Indigenous students who were attempting to make the transition into public schools. Although the University of Alberta had begun offering courses for teachers who would be working with students from reserves, "the fruits of this new curriculum will not be seen for a few years and, even then, they will not be widespread," the report noted. "The people who are teaching in Indian areas at present have little training in this sphere and have no opportunity to acquire the adequate training."[24]

These findings echoed comments made a year earlier by University of Alberta student Annie Minoose. Speaking at an education conference held in St. Paul in March 1966, Minoose observed that Indigenous students were caught between two differing world views, which led to a conflicted sense of identity and made it difficult for them to adapt to mainstream Canadian society.[25] In short, if residential schools were fundamentally oppressive institutions, neither did public schools provide an environment conducive to the well-being of Indigenous students. Both rested on the premise that schooling should serve to promote assimilation.[26]

Disputes surrounding Canada's Indian policy, including its approach to the provision of education, escalated dramatically following the June 1969 release of *Statement of the Government of Canada on Indian Policy, 1969*, otherwise known as the White Paper. As Leon Crane Bear explains in the previous chapter, the White Paper proposed eliminating Indian status entirely, thereby assimilating Indigenous people into Canadian society by legal fiat. According to this plan, within the space of only a few years the Department of Indian Affairs would be dissolved, the Indian Act would be repealed, and the provinces would become responsible for providing services to Indigenous peoples, including education. In fact, the federal government had already begun negotiating agreements with the provinces regarding the integration of Indigenous students into provincial schools.[27] According to a March 1969 departmental memorandum, these agreements would enable Indian Affairs to "relinquish the responsibility of actively providing educational services to Indians."[28]

In a forceful response to the White Paper, titled *The Unjust Society*, Harold Cardinal, president of the Indian Association of Alberta, argued that Indigenous peoples wanted autonomy, not integration. Although willing to contribute to and participate in Canadian society, Indigenous people were "acutely aware of the threat—the loss of our Indian identity." They also wanted control over their own destiny. As Cardinal went on to point out, "We want better education, a better chance for our children and the option to choose our own pathway in life."[29] But no longer would Indigenous people "trust the government with our futures," he warned. Rather, it was time for the government to "listen to and learn from us."[30] Cardinal's book appeared in December 1969, and it rapidly became a manifesto.

Unrest at Blue Quills

In the mid-1950s, Indian Affairs had begun to set up school committees on reserves that would ostensibly "exercise control over certain aspects of school affairs and the expenditure of school funds," while also serving "to stimulate an interest in school work amongst parents."[31] Although, in practice, these committees had little real power, they did open a channel for communication between parents and school administrations. By the mid-1960s, the Saddle Lake community had grown alarmed by the high dropout rate at Blue Quills. Parents blamed the administration for this situation, arguing that discipline at the school was unduly strict and that boys and girls were too rigidly segregated. But parents were also concerned about the favouritism shown toward some of the girls by the priest in charge of Blue Quills. Several older girls had apparently stopped attending school to avoid his unwelcome advances.[32]

In the summer of 1966, the Saddle Lake branch of the Catholic Indian League petitioned to have the principal removed.[33] Evidently, his replacement, Father S. R. Gagnon, held Indigenous people in rather low regard. As one Indian Affairs official put it, Gagnon was of the opinion that "Indian people were not very capable or reliable."[34] At the time, Blue Quills had only a handful of Indigenous staff, all of them employed in maintenance and service jobs. One of these employees was Stanley Redcrow, who had worked at the school for many years and was also the president of the Saddle Lake School Committee during the late 1960s. As Redcrow later recalled, when he approached the principal to ask whether he would be willing to hire more Indigenous staff, Gagnon rejected the idea. This led to a special meeting of the school committee at the end of September 1969, at which Gagnon reiterated his position—that "Indian people were not qualified and that they would not be able to do the work."[35]

In the meanwhile, Indian Affairs had, in 1966, resolved to close Blue Quills and turn the school into a residence hall. This decision was not communicated to the local community, however, which found out about it only three years later. It appears in October 1969, Alice Makokis—a member of the Saddle Lake School Committee who was also employed by Indian Affairs as a school counsellor—overheard department officials discussing a plan to sell Blue Quills to St. Paul for the token of one dollar.[36] Rumours were also circulating about the possibility that Blue Quills students would be sent to a new regional high school in the town, scheduled to open the following year. At the end of October, representatives from all the school committees in the Saddle Lake–Athabasca district assembled in St. Paul for a three-day meeting, present at which was someone from Indian Affairs. When asked about the truth of these rumours, he made a telephone call to Edmonton and then confirmed that the plan was to close the school and turn it into a residence.[37] Even though a motion in support of this proposal was adopted at the meeting, "subsequent discussion revealed unhappiness with the administration of the school and a desire to see some schooling continue at Blue Quills."[38]

Discontent simmered until a meeting of the Saddle Lake community on 7 December. At that meeting, it was unanimously resolved that Blue Quills should continue to operate as a school, that its service staff should be entirely Indigenous, and that the administration of the school "should be turned over to Indian people."[39] As Redcrow later recalled, "when Indian people understood what we were trying to do, they came along with us with the idea of taking the School over and running it ourselves."[40]

Another district-wide meeting of school committees took place early in April 1970. In attendance were representatives from reserve communities in which students had been integrated into the public school system. Hearing critical reports about the education provided in provincial schools, those present at the meeting resolved to take over control of Blue Quills. This resolution was telegraphed to the minister of Indian Affairs, Jean Chrétien, the next day.[41] Shortly afterward, the Blue Quills Native Education Council was formed to represent the reserves in the Saddle Lake–Athabasca district and organize the next steps in the struggle. "We can no longer be content to let others do our thinking for us," its constitution stated. "We, ourselves, must take the action which will remove the discrepancies which have existed in education for Indians in the past."[42] The council set a target date of 1 August 1970 for the takeover.[43]

Meetings were subsequently held with representatives from both Indian Affairs and the Alberta Department of Education in an effort to work out an agreement. Indian Affairs pushed for an arrangement whereby reserves would operate like local school districts and follow provincial regulations. This proposal was unacceptable to council members, who viewed it as an attempt to implement the plans laid out in the government's White Paper on Indian policy.[44] By this point, the Indian Association of Alberta and its president, Harold Cardinal supported the movement at Blue Quills. Only a month earlier, the association released *Citizens Plus*, in which the Indigenous chiefs of Alberta decisively rejected the assimilatory vision of the White Paper. Included in the Red Paper, as it came to be called, was a detailed proposal for an Indian Education Centre that would "provide a setting and a learning environment in which Indian men, women and children may develop a deep understanding of themselves, of their history, and of their individual potential."[45] The Red Paper was especially critical of provincial schools, where Indigenous students were routinely "subjected to various types of discriminatory behaviour" as well as to "educational policies that have the effect of emphasizing the social gap between Indigenous reserve communities and town populations."[46]

On 14 July, Harold Cardinal and members of the Blue Quills Native Education Council met with J. B. Bergevin, the assistant deputy minister of Indian Affairs, along with other department officials. These negotiations ended when the council demanded to meet with the minister himself, Jean Chrétien, or else with the deputy minister, H. B. Robinson, for the purpose of arriving at a final agreement regarding the future administration of Blue Quills.[47] It was, in fact, Robinson to whom Redcrow had written with an invitation to this meeting. Instead, Chrétien had chosen to send Bergevin—Robinson's subordinate. From the standpoint of protocol, this was a mistake. In a letter, Redcrow wrote that activists were "prepared to sit there till someone at the ministerial or deputy ministerial level comes to consult with us."[48]

Reclaiming Territory

On that same day, 14 July 1970, roughly sixty protesters occupied the Blue Quills gymnasium. In the days ahead, their numbers swelled. According to one estimate, more than a thousand people eventually took part in the protest. People came and went, with at least two hundred occupying the site at any particular time. Protesters remained on the property both day and night, sleeping in the empty school residence or camping in tents and tipis set up on the lawn. The sit-in attracted not only residents of nearby reserves but also Indigenous people from elsewhere in Alberta as well as Saskatchewan, along with many non-Indigenous allies who travelled to Blue Quills to participate. Free meals were prepared, with people contributing venison or heading out to fish or gather berries and rhubarb. Elders led prayers, there was singing and dancing and storytelling, and the protest acquired a festival-like atmosphere.[49]

The events at Blue Quills generated considerable attention in the media. Articles appeared regularly in both the *St. Paul Journal* and the *Edmonton Journal*, featuring interviews with protesters and photographs of the sit-in. The response of Minister Jean Chrétien—a man known to be one of the driving forces behind the White Paper issued a year earlier—also came under criticism. His refusal to travel to Blue Quills to negotiate an agreement was widely perceived as evidence of the government's lack of any genuine respect for Indigenous people and their concerns. Chrétien's apparent indifference only increased public support for the sit-in, with people writing letters urging him to visit Blue Quills.[50] Supporters organized pickets outside the regional office of Indian Affairs in Edmonton, where they handed out pamphlets supporting the right of Indigenous people to control their own education.[51]

As the protest gained both strength and media coverage, Chrétien finally agreed to meet in person with representatives from Blue Quills, provided that they would come to him. After eliciting a promise that Indian Affairs would cover the cost of the airfare, twenty Blue Quills representatives travelled to Ottawa in late July to negotiate with Chrétien. The group insisted that the meeting continue until the government conceded the right of First Nations to educational autonomy and agreed to turn Blue Quills over to the local community.[52] After two days of meetings, the government capitulated. On 31 July, Chrétien officially informed Redcrow that the school's operations would be transferred to the Blue Quills Native Education Council, with Indian Affairs continuing to provide financial backing. Chrétien added that "I will give immediate and serious considerations to the council's request for additional funds to hold board meetings and to cover training programs and legal services for the coming year."[53] In the wake of this victory, the sit-in ended in early August. Six months later, at the time that the final agreement was signed, Harold Cardinal rightly observed that "the success of our sit-in last summer at Blue Quills was due to our persistence in spite of the many obstacles that were placed before us."[54]

It is easy to lose sight of the momentous significance of this achievement. Success was by no means guaranteed, and some doubted whether the attempt was wise. At one point during the protest, when spirits seemed in danger of flagging, Elder Jonas Cardinal stood up and addressed the crowd. Over the past forty years, he began,

> since the department has had control over our schooling, how many of us completed grade 12? If you have stand up." No one stood up. He went on to enquire, "How many of us completed grade 8? Let's stand up!" One person sheepishly arose from his chair. "How many of us completed grade 6?" A handful of people stood up. Then he said, "Look around. We can't do any worse by taking over this school!

As he went on to say, "We need graduates who will return to our reserves to teach our people so that we can become strong as nations."[55] When asked why she was participating in the protest, Margaret Quinney, a member of the Blue Quills Native Education Council from the Frog Lake reserve, voiced similar sentiments. "If we do not do what we are doing," she replied, "we are going to risk losing what little of our culture, traditions, and spirituality we have left. We want to re-establish our ways and our values. We want a place where we can teach it our way."[56]

The Legacy of Blue Quills

The Blue Quills Native Education Centre opened its doors at the start of September 1971. In the coming years, several other residential schools would follow the pattern set by Blue Quills, at least to the extent that local First Nations assumed control over the residence facilities associated with these schools. The first of these was the Qu'Appelle Indian Residential School, at the White Calf reserve in Saskatchewan's Qu'Appelle Valley, northeast of Regina. In 1972, a council was formed to negotiate the transfer of the school to local control, and the following year White Calf Collegiate opened, with the band administering the residence and, eventually, the school itself. Very shortly thereafter, First Nations bands in the Prince Albert area reached a similar agreement with Indian Affairs regarding the residence at the Prince Alberta Indian Residential School.[57] Yet, as Milloy points out, in the end "only five schools, all in Saskatchewan, followed the Blue Quills–Qu'Appelle lead."[58] For the most part, residential schools were simply shut down, with students either moving to band-controlled day schools or else into provincial schools.

The legacy of Blue Quills largely lies elsewhere, however. Even if only a limited number of residential schools ultimately passed into the hands of First Nations communities, the victory at Blue Quills inaugurated a new era, one in which Indigenous people would come to gain greater control over their education. In the aftermath of the protest at Blue Quills, the National Indian Brotherhood established a working group on education. The result was *Indian Control of Indian Education*, a landmark position paper submitted to Indian Affairs late in 1972. Enshrined in it were two fundamental principles—that parents are responsible for setting the goals of their children's education and that local communities must exercise control over that education. "We want education to provide the setting in which our children can develop the fundamental attitudes and values which have an honored place in Indian tradition and culture," its authors wrote. The values that First Nations parents wish to instill in their children "are not written in any book. They are found in our history, in our legends and in the culture."[59] *Indian Control of Indian Education* would set the direction for future educational policy. At Blue Quills, First Nations had drawn a line. No longer would they allow others to dictate the terms of their education.

These events occurred at a time when well over half of all First Nations students—more than forty thousand of them—were already enrolled in provincial schools.[60] While Indian Affairs had now shown itself willing to consider band-controlled schools as an alternative to integration, it was also committed to closing residential schools, and it was not prepared to fund the construction of an entirely new First Nations–only school system that would serve children at all grade levels. Inevitably, then, many First Nations students were destined to remain in provincial schools. At the same time, as the report of the Truth and Reconciliation Commission observes, "debates over the effectiveness of the federal government's integration policy had highlighted both the direct and institutional racism that students were subjected to in public schools."[61] In other words, the protest at Blue Quills, in tandem with position papers such as *Citizens Plus* and

Indian Control of Indian Education, had brought the truth out into the open. Through words and actions, First Nations had collectively initiated a process of consciousness-raising that would irrevocably alter provincial education policy and programming.

In 1975, for example, the Task Force on the Educational Needs of Native Peoples of Ontario began by soliciting input from Indigenous organizations throughout the province. Its report, tabled on 30 June 1976, made numerous recommendations about changes to school curricula that would be needed to incorporate Indigenous perspectives and history. The task force also insisted that schools serving Indigenous students must employ Indigenous teachers and counsellors and that students must have access to adequate financial assistance.[62] Other such initiatives followed, as provincial authorities gradually came to recognize that Indigenous communities must be allowed to take part in curriculum development and policy planning. In Alberta, the Native Education Project, established in 1984, undertook province-wide consultations with Indigenous communities, the results of which were summarized in *Native Education in Alberta: Native People's Views on Native Education,* a report prepared in 1985.[63] In 1987, Alberta Education released an aspirational policy statement titled *Native Education in Alberta's Schools.* In it, Alberta Education professed its commitment to working with school boards and Indigenous communities to develop classroom materials, including resources for the teaching of Indigenous languages, and to providing opportunities for parents to become more closely involved in their children's education.[64]

The protesters who occupied Blue Quills did not, however, set out to improve provincial education, although they were probably pleased to see public schools become more responsive to the needs of Indigenous students. Rather, they wanted to create their own model of education. In 2015—close to half a century after the protest at Blue Quills—the Truth and Reconciliation Commission issued its ninety-four calls to action. Of the seven that pertain directly to education, one calls for federal legislation dedicated to principles such as "Improving education attainment levels and success rates," "Developing culturally appropriate curricula," and "Enabling parents to fully participate in the education of their children."[65] Another challenges the government to eliminate the gap in federal funding for on-reserve education as opposed to education off reserve. Amidst talk of the need to "Indigenize" the academy, questions still remain about how well the policy of integration truly answers the needs of Indigenous students and honours Indigenous perspectives.

The original Blue Quills school building still stands in the open fields to the west of St. Paul, its red brick walls a reminder of a system that no longer exists but whose effects continue to reverberate across the generations. Inside those walls, however, is a world transformed—a world that centres Indigenous ways of knowing and being while at the same time incorporating elements of Western knowledge systems. Perhaps integration began in the wrong place. Perhaps, as the treaties envisioned, it is up to Indigenous peoples to decide how far to "Westernize" their academy.

NOTES

1. *Pimohteskanaw, 1971–2001: Blue Quills First Nations College*, commemorative ed. (St. Paul, AB: Blue Quills First Nations College, 2001), http://www.bluequills.ca/wp-content/uploads/2012/02/BQ-30th-Anniversary-Book.pdf, iii. According to this account, much of which was provided by Elder Stanley Redcrow, the people of Saddle Lake wanted to have a school in their own community, to avoid the need to travel all the way to Lac La Biche.

2. Lucy Bashford and Hans Heinzerling, "Blue Quills Native Education Centre: A Case Study," in *Indian Education in Canada*, vol. 2, *The Challenge*, ed. Jean Barman, Yvonne Hébert, and Don McCaskill (Vancouver: University of British Columbia Press, 1987), 126.

3. There are a few terms used in this chapter that need explanation. The term "Indian" was first used when colonizers thought they had arrived in India; thus, they called the natives of the land "Indian." This term was used well into the nineteenth century and is still present in government acts, titles, and department names. For instance, the term is still used in the *Indian Act*. During the 1970s, the term "First Nations" replaced the term "Indian" because many people found the term to be derogatory and offensive. The terms "nation" and "band" are sometimes used interchangeably since they refer to a group of Indigenous people recognized under Canada's *Indian Act*. "Nation" refers to the entire group, while "band" is a sub-group of the nation that lives on reserves. Each band has an elected band council that governs the collective use of lands in reserve territory. I use the term "Indigenous" when the legal term "First Nations" seems restrictive. "Indigenous" is a broader term that includes those recognized and not recognized by the federal government.

4. *Dominion of Canada Annual Reports of the Department of Indian Affairs for the year ended June 30, 1889*, Library and Archives Canada [hereafter LAC], Department of Indian Affairs [DIA], Annual Reports, 14. http://www.bac-lac.gc.ca/Pages/default.aspx

5. Ibid.

6. *Annual Report*, 1932, LAC, DIA. The number of school-aged children in the Dominion of Canada in 1889 was 15,835. Out of 107 students enrolled in boarding schools, the daily attendance average was 81 students. Out of 593 students enrolled in industrial schools, the daily attendance average was 569. And, of 5,759 students enrolled in 250 day schools across the Dominion, the daily average attendance was 2,980. Average low attendance in day schools was used as evidence that boarding schools and industrial schools were providing children with better education. The assumption was that a child's family home and community—where they could speak their native language and participate in cultural activities—were not sites of learning and education.

7. Sheila Carr-Stewart, "A Treaty Right to Education," 138. Broadly speaking, First Nations viewed the treaties as agreements between equals, whereby their communities would receive certain benefits—including access to Western knowledge and skills—in exchange for sharing their land with settlers. Carr-Stewart writes that Indigenous people also thought they could "supplement their community educational practices with the linguistic and literacy skills of the settlers" (3). Yet, as Carr-Stewart goes on to point out, First Nations students were instead "forced into an educational system that sought to eliminate their traditional educational practices, languages, culture, and customs, something that had not been a part of the treaty negotiations" (138).

8. J. R. Miller, *Shingwauk's Vision: A History of Native Residential Schools*, (Toronto: University of Toronto Press, 1997), 10.

9. Celia Haig-Brown, *Resistance and Renewal: Surviving the Indian Residential School* (Vancouver: Tillacum Library, 1988), 56.

10. TRC, AVS, Andrew Bull Calf, Statement to the Truth and Reconciliation Commission of Canada, Lethbridge, Alberta, 10 October 2013, Statement Number: 2011-0273. 49.

11. Mary-Ellen Kelm, "'A Scandalous Procession': Residential Schooling and the Re/formation of Aboriginal Bodies, 1900–1950," *Native Studies Review*, vol. 11 (1996), 51.

12. John S. Milloy, *A National Crime: The Canadian Government and the Residential School System, 1879 to 1986* (Winnipeg: University of Manitoba Press, 1999), 158.

13. See Truth and Reconciliation Commission of Canada (hereafter TRC), *Canada's Residential Schools*, vol. 1, pt. 2, *The History: 1939 to 2000* (Montréal and Kingston: McGill-Queen's University Press, 2015), 3–4; the quotation is from p. 4.

14. John F. Leslie, "Assimilation, Integration or Termination? The Development of Canadian Indian Policy, 1943–1963" (PhD diss., Department of History, Carleton University, 1999), 112.

15. Quoted in J. R. Miller, *Shingwauk's Vision: A History of Native Residential Schools* (Toronto: University of Toronto Press, 1997), 389–90. On the work of the committee, see Jim McMurtry, "The 1946–48 Special Joint Committee on the Indian Act and Educational Policy" (MEd thesis, Department of Educational Foundations, University of Alberta, 1985); and Leslie, "Assimilation, Integration or Termination?" chap. 3.

16. Miller, *Shingwauk's Vision*, 391–92.

17. *The Indian Act*, SC, 1951, c. 29, s. 113(b).

18. Ibid., s. 117. For a discussion of the implementation of the new policy during the 1950s, see TRC, *Canada's Residential Schools*, vol. 1, pt. 2, *The History: 1939 to 2000*, 56–59. As the commission notes, "just as Aboriginal people had been granted no input into the Indian Affairs school system, they had little ability to influence the provincial schools" (59),

19. Miller, *Shingwauk's Vision*, 135.

20. *Report of the Royal Commission on Aboriginal Peoples*, vol. 1, *Looking Forward, Looking Back* (Ottawa: Minister of Supply and Services Canada, 1996), 319–20, citing R. F. Davey, "Residential Schools—Past and Future," 8 March 1968.

21. Ibid., 320.

22. "Silver Jubilee Encouraging Progress Toward Integration," *St. Paul Journal*, 31 May 1956, 1. On the evolution of education at Blue Quills during the 1950s and the growth of tensions between the Catholic Church and Indian Affairs, see Diane Persson, "The Changing Experience of Indian Residential Schooling: Blue Quills, 1931–1970," in *Indian Education in Canada*, vol. 1, *The Legacy*, ed. Jean Barman and Don McCaskill (Vancouver: University of British Columbia Press, 1986), 157–63.

23. *Report of the Royal Commission on Aboriginal Peoples*, vol. 1, *Looking Forward, Looking Back*, 320.

24. Morton Newman, *Indians of the Saddle Lake Reserve: Community Opportunity Assessment* (Edmonton: Government of Alberta, Executive Council, Human Resources Research and Development, 1967), 88. Newman's findings are based on interviews conducted in the latter half of 1966 (7). His research formed part of a broader community opportunity assessment

study directed by C. W. Hobart, and his report on Saddle Lake appeared as appendix F in Hobart's final report.

25. "Education Bridge for Integration Says U of A Professor," *St. Paul Journal,* 31 March 1966, 1, 3.

26. In recent years, scholars have expanded the conceptual boundaries of this problem. In her groundbreaking study *Decolonizing Education: Nourishing the Learning Spirit* (Saskatoon: Purich Publishing, 2013), for example, Mi'kmaw scholar Marie Battiste argues that Western education itself is detrimental to Indigenous students in that it is founded, in both theory and practice, on a Eurocentric world view that denies the value of Indigenous knowledges and promotes assimilation by forcing students to work within a colonial framework to succeed. Even in the absence of overt racism and discrimination, this process of colonization continues to undermine the psychological integrity of Indigenous students, who find themselves split between two worlds. This is especially the case when considering Indigenous pedagogical practices as a reflection of worldview and the emphasis on orality. On Indigenous pedagogical practices, see Donald Fixico, *The American Indian Mind in a Linear World: American Indian Studies and Traditional Knowledge* (New York: Routledge, 2003). On oral history and storytelling, see Keith Thor Carlson, Kristina Rose Fagan, and Natalia Khanenko-Friesen, eds., *Orality and Literacy: Reflections Across Disciplines* (Toronto: University of Toronto Press, 2011) and Julie Cruikshank, *The Social Life of Stories: Narrative and Knowledge in the Yukon Territory* (Lincoln: University of Nebraska Press, 1998), 64.

27. On the federal government's initial efforts to promote integration, see Milloy, *National Crime,* 200–202. As he points out, Indian Affairs had been pursuing "joint schools" arrangements with local school boards since 1949 and began pursuing formal arrangements with provinces early in the 1960s.

28. "Educational Services for Indians," memorandum, Department of Indian Affairs, 24 March 1969, quoted in ibid., 202.

29. Harold Cardinal, *The Unjust Society,* 2nd ed. (Vancouver: Douglas and McIntyre; Seattle: University of Washington Press. 1999), 12, 13. First published 1969 by M. G. Hurtig (Edmonton).

30. Ibid., 15.

31. *Annual Report of the Department of Indian Affairs, 1956–57,* quoted in TRC, *Canada's Residential Schools,* vol. 1, pt. 2, *The History: 1939 to 2000,* 86.

32. Newman, *Indians of the Saddle Lake Reserve,* 86. As Newman goes on note, researchers interviewed five teenage girls who had dropped out of Blue Quills, and "all stated that advances made to them by the priest had been the

main reason for their leaving"—a situation for which Indian Affairs was able to supply supporting evidence (86).

33. TRC, *Canada's Residential Schools*, vol. 1, pt. 2, *The History: 1939 to 2000*, 86.

34. V. G. Boultbee to M. G. Jutras, 12 March 1970, quoted in ibid., 88.

35. "An Interview with Stanley Redcrow," *Saskatchewan Indian* 3, no. 2 (February 1972): 8.

36. Bashford and Heinzerling, "Blue Quills Native Education Centre," 127.

37. TRC, *Canada's Residential Schools*, vol. 1, pt. 2, *The History: 1939 to 2000*, 86–87. The meeting took place 29–31 October 1969. According to Bashford and Heinzerling, this news was communicated by the acting district school superintendent: see "Blue Quills Native Education Centre," 127.

38. TRC, *Canada's Residential Schools*, vol. 1, pt. 2, *The History: 1939 to 2000*, 87.

39. Ibid.; the quotation is from the minutes of the meeting.

40. "Interview with Stanley Redcrow," 8.

41. TRC, *Canada's Residential Schools*, vol. 1, pt. 2, *The History: 1939 to 2000*, 88. The telegram elicited only a request for further information.

42. Indian Association of Alberta (IAA), Treaty and Aboriginal Rights Research Program (TARR), Blue Quills Administrative Take-Over, 12 June 1970.

43. TRC, *Canada's Residential Schools*, vol. 1, pt. 2, *The History: 1939 to 2000*, 88.

44. Ibid., 89.

45. Indian Chiefs of Alberta, *Citizens Plus* (Edmonton: Indian Association of Alberta, 1970), reprinted *Aboriginal Policy Studies* 1, no. 2 (2011): 242.

46. Ibid., 272.

47. Ibid., 89–90.

48. Stanley Redcrow, 9 July 1970, School Buildings, Blue Quills Student Residence, vol. 11, Library and Archives Canada, Department of Indian Affairs, RG10, R216, file 779/6-1-009.

49. TRC, *Canada's Residential Schools*, vol. 1, pt. 2, *The History: 1939 to 2000*, 90, citing a Canadian Press report by Dennis Bell, "Indian School," 15 September 1970. See also: Milloy, *National Crime*, 236; 10 July 1970, Blue Quills Administrative Take-Over, Sub-series 5: Blue Quills Residential School, Special Committees, Indian Association of Alberta, Treaty Aboriginal Rights Research Program.

50. Chief Deiter to Jean Chrétien, 20 July 1970, Library and Archives Canada, Department of Indian Affairs, file 779/6-1-009, vol. 11. 01/70-11/74; Jim Shot Both Sides to Jean Chrétien 22 July 1970, Library and Archives Canada, Department of Indian Affairs, file 779/2, 03/60-12/70, vol. 2; Paul Yewchuk to Jean Chrétien 20 July 1970, Library and Archives Canada, Department of Indian Affairs, file 779/25-1-1, vol. 1, 04/70-02/71.

51. 9 July 1970, School Buildings, Blue Quills Students Residence.

52. "Blue Quills Native Education Council," 27 July 1970, Blue Quills
Administrative Take-Over, Sub-series 5: Blue Quills Residential School,
Special Committees, Indian Association of Alberta, Treaty Aboriginal Rights
Research Program.

53. For the text of Chrétien's letter, see *Pimohteskanaw, 1971–2001*, 3. See also
"Indians Will Operate Blue Quills School," *Edmonton Journal*, 1 August 1970,
28. The transfer of the residence facility at Blue Quills was scheduled for 1
January 1971, while school operations would be transferred on 1 July 1971.

54. "Final Agreement of Blue Quills Take-Over Is Officially Signed," *St. Paul
Journal*, 10 February 1971, 1.

55. Quoted in *Pimohteskanaw, 1971–2001*, 2–3, as part of an account provided
by Mike Steinhauer. Charles Wood, manager of the Saddle Lake band, also
remembered Jonas Cardinal's speech. See "Native Awakening: Alberta
Indians Occupy a Rural Residential School and Signal a New Era in Native
Activism," CBC Learning, *Canada: A People's History*, 2001, http://www.cbc.
ca/history/EPISCONTENTSE1EP16CH2PA3LE.html.

56. Quoted in *Pimohteskanaw, 1971–2001*, 2.

57. For more on these examples and others, see TRC, *Canada's Residential
Schools*, vol. 1, pt. 2, *The History: 1939 to 2000*, 93–97. The desire to see
residences remain open reflected concerns about alternative housing for
children who had to travel some distance to attend school. Very often, when
a residential school closed, Indian Affairs handed over responsibility for the
children enrolled in it to provincial child welfare authorities, who proceeded
to place the children in foster homes—an arrangement that many parents
found unacceptable (93–94).

58. Milloy, *A National Crime*, 238.

59. National Indian Brotherhood, *Indian Control of Indian Education* (Ottawa:
National Indian Brotherhood, 1972), 2. See also TRC, *Canada's Residential
Schools*, vol. 1, pt. 2, *The History: 1939 to 2000*, 91–92.

60. According to the annual report of Indian Affairs for 1973–74, there were
42,022 students enrolled in provincial schools, compared to only 32,563 in
schools run by Indian Affairs. Cited in TRC, *Canada's Residential Schools*,
vol. 1, pt. 2, *The History: 1939 to 2000*, 92.

61. Ibid., 93.

62. Chiefs of Ontario, "Elements of Quality First Nations Education Systems,"
2–3, in *The New Agenda: A Manifesto for First Nation Education in Ontario*,
April 2005, http://education.chiefs-of-ontario.org/article/manifesto-269.asp.

63. Native Education Project, *Native Education in Alberta: Alberta Native
People's Views on Native Education*, 1985, https://archive.org/details/
nativeeducationiooalbe, 3. (The report was released by Alberta Education

in March 1987.) The Native Education Project was initiated in the wake of recommendations contained in *Native People in the Curriculum,* a 1982 ad hoc committee report on learning resources.

64. See Alberta Education, *Native Education in Alberta's Schools: Policy Statement on Native Education in Alberta,* March 1987, https://archive.org/ details/policystatementoooalbe, 4–5.

65. *Truth and Reconciliation Commission of Canada: Calls to Action* (Winnipeg: Truth and Reconciliation Commission of Canada, 2015), nos. 10 (ii, iii, and vi) and 8.

3

"We are on the outside looking in [. . .]. But we are still Indians"

Alberta Indigenous Women Fighting for Status Rights, 1968–85

Corinne George

In November 1973, Nellie Carlson wrote a letter to Jean Chrétien, minister of Indian and Northern Affairs, on behalf of the Alberta committee of Indian Rights for Indian Women (IRIW), saying, "At the present time, Indian women are denied the freedom of marriage and should they choose to exercise that right despite section 12(1)(b) of the Indian Act, she faces exclusion from her home, the deprivation of her rights and most importantly her identity as an Indian is diminished."[1] Carlson's letter was one of many requests made to the federal government to address the oppressive elements of the Indian Act. She and a number of Indigenous women in Alberta and throughout the country rallied specifically to ensure that their identity as "Indian women" was acknowledged in the act.

This chapter focuses on the activism of Nellie Carlson, Jenny Margetts, and Christine Daniels, three Alberta women who were central to the formation of both the Alberta committee of IRIW and the national organization. Their aims were to lobby for changes to the Indian Act and educate others on the plight of Indigenous women. Women like Carlson, Margetts, and Daniels who were involved in IRIW maintained their identities as "Indian" (hereafter Indian) women, retained a strong connection to Indigenous culture and identity, and resisted forced assimilation through the Indian Act, which had caused them to move from their home communities. After years of struggle, in 1985 the Indian Act was amended through Bill C-31. While the women involved in IRIW were ultimately successful, they faced opposition along the way. Much of the opposition to the IRIW stemmed from personal and community connections to oil and gas resources, concerns about potential overcrowding on reserves, and fear that changing the Indian Act would have negative impacts on treaty rights.

Historian Olive Dickason contends that the main purpose of the Indian Act was assimilation.[2] That goal made the act contentious. Another aspect was also controversial: the act discriminated against Indigenous women and their freedom to marry whomever they chose. Starting in 1869, section 6 decreed that if an Indian woman married a non-Indian, she would lose her status.[3] From 1869 to 1951, this portion of the act underwent minor revisions. In 1876, this section became part of the Indian Act, as section 3(3)(c) of which read as follows:

> Provided that any Indian woman marrying any other than an Indian or non-treaty Indian shall cease to be an Indian in any respect within the meaning of this Act, except that she shall be entitled to share equally with the members of the band to which she formerly belonged, in the annual or semi-annual distribution of their annuities, interest moneys and rents; but this income may be commuted to her at any time at ten years' purchase with the consent of the band.[4]

This meant that even after losing their status by "marrying out," Indigenous women could still receive shares of the bands' annual payments. They could also opt to receive a lump sum worth approximately ten years of their annual share. The sums offered were normally quite low, however.

From 1876 to 1951, this provision remained largely unchanged. In the 1951 revisions to the Indian Act, the section 12(1)(b) was amended to read "the following persons are not entitled to be registered, namely a woman who is married to a person who is not an Indian."[5] The 1951 change stripped the few remaining band rights of non-status Indigenous women. An Indian woman who "married out"—married a man who was not Indian (or did not have Indian status)—was no longer registered or recognized as an Indian under the Indian Act. This 1951 amendment also provided that if an Indian woman's husband died or abandoned her, she would lose Indian status; her status was conditional on his.[6] These are only some examples of gender discrimination within the Indian Act. Kathleen Jamieson outlined further elements of the Indian Act that discriminated against Indigenous women:

> The woman, on marriage must leave her parents' home and her reserve. She may not own property on the reserve and must dispose of any property she does hold. She may be prevented from inheriting property left to her by her parents. She cannot take any further part in band business. Her children are not recognized as Indian and are therefore denied access to cultural and social amenities of the Indian community. And most punitive of all, she may be prevented from returning to live with her family on the reserve, even if she is in dire need, very ill, a widow, divorced or separated. Finally, her body may not be buried on the reserve with those of her forebearers.[7]

Indigenous women in Alberta and across the country who were discriminated against in the Indian Act outwardly challenged a system designed to marginalize them and their identities. Through actively challenging the Indian Act, these women were in fact challenging colonialism at all levels; politically, culturally, and socially. Yet, like the broader history of Indigenous women in urban areas, the story of the Alberta activists is only partially told. In 2013, Linda Goyette shared the experiences of Nellie Carlson and Kathleen Steinhauer, writing that "throughout their lives, Nellie and Kathleen have rejected the Canadian government's never-ending attempts to define, legislate, and restrict the identity of First Nations, Métis and Inuit peoples."[8] Goyette outlines Carlson's and Steinhauer's engagement in the struggle but acknowledges that the account is somewhat fragmented because some details were based on conversations, while others were based on notes and other recordings.[9]

Using oral history interviews carried out with seven Indigenous women, this chapter builds on and adds to the scholarship on Indigenous women activists in urban settings, particularly in Edmonton from 1951 to 1985. During that time, Indigenous women still contended with stereotypes and discrimination, yet they were vocal in addressing these issues and worked to dispel myths and create a more welcoming environment for Indigenous people in urban settings.

Carlson, Daniels, and Margetts were Cree from Saddle Lake reserve in Alberta. All eventually lost their status and moved away from the reserve. Carlson was born on 3 July 1927.[10] In 1947, she married a man whose mother was Indian and whose father was Swedish, which meant that Carlson's husband and their children were non-status.[11] She became what was described as a "red ticket holder"—married to a non-status man yet living on reserve.[12] When she moved off reserve in 1956, Carlson removed her name from the band list. One of the reasons she chose to move away from the reserve was that her doctor (who was Métis) had informed her that she could not actively speak out against the Indian Act if she was a status Indian.[13] In 1963, Carlson and her husband moved farther away from her family and reserve, to Edmonton, to attend to her husband's health problems. Carlson's husband was unable to access health services on the reserve because he was not recognized as a status Indian.

Daniels (née Whiskeyjack) was a co-founder of the Voice of Alberta Native Women's Society (VANWS), where she addressed concerns about treaty women losing their rights when they married non-treaty men.[14] VANWS was created in 1968, after a group of Alberta Indigenous women congregated at the Mayfair Hotel in Edmonton for the First Alberta Native Women's Conference.[15] VANWS, like IRIW, was created as a way for Indigenous women to come together and fight the discrimination they experienced as the result of sexism, racism, and colonialism. However, while IRIW focused on the issue of Indigenous women's status, VANWS focused on multiple issues that affected Indigenous women and families, such as Native foster care programs, ways to keep one's Indigenous identity while working in modern jobs or attending university, and, of course, the issues around marriage and status in the Indian Act. VANWS took up both treaty and Métis women's interests.

Margetts, a co-founder of IRIW, was born on 14 June 1936. She lost her Indian status in 1960 after marrying a non-Indian man and moving to Edmonton.[16]

One of the events that helped to stimulate the formation of IRIW was the First Alberta Native Women's Conference in Edmonton in 1968. Organized by the same group of women who formed VANWS following the conference, this gathering of Indigenous women was one of the first forums where Indigenous women could discuss the discrimination they experienced.[17] Some of the presentations given at the conference were "The Role of Native Women," by Mary Anne Lavelle; "Challenges Facing Native Women Today," by Alice Mustos; and "Challenges Facing Métis Women," by Clara Yellowknee.[18] The conference sparked further grassroots organization among Indigenous women. Another precedent to IRIW was the formation of

Equal Rights for Indian Women in 1969 by Mary Two-Axe Early, a Mohawk from Kahnawake, Québec, who founded the group to address discriminatory sections of the Indian Act.[19]

Another catalyst was the Jeanette Lavell legal case, which was initiated in 1970.[20] Lavell was an "Ojibwa woman" who had married a non-Indian, lost her status, and then challenged the deletion of her name from the band list. Lavell was joined in her case by Yvonne Bédard, a Six Nations woman who had lost her Indian status upon marrying out but who had subsequently separated from her husband. Bédard was fighting the Six Nations band council's attempts to evict her from the reserve and from the house that had been willed to her by her mother.[21] During the court process, the number of Indigenous women and children who had lost their status because of section 12 was revealed to be six thousand.[22] Lillian Shirt, also from Saddle Lake and a sister of Jenny Margetts, recalled the personal impact on her family and the pain caused by that section of the Indian Act:

> We could not go back to the reserve, if the woman married, we were not an Indian, if we married a white man. And that was unjust also. So, she [Jenny] registered an organization called 'Indian Rights for Indian Women.'. . . At that time, my sister Ursula had two children, had just had a miscarriage, got chased off the reserve . . . and my dad cried. And I remember my dad looking at my sister Ursula and her family in the wagon . . . the team of horses pulling this cow and rope and a couple of horses and a rope. And my dad standing at the window . . . "Ah-hu-ya!! . . ." and he held . . . he put his hand to his heart, he said, "it hurts."[23]

As part of the education and activism stimulated by the Lavell case, in 1972 a panel was organized by Daniels and others at the University of Calgary. The panel heard from Margetts, Lavell, and Philamene Ross, along with two status women who opposed their views. Margetts explained, "I strongly recommended this kind of exposure before the Supreme Court hearing in April. [. . .] Strong action is definitely needed to make the government aware of this injustice done to Indian women."[24] In January 1973, another step was taken when a newsletter authored by Margetts announced the formation of the Alberta Committee of IRIW. Its first act was to conduct a workshop to promote understanding of the Indian Act and the Canadian Bill of Rights, which had been passed in 1960. She hoped that women in other provinces would commit to similar approaches to educate the public on the Indian

Act's injustices toward Indian women.[25] Reflecting on that critical juncture, Carlson recalled that Alberta Indigenous women responded to the call to support Lavell by formally registering the Indian Rights for Indian Women as an organization: "There were fifteen of us that were really determined in the Alberta committee. We registered the organization, and we went and supported the Supreme Court case . . . Jeanette Lavell's case."[26]

It came as a shock to Lavell and her supporters when, on 27 August 1973, a majority (but not unanimous) decision of the Supreme Court of Canada ruled that section 12 of the Indian Act did not in fact discriminate against women. Carlson and others, however, were encouraged that a minority opinion, held by Chief Bora Laskin, argued that—in Carlson's words—"it's up to the parliament to change this Act. And so, again, we started all over again and we lobbied the government. [. . .] [F]or seventeen years we lobbied."[27]

Through the IRIW, Indigenous women activists in Alberta sought to protest the decision and educate other Indigenous people as well as other members of Canadian society about the legal discrimination in the act. On 22 October 1973, IRIW staged a demonstration in front of the legislative buildings in Edmonton to protest the Lavell decision.[28] The action was among many that took place simultaneously across Canada. Brief and peaceful, the demonstration was described by the *Native People*, a publication of the Alberta Native Communications Society, as "a day of mourning in reference to the Canadian Bill of Rights which until the August 27th decision assured equality before the law as a right belonging to all Canadians."[29] Some demonstrators wore black to illustrate their feelings of disappointment. Carlson, who was a prominent figure at this demonstration, once again pledged her commitment to continue to fight.[30]

Education was an important vehicle in the campaign. In March 1977, Margetts spoke at a Native Land Claims conference at the University of Alberta. She stressed her Indigenous identity despite the fact that the Indian Act did not recognize her as such. The *Native People* reported that although she was married to a non-Native, "Mrs. Margetts refuses to consider herself and women like her as anything other than Indians in spite of enfranchisement regulations."[31] So important was the issue, Margetts argued, that it needed to be addressed before land claims were pursued.

In November 1977, Margetts requested federal funding to allow IRIW to undertake a national research project on the issue of Indigenous women's rights across Canada. She added that if funding were to materialize, it should be used to gather historical, ethnographic, and sociological data on Native women's rights.[32] The *Native People* published an article describing a workshop organized by IRIW, titled "National Indian Rights for Women," held in April 1978 in St. Albert, Alberta.[33] Twenty-nine women from across Canada attended this workshop to discuss issues surrounding the status of Indian women, their spouses, and their children. The experiences shared at the 1978 workshop were used in Kathleen Jamieson's book *Indian Women and the Law in Canada: Citizens Minus*. In November 1978, IRIW held its fifth annual conference in Edmonton. Sixty delegates from the western Prairie provinces attended. In an interview published in the *Native People*, Margetts explained,

> We are told that the government recognizes the injustices of the present situation and that they are prepared to make changes. But what changes? Now is the time to put on the pressures to make sure that the changes made are ones that will meet our needs and help eliminate discrimination. Our children cannot be deprived of their heritage and inheritance. They deserve a promising future and only we can make it happen for them.[34]

In these efforts to revise the Indian Act, Margetts strongly recommended unity among Indigenous people. A common response was critical to effecting change. Margetts also sought more open discussion among Indigenous people. Her group had approached reserve communities in the province to hold informational and consultative meetings, but some communities denied them permission. The delegates left the conference determined to be involved in the consultative process and to continue lobbying for changes to the Indian Act.[35]

The women of IRIW faced tremendous opposition. As they vocalized their grievances, opposition from some Indigenous organizations and the federal government emerged. A 1978 *Edmonton Journal* article explained that some Indigenous leaders in Alberta feared an influx of women and their non-Indigenous husbands returning to the reserves and sharing in the band resources, which often included oil and gas revenues. Although a number of Indigenous organizations supported Indigenous women, some leaders were unsympathetic, arguing, "They knew what they were giving up when they decided to get married."[36] Carlson reflected on her experiences during this period of conflict: "We were followed everywhere, our phones were tapped, our mail was confiscated . . . simply because we said, 'We are Indian women of Canada and we lost the rights that we were rightfully born with.' That was the punishment we received."[37] To this day, Carlson does not know who tapped their phones or who was sent to follow her and others. But even without these specifics, her recollection illuminates the hostility felt by some toward the activism of Carlson and others like her.

A breakthrough came in 1981, when Sandra Lovelace, a Maliseet woman who lost her status and band membership when she married a non-Indian man, challenged the Canadian government through the United Nations Human Rights Committee. The UNHRC found the government of Canada in breach of the International Covenant on Civil and Political Rights and concluded that section 12(1)(b) of the Indian Act was sexually discriminatory. Shamed domestically and internationally, in 1985 the government of Canada finally yielded.[38] On 28 June 1985, Bill C-31 was passed to end sexual discrimination in the Indian Act. It also eliminated regulated enfranchisement of Indigenous people, provided for the reinstatement of women who had lost their status, and, for the first time since Confederation, gave power to the bands to formulate and administer their own membership codes.[39] In other words, the legal process for terminating a person's Indian status and conferring full Canadian citizenship no longer existed.[40] As a result of the change, 16,200 people who had been disinherited regained their status. Complications remained, including the termination of status after two generations of intermarriage between Indians and non-Indians and the restrictive membership codes of some, but not all, bands.[41] Yet despite the challenges, Indigenous women won a significant fight to address some of their grievances against the discriminatory sections of the Indian Act.

Carlson, Daniels, and Margetts were among the many women across Canada active at the grassroots level of the IRIW. These women were unrelenting in their efforts, with their activism taking the form of lobbying and education. Connection to community and family and economic well-being were among the reasons why having status, keeping band membership, and maintaining the option to live on the reserves were so significant. In striving to reclaim a place in Indigenous society and within the community that was rightfully theirs, they were adamant that discriminatory federal legislation would not dictate their identities as Indian women.

NOTES

1. Linda Goyette, "Chiefs' Stand Divides Native Women," *Edmonton Journal,* 16 May 1984. This article is also the source of the quotation in this chapter's title. The comment was made by Indigenous activist Jenny Margetts, in reaction the adverse discriminatory elements of the Indian Act towards Indian Women.

2. Olive Patricia Dickason, *Canada's First Nations: A History of Founding Peoples from Earliest Times,* 3rd ed. (Toronto: Oxford University Press, 2002), 263.

3. Sharon Helen Venne, comp., *Indian Act and Amendments, 1868–1975: An Indexed Collection* (Saskatchewan: University of Saskatchewan Native Law Centre, 1981), 12.

4. The Indian Act, 1976, https://www.aadnc-aandc.gc.ca/DAM/DAM-INTER-HQ/STAGING/texte-text/1876c18_1100100010253_eng.pdf. In a subsequent amendment, "with the consent of the band" was replaced with "with the approval of the Superintendent General" (of Indian Affairs). See Venne, *Indian Act and Amendments,* 249.

5. Venne, *Indian Act and Amendments,* 319.

6. "Bill C-31," IndigenousFoundations.arts.ubc.ca, First Nations Studies Program, 2009, http://indigenousfoundations.arts.ubc.ca/bill_c-31/.

7. Kathleen Jamieson, *Indian Women and the Law: Citizens Minus* (Ottawa: Minister of Supply and Services, 1978), 1.

8. Nellie Carlson and Kathleen Steinhauer, as told to Linda Goyette, *Disinherited Generations: Our Struggle to Reclaim Treaty Rights for First Nations Women and Their Descendants* (Edmonton: University of Alberta Press, 2013), xxii.

9. Carlson and Steinhauer, *Disinherited Generations,* xxii–xxiii.

10. Nellie M. Carlson, interview by the author, 2 August 2006, transcript.

11. "Committed to Her People," *Edmonton Journal,* 4 November 1988, Newspaper Clippings, Alberta: 1968–2004, City of Edmonton Archives (hereafter EA).

12. Red ticket holder: "Some Indian agencies had issued prior to 1951 an identity card called a 'Red Ticket' to such women (Indian women who 'married out' prior to 1951 who retained the right to collect annuities and band monies." Jamieson, *Indian Women and the Law,* 61. Indian women who married out prior to 1951 could retain their red ticket status; in 1956, an amendment to the Indian Act stopped this practice. Government of Canada, *Report of the Royal Commission on Aboriginal Peoples,* vol. 4, *Perspectives and Realities: Women's Perspectives* (Ottawa, 1996), http://data2.archives.ca/e/e448/e011188230-04.pdf.

13. Carlson, interview.

14. "Let's Meet Christine Daniels," *Native People,* April 1971, 6.

15. "Report of the First Alberta Native Women's Conference, Mayfair Hotel, Edmonton, March 12–15, 1968," Ralph Garvin Steinhauer fonds, M-7934-46, Glenbow Archives, Calgary; "History of the V.A.N.W.S.," Stan Daniels fonds, PR1999.465, box 8, file 78, Provincial Archives of Alberta, Edmonton.

16. "Jenny Margetts," *Edmonton Journal,* 3 October 2004, Newspaper Clippings, Alberta: 1968–2004, EA.

17. Kathleen Jamieson, "Multiple Jeopardy: The Evolution of a Native Women's Movement," *Atlantis: A Women's Studies Journal* 2, no. 2 (1979): 164.

18. "Report of the First Alberta Native Women's Conference."

19. Mary Two-Axe Early, "Indian Rights for Indian Women," in *Women, Feminism and Development,* ed. Huguette Dagenais and Denise Piché (Montréal and Kingston: McGill-Queens University Press, for the Canadian Research Institute for the Advancement of Women, 1994), 432.

20. Jamieson, "Multiple Jeopardy," 166.

21. Kathleen Jamieson, "Sex Discrimination and the Indian Act," in *Arduous Journey: Canadian Indians and Decolonization,* ed. J. Rick Ponting (Toronto: McClelland and Stewart, 1986), 126.

22. "Lavell Loses Status Case," *Native People,* 31 August 1973.

23. Lillian Shirt, interview by the author, 4 July 2006.

24. Shirt, interview.

25. "Plans for National Committee on Indian Rights for Indian Women: Newsletter, January 15, 1973," 1, 2, Stan Daniels fonds, PR1999:465, box 9, file 82 (2 of 2), Provincial Archives of Alberta, Edmonton.

26. Carlson, interview.

27. Ibid.

28. "Lavell Supporters Demonstrate," *Native People,* 26 October 1973. The article does not specify the number of protesters.

29. Ibid.

30. Ibid.

31. "Native Women's Rights," *Native People,* 1 April 1977.

32. "Native Women's Rights, Status 'Not Ignored,'" *Edmonton Journal,* 15 July 1975, Newspaper Clippings Alberta: 1968–2004, EA.

33. "A.N.C.S. Students . . . Indian Rights for Indian Women," *Native People,* 21 April 1978.

34. "Revision to the Indian Act IRIW's Priority," *Native People,* 10 November 1978.

35. Ibid.

36. "Indian Women's Fight Continues in Alberta," *Edmonton Journal,* 28 July 1978, Newspaper Clippings Alberta: 1968–2004, EA.

37. Carlson, interview.

38. Cora J. Voyageur, "Contemporary Aboriginal Women in Canada," in *Visions of the Heart: Canadian Aboriginal Issues,* 2nd ed., ed. David Long and Olive Patricia Dickason (Toronto: Harcourt Brace, 2000), 92.

39. Jamieson, "Sex Discrimination," 128.

40. "Enfranchisement," IndigenousFoundations.arts.ubc.ca, First Nations Studies Program, 2009, http://indigenousfoundations.arts.ubc.ca/enfranchisement/.

41. Please note that the sources do not identify particular bands limiting membership. See Carlson and Steinhauer, *Disinherited Generations,* xlii–xliii.

PART II

Defying Heteropatriarchy

Lillian Dick objects to Super S Drugs sign, Calgary, March 1970. Courtesy of Calgary Herald Photograph Collection, Glenbow Archives, Calgary, NA-2864-5209.

Calgary Police Chief Inspector Andy Little on Homosexuality, 1968

Speaking to the University of Calgary Psychology Club in October 1968, Calgary Police Chief Inspector Andy Little decried the move to liberalize the Canadian Criminal Code to permit same-sex relations between consenting adults.

"Any homosexual is a potential murderer," he claimed. Questioned by club members, he added that "in order to gratify his alleged need, he will frequently assault a child."

> Nigel Roberts, "Public Blamed for Crime: An Interview," *The Gauntlet*, 2 October 1968, 3.

Calgary Board of Education's Survey on Sexual Activity, 1969

In 1969 the Calgary Board of Education asked students at the city's Crescent Heights High School to give their opinions about a number of aspects of sexual activity. Question number 21 on the form asked: "Now that England no longer regards as criminal homosexuality among consenting adults in private, do you feel that their civilization will collapse on this account? Explain."

> Joanne Hatton, "Progressives and Traditionalists Battle for Control of Education," in *Alberta in the 20th Century: A Journalistic History of the Province*, vol. 10, *The Sixties Revolution and the Fall of Social Credit*, ed. Paul Bunner (Edmonton: United Western Communications, 2002), 135.

Introduction

In Alberta, as elsewhere, challenges to heteropatriarchy mounted by women, on the one hand, and by lesbian and gay persons, on the other, initially evolved along two separate paths. Women activists of the 1960s and 1970s could point to what was, in many respects, an enviable record of feminist agitation. During the early decades of the century, the so-called Famous Five—Henrietta Muir Edwards, Nellie McClung, Irene Parlby, Louise McKinney, and Emily Murphy—advocated in the province for women's rights, including the right to vote and to hold office. Edwards, born a generation before the others, was instrumental in the 1893 founding of the National Council of Women of Canada. McClung fought for women's suffrage, first in Manitoba and then in Alberta, where she was subsequently elected, in 1921, to the Legislative Assembly. In part as a result of her spirited efforts, in January 1916, Manitoba became the first province to extend the franchise to women, followed in March by Saskatchewan and in April by Alberta. That same year, Parlby became the founding president of the United Farm Women of Alberta and, in 1921, Alberta's first female cabinet minister, while McKinney, also a suffragist, founded the Women's Christian Temperance Union, which sought to protect women and children through the prohibition of alcohol. Trained in law, Murphy fought for women's property rights and, in 1916, became Canada's first female judge—indeed, the first female judge anywhere in the British Empire. Collectively, the Famous Five are known for challenging the Supreme Court to decide whether women were "persons" (and therefore eligible for membership in the Senate). When the court ruled in 1928 that women were not, in fact, persons, the group appealed the decision to England's Privy Council, which, in 1929, overturned the Supreme Court's decision, thereby opening the door of the Senate to women.

Yet, despite their many achievements, the Famous Five were undeniably products of the era in which they lived—women whose vision of social progress was deeply conditioned by White, middle-class, Protestant values. Emily Murphy, for example, harboured racist attitudes toward the Chinese, whose opium dens she blamed for the social ill of drug addiction. The Famous Five have also earned a measure of infamy for their support of Alberta's Sexual Sterilization Act, passed in 1928 (and repealed only in 1972). As Erika Dyck notes, during this period, "discourses about sexual sterilization formed part of social reform movements, including maternal feminism," with the passage of the act resting on "a delicate constellation of unlikely supporters, from feminists to social gospellers to farmers."[1] At the time, a host of traits deemed undesirable, from feeble-mindedness to promiscuity to criminal behaviour, were believed to originate in inferior genetic stock, of a sort frequently associated with racialized peoples.[2] By allowing a provincial eugenics board to approve the sterilization of individuals deemed "unfit" to be parents, the act promised to produce a suitably wholesome, and suitably White, society. One such objectionable trait was, of course, homosexuality, then more or less universally condemned as a character defect that threatened both public morals and the sancity of the nuclear family. Ironically, then, these early feminists would have had little sympathy for lesbian and gay activism.

Discrimination against gay and lesbian people was alive and well in Alberta when the 1960s rolled around. Yet, as several of the following chapters attest, the province was also home to much gay and lesbian activism. Indeed, one Calgary man, Everett George Klippert, inadvertently played an unfortunate but integral role in the national decriminalization of homosexuality in 1969. First arrested for gross indecency in 1960, Klippert was eventually found by the Supreme Court to be a "dangerous offender" and sentenced in 1967 to life imprisonment. His sad story points to the legal discrimination that gay people faced at the time—yet, as Kevin Allen, the lead researcher for the Calgary Gay History Project, points out, "the reforms which led to Canadian legalization of homosexuality were a direct result of the Klippert case."[3] Although not himself an activist, Klippert has amply earned his place in the history of gay activism in Canada.

In December 1967, just six weeks after Klippert's final sentencing, Pierre Trudeau—then minister of the Department of Justice—famously declared that "there's no place for the state in the bedrooms of the nation."[4] Trudeau was speaking to the press following the introduction of Bill C-195 into the House of Commons—an omnibus bill that aimed, among other things, to legalize both abortion and acts of homosexuality, if only under certain circumstances. After Trudeau was elected prime minister, the bill was reintroduced in December 1968 as the Criminal Law Amendment Act, otherwise known as Bill C-150, together with a related bill that further proposed to decriminalize the sale and use of oral contraceptives. After months of rancorous debate, Bill C-150 was eventually passed, receiving royal assent on 27 June 1969.

The passage of Bill C-150 was a watershed moment for both the women's liberation and gay liberation movements in Canada. Activists in both movements used this moment to embark on a struggle for rights that remained out of their grasp, establish needed services in their communities, and raise public consciousness about the issues with which they were grappling. As Erin Gallagher-Cohoon points out in her chapter below, lesbians—as neither gay men nor heterosexual women—sometimes struggled to find a home in either movement. But, as the 1970s progressed lesbians began to create their own organizations and public platforms, distinct from those created by gay men and straight women. In short, while the feminist movement and the movement for gay rights evolved along different trajectories, the passage of the Criminal Law Amendment Act in 1969 opened a space in which these movements could organize more publicly.

The energy generated in 1969 propelled feminist and gay liberation activism into the 1970s and built up activist support networks would be needed in the battles yet to come. Although the passage of Bill C-150 created a sense of hope and possibility, it did not translate into wholesale change on the ground. Indeed, as victories go, this was a decidedly limited one. Even after the legal reforms of 1969, both abortion services and homosexual practices continued to be regulated and policed. Women could not, for example, simply decide to have an abortion and then make an appointment at a clinic. Rather, women seeking abortions had to present their cases to a Therapeutic Abortion Committee (TAC) made up of at least three doctors, who had the power to decide whether an abortion was "necessary" on a case-by-case basis. In the meanwhile, acts of homosexuality and "gross indecency" were now legal only if they occurred in private between two consenting adults. Police therefore continued to harass gay men, not merely by surveilling gay bars and other popular cruising spots but also by raids on bathhouses.[5] Indeed, in view of the situation put in place by the passage of Bill C-150, Trudeau may have meant, quite literally, that the state had no place in the *bedrooms* of the nation. When it came to pregnancy and to homosexual behaviour in public spaces, the state still insisted on having a presence.

Laws change in response to shifts in dominant social attitudes, but social attitudes can be notoriously slow to evolve. Inevitably, efforts to liberalize the laws in the 1960s reflected contemporary heteronormative and patriarchal presumptions about what were, and were not, acceptable sexual relationships. The ideal remained the married heterosexual couple, in which the father was the primary breadwinner and the mother the principal caregiver, and attempts were made to police sexual behaviour that did not conform to this ideal. Unlike men, women were not supposed to engage in sexual activity outside of marriage, and limiting access to abortion (and, previously, to contraceptives as well) was one way to discourage female sexual freedom—while labelling a child born out of wedlock "illegitimate" further stigmatized the behaviour. Restrictions around abortion also safeguarded against the culturally unthinkable possibility that a married woman who found herself pregnant might seek to terminate the pregnancy. Even after homosexual acts were technically legal, at least in some circumstances, construing public expressions of homosexuality as gross indecency effectively coded same-sex relationships as deviant. As "indecency" implies, any public display of homosexuality was deemed to be offensive and potentially corrupting. If policing women's fertility aimed to ensure that women would seek personal fulfillment only in the context of marriage and motherhood, policing homosexual behaviour aimed to contain what continued to be perceived as some form of moral pollution.

In the face of the unfinished victory represented by Bill C-150, gay activists showed a growing determination to step out of the closet, while women insisted on greater equity and the right to a life beyond motherhood—and what was happening all across the country was happening equally in Alberta. In "Fed Up with the Status Quo," Tom Langford describes the coalitions formed among professional and working women's organizations, social workers, and civil servants in Alberta as they took up the campaign for affordable high-quality daycare. As Nevena Ivanović, Kevin Allen, and Larry Hannant similarly reveal, in "Gay Liberation in Conservative Calgary," the University of Calgary's student newspaper, *The Gauntlet*, became a site for building community solidarity, a place where activists could raise public consciousness, combat discrimination, and dismantle stereotypes about gay and lesbian people.

Other activists in Alberta worked to establish safe spaces and adequate services tailored to local needs. Community-centred initiatives such as the Lethbridge Birth Control and Information Centre (LBCIC) and Edmonton's Gay Alliance Toward Equality (GATE) were created in response to specific needs and desires within their respective communities. As I explain in my own chapter, "Contraception, Community, and Controversy," in the small Bible-Belt city of Lethbridge, the LBCIC offered literature, workshops, and counselling assistance regarding sexuality, birth control, and abortion. In "'Ultra Activists' in a 'Very Closeted Place,'" Gallagher-Cohoon describes the work of GATE, which provided phone lines and other counselling opportunities while at the same time lobbying the Alberta Human Rights Commission for the inclusion of homosexuals under the Individual's Rights Protection Act. The community services offered by LBCIC and GATE illustrate the very concrete achievements of Alberta activists, who worked hard to provide on-the-ground resources that offered immediate aid to anyone in need.

These tangible, community-based forms of activism are often overshadowed by mass demonstrations and national campaigns for legal change, but in the chapters to follow they are highlighted and celebrated. Although these chapters explore only a few examples of Alberta activists who pushed against a conservative heteropatriarchal social order, they enhance our understanding of Prairie attitudes toward gender and sexuality. Hopefully, they will also inspire further research into the communities and coalitions and the local services established and maintained by activists in the province.

Karissa Robyn Patton

NOTES

1. Erika Dyck, *Facing Eugenics: Reproduction, Sterilization, and the Politics of Choice* (Toronto: University of Toronto Press, 2013), 18, 11–12.

2. As has been well documented, not only were women more at risk of sterilization than men, but Indigenous women were considerably overrepresented among the women who were sterilized. In addition, especially prior to World War II, immigrants—notably those of Eastern European origin—were disproportionately targeted. For a useful overview, see Jana Grekul, Arvey Krahn, and Dave Odnyak, "Sterilizing the 'Feeble-Minded': Eugenics in Alberta, Canada, 1929–1972," *Journal of Historical Sociology* 17, no. 4 (2004): 358–84.

3. Kevin Allen, "Calgary's Role in Decriminalizing Homosexuality in the '60s," *Calgary Gay History Project*, 17 October 2012, https://calgaryqueerhistory. ca/2012/10/17/calgarys-role-in-decriminalizng-homosexuality-in-the-60s/.

4. Trudeau's comment was made during a press conference: see the clip from a news broadcast on 21 December 1967 in the CBC Archives, https://www. cbc.ca/archives/entry/omnibus-bill-theres-no-place-for-the-state-in-the-bedrooms-of-the-nation. As Kevin Allen rightly notes, while people still remember Trudeau's "bedrooms" remark, they often fail to realize that he was speaking directly to homosexuality. Kevin Allen, "Klippert Month: Finale," *Calgary Gay History Project*, 30 October 2017, https:// calgaryqueerhistory.ca/2017/10/30/klippert-month-finale/.

5. Tom Warner, *Never Going Back: A History of Queer Activism in Canada* (Toronto: University of Toronto Press, 2002), 100; Thomas Hooper, "'More Than Two Is a Crowd': Mononormativity and Gross Indecency in the *Criminal Code*, 1981–82," *Journal of Canadian Studies* 48, no. 1 (2014): 68. The prohibition on acts of "gross indecency" was part of the original Criminal Code (1892), section 178 of which explicitly restricted the offence to acts committed by males. Although the 1953–54 revisions to the Criminal Code eliminated this restriction, such that anyone could be charged with the crime, charges continued to be brought primarily against men. The "gross indecency" law survived as section 157 of the 1970 Criminal Code, which was repealed only in 1985, with the repeal coming into force in 1987. In all this time, the Criminal Code never defined what constituted an act of gross indecency: this was left to the courts to decide in individual cases.

4 Fed Up with the Status Quo

Alberta Women's Groups Challenge
Maternalist Ideology and Secure Provincial
Funding for Daycare, 1964–71

Tom Langford

It is a list of organizations that are not usually thought of as incubators of radical critique and activism: the University Women's Clubs of Edmonton and Calgary, the Business and Professional Women's Club of Edmonton, the National Council of Jewish Women, branches of the United Church Women, the Federation of Medical Women, the Calgary Home Economists Association, the Calgary Local Council of Women, and the Junior League of Calgary. Nevertheless, this wide range of women's organizations played a crucial role in challenging the entrenched maternalist notion in Alberta of the 1960s that, inasmuch as mothers provide the ideal care for young children, full-scale, government-supported daycare programs "are for the birds."[1]

Admittedly, these women's groups did not act alone in challenging maternalist orthodoxy in Alberta; they participated in a diverse coalition that included social workers, pediatricians, educators, and young people politicized during the 1960s. Social workers, particularly those employed in municipal social services departments, were forceful proponents for public investment in daycare to support working mothers. Their leadership in advocating for daycare in Alberta, beginning in the mid-1960s, parallels a key development on the national stage, where a network of social workers shaped the demand for child care in Canada before women's liberation activism became widespread in Canada.[2] Also challenging the sanctity of maternalism were pediatricians like Dr. Gerry Holman of the University of Calgary and Dr. Jean Nelson, who served together on the Day Care Centres Committee of the Canadian Pediatric Society in the early 1970s.[3] The coalition also included members of a nascent movement for quality in early childhood education, led by educators such as Sheila Campbell of Edmonton (who was active in the Canadian chapter of OMEP—Organisation mondiale pour l'éducation préscolaire) and British-trained "nursery nurses" Mary Hull (director of the Community Day Nursery in Edmonton between 1966 and its closing in 2001) and Nancy Hall (the first director of the Bowness-Montgomery Day Care in Calgary), both of whom were strong advocates of a "learn through play" curriculum. Finally, this diverse coalition was topped off by young people, many of them women with preschool-age children, who had been politicized in the 1960s and accordingly brought the values of participatory community development and women's liberation to the struggle for quality daycare. These young activists also brought a sense of urgency to the struggle against an untenable status quo. Al Hagan, who was appointed as the city of Calgary's first daycare counsellor in 1969, recalled that during his early years on the job there was a steady stream of traffic into his office at city hall: "I'd come to work and there'd be about six people in my office to bug me about some issue or other."[4]

As will be described below, the coalition challenging maternalist orthodoxy formed episodically at different crucial junctures between 1964 and 1971. At these junctures, an important strength of the coalition was its inclusion of a number of women's organizations that were connected to well-established social institutions (such as universities, the medical profession, and faith communities). Consequently, these women's organizations could agitate in favour of enhanced provincial government support for daycare while being treated respectfully and attentively by the powers that be. In other words, they could "buck conservatism" from a position inside rather than outside Alberta's institutional status quo. Hence, the women's organizations that joined the coalition helped to legitimate the movement against maternalist thinking and policies. They made it much easier for Premier Ernest Manning to justify making initial provincial investments in high-quality daycares and family day home programs during his last years in office, between 1965 and 1968, and paved the way for significant growth of those investments after Premier Peter Lougheed assumed power in 1971.

This chapter first sets the context for activism on daycare by women's organizations in the 1960s: it discusses the history of women's maternalist philanthropy in Alberta, with particular attention to the establishment and operation of the Edmonton Creche, which existed from 1930 to 1964. It then addresses three questions about the wave of activism for quality daycare in the 1960s. First, how and why did these women's organizations become concerned about and involved in the question of daycare in the province? Second, how far did they go in challenging maternalist orthodoxy, how successful were they, and how long did they stay involved in the struggle for significant provincial government support for quality daycare? Third, was the experience of activism transformative for any of the members of these women's organizations? Specifically, were any of them politicized by their positive interactions with the social movements of the 1960s and early 1970s (including feminism) and their frustrating encounters with government officials, and thereby transformed into a deeper hue of radical in the 1970s and beyond? My affirmative answer to the third question will be illustrated by the profile of Sheila Campbell that concludes the chapter. Campbell transitioned from volunteer work with organizations like the University Women's Club of Edmonton in the late 1950s and early 1960s to roles as early learning professional and administrator beginning in the early 1970s (while still actively participating in the movement for quality child care). Her early years of volunteer activism and subsequent career experiences helped Campbell to develop a radical critique of the ill effects of conservatism and patriarchy in Alberta.

Backstory: Women's Philanthropy and the Edmonton Creche, 1930–64

What made the women's organizations listed at the beginning of the chapter so "radical" on the question of daycare in the 1960s is that they challenged the logic and past practices of women's philanthropic sponsorship of daycare in Alberta. This may seem to be a low bar for defining what is "radical," but it is a meaningful one because of the ways that conservatism had become deeply entrenched in Alberta under the extended premiership of Ernest Manning between 1943 and 1968. Combining the perspectives of Christian evangelism and economic individualism in his worldview, Premier Manning consistently resisted federal proposals for new universal social programs such as the Canada Pension Plan and medicare.[5] He instead favoured private initiatives to meet human needs. In the field of child care, this meant that the Manning government preferred maternal care of young children whenever possible. When maternal care was impractical, however, the government preferred daycares run by private organizations like the Edmonton Creche rather than government sponsorship.

There is a long history of women's philanthropic involvement in the provision of daycare in Edmonton. Indeed, Alberta's first day nursery was an initiative of the Local Council of Women in Edmonton. In 1908, this group established a crèche "patterned after the highly successful day nurseries of eastern cities."[6] Located near the city's Immigration Hall, it was designed to serve the children of newly arrived women who needed to engage in paid labour for their families to survive. The philanthropy behind this early crèche included the establishment of "a free employment bureau" that linked registrants seeking domestic work to any "ladies requiring workwomen who telephoned." The project was thus animated by the somewhat self-serving benevolence of Edmonton's "ladies" with telephones—the elite.[7]

The first Edmonton crèche went through several incarnations during the First World War and then disappeared, with the result that, during the 1920s, no subsidized daycare existed in Edmonton.[8] However, a new crèche was established in 1930. According to a story recounted by Campbell, in 1929, in Edmonton, "five small children, left home alone while their mother worked, were barely rescued from their burning home by a passerby." This prompted Lady Rodney, convener of child welfare in the Local Council of Women, to personally investigate the care of young children in the inner city. She reported finding "unsanitary conditions, children locked in rooms while their mothers worked, irresponsible caregivers, overcrowded care situations and, in one case, six or seven babies in a home, some lying on the floor holding their bottles." Lady Rodney's investigation led to the establishment, in 1930, of the Edmonton Creche and Day Nursery Society, which, with support from the city, opened a new crèche with a capacity for eighteen children.[9] This account of the origins of the Edmonton Creche illustrates the combination of "noblesse oblige, pity, and sense of women's particular responsibility for children" that likewise infuses stories about the origins of the first day nurseries in the mid-nineteenth-century United States— an ideology that has been described as "sentimental maternalism."[10] As illustrated in the impulse behind Lady Rodney's initiative in Edmonton, sentimental maternalism represents elite women as showing leadership by extending their maternal role into the public realm, thereby protecting little children whose working-class parents were presumed to be unable or incapable of doing so.[11]

The Edmonton Creche operated continuously for thirty-four years, until 1964; during these years it was the only subsidized daycare in Edmonton and indeed in all of Alberta. It represented the privatized, philanthropic alternative to provincially funded and organized daycares. Demand for subsidized daycare in Edmonton always exceeded the capacity of the Edmonton Creche, at no time more than during the Second World War, when women's labour was needed to keep wartime industries going. I estimate that in 1944 there were thirteen thousand female industrial workers in Edmonton and Calgary, with the working mothers in this group numbering in the low thousands.[12] Despite the recognition at that time that government-subsidized daycares would facilitate mothers' entering and remaining in the labour force, the Manning government decided against joining with the federal government to establish wartime day nurseries in the province.[13] It is noteworthy that even the women's groups that favoured the establishment of wartime day nurseries in Alberta did not challenge the prevailing maternalist orthodoxy. For instance, in 1944, the Catholic Women's League (CWL) of Edmonton, although supportive of wartime day nurseries because of the large number of women with young children in the labour force, asserted "that women's proper sphere is her own home and that her work as the mother of a family is her noblest career."[14]

However, both the logic of maternalism and the efficacy of the care provided by lightly regulated daycares lacking structured programs (whether the Edmonton Creche or commercial alternatives) came under increasing scrutiny in the late 1950s and into the 1960s. At the economic level, the economy and population of Alberta had expanded rapidly after the discovery of oil at Leduc in 1947. Between 1951 and 1961, the number of married Alberta women in the paid labour force grew from 21,000 (just 10 percent of all married women) to 77,000 (26 percent of all married women). By 1971, there would be 157,000 married women in the paid labour force (43 percent of all married women).[15] What this trend implies is that the male-breadwinner ideal of yesteryear was now under challenge from the two-wage-earner family norm. Both the job opportunities in the expanding economy and the desire of families for increased disposable income made the involvement of such a high proportion of married women in the paid labour force a permanent rather than a temporary phenomenon. Maternalist orthodoxy could not handle this new reality.

A companion social change was the growing number of educated, married women who aspired to the challenge of a career alongside their mothering responsibilities. As will be shown below, these women were initially influential as volunteers in groups that raised searching questions about the status quo in daycare in Alberta in the late 1950s and early 1960s. This women's activism was quite distinct from the "sentimental maternalism" of the Edmonton Creche and Day Nursery Society of the early twentieth century in that it was ignited by professional working women (rather than philanthropic, elite homemakers) and searched for the latest research and opinion on how daycares should be organized, regulated, and funded (instead of assuming that cheap, custodial care would suffice). This change in focus reflected the fact that the professional women of the early 1960s had a vision of daycares that would be suitable for their own children (and by extension, all children) while the crèche had been designed as a bare-bones service for the children of low-income women. For educated, professional women in the 1960s, establishing high-quality, publicly subsidized daycares was both a matter of women's empowerment (allowing women with young children to continue on career paths) and a question of children's rights. The "sentimental maternalism" behind the crèche, in contrast, saw daycare in a far more limited way—as a means to foster individual responsibility and labour market participation by poor working-class women.

A third change of import was a shift in social scientific portrayals of the effects of non-maternal care on young children. During the 1950s and into the early 1960s, many of those concerned about the care of young children in Alberta accepted what was then the conventional interpretation of John Bowlby's research on children institutionalized during the Second World War: "that it is essential for young children and babies under three years of age to have the constant and consistent mothering of one person, that the child recognizes as belonging specifically to him."[16] However, as noted by Campbell, the applicability of Bowlby's research on wartime orphans to the experience of children in daycare was being seriously questioned in the early 1960s.[17] Indeed, new research began to establish that daycare organized on a sound basis could have a number of positive benefits for young children, like improving readiness for school. By the mid-1960s, a new cultural understanding of daycare was in wide currency: rather than being a poor substitute for maternal care in the home, high-quality daycare could be a positive intervention, enhancing children's cognitive, social, and emotional development and potentially compensating for any deficiencies in their family situation.[18]

Despite the magnitude of the economic, social, and cultural changes discussed above, both the provincial government of Ernest Manning and the philanthropic women of the Edmonton Creche Society tried to carry on into the 1960s with a maternalist orthodoxy that was no longer in step with the times. Their obduracy was a key factor in mobilizing professional women's groups to become strong advocates for high-quality, government-subsidized daycare. As shown in the next section, the strange end to the Edmonton Creche in 1964 was the first turning point in the struggle to get the provincial government to subsidize the care of young children.

Professional Women Challenge the Status Quo on Daycare

In Edmonton in the late 1950s, a number of groups of professional women began to take an active interest in the state of daycare in the province. In addition to the University Women's Club, which made its first submission on daycare to the provincial government in June 1958, two other such groups were active at this time. The Study Group on Family Welfare Services—led by Marg Norquay, a minister's wife who held a master's degree in sociology from the University of Toronto—conducted a study on daycare in 1960. A third group was based at St. Paul's United Church and led by Anne Lightfoot; among its accomplishments was the creation of a study guide on daycare for United Church Women groups.[19]

During these years, Campbell participated in all three Edmonton groups and also began her association with OMEP-Canada. She offered the following explanation for the commitment of professional women to daycare advocacy at that time:

I think we felt some obligation to do something in the community. I think we wanted some interest outside the home. We were all of us at that time stay-at-home moms. I think we just had to have something else in your life, especially professional women. We'd all been doing professional things, then all of a sudden you're not doing them. This is a way to do something that's rather meaningful. Like there were also book groups for reading, but this is more meaningful. I think the University Women's Club itself had had an orientation towards that kind of activity, more meaningful kind of activity than bridge playing and so on.[20]

The involvement of these women's organizations with daycare was encouraged by an early success. The University Women's Club's submission to the provincial government in 1958 was based upon a study of child care offered through advertisements in the *Edmonton Journal*. Until this time, the province had not enforced its requirement that facilities caring for four or more children be licensed, and as a consequence, only one of the fifty-four businesses surveyed in 1958 held a licence. In response to continued lobbying by the University Women's Club, the province promised to license all day nurseries and to investigate those that advertised child care services. Then, in 1960, the province hired a civil servant, Frances Ferguson, to take charge of the area, and in 1961 the first set of standards for daycare was issued, standards that were upgraded in 1963. Nevertheless, those standards fell far short of what was recommended in the latest research on early childhood education and care. In Alberta at that time, the only qualification for staff was that they be "sympathetic to the children's welfare," and the minimum staff-to-child ratios were set at one to twenty for children between two and seven years of age and one to ten for children less than two years old.[21]

The intense study of daycare standards and needs by Edmonton organizations in the late 1950s and early 1960s led to the opening of a second front of advocacy: the quality of care at the Edmonton Creche (which by this time was caring for over 120 children). The Creche Society had turned its back on education by discontinuing employment of a kindergarten teacher and used a television set to keep the children amused during long unstructured stretches in the daily schedule. A formal complaint about the quality of the Edmonton Creche's program was investigated by the Council of Community Services in 1962, and although the investigation did not find major fault with the crèche, the volunteer members of the crèche's board, as well as the staff, felt they were under attack. In the words of the chair of the board at the time, Mrs. H. H. Stephens, "We just got fed up. We had all worked very hard and were getting nothing but abuse for our troubles."[22] The matter came to a head on 31 March 1964, when the board of the Edmonton Creche Society made the shocking announcement that it intended to close its daycare. This decision showed there was a limit to the noblesse oblige of the philanthropists on the board. It also demonstrated that "sentimental maternalism" was incapable of adjusting to the new societal needs for daycare and contemporary understandings of how a "learn through play" curriculum led by well-trained teachers could benefit young children. The crèche had been established in 1930 to provide custodial care of young children so that poor, female lone parents could take on paid work. This was philanthropy with a class agenda. In 1964, the members of the board of the Creche Society were unwilling to rethink this dated and extremely restrictive view of which families deserved help with daycare. They wanted no part in facilitating any woman's engagement in paid work when that woman could afford to pay the market rate for commercial daycare. The implication of this position was that no daycare subsidy should be granted to a woman who willfully chose the independence and fulfillment of paid work ahead of the maternalist ideal. Indeed, in defence of families that sacrificed to maintain that ideal, the board rejected the notion of subsidized daycare for families with two working parents, on the grounds that such a "family is maintaining a higher standard of living at public expense."[23]

The tumult caused by the decision to close the crèche led to further study and heated rhetoric in Edmonton. After the Edmonton Creche closed for good at the end of May 1964, Community Day Nursery immediately opened in the same location, sponsored by the City of Edmonton and two community service agencies. The next year, when a new location for Community Day Nursery needed to be found, provincial officials agreed to contribute to building-renovation costs and to share the cost of the daycare's yearly operating deficit with the City of Edmonton and United Community Fund. For the first time in Alberta's history, the provincial government had agreed to financially support a daycare.

Despite this approval, however, considerable support remained for the ideals of maternalism and family responsibility for young children around the provincial cabinet table. Indeed, in 1965, the minister of public welfare, L. C. Halmrast, reported to Edmonton's mayor, "When discussing the matter with Cabinet there was a definite feeling that there should be no subsidy for those who could well afford to pay for the care of their children from their own resources."[24] That sentiment re-emerged with a vengeance in 1967 after the premier appointed Alfred Hooke as the new minister of public welfare. Minister Hooke attempted to put the brakes on the expansion of provincial subsidization of daycares by rejecting the City of Edmonton's application for Preventive Social Service (PSS) funding for a city-run daycare to be located in the Glengarry recreation centre.[25] This unexpected decision, along with the minister's inflammatory arguments—including the "for the birds" comment quoted at the beginning of this chapter and a remark to the effect that he would rather pay needy mothers to stay at home with their children than support daycare centres—sparked an avalanche of protest from women's and social service organizations.[26]

Letters opposed to Minister Hooke's position flooded into the premier's office; the writers included eight women's organizations, three church groups, three non-profit social service agencies, two community groups, and thirty-four citizens, including Judge Marjorie Bowker. After weeks of controversy, Premier Manning called a meeting to discuss this matter with city officials. Keith Wass, then Edmonton's director of social services, believed that the premier came around to supporting the Glengarry Day Care Centre proposal after a chance remark by Wass about how children in city-run daycares would not watch TV. Even if serendipity factored into Manning's reversal of Hooke's initial decision, the overwhelming support for the daycare from women's professional and church organizations in Edmonton undoubtedly helped to pave the way. The widespread protest against Minister Hooke's original decision demonstrated that many urban women's organizations were no longer comfortable with maternalist orthodoxy as the guide for provincial policy on daycare; as a consequence, the premier was forced to recognize that continuing rejections of municipal applications for PSS daycares would threaten his party's political fortunes in urban areas.[27]

Women's professional and church organizations also actively contributed to the establishment of a trail-blazing, community-run daycare in Calgary. In 1968, there were two separate initiatives aimed at establishing PSS daycares in Calgary. The first was led by Phil Lalonde, a community organizer with the Company of Young Canadians (CYC), who used a list of fifty names of residents of the neighbourhoods of Bowness and Montgomery, gathered during a survey by the Social Planning Council, to start "organizing the community around the issue of day care."[28] The CYC's involvement in this project demonstrates the importance of young people politicized during the 1960s to the growing movement for expanded provincial subsidization of daycares.

Initial meetings organized by Lalonde in March 1968 led to an ambitious plan to develop a proposal for a PSS daycare using widespread community input: a number of subcommittees were struck, each charged with research-ing and writing a section of the proposal. So many community volunteers were needed for this effort that Lalonde recruited other CYC members in Calgary to find additional residents of Bowness and Montgomery who would be willing to contribute to the project. A great deal of work was accomplished in a short time, and a formal proposal "for a community day care centre in Bowness-Montgomery" was submitted to the City of Calgary's Social Ser-vices Committee in June. Furthermore, in September 1968, a door-to-door canvass was organized to confirm community support for the initiative.[29]

The second initiative on daycare in Calgary in 1968 involved six women's organizations, including the University Women's Club, the Local Council of Women, the National Council of Jewish Women, and the Junior League of Calgary. They first met in May to begin organizing a proposal for a "model day care" in the city. Quality programming in daycare had now become a primary focus of women's organizations, demonstrating how the focus of these groups differed from the "sentimental maternalism" of yesteryear. The initial proposal for this "model day care" was quickly pulled together and submitted in July 1968; shortly thereafter, the city rejected it because it would have been too costly and the group did not have a location in which to house the daycare. After a few months of trying to find a way to sal-vage their model daycare, the sponsoring organizations finally accepted the Social Planning Council's suggestion that they amalgamate forces with the Bowness-Montgomery Day Care Association (B-MDCA). This merger, in early 1969, brought significant benefits to the B-MDCA. The Junior League donated fifteen thousand dollars and promised to provide volunteers to improve the quality of care in the centre. The National Council of Jewish Women donated six thousand dollars. Furthermore, the involvement of these women's organizations increased the credibility of the proposal and meant that there was a strong push to make the project a model for quality care. Both the city and province approved a revised proposal from the B-MDCA in 1969, and a combined daycare/satellite family day home agency opened with PSS subsidization in a converted elementary school on 1 May 1970.[30]

Government sponsorship of daycares through the PSS program had started to increase during the final years of Social Credit's hold on the prov-incial government but really took off during the first term in office of Premier Peter Lougheed (1971–75). By 1975, there were forty-seven PSS daycare cen-tres across the province, licensed to care for over two thousand children.

PSS centres held about one-quarter of the licensed spaces in Edmonton and Calgary and fully half of the licensed spaces in the rest of the province.[31] A high-quality alternative to often-inferior commercial daycares had become firmly established in Alberta by 1975, with three Alberta cities—Edmonton, Medicine Hat, and Calgary—recognized as being among the national leaders on quality daycare. The PSS sector had the expertise and person-power to champion its own cause and was effectively supported in advocacy by municipal social services bureaucrats (many of whom were social workers) and a new specialized interest group, the Alberta Association for Young Children (AAYC), founded in 1971. The resources that professional and church women's organizations brought to struggles over daycare in Alberta in the late 1950s and 1960s—political credibility and committed volunteer work that could embarrass under-resourced civil servants—were no longer of decisive import in the 1970s. Nevertheless, these women's organizations had played a key role not only in helping to convince the Social Credit government in the 1960s and early 1970s to abandon maternalist orthodoxy and subsidize high-quality daycares but also in getting the new Progressive Conservative government of Peter Lougheed to see expansion of PSS daycares as a way to solidify its support in urban areas.[32]

Sheila Campbell's Professional and Political Educations

Sheila Campbell was one of the Edmonton-based women whose persistent volunteer activism in the late 1950s and the 1960s helped to change the landscape for the care of young children in Alberta.[33] Campbell learned a great deal from these experiences and subsequently became an early childhood educator and administrator. Simultaneously she deepened her advocacy for young children. Her life's trajectory demonstrates how individuals involved in issue-based activism in the 1960s (such as the movement for quality daycare) could become politicized in a fundamental way. This happened not only because of the lessons learned from fighting a stubborn and oftentimes reactionary provincial government, or from personal experiences of sexist organizational cultures but also through eye-opening interactions with activists connected to some of the prominent social movements of the era.

Sheila Campbell graduated with a Bachelor of Education degree in 1952. She taught for a short while before leaving the paid labour force for about a decade while her children were young. During these years, her volunteer activities focused increasingly on early childhood education (ECE) and day-care. Her professional career from the mid-1960s onward included earning her master's degree (1972) and her doctorate (1981) in ECE, designing and founding the ECE program at Grant MacEwan College in 1971–72, working for a year as director of daycare services for the City of Edmonton, serving as an assistant professor in early childhood curriculum instruction at the University of Alberta for seven years, and working as a self-employed daycare consultant for the remainder of her career.[34]

Campbell's politicization included interacting with activists from the new movements of the 1960s. For instance, she commented that a meeting on daycare she attended in Washington, DC, in 1970 was her "first experience with Black Power."[35] Further, in her leadership role in the AAYC as well as her year as director of daycare services for the City of Edmonton, Campbell had a great deal of interaction with young people who had been politicized through participation in the social and political movements of the 1960s and early 1970s and were now the backbone of support for the expanding network of PSS daycares in the city. Among the youthful activists pushing forward the quality daycare agenda at that time was David Leadbeater, a left-wing economist with master's degrees from the University of Alberta and Oxford University. Leadbeater, who had been active in student politics while at the University of Alberta, served a term as an Edmonton alderman from 1974 to 1977. As an alderman he was the most reliable advocate for PSS daycares at city hall, even arguing—unsuccessfully—that Edmonton should continue to build more PSS daycares in the face of provincial funding cutbacks.[36]

Campbell was also politicized by her experiences of sexism in the labour force. First, she left Grant MacEwan College in 1972 after she perceived that an all-male hiring committee had made fun of her candidacy for the position of chair of the community services department. Second, she bristled at the sexist culture she encountered while working at the City of Edmonton in 1972–73 that included a male co-worker withholding crucial information from her, exclusion from decision making that occurred in informal male networks ("in the washroom, the beer parlour, someplace"), and instructions to skip the city's administrative staff meetings since they involved male administrators playing poker and telling jokes.[37]

Campbell also developed a finely tuned political consciousness through her many years working to educate parents, politicians, and civil servants on what daycare in Alberta should look like. She commented that she and other activists were initially politically naïve in the way they "misjudged parents. I never realized that they were so much more interested in how much it cost them to pay for their kids' care than in what kind of care their kids got." She also argued, "I don't think any of us really understood the political process. That what we were up against was, you know, a mind-set in favour of private enterprise, against rocking the boat."[38] She even learned, after Lougheed's historic victory in the 1971 provincial election, that "the mind-set of the cabinet that came in was still very traditional [. . .]. 'Yeah, mothers should be at home with their children.'"[39] Old-fashioned maternalism therefore continued to haunt advocacy for quality daycare even after the historic change in government of 1971. Campbell and other advocates navigated this perilous situation by adopting techniques that would get the attention of MLAs regardless of their underlying beliefs, such as advocacy campaigns that mobilized local residents to pressure every MLA in the province. However, as someone with a professional's interest in the latest research on child care, Campbell was consistently frustrated by the orientation of many provincial civil servants in the 1970s: "You were dealing with professional civil servants [who] had no professional background and they didn't relate to the issues at all, except in the light of 'Is this going to cause trouble? Is this something the Minister isn't going to like?'"[40] This situation perturbed Campbell and other leaders of the AAYC who were trying to steer the Lougheed government toward sound policies on the education and care of young children.

Campbell's days of interacting directly with and lobbying provincial civil servants ended when one of the senior provincial bureaucrats lacking professional training on daycare informed her, "We're tired of seeing you people around here. It's the same old faces all the time, and telling us the same old thing. We don't want to see you anymore." Campbell continued, "And that's when I vowed I would never show my face before the government again, which I didn't."[41] Instead, from the late 1970s onward, she continued her professional career and advocacy on behalf of young children while eschewing the work of directly lobbying the politicians and civil servants who found her so troublesome. Her committed work with the AAYC, Early Childhood Professional Association of Alberta, and Clifford E. Lee Foundation stretched into the new century and helped to keep alive the tradition of quality child care in Alberta at a time when the provincial government was reducing spending, loosening regulations, and cutting the capacity of regulatory staff.[42]

Campbell's radical views on defending the rights of young children still shone through in my interviews with her in the late 1990s, some forty years after she first became involved in daycare advocacy. For instance, this is how she explained the position she took on the disputed issue of the long-term effects (if any) of daycare on children: "I always used the argument that I don't give a damn about the long-term effects, what I care about is right now. I don't like being in an uncomfortable setting. Do you like being in an uncomfortable setting? Then why do we do that to children? [. . .] As long as I can show you that [a] setting is uncomfortable for the child right now, who cares if eight years down the road it's bad or good? Children matter now."[43]

In the 1960s, Campbell and her colleagues in professional and church women's groups challenged conservative and maternalist orthodoxy and argued in favour of provincial investments in high-quality daycares in Alberta. They were a crucial part of the coalition of advocates who worked to secure the extensive network of PSS daycares, including the Glengarry Day Care Centre in Edmonton and the Bowness-Montgomery Day Care Centre in Calgary, that by the mid-1970s had made Alberta a national leader in daycare services. In their daycare activism, Campbell and her colleagues simultaneously asserted the right of women with young children to professional careers and the right of young children to early childhood education and quality care. In Campbell's case, volunteer issue-based activism in the 1950s and early 1960s set the trajectory for a professional career as an early childhood educator and administrator, as well as forty years of activism on behalf of young children. Over these decades, she deepened her critical understanding of conservatism in Alberta, ran into sexist treatment that is still all too common in today's world, and challenged the status quo on daycare so effectively that a senior provincial civil servant told her, "We don't want to see you anymore." Campbell's subversive answer was to leave the lobbying to others while diligently working behind the scenes to keep alive a legacy of quality daycare around the province.[44]

NOTES

1. The assessment was offered by Alfred J. Hooke, then minister of Alberta's Department of Public Welfare: "Province-Backed Day Care Plans 'Are for the Birds,' Says Hooke," *Edmonton Journal*, 23 October 1967.

2. Rianne Mahon, "The Never-Ending Story: The Struggle for Universal Child Care Policy in the 1970s," *Canadian Historical Review* 81, no. 4 (2000): 588.

3. "Standards for Child Development Programs, Including Day Care Centres and Family Day Homes," Alberta Association for Young Children [AAYC], April 1973, AAYC fonds, PR2377, Provincial Archives of Alberta [PAA], Edmonton. Dr. Nelson, appointed as deputy minister of community health in 1975, was the first woman ever to be appointed to a deputy minister position in the Alberta government. Her distinguished career as a civil servant was cut short when she died of cancer in 1979. W. H. Hunley, "Dr. Jean Nelson: Courage and Spirit," *CMA Journal* 120, no. 10 (19 May 1979): 1276.

4. "'Day Care Has Turned Full Circle,' Says City Consultant," *Calgary Herald*, 3 August 1978.

5. Alvin Finkel, *The Social Credit Phenomenon in Alberta* (Toronto: University of Toronto Press, 1989), chap. 6; Leslie Bella, "The Origins of Alberta's Preventive Social Service Program" (Department of Recreation Administration, University of Alberta, 1978).

6. "The Edmonton Creche," *Edmonton Bulletin*, 5 December 1908.

7. "Is Not the Proper Maintenance of This Institution Worth a Thousand Dollars Annually to Edmonton?" *Edmonton Bulletin*, 17 April 1909. Tom Langford, *Alberta's Day Care Controversy: From 1908 to 2009 and Beyond* (Edmonton: Athabasca University Press, 2011), 15–16.

8. Nor was there subsidized daycare in Alberta's other larger cities (Calgary, Medicine Hat, and Lethbridge) at that time. However, a different sort of non-profit, group initiative led to the organization of a new daycare in Drumheller in the mid-1920s. A women's organization associated with the communist movement, the Women's Labour League, established a daycare with a strong political mission: the group depicted the daycare as "free from bourgeois influence" (*The Worker*, 12 July 1924, as cited in Charles A. Seager, "A Proletariat in Wild Rose Country: The Alberta Coal Miners, 1905–1945" [PhD diss., York University, 1981], 378).

9. Sheila Campbell, "Acting Locally: Community Activism in Edmonton, 1949–1970," in *Changing Child Care: Five Decades of Child Care Advocacy and Policy in Canada*, ed. Susan Prentice (Halifax: Fernwood, 2001), 82–83. Campbell's account is based on a letter written by Lady Rodney in May 1929, RG 11, class 32, file 2, City of Edmonton Archives [EA]. See also Langford, *Alberta's Day Care Controversy*, 18–19.

10. Sonya Michel, *Children's Interests/Mothers' Rights: The Shaping of America's Child Care Policy* (New Haven: Yale University Press, 1999), 12. Michel (314n4) credits the term "sentimental maternalism" to Molly Ladd-Taylor, in *Mother-Work: Women, Child Welfare, and the State, 1890–1930* (Urbana: University of Illinois Press, 1994), 7.

11. Michel, *Children's Interests/Mothers' Rights*, 11–14.

12. Langford, *Alberta's Day Care Controversy*, 20, drawing upon Donna J. A. Zwicker, "Alberta Women and World War Two" (MA thesis, University of Calgary, 1985).

13. Order-in-Council PC 6242, dated 20 July 1942, authorized the federal minister of labour to enter into a cost-sharing agreement with any province for the establishment of "day nurseries, crèches and recreation centres for children." In August 1943, Alberta became the third province, after Ontario and Québec, to enter into such an agreement. However, in the spring of 1944, the Alberta cabinet decided against implementing the agreement following a negative recommendation by a provincial advisory committee that "deliberately ignored the strong evidence that one wartime day nursery was needed in Calgary, at least two were needed in Edmonton, and extensive out-of-school care programs were needed in Edmonton." Tom Langford, "Why Alberta Vacillated over Wartime Day Nurseries," *Prairie Forum* 28, no. 2 (2003): 191n1, 185.

14. From a resolution passed at the CWL of Edmonton's annual meeting as reported in a letter from president Rosemary G. Gaboury to A. Miller, 22 April 1944, attached to a letter from S. W. Field, president of the Edmonton Council of Social Agencies, to R.A. Andison, clerk, executive council, 1 May 1944, GR1969.289/0882, PAA.

15. Langford, *Alberta's Day Care Controversy*, 40, table 3.1, which is mainly based on Alberta Bureau of Statistics, *An Historical Profile of the Alberta Family* (Edmonton: Government of Alberta, 1981).

16. "Report to the By-Laws Committee of the City of Edmonton from the Study Group on Family Welfare Services," 8 December 1960, MS 323, class 2, file 18, EA.

17. Campbell, "Acting Locally," 87. For additional details of Bowlby's research findings, see Michel, *Children's Interests/Mothers' Rights*, 155.

18. A summary of the research supporting this new cultural understanding of daycare was published by Howard Clifford, then the director of daycare services for the City of Edmonton, in the early 1970s. Clifford, *Let's Talk Day Care* (Edmonton: Canadian Mental Health Association, n.d. [1972]).

19. Langford, *Alberta's Day Care Controversy*, 44.

20. Sheila Campbell, interview by the author, 17 April 1996, tape recorded.

21. "Report to the By-Laws Committee"; Campbell, "Acting Locally," 86; Langford, *Alberta's Day Care Controversy*, 45–46.

22. "Final Chapter Written in the History of the Edmonton Creche and Day Nursery," *Edmonton Journal*, 4 December 1968.

23. "Creche Board Explains Closure," *Edmonton Journal*, 15 May 1964; Langford, *Alberta's Day Care Controversy*, 47–48; Larry Prochner, "A History of Early

Education and Child Care in Canada, 1920–1966," in *Early Childhood Care and Education in Canada*, ed. Larry Prochner and Nina Howe (Vancouver: University of British Columbia Press, 2000), 47.

24. L. C. Halmrast to V. Dantzer, 7 June 1965, RG 11, class 32, file 16, EA.

25. Introduced in 1966 to coincide with the Canada Assistance Plan, the Preventive Social Services Act allowed municipalities to initiate new preventive social services that would be cost-shared by the federal government (50 percent), provincial government (30 percent), and municipality (20 percent). However, both senior levels of government had to approve a PSS project proposed by a municipality. See Langford, *Alberta's Day Care Controversy*, 51.

26. Bella, "Origins," 227, 243; Langford, *Alberta's Day Care Controversy*, 60. On the involvement of women's organizations in the fight to secure provincial funding for the proposed Glengarry Day Care Centre, see the letters in the PAA, 77.173, file 702.

27. Keith Wass, interview by the author, 13 April 1996, taped; Langford, *Alberta's Day Care Controversy*, 60–62.

28. Ada Brouwer and Howard McDiarmid, "The Founding of a Day Care Programme: A Documentation of the States of Development of the Bowness-Montgomery Day Care Association" (School of Social Welfare, University of Calgary, 1970), 8–9.

29. Langford, *Alberta's Day Care Controversy*, 67–68; Brouwer and McDiarmid, "Founding of a Day Care," 10–14.

30. Langford, *Alberta's Day Care Controversy*, 69–70, 96; "Bowness-Montgomery Day Care Program: City of Calgary Preventive Project Submission," August 1969, box 28431, Preventive Services Reports binder, City of Calgary Archives. It should be noted that combining the forces of community members and conventional women's organizations did not always go smoothly. The first director of the Bowness-Montgomery Day Care, Nancy Hall, recalled that a Junior League member on one of the early boards of the B-MDCA proved to be difficult to work with and was quietly removed. Hall, interview by the author, 19 April 1996, taped.

31. Langford, *Alberta's Day Care Controversy*, 91, table 4.2.

32. Prior to the 1971 election that ended the thirty-six-year run of Social Credit government, Peter Lougheed told Calgary's daycare counsellor, Al Hagan, that his party "was going to push day care and that was part of their platform." Hagan also recalled, "Prospective candidates for the Conservative Party . . . wanted a lot of information about day care, and wanted to make that a major platform item." Hagan, interview by the author, 16 April 1996, taped.

33. Except when otherwise noted, the information in this section comes from taped interviews I conducted with Campbell on 17 and 25 April 1996 and from my notes on conversations we had in the AAYC office on 12 and 13 November 1998. It is unlikely that Campbell and other advocates for quality daycare in the late 1950s and the 1960s self-identified as "activists" or saw their demands as "radical." However, their political interventions fit the definition of activism proposed by Jennifer Baumgardner and Amy Richards: "A regular woman becomes an activist when she rights some glaring human mistake, or recognizes a positive model of equality and takes the opportunity to build on it." Baumgardner and Richards, *Manifesta: Young Women, Feminism, and the Future* (New York: Farrar, Straus and Giroux, 2000), 282.

34. Campbell resigned from her assistant professor position because of a family move and the frustration of not being able to finish her dissertation because of the grind of teaching and administrative responsibilities. She later regretted leaving the University of Alberta, however, because she missed conducting research (her specialization was the organization of space in daycare centres); she had expected that she could readily secure research grants as a researcher unaffiliated with a university—an expectation that proved mistaken.

35. Campbell, interview, 17 April 1996.

36. David Leadbeater to Edmonton commissioner A. H. Savage, 14 September 1977, Children's Services 1975–78, box 5, file: City Council Correspondence and Memos, Edmonton Community and Family Services; Langford, *Alberta's Day Care Controversy*, 90–93.

37. Campbell, interview, 17 April 1996.

38. Campbell, interview, 25 April 1996.

39. Ibid.

40. Ibid.

41. Ibid.

42. Campbell joined the board of directors of the Clifford E. Lee Foundation in 1973. Clifford E. Lee had been a leader of the Alberta CCF during the Second World War. After the war he made a large amount of money through a chain of pharmacies and as a land developer and house builder. The Lee family established the foundation in 1969 "to give back to the community the prosperity Clifford achieved" (Lila Lee obituary, *Edmonton Journal*, 19–22 July 2006). Mr. Lee died in 1973 but the foundation continued to operate until 2004. In 1998, the foundation's executive director (and daughter of Clifford E. Lee), Judy Padua, stated, "It was basically Sheila who shaped our policy on, or thrust, in the area of day care, absolutely, for years." During this time the Clifford E. Lee Foundation made many grants to daycares and

child care organizations, supporting initiatives such as new playground equipment, conferences, and strategic planning exercises. Padua, interview by the author, 3 March and 18 August 1998, taped.

43. Campbell, interview, 25 April 1996.

44. Sheila Campbell died on 18 April 2020 at the age of 90. To honour Sheila's "dedication and passion in a profession that has a lasting impact on so many lives," MacEwan University has established the Dr. Sheila D. Campbell Founders Award.

5 Gay Liberation in Conservative Calgary

Nevena Ivanović, Kevin Allen, and Larry Hannant

The 1960s would be a time of dramatic and positive change for lesbians and gays. But in Wild Rose Country, the decade began with an arrest that seemed to presage the continuing reign of conservatism and repression in the province. For a thirty-four-year-old Calgary bus driver whose ready smile made him a favourite of many passengers, the tragedy came in a trial that saw the considerable weight of legal and moral prejudice brought down on him. Everyone who knew him considered Everett Klippert to be friendly, thoughtful, and polite. Yet Klippert lived in a city that cherished its cowboy heritage. *Brokeback Mountain* was half a century away. It was dangerous to be gay in a town that showed little tolerance for queers.

Beyond Alberta, legal discrimination against homosexuals had been steadily intensifying in Canada since the 1930s, as interest in sexual "deviancy" grew, partly in the context of the eugenics movement. In 1948, the Canadian Criminal Code, which had from the beginning banned "buggery" (that is, sodomy) and "gross indecency," was amended to include a section on "criminal sexual psychopaths," aimed largely at men. Gay men, in particular, were assumed to be unable to control their sexual impulses and therefore potentially dangerous. In 1953, buggery and gross indecency were incorporated into the list of offences that could be interpreted as evidence of criminal sexual psychopathology. Further revisions occurred in 1961, when the term "criminal sexual psychopath" was replaced by "dangerous sexual offender" and the definition expanded to include anyone who "is likely to commit another sexual offence."[1]

In addition, the Cold War contributed to a moral panic that saw fear of communism linked to homosexuality in the minds of government officials, including police authorities. During this period, homosexuals came to be considered a threat to national security, with gays regarded either as probable communists or as potentially vulnerable to blackmail by Soviet agents. At the behest of Canada's Security Panel, the security and intelligence arm of the Royal Canadian Mounted Police (RCMP) actively hunted for, identified, and surveilled queers, who were not only fired from civil service positions and dismissed from the military but also subjected to criminal prosecution. In its effort to track down suspects, the RCMP exerted tremendous pressure on people, turning friends against friends and driving those of queer orientation further underground. Secrecy became a necessity for queers.[2]

Everett Klippert was not well positioned to engage in hookup subterfuge. A working-class man from a rigidly Baptist background, he had no access to the survival strategies of Calgary's better-off homosexuals. Those men typically met at the bar of the venerable Palliser Hotel and then made their way to a private home to avoid detection by the police. Klippert, by contrast, frequented boxing and wrestling matches and local swimming pools, pursuing his preference for men over women as sexual partners while still attempting to remain discreet.[3]

In 1960, his pursuits caught up with him. Denounced to police by the father of a young man with whom he was in a sexual relationship, Klippert admitted, under questioning, that he had committed homosexual acts with the eighteen men listed in his little black book. He was convicted of "gross indecency"—the charge typically brought against gay men—and sent to prison for four years. Once released, he moved to the Northwest Territories, hoping to make a new start. But, as a known homosexual, Klippert would find it difficult to escape his past.

In August 1965, only a year after his release, Klippert was working in the town of Pine Point when the RCMP brought him into custody in connection with an arson case. Klippert actually had no involvement in the case, but questioning soon turned to details of his sex life. During a lengthy interrogation, Klippert was pressured into naming all his sexual contacts and was again charged with gross indecency. The fact that his liaisons were consensual did not sway the court, which sentenced him to another jail term. At the same time, the Yellowknife Crown attorney also initiated proceedings to have Klippert declared a "dangerous sexual offender"—the term that, in 1961, had replaced "criminal sexual psychopath." Fought all the way to the Supreme Court of Canada in 1967, the case shocked many who followed it, especially after the Supreme Court upheld Klippert's conviction as a dangerous sex offender even though the two psychiatrists who had examined him agreed that he had no violent tendencies whatsoever.[4] Klippert was duly sentenced to indefinite imprisonment, quite possibly for life.

In December 1967, in the wake of Klippert's November sentencing, Pierre Trudeau, then justice minister, launched Bill C-150 to amend portions of the Criminal Code, including its unqualified condemnation of both sodomy and gross indecency. In a statement that's widely quoted, without citing the key introductory phrase, Trudeau said: "Take this thing on homosexuality, I think the view we take here is that there's no place for the state in the bedrooms of the nation."[5] Only five months earlier, Britain's Sexual Offences Act 1967 had legalized homosexual acts provided they were committed in private between two consenting adult men (men merely because, in Britain, no legislation had ever targeted homosexual acts between women), and Trudeau's bill neatly mirrored those reforms.

The proposed changes—while long planned and supported by associations speaking for professionals such as lawyers and psychiatrists, as well as by the Canadian Council of Churches—were nevertheless strongly contested in Parliament. Among the leading opponents were members of Parliament from Ralliement créditiste, originally the Québec branch of the Social Credit Party of Canada. Eventually, however, the bill—reintroduced in December 1968, after Trudeau became prime minister—passed its third reading, in May 1969, receiving royal assent in late June. The legal reform was of no benefit to Klippert, who would languish in prison until 1971. The success of the bill gave a tremendous boost to a sense of change that was sweeping through many political, social, and cultural organizations.[6] Gay liberation and lesbian feminist networks started to form more openly and began to proclaim that "Gay is Good."

Many young women and men who were gay-curious gravitated to cities in the 1960s, where they sought some relief from the puritanical gaze, and to universities, where they hoped for more liberal social outlooks. Yet Calgary and Edmonton—still relatively small cities of 300,000 and 350,000, respectively, in the mid-1960s—were far from bastions of liberalism, and even university students, especially at the University of Calgary (U of C), were often quite conservative in their outlook. The loneliness and isolation faced by gays was described in a candid letter to the U of C student newspaper, *The Gauntlet*, in March 1971 from "Ramonn," who wrote that he knew "from experience just what a frustrating lonely life it can be at a university if you are gay and don't know any others." Ramonn was a third-year student who had spent the past two years on campus, then home to about five thousand students. In all that time, he wrote, he had not known "a single gay guy let alone friend."[7]

Off campus, by the late 1960s gays and lesbians had already taken steps to create their own safe socializing spaces. Until 1970, these were temporary or operated by businesspeople who were not consistently gay-friendly and sometimes exploitive. Police raids and harassment were constant threats, but that changed in 1970 with what Kevin Allen celebrates as "a collective declaration of independence for the first time from the culture of homophobia, repression and intimidation in Calgary."[8] The social venue Club Carousel, which opened in March of that year, was initiated and legally controlled by gays who had formed a non-profit charitable society to operate it.[9] By 1972, the society had almost 600 members and they had begun to publish their own monthly newsletter, *Carousel Capers*, which appeared until at least 1975.

The two initiatives would contribute—if only by creating a space for networking and conversation—to the founding in 1975 of Gay Information and Resources Calgary, which published its own newsletter, *Gay Moods*, in 1977 and subsequently *Gay Calgary*.[10] Cowtown, which had been hostile to gays and bereft of gay activism before the late 1960s, had in short order created a permanent gay support network. By the late 1970s, an active, if more closeted, scene existed even in smaller Alberta cities like Medicine Hat.[11]

Change was also occurring on the U of C campus. In February 1969, the campus was the site of a lecture by Hal Call, leader of the Mattachine Society, the pioneering gay civil rights organization founded in Los Angeles in 1950. The lecture and post-lecture panel discussion was sponsored by the University of Calgary Civil Liberties Association, although it is unclear precisely who took the forward step of inviting Call to speak. His talk, "Homosexuality: A Police Industry," was part of a vigorous discussion going on throughout the country on the issue of the criminalization of sexual behaviour.

Reflecting the theme of Call's lecture, three Calgary city detectives stood out among the three hundred students in the audience, although the police left soon after being invited to join the panellists commenting on the situation in the city. But one of the panel members, lawyer Max Wolfe, observed that there were relatively few prosecutions for homosexuality in the city, reflecting the fact that "either the police are shutting their eyes to it or the homosexuals are being reasonably circumspect about their activities, or both." He warned, however, that any bar that became known for being openly gay "would be closed in double-quick time," like one popular coffee shop that had run afoul of city authorities for catering to countercultural patrons.[12] The other panellists, it should be added, were local clergymen—no openly gay person was included.

Late in 1970, Calgary and the U of C campus saw the first exchanges in a years-long debate about human rights—not merely the right to one's own sexual practices but also the right to freedom of speech associated with sexuality. The discussion was sparked by "Ramonn," the U of C student who was bravely reaching out to connect with fellow gay students and open-minded straights. In a letter to *The Gauntlet*, Ramonn expressed his frustration with the censorship exercised by the city's two daily newspapers, the *Calgary Herald* and *The Albertan*. He had attempted to place classified advertisements in the newspapers giving a post office box where lonely gays and curious straights could write to him. The ads were rejected, he reported, because they were "against regulations" enforced by the newspapers. Would *The Gauntlet* run the ad? It not only would, but it would also become a venue for commentary and criticism of the environment of petty censorship dominating the city, which, unsurprisingly, persisted despite the legal changes that had occurred eighteen months earlier.[13]

Headlined "Gay is Good," Ramonn's ads were a sign of the rising tide of the gay liberation movement, in which "homosexuals" renamed themselves gays, lesbians, and queers in a spirit of celebration that rejected shame about one's sexuality. Coined two years earlier, in 1968, by US gay rights activist Frank Kameny, the slogan "Gay is Good" was a deliberate echo of the Black Power movement's proud affirmation "Black is Beautiful."[14] Ramonn reached out again to students in a front-page *Gauntlet* article headlined "Homosexuality: An Offer of Help to Others," which appeared in the 20 January 1971 issue. The same issue also carried an article—ironically headlined "Are You a Sex Criminal?"—from the Canadian University Press student news service that described, with a mixture of sensationalism and outrage, California's oppressive Mentally Disordered Sex Offender Law and the deplorable treatment of homosexuals under it.

This open criticism of the prejudice against gays prompted the conservative newspaper columnist Fred Kennedy to write, in *The Albertan*, a condemnation of homosexuals on campus. They were nothing but "low-lifers," he insisted—evidence of what he described as the "breakdown of the moral code on the part of university students," as well as elsewhere in society. Although *The Gauntlet*'s reaction was curiously conciliatory, it did voice its opposition to Kennedy. It reprinted his column, accompanied by an appeal from the newspaper's editor urging Kennedy to try to understand the "code of behaviour of the homosexual." At the same time, the unnamed author was careful to add that "I am in no way advocating homosexuality."[15]

Despite the editor's sentiments, the next year saw increasingly open support for gay rights in the pages of *The Gauntlet*. A classified ad announcement, published in the 19 September 1972 issue, urged "gay men and women" to "Come out! Out of your closets before the door is nailed shut." The ad was signed by the Gay Liberation Front—a short-lived Calgary chapter, consisting of about a dozen activists, of a coalition that had formed in the United States three years earlier.[16]

Shortly thereafter, in early October, controversy erupted when *The Gauntlet* published an article and photo spread that was intended, the article said, "as a Saul Alinsky style protest" against the sexual stereotyping promoted by Frosh Queen contests. The spoof—headlined "Beautiful Isn't (S)he?"—was the work of the residents of one floor in a U of C dormitory, who had decided to enter their own candidate in the contest. One photo—titled "The it"—showed a male with his back turned to the camera, wearing nothing but sunglasses, a polka-dot hairband, and a shoulder-length wig. The accompanying article, written by one of the dorm residents, mentions another student's reaction to the spoof—a "suggestion that after supper we should hang a faggot" —to which the authors offered a "demur blush."[17]

The following week, a critical letter appeared on the front page of *The Gauntlet*. Its author, Rick Sullivan—at the time, the only openly gay activist at U of C—had only recently arrived on campus and had already been instrumental in the formation of the Gay Liberation Front. Sullivan began by praising the subversion of the anti–Frosh Queen project, which he thought to be "an excellent bit of guerrilla theatre directed at the sexist 'meat parades' involved in the selection of a campus queen." But the organizers of the protest had failed to deal with "their own sexism," he noted. "Heterosexuals are going to have to realize that we are not 'its.' Nor are we a minute coterie of drag queens, hair-dressers and dancers. We are your classmates; your workmates; your neighbours; your relatives." He concluded on a passionate note: "We are human beings deeply committed to the transformation of society that to date has denied us the right to our freedom. We are angry and we are on the way up. Move over brother, the time has come!"[18]

Sullivan's candour was another, more explicit sign of gays' determined fight to beat down the walls of the social closet. Yet his views were expressed in a moment when police were still monitoring those at the political forefront of the gay liberation movement. The intensity of the surveillance was evident in an RCMP report that documented the details of Sullivan's arrival by train in Calgary to take up graduate studies in the fall of 1972. As Sullivan was aware, the police targeted him because they suspected that his politics were left-wing and that he was gay. Indeed, the RCMP attempted to extract more information about him from the U of C administration, although they were denied it.[19]

Sullivan's impassioned plea received a prompt response. In a "personal reply to gay lib," *Gauntlet* staff member Shari Meakin interviewed Sullivan to get a better sense of both "[w]hat it means to be gay at U of C" and what the GLF wanted. The article was a sympathetic overview of the demands of the gay liberation movement, emphasizing the need for a "clean-up of the social vocabulary" and educational, political, and legal reform.[20] The issues had never before been so visible on the campus. Sullivan himself began to write regularly in *The Gauntlet* on a wide range of issues, including the social and political condition of gays, reviews of both books and film, and the causes and alleviation of international poverty. In an op-ed piece, "Campus Gays an Oppressed Minority," he described two approaches for activists: continue to focus on legal reforms and work to "develop gay as a revolutionary life form and make it viable."[21] He was also often quoted in *The Gauntlet*, variously described as a "gay militant," "gay liberationist," and "gay Calgarian."

In the fall of 1973, an apparently short-lived lesbian feminist group formed on campus, whose contact person, Myra ("My") Lipton, had also been involved in the founding of the Gay Liberation Front. Near the end of the term, she and Sullivan appeared as guest speakers in a human sexuality course taught by Larry MacKillop, a sessional instructor in what was then the School of Social Welfare. The writer of a "Course of the Week" review for *The Gauntlet* said that he found the course to be a "personal education experience" and noted that the opportunity to hear Lipton and Sullivan was for many students the "first exposure to this aspect of human sexuality."[22] Evidently, MacKillop was pleased with their talk, as they were invited to speak again when the course was taught the following fall.

In November 1974, an article about the second Lipton-Sullivan presentation appeared in *The Gauntlet*. It reported that their remarks exposed students to gay and lesbian political demands—demands that were, Sullivan later recalled, regarded in the early 1970s as "too pushy" and "aggressive," even within the Calgary gay community.[23] The writer reports Lipton saying that "just as women should have control over their own bodies in the abortion issue, so should they be able to 'engage in whatever sexual activities they prefer.'" Lipton added that the "greatest threat to the male role is solidarity among women" and that "lesbianism epitomizes that solidarity." For his part, Sullivan attacked the "supposedly progressive left for avoiding the issue of gay liberation."[24] But he also spoke more broadly about the anti-gay attitudes still embedded in the legal system and about how gay groups often had a hard time finding a public outlet for their views.

Sullivan's criticism of the legal system's treatment of gays probably was shared by some U of C faculty members. An unidentified group of them issued an invitation to Sir John Wolfenden to speak on campus as a distinguished lecturer, which he did in April 1973. It was Wolfenden's 1957 report to the British government that had served as the key impetus for the 1967 decriminalization of homosexual acts in England and Wales. Yet Sullivan was rebuffed when he lobbied U of C faculty members to support a campaign urging the American Psychiatric Association to strike homosexuality as a mental illness from the *Diagnostic and Statistical Manual of Mental Disorders* (DSM). The rejection stung "at a personal as well as a political level," he later reported.[25] As he wrote many years later, "U of C gave us a chance to cut our teeth before moving on to communities that were more ready for our kind of activism."[26]

The debates that unfolded in *The Gauntlet* did not, of course, take place in a vacuum. Elsewhere in the city, early 1973 saw the formation of the People's Liberation Coalition (PLC), one of Calgary's first activist groups, which set up a phone line that offered information and counselling to lesbians and gays. Many of the activists involved with the Gay Liberation Front went on to become active with the PLC.[27] Both the PLC and its successor, Gay Information and Resources Calgary, established in June 1975, regularly advertised their support services in *The Gauntlet*. Although in 1975 the *Herald*, the city's leading mainstream newspaper, still refused to accept such ads, *The Albertan* had by then agreed to print them.[28]

Calgary gay activists were, moreover, sometimes front and centre in places that were decidedly hostile to gays. When, for example, the US-based anti-gay crusader Anita Bryant visited Edmonton on 29 April 1978 as part of a Canadian tour, forty Calgarians joined protesters outside of Northlands Coliseum. Independently of them, two very determined Calgary militants, Windi Earthworm—one of the founders of Gay Information and Resources Calgary—and My Lipton, hatched a bolder plan. They bluffed their way inside, and, with Lipton's assistance, Earthworm chained his neck to a post, isolated among six thousand Bryant worshippers. When Lipton asked whether he was okay, Earthworm replied, "Yeah, except these really kind Christian folk are ready to hang me." Newspaper photos show him standing defiant at the event, where he took on Bryant, shouting, "You love me so much you want me in prison."[29]

At the time of Bryant's appearance in Edmonton, Everett Klippert had been out of prison for nearly seven years: he was released on probation in July 1971 and moved to Edmonton. Since his release, he had found his way to a less turbulent life, albeit only by a return to the closet. He categorically refused to take part in gay rights activism and eventually, at the age of about sixty, married a long-standing friend, Dorothy Hagstrom. In the meanwhile, his fellow queers continued their lives, some staying under the radar and some actively fighting for their rights. By the mid-1970s, Calgary was beginning to learn tolerance for a minority that had endlessly been persecuted, shamed, or, at best, ignored. But the town was still decades away from a more progressive legal environment and widespread social acceptance.

NOTES

1. See Gary Kinsman and Patrizia Gentile, *The Canadian War on Queers: National Security as Sexual Regulation* (Vancouver: University of British Columbia Press, 2010), 73. See also Elise Chenier, "The Criminal Sexual Psychopath in Canada: Sex, Psychiatry and Law at Mid-Century," *Canadian Bulletin of Medical History* 20, no. 1 (2003): 75–101, esp. 76–78.

2. On RCMP surveillance and the Canadian security regime, see Kinsman and Gentile, *Canadian War on Queers*, 76–79; and Gary Kinsman, "The Canadian War on Queers: Sexual Regulation and Resistance," in *Queerly Canadian: An Introductory Reader in Sexuality Studies*, ed. Maureen

Fitzgerald and Scott Rayter (Toronto: Canadian Scholars' Press, 2012), 65–79, esp. 65–66.

3. Kevin Allen, *Our Past Matters: Stories of Gay Calgary* (Calgary: Calgary Gay History Project, 2018), 18–19. Considerable documentary evidence about Klippert's case, and his personal, family and work history, and press coverage of his case is at the "Calgary Gay History Project: Our Past Matters, https://calgarygayhistory.ca/2017/11/03/klippert-month-the-recap/."

4. John Ibbotson, "In 1965, Everett Klippert was Sentenced to a Life Behind Bars. His Crime? Being Gay," *Globe and Mail*, 27 February 2016, F4. For the testimony of the two psychiatrists, see *Klippert v. The Queen*, [1967] SCR 822 at 827–29.

5. "Trudeau: 'There's No Place for the State in the Bedrooms of the Nation,'" *CBC News*, 21 December 1967, CBC archives, https://www.cbc.ca/archives/entry/omnibus-bill-theres-no-place-for-the-state-in-the-bedrooms-of-the-nation.

6. Kinsman and Gentile, *Canadian War on Queers*, 221–22. The 1969 law reform also allowed abortion under certain conditions and created no-fault divorce, ending the necessity for couples to endure a criminal trial to end a marriage. A related bill, passed at the same time, reconfigured the law on the sale and use of contraceptives. Tom Hooper argues that the phrase "decriminalization" of homosexuality is erroneous. Instead the bill should be considered "the recriminalization of homosexuality" since it "enabled the expanded role of the criminal justice system in the everyday lives of queer people." Tom Hooper, "Queering '69: The Recriminalization of Homosexuality in Canada," Canadian Historical Review, Vol. 100, No. 2, June 2019, 258.

7. Ramonn, "A Problem for Gays—Making Friends," *The Gauntlet*, 3 March 1971, 3. "Ramonn" also actively took up the debate about gay life and organizations in a 29 October 1973 letter to Edmonton's alternative newspaper, *Poundmaker*. See the chapter by Erin Gallagher-Cohoon elsewhere in this volume.

8. Allen, *Our Past Matters*, 31–33, 36.

9. Perhaps referring to earlier bids to create gay-operated safe social spaces, Gens Hellquist dates the opening of Club Carousel to 1969, but legal documents suggest that it was in 1970. Hellquist, "The Prairies," in *Gay on the Canadian Prairie: Twenty Years of Perceptions, 1983–2002*, comp. Alex Spence (Saskatoon: Perceptions Publications, 2003), 49.

10. "Before the Net: Calgary's 70s Gay Press," CGHP, 2 March 2017, https://calgaryqueerhistory.ca/2017/03/02/before-the-net-calgarys-70s-gay-press/.

11. "Earning Toasters in 'The Hat,'" CGHP, 9 March 2017, https://calgaryqueerhistory.ca/2017/03/09/earning-toasters-in-the-hat/.

12. Graham Pike, "U of C Hears Pitch for Homosexuality," *The Albertan*, 12 February 1969. The RCMP Security Service in Calgary took note of Call's lecture, sending a news clipping about it to the RCMP commissioner in Ottawa. LAC ATIP A2016-00880, Vol. 2, p. 134.

13. "Gay Student Has Trouble with *Herald*," *The Gauntlet*, 4 November 1970, 5. Calgary newspapers were not alone in their censorship. Newspapers in Edmonton had a similar policy, as did those in Vancouver until 1975, when a BC legal tribunal ruled them illegal. W. W. Black, "Gay Alliance Toward Equality v. Vancouver *Sun*," *Osgoode Hall Law Journal*, Vol. 17 No. 3, December 1979, https://digitalcommons.osgoode.yorku.ca/cgi/viewcontent.cgi?article=2057&context=ohlj.

14. "Gay Is Good: How Frank Kameny Changed the Face of America," interview by Will O'Bryan, *Metro Daily* (Washington, DC), 4 October 2006, http://www.metroweekly.com/2006/10/gay-is-good/. On the connection to "Black is Beautiful," see Frank Kameny to Randy Wicker and Peter Ogren, 23 August 1968, in *Gay Is Good: The Life and Letters of Gay Rights Pioneer Franklin Kameny*, ed. Michael G. Long (Syracuse, NY: Syracuse University Press, 2014), 165–66; and Elizabeth A. Armstrong, *Forging Gay Identities: Organizing Sexuality in San Francisco, 1950–1994* (Chicago: University of Chicago Press, 2002), 53–54. A veteran of World War II, Kameny had gone on to earn a PhD in astronomy, only to be fired in 1957 from his job with the US Army Map Service because he was a homosexual. As part of a determined effort to fight his dismissal, in 1961 he wrote the first gay-rights legal brief ever to be filed with the US Supreme Court, as well as founding, later that same year, the Washington, DC, branch of the Mattachine Society. He remained active politically for the rest of his life, defending gay and lesbian rights right up to his death, in 2011.

15. "Filth and obscenities," *The Gauntlet*, 3 February 1971. Kennedy's column was reprinted next to the unsigned *Gauntlet* reply. It should be noted that not everyone at *The Albertan* shared Kennedy's animosity toward gays. In late October 1969, *Albertan* city editor Paul Jackson had been discreetly invited to a gay costume ball at one of the short-lived clubs predating Club Carousel, which he described as "a quiet oasis in the midst of an alien world of fear, hate, insecurity and often bitter loneliness." Paul Jackson, quoted in Celeste McGovern, "Out of the Closets and onto the Streets," in *Alberta in the 20th Century: A Journalistic History of the Province*, vol. 10, *The Sixties Revolution and the Fall of Social Credit*, ed. Paul Bunner (Edmonton: United Western Communications, 2002), 76.

16. Richard (Rick) Sullivan, telephone interview by Kevin Allen, 23 May 2017.

17. Dave Simpson, "Beautiful Isn't (S)he?" *The Gauntlet*, 4 October 1972, 7–10.

18. Rick Sullivan, "*Gauntlet* Offends Campus Minority," *The Gauntlet*, 11 October 1972, 1. Sullivan, who hailed from Ontario, was in Calgary only briefly for a master's degree. He went on to have a career as a social worker and later an academic in British Columbia, focusing on the community experience of LGBTQ youth. In the interview cited above, he mentioned that, in his recollection, it was he who called the first meeting of the Gay Liberation Front.

19. Sullivan interview. Evidence of the RCMP Security Service's file on Sullivan is confirmed in documents from a review of the political groups and individuals on the U of C campus that was conducted by the RCMP in August 1973. The review names Sullivan and two other students as active in the People's Liberation Coalition, a group "which promotes equality for homosexuals." RCMP Security Service, Calgary, "University of Calgary," 28 August 1973, LAC ATIP A2016-00880, Vol. 5, p. 560. Sullivan's situation appears to be described in a remarkable letter by U of C registrar W.F.M Stewart of 15 February 1973. Following an RCMP request to the university for personal data, Stewart went so far as to request a meeting with two RCMP Security Service officers to alert them to a deviation from the established protocol between the university and the RCMP about what information U of C would provide. In a follow-up letter to the officer in charge of the RCMP in Calgary, Stewart reminded the police that U of C had agreed to provide only publicly-available information about people employed at the university. Instead, Stewart wrote, there was a "disquieting inference" in what the RCMP had requested that they were investigating someone who held opinions "unpopular, orthodox, or in one of its many senses, 'subversive'" and who exhibited "behaviour which might be regarded as, to one degree or another, deviant." In order to avoid "an invasion of academic freedom," U of C would not respond to any "request for 'background' information, or personal information" other than what was already publicly available. See Stewart to Officer Commanding, RCMP, Calgary, 15 February 1973, LAC ATIP Act A2016-00880, Vol. 5, p 582–84.

20. Shari Meakin, "What It Means to Be Gay at U of C," *The Gauntlet*, 18 October 1972, 9.

21. "Campus Gays an Oppressed Minority," *The Gauntlet*, 27 November 1973, 2.

22. David Wolf, "*Gauntlet* Evaluates Course of the Week," *The Gauntlet*, 25 January 1974, 5.

23. Sullivan interview.

24. Don Moules, "Gay Liberation as a Threat to Present Society," *The Gauntlet*, 8 November 1974, 6.

25. Sullivan interview. In December 1973, the American Psychiatric Association's board of trustees voted to remove homosexuality from the DSM. Early the next year, opponents tried to overturn the decision by means of a referendum of members, but the attempt failed: the trustees' decision was upheld, albeit by a relatively slim majority (58%). Jack Drescher, "Out of DSM: Depathologizing Homosexuality," *Behavioral Sciences* 5, no. 4 (2015): 571, doi: 10.3390/bs5040565.

26. Richard (Rick) Sullivan, personal correspondence with Kevin Allen, 23 May 2017.

27. Sullivan interview. For more information, see "Before GIRC: YYC Gay Support in the 70s," CGHP, 11 February 2016, https://calgarygayhistory.ca/2016/02/11/before-girc-yyc-gay-support-in-the-70s/.

28. "GIRC Origins," CGHP, 14 January 2016, https://calgarygayhistory.ca/2016/01/14/girc-origins/.

29. Allen, *Our Past Matters*, 60–61; "1978: A Windi Blowback for Anita Bryant," CGHP, 15 June 2018, https://calgaryqueerhistory.ca/2018/06/15/1978-a-windi-blowback-for-anita-bryant/. Earthworm was replying to Bryant, who had just said, "I love you, and I know enough to tell you the truth so you will not go to eternal damnation."

6 Contraception, Community, and Controversy

The Lethbridge Birth Control and
Information Centre, 1972–78

Karissa Robyn Patton

In January of 1973, the small city of Lethbridge was abuzz with anticipation over the grand opening of the new Lethbridge Birth Control and Information Centre (LBCIC). *The Meliorist*, the University of Lethbridge (U of L) student newspaper, ran an enthusiastic story about the new birth control centre. "Birth control centre at last," featured on the front page of the 19 January issue, provided information about the centre's open house, upcoming workshops, and a comprehensive list of the services the centre would soon provide.[1] The student journalists' enthusiasm for the new LBCIC, evident in the article's headline, illustrates the demand for such services and education by youth and students in the Lethbridge area. The local daily, the *Lethbridge Herald*, wrote less enthusiastically about the LBCIC but still ran a short but informative piece on the centre's first week of operation. The *Herald* article, headlined "Ten use clinic," had fewer than one hundred words and was placed on page 15 (toward the end of the issue) of the 1 February edition. It explained where the centre was located, pointed out that all of the LBCIC's services were confidential, and noted that ten people had used the centre's services in its first week of operation.[2] The stark contrast between these two news articles reflects a variety of local reactions to the LBCIC: for some, it evoked enthusiasm; for others, it piqued interest; for not a few, it generated anxiety.[3] Over the next five years, the LBCIC would be featured in student and local newspapers and celebrated for bringing topics like birth control, abortion, and sexuality into the public eye—yet it also provoked controversy. This chapter will convey the story of the LBCIC and explore the ways it supported larger goals of activism for reproductive rights, fostered coalition building, and sparked important and provocative discussions about reproductive and sexual health.

The newly opened centre was the brainchild of three local health professionals: registered nurse Judy Burgess, Dr. Lloyd Johnson, and Dr. Robert Hall. With Burgess at the helm, the three came to the conclusion that Lethbridge needed a community space where people of any age could get information about birth control, reproduction, human sexuality, pregnancy, and abortion. At its opening, the centre offered pregnancy tests, birth control information (including which local doctors to go to for prescriptions), birth control and abortion counselling, and a library containing materials on a variety of topics related to reproductive health and human sexuality.[4] It very quickly expanded its services to include prenatal care, information for unwed mothers, and a variety of educational seminars on sexuality. In the minds of the three instigators, the birth control and information centre filled some important gaps in their city. On a medical level, they hoped it would help curb the climbing rates of teenage pregnancy and venereal diseases (VD) in Lethbridge and beyond. As local health professionals, all three had seen the fallout from poor human sexuality education in the region. And, on a human rights level, they believed that everyone had a right to such education and resources as a means to be healthy autonomous and sexual beings.[5]

Burgess, Johnson, and Hall were not alone in recognizing the need for public services provided by the LBCIC and similar centres across Canada and the United States. Indeed, as Sandra Morgen wrote in *Into Our Own Hands*, during the 1970s, birth control, abortion, and women's health centres were opening their doors across North America. She explained that these centres, like the LBCIC, were part of a larger international grassroots movement in the 1970s working to create better reproductive and sexual health services that were accessible to the general public. Moreover, because most of these centres were linked to the women's liberation and women's health movements in the 1970s, activists like Burgess recognized that the services offered more autonomy for everyone, particularly women. Burgess and other reproductive health activists knew that offering these services would destigmatize conversations about bodies and sexuality.[6] The centre's potential to elevate women's, reproductive, and sexual rights in Lethbridge was one of the many reasons Burgess was intent on making the LBCIC a reality.[7]

Perhaps the best evidence of Burgess's devotion to the LBCIC and the many causes it represented is the fact that she worked unpaid for several months to create it. She worked on grant applications to fund the centre, looked for qualified staff and volunteers to help run the centre once it opened, and sought materials for the educational seminars and information library she hoped the centre would run. Finally, Burgess, Johnson, and Hall received a Local Initiatives Program (LIP) grant to fund all aspects in the centre—including Burgess's salary. In November 1972, when the grant was approved and Burgess received her first paycheque, she recalls with laughter the joy "of being paid for the first time in years because I had been going to school. I cashed the whole paycheque and I put the money on my bed and I yelled 'Ah I got paid!' It was six hundred dollars or something."[8] Burgess's elation speaks volumes about her commitment and dedication in establishing the centre.

The successful LIP grant gave Burgess, Johnson, and Hall the means to begin their centre in 1972, but the municipal funding of the centre eventually led to controversy. In the 1970s, the LIP grant was a common form of funding for community programs, because it allowed joint municipal, provincial, and federal collaboration and funding. However, the multiple funding bodies often made for a complicated application and reapplication process from year to year, depending on who sat on city council or provincial and federal committees. In Lethbridge, the LBCIC was lucky enough to have a mayor and city council who supported it financially from 1972 to 1978, providing not only a gateway to funding the centre but also a foundation of community backing for it. Indeed, during its operation, the LBCIC was also supported by community collaborations between southern Alberta feminists, student activists, and local professionals, who all rallied behind the need for good reproductive and sexual health services and education. However, the centre was not without its detractors. From vandalism of LBCIC advertisements on city buses to letter-writing campaigns demanding an end to municipal funding, some Lethbridge citizens were less than happy—some even deeply offended—with the local presence of open-access reproductive and sexual health services.[9]

This chapter is organized around three themes: contraception, community, and controversy. Drawing on oral history interviews, local and student newspapers, and the few surviving archival documents on the LBCIC, I will explore the themes and discuss how the particular setting of the small city of Lethbridge (with a population just over 46,000 in 1976) made for a great hotbed of feminist and student collaboration and activism.[10] The contraception section reviews the reasons why many people at the time believed the city needed reproductive and sexual health services. The section recognizes that the LBCIC offered much more than birth control counselling and sexuality education; it also provided new avenues for autonomy for some citizens in Lethbridge, especially young women. The section on community investigates the ways that student and feminist activists worked with the city's main players and organizations to increase popular support for the LBCIC. Additionally, the section looks at how these forces cumulatively contributed to the centre's success. My exploration of how that community factored into the success of the LBCIC reveals why the small city of Lethbridge, known more popularly as part of the so-called southern Alberta Bible Belt and a bastion of conservatism, actually became a space that fostered coalition building.[11] The last section, on controversy, describes public anxiety and populist pushback regarding the municipal funding of, and the public access to, services provided by the LBCIC. Specifically, I draw upon the 1974 local controversy around municipal funding of the centre. Ultimately, these three sections come together to illustrate how community collaboration triumphed over pushback, controversy, and, in many ways, conservatism.

Recognizing Alberta's Reproductive Health Activism: Oral Histories and Activist Voices

Personal stories and memories gathered from oral history interviews feature prominently in my telling of the LBCIC's story. Oral histories are often significant in a topic of this kind. However, it is important to note that while I highlight voices of a few activists involved with the LBCIC, these voices focus on feminist student activist communities. Indeed, there are many voices left out of the conversation and many voices that need to be added to the conversation around reproductive health activism in Alberta. For instance, this chapter focuses only on Lethbridge, one starting point for broader research on similar activism in the entire province. Further, the stories of the many professional supporters of the LBCIC and similar causes are discussed, but their voices are not featured here.

Perhaps more significantly, Indigenous stories are often left out of the narrative about reproductive health activism. It is not clear to what extent Indigenous people used the services at the LBCIC, or if they volunteered there. However, the history of Indigenous people and the politics of choice in Canada is an important one to consider in connection to the story of the LBCIC. Canada and Alberta have a history of cultural genocide, residential schools, eugenics, and coercive sterilization of Indigenous people.[12] Moreover, in the 1970s, Indigenous communities were still devastated after the infamous Sixties Scoop, when an estimated twenty thousand Indigenous children were taken from their homes and placed with White families who were deemed "more suitable."[13] Because of the federal and provincial legacies of genocide, eugenics, and the Sixties Scoop, Indigenous communities faced complicated realities in terms of reproductive politics in the 1970s. Faced with a legacy of population control, neglect, and having loved ones physically taken from them, Indigenous communities were not only looking for ways to limit their fertility through contraception and to access good reproductive and sexual health services and education but simultaneously fighting for their right to have children and parent the children they already had.[14] Their stories are significant and many of their stories still need to be told.

In the meantime, I focus here on the somewhat limited but still significant story and oral histories of the LBCIC. The LBCIC, like feminist activism in Alberta in the 1960s and 1970s more generally, has often been left in the shadows of high-profile feminist activism in the larger urban centres of Toronto, Vancouver, and Montréal. Thus, the story of the LBCIC has yet to be told. Using oral histories to tell the story of the LBCIC is important because, as historian Ruth Roach Pierson states, using oral history interviews brings the historian and the reader "closest to the 'reality' of women's lives."[15] The voices of six women who were involved in the LBCIC during the 1970s play a large role in this recounting of the centre's story. These six women illustrate that organized feminist and community activism was happening and, indeed, was successfully making changes in their local and provincial communities. By sharing their stories, I am adding these southern Alberta activists to the larger historical narrative and highlighting their activism as influential and significant in the national and international histories of activism in the 1960s and 1970s.

Contraception: Creating Dialogue and Fighting for Reproductive and Sexual Autonomy

From its inception, it was clear that the LBCIC fed an appetite for access to information on contraception and sexuality in Lethbridge. Women's liberation activist and *Meliorist* journalist Luba Lisun remembers that a lack of reproductive and sexual health services and education made for some dire situations. The social stigma that barred unmarried youth from seeking contraceptives at the time did not deter them from engaging in sexual activity. She recalls that the result of inaccessible contraceptives was often unwanted pregnancy and, sometimes, marriage:

> Yeah, the other side of being raised in a Catholic world was that girls got pregnant. [. . .] People I knew got pregnant as teenagers and either went away and had the child or they kept the child. Others got married right after school. I mean we still lived close enough to that period of time that that's what you did. And it wasn't until the mid-to-late '60s that that started to change—thinking about how to deal with that, or how things should change.[16]

Unwanted pregnancies resulting from inaccessibility to contraceptive and sex education services were part of the reason that the members of the Lethbridge community, especially young women like Lisun, embraced the LBCIC with open arms.

For women such as Lisun and Mary Bochenko, the LBCIC also became a means to increase their autonomy. Birth control services and education offered them independence, while also allowing them to embrace their own sexuality. Lisun and Bochenko remember that the expectation was that they (and all young, unmarried women) would practice abstinence. And many young women were encouraged to marry young so that they could begin to have sex—with the expectation that they would also bear children—without breaching familial and social moral expectations. Bochenko, a student journalist and activist at the Lethbridge Community College's *The Endeavour*, recalls that "my mom was always on my case: 'Okay, now you're finished school, now you get married, you have a family. You do all of those things,' and I was like: I don't think so. There was this whole world out there that I knew nothing about, right."[17] Lisun also remembers her feelings of resistance to her family's pressure: "You just felt like: I'm a girl and I work hard and I should have the same rights and I shouldn't be expected to get married. I don't want to get married. [. . .] Just don't tell me what to do, I'm going to choose."[18] For Lisun and Bochenko, better access to birth control and sexuality information gave them the autonomy to pursue education, careers, travel, and life outside of wifehood and motherhood.

Similarly, Rita Moir, an activist involved in women's liberation and a student journalist at *The Meliorist* in the 1970s, remembers the opening of the LBCIC as a triumph not only of reproductive health activism but of women's liberation more broadly. She describes the LBCIC as a "tremendous service being offered to women of all ages." More than that, "for us as young women and women dealing with issues of birth control, and rape, and unwanted pregnancy—it sounds melodramatic—but we were fighting for our lives, our futures."[19] Her memories of the LBCIC capture the gravity of the situation for young women in particular but really for the public in general: by breaking free from moral regulations, people's sexual and social autonomy would increase.

Like Moir, Lisun, and Bochenko, medical professionals in Lethbridge noticed and recognized the need for better reproductive and sexual health and sought to improve it. Burgess states, "I got to know a couple of the gynecologists who were very interested in supporting women's health [. . .] because they were seeing the fallout of it: unwanted pregnancies and whatnot."[20] Terri Forbis, director of the Lethbridge Family Planning Centre in the late 1970s, remembers "the lack of information and how that was affecting young people, and not just young people, older women too. I had clients that were forty-four years old that had so little information about their bodies and about reproduction and what was happening."[21] Forbis says she found solidarity with other professionals who were seeing the same consequences of a lack of reproductive and sexual health information.

Forbis also remembers not only public need but significant public desire for reproductive and sexual health information.

> At the time, the Kinsey studies were a huge big deal for people. Or Woody Allen movies where he actually started introducing sex into movies and providing people with information about sexual functioning and relationships. And it was just so not talked about anywhere that people were really hungry for it. Really hungry for it. But they still had to get it served under the table. That's why the Birth Control

and Information Centre was so controversial—this was really putting everything on the table.[22]

Her memories reveal that desire for information was increasing rapidly through the 1960s and 1970s. Moreover, as Forbis explains, the LBCIC provided essential services related to reproduction, contraception, and sexuality that citizens desperately wanted and needed. However, social stigma surrounding topics like contraception, sexuality, VD, and abortion made the services and education taboo. According to Forbis, the LBCIC was seen as controversial because it offered these desired services openly and unashamedly. While working at the Lethbridge Family Planning Centre, Forbis recognized that the LBCIC was the first organization in the region to offer this type of comprehensive and judgment-free reproductive and sexual health education.

The LBCIC also provided training in reproductive and sexual health service provision and education for its volunteers and employees. Thus the centre became a space where specialized skills in human sexuality education were learned and practised. According to Forbis, "At that time, there were so few of us that had any skill set in how to talk about sexuality that we were really sought after by different professional groups and agencies that didn't have that skill set and wanted it."[23] As Forbis remembers it, the LBCIC was a model for what comprehensive sex and reproductive health education should look like. In laying that foundation, employees and volunteers at the centre developed specific skills that distinguished them from other kinds of health and education professionals.

Community: Coalition Building and the Significance of Place

Because such a variety of communities came to support the LBCIC, it also became a site for coalition building. Women such as Burgess, Moir, Lisun, and Bochenko came together within a strong and supportive network of like-minded activists. The supporting community was not limited to feminist activists. Indeed, many Lethbridge citizens, including progressive local professionals, came together in support of the centre and often built coalitions across communities and causes. In fact, according to the oral history narrators, it was the strength of these coalitions and communities that made the centre such a success during its six years of operation.

Lethbridge coalitions and communities built around reproductive and sexual health activisms resembled coalitions built in many cities across Canada and the United States at the time. Historian Christabelle Sethna has traced important work achieved through student and feminist collaborations in Canada including the McGill *Birth Control Handbook* (first published in 1968) and the Abortion Caravan in 1970 initiated by the Vancouver Women's Caucus.[24] While Lethbridge was a much smaller city, and located in a Bible Belt, the unity of students, youth, and feminists there was just as significant as those in Vancouver or Montréal. Moir explains that, in part, these coalitions were built into the culture of the late 1960s and early 1970s: "So, there were a lot of student activists, the newspaper [*The Meliorist*] was a student activist newspaper [. . .] and so we actively supported places like the Birth Control and Information Centre."[25] Local feminists, students, and youth comprised the largest community of support.

While activists provided the numbers and volunteer power to run the centre, support from them—as people sometimes deemed too radical—was not enough to maintain it. Burgess, Moir, and Forbis emphasize that it was the support and advocacy of local professionals, doctors and nurses especially, that really won the city's approval to fund the LBCIC and initially safeguarded it. Lethbridge doctors like Johnson and Hall recognized the need for a birth control centre and supported the movement through referrals for birth control and abortions.[26]

Local professionals also helped to combat the inevitable voices of criticism against the centre. A typical complaint was registered in an April 1974 letter to city council. "As a realist," the writer declared, "I believe that if society demands that birth control (conception) [*sic*] information should be given to unmarried teen-agers, then a clinic operated by medical doctors (and never by hippie type unqualified persons) is the only proper answer."[27] The theme was repeated, with an added pejorative, by another complainant, who told council that "I do not want my children taught by a bunch of hippys or second class people that run this centre."[28] These were obvious efforts to discredit the young student and feminist activists who supported the LBCIC.

Burgess, then in her early to mid-twenties, remembers that, for some, her youth and appearance undermined her authority as head of the LBCIC. As a result, she and the board members agreed to hire Claranne (Tinky) Bush, a young academic with a PhD in physiology, to increase the centre's credibility.[29] Once reputable doctors and other professional figures from local schools, clinics, and the municipal government threw their support behind the reproductive and sexual rights mandate of the LBCIC, perceptions of respectability followed, and other citizens joined the campaign.

In fact, according to the oral history narrators, the small population and rural surroundings of Lethbridge brought communities together and was ideal for coalition building. Moir describes the unique way that the small city and rural surroundings of Lethbridge in particular, and Alberta more generally, were places where coalitions and collaborations became an integral part of local activism. She argues that the smaller rural population in Lethbridge and southern Alberta actually strengthened their community:

> Lethbridge was pretty rural compared to Montreal or big cities. We were far more likely to form coalitions because we didn't have a critical mass of people that you could have groups that were all 22 year olds or you know all 30 year olds or all 70 year olds. You brought together people who wanted to talk about the same thing and grapple [with] the same issues [. . .]. And in Lethbridge that [separate activist groups] just couldn't have worked—there wouldn't have been enough people.[30]

While Lethbridge may not be commonly recognized as an activist space, given its location in the Canadian Bible Belt, the rural location and setting contributed to fostering strong activist coalitions and bringing together communities of activists and local professionals. For example, the different communities supporting the LBCIC found solidarity in 1974 when a group called Citizens in Action (CIA) pressured the city to pull funding from the centre. Burgess and Moir both explain that the strength of their communities ultimately overwhelmed the protest. Moir recalls that she did not feel ostracized "because we had such a broad base within our women's movement in Lethbridge."[31] Similarly, Burgess notes that "there was always a group of people to support you. And I really felt supported."[32] This supportive activist community proved stronger than social anxiety, public pushback, and controversy.

Controversy: Resolve and Resiliency in the Face of Opposition

Commitment to the LBCIC was key to defeating the intense controversy that erupted in 1974 over its municipal funding. That year, the centre became a target of CIA when its LIP grant came up for renewal. Citizens in Action put forward a recommendation that the city withdraw all municipal funding from the LBCIC. Without that, the provincial and federal monies would also be lost and the centre forced to close.[33] The CIA campaign led to a public debate between supporters and opponents of the centre. In April and May, the debate played out in newspaper editorials and in letters to city council.[34] This local debate reveals important aspects of both opposition and support.

Opposition was largely fuelled by anxiety around youth having access to such reproductive education and services. Moir recalls public apprehension that the centre was "promoting promiscuity" and "teen sexuality or irresponsible sexuality."[35] In letters to council, some citizens referred to the LBCIC and the literature it distributed as immoral. Letter writer Rosemary R. Edmunds went as far to charge that the "literature made available with regard to this project is obscene. We should all be enraged at such pornographic material being available to adults, let alone children."[36] Forbis also remembers people's concerns

> about sex education and "What are you saying to our kids? And what about values? What values are you going to be imparting? You're going to be telling our kids it's OK to have sex. And if you talk about birth control they're going to want to go out and do it. And we want you to be abstinence only [education]. And then, what about the abortion issue? Are you going to be talking about abortion?"[37]

These questions illustrate the social anxieties around contraceptive and sexuality education of youth that partially fuelled protest against the LBCIC.

At the same time, the debate and the opposition to the centre actually worked to strengthen the resolve of LBCIC supporters and enhance the coalitions built around it. Indeed, CIA was unsuccessful in getting the LBCIC's funding pulled and the centre continued to be supported by the city until 1978. Moir and Burgess both remember overcoming such controversies with the unyielding affirmation of their cohorts of feminists, students, and local progressive professionals.

In 1978, as a result of two political shifts, the LBCIC lost its LIP funding and closed its doors. By then, the Alberta government included reproductive and sexual health services as part of provincial health care. The services were then regulated by provincial legislation and bureaucracy. At the municipal level, the centre's closure was caused largely by a change in municipal leadership. A new mayor and council were less sympathetic to the LBCIC and used the new provincial legislation to justify closing the centre in favour of opening the Family Planning Centre (FPC), a provincial health service that both levels of government could regulate more closely. The new FPC tried to fill the same gaps that the LBCIC had filled during its operation, but the new municipally run board, often acting as gatekeepers, sometimes limited what the FPC could accomplish.[38]

While government regulation of these services presented new limitations, it also represents a broader acceptance of these issues on an official level in Alberta society. Seen from the perspective of reproductive and sexual health activism, the closure of the LBCIC and the increased regulation of the FPC were defeats. However, the inclusion of these services under provincial health care meant a reduction in costs to both the centres and citizens. And the inclusion of such health services in the provincial health-care system illustrates that reproductive and sexual health were becoming part of a normalized model of health and wellness—in large part thanks to the activists, including those at the LBCIC, who brought public attention to sexuality, contraception, abortion, and VD and made these health services legitimate.

While the LBCIC closed its doors in 1978, the stories shared about its six years of operation illuminate a significant instance of feminist reproductive rights activism in southern Alberta. The history of these activists demonstrates initiative, political dedication, and commitment to their communities. Additionally, the story of the LBCIC illustrates that this activism persisted in the face of both inertia ("we do not need this here") and conservative opposition ("we do not want this here"). Lethbridge may not be the first place that comes to mind when one thinks about activism in Alberta, let alone Canada. But as the story of the LBCIC shows, the small city was home to some dedicated feminists in the 1970s.

Acknowledgements

Thank you to all of the oral history narrators whose stories inform this work. Also, thank you to the Glenbow Archives and the Galt Museum and Archives, especially archivist Andrew Chernevych, for the invaluable assistance over the years. Thank you to Anastasia Sereda, Erin Gallagher-Cohoon, and Tarisa Little for valuable feedback on this piece. Thank you to Erika Dyck and Carol Williams for your mentorship and guidance throughout my research on the LBCIC. Thank you to the Social Sciences and Humanities Research Council of Canada, which funded part of this research throughout my MA and PhD through the Joseph-Armand Bombardier Master's Award and the Canadian Graduate Student Doctoral Award.

NOTES

1. Rita Moir, "Birth Control Centre at Last," *The Meliorist*, 19 January 1973.
2. "Ten Use Clinic," *Lethbridge Herald*, 1 February, 1973, 15.
3. See also "Of Cash and Clubs," *The Meliorist*, 6 October 1972, 2; "The New Birth Control and Information Centre," *The Meliorist*, 26 January 1973, 4; Rita Moir, "Clinic Petition Planned," *The Meliorist*, 2 February 1973, 1; "Sexuality Seminar Planned," *The Meliorist*, 5 March 1973, 2; Rita Moir, "If You Think Gay People Are Revolting You Can Bet Your Sweet Ass They Are!" *The Meliorist*, 22 March 1973, 1; "Child Care Offered at Sex Seminar," *Lethbridge Herald*, 30 March 1973, 18; "Birth Control Info Coming . . . ," *The Endeavour*, 20 October 1972, 2; Mary Bochenko, "Birth Control Centre Serves Purpose," *The Endeavour*, 16 February 1973, 2.
4. The centre provided abortion counselling; that is, it counselled pregnant women on the various options (i.e., abortion, adoption, keeping the baby). If the woman chose abortion, the volunteers and staff would counsel her on what to expect of the methods and the procedure itself. The centre did not perform abortions but did know which doctors in the city were pro-choice and thus could counsel women on which physician to see.
5. Judy Burgess, interview by the author, 8 December 2012, transcript. Recordings and transcripts of the interviews cited in this chapter can be found in Oral History Project: Students' Reproductive Rights Activism in Southern Alberta During the 1960s and 1970s, Galt Museum and Archives, Lethbridge, acc. no. 20171019.
6. Sandra Morgen, *Into Our Own Hands: The Women's Health Movement, 1969–1990* (New Brunswick, NJ: Rutgers University Press, 2002), 70.

7. Burgess, interview.

8. Ibid.

9. Rita Moir, "Support for Centre Looks Favourable," *The Meliorist*, 4 April 1974, 4.

10. In the 1970s, Lethbridge was still a small city, although it had grown considerably since the start of the 1960s. From 1961 to 1976, the city's population increased by nearly a third, from 35,454 residents to 46,752. This pattern of growth was even more visible in Calgary, which witnessed an 88 percent increase in population during the same period (from 249,641 people to 469,917). "Table 6: Population by Census Subdivisions, 1901–1961," *1961 Census of Canada*, vol. 1, *Population* (Ottawa: Statistics Canada, 1963), 6.77–6.83; "Table 3: Population for Census Divisions and Subdivisions, 1971 and 1976," *1976 Census of Canada*, vol. 1, *Population, Geographic Distributions* (Ottawa: Statistics Canada, 1977), 3.40–3.43.

11. In 1972, Lethbridge (then a city of 42,816) housed forty churches, including several Ukrainian Orthodox churches, one Jewish synagogue, one Buddhist temple, one Japanese United Church, a handful of Mormon and Catholic churches, and the majority of Protestant denomination churches. Thus, while the ratio of churches to population is high, the city did have a somewhat diverse religious makeup. See *Henderson's Lethbridge Directory* (Calgary: Henderson Directories Alberta, 1974). Moreover, scholars have linked religion and politics in the history of Alberta. In "Evangelical Christianity and Political Thought in Alberta," Clark Banak argues that deeper understandings of the religious influence on Alberta's political leaders in the twentieth century—Henry Wise Wood, William Aberhart, and Ernest Manning—can illuminate how the right-wing monopoly on Alberta's legislature sustained itself across the twentieth century. In *God's Province*, Banak similarly highlights the important role religion has played in the province's "tradition of protest and experimentation" (3). While Banak's focus is on religion and how it influenced populist democracy and conservatism in Alberta, he is quick to remind readers of three important things: his focus is on political thought of political leaders, rather than smaller-scale population-based politics; "Alberta was not an unusually religious place in the early twentieth century; nor is it today" (6); and "pundits who often bemoan long stretches of one-party rule often fail to note the significant differences in approach and policy" between many of Alberta's twentieth-century political leaders. In particular, he highlights "the wide gulf between the activist administrations of PC leader Peter Lougheed (1971–85) and the neoliberal approach of Ralph Klein's PCs (1992–2006)." Thus Banak offers a nuanced discussion of how Alberta can simultaneously

be home to a Bible Belt while also breaking down assumptions of how religiously influenced politics work on the ground during different eras. See Banak, "Evangelical Christianity and Political Thought in Alberta," *Journal of Canadian Studies* 48, no. 2 (2014): 70–99; *God's Province: Evangelical Christianity, Political Thought, and Conservatism in Alberta* (Montréal and Kingston: McGill-Queen's University Press, 2016).

12. Erika Dyck, *Facing Eugenics: Reproduction, Sterilization, and the Politics of Choice* (Toronto: University of Toronto Press, 2013), chap. 2, "Race, Intelligence, and Consent: George Pierre."

13. Allison Stevenson, "Intimate Integration: A Study of Aboriginal Transracial Adoption in Saskatchewan, 1944–1984" (PhD diss., University of Saskatchewan, 2015), chap. 5, "Adopting a Solution to the 'Indian Problem': From Adopt Indian and Métis (AIM) to REACH in Saskatchewan, 1951–1973."

14. This is clear in the Voice of Alberta Native Women's Society files, which identify Indigenous foster care as one of its main concerns in the 1970s, see "Report of the VANWS Foster Care Program (October 1975-June 1976)," pg. 1, PR1999.0465.78, at the Provincial Archives of Alberta, Edmonton, Alberta. Also see Loretta Ross, "Understanding Reproductive Justice: Transforming the Pro-Choice Movement," *Off Our Backs* 36, no. 4 (2004): 14–19 for a more general discussion of Indigenous and Black women's calls for reproductive justice.

15. Ruth Roach Pierson, "Experience, Difference, Dominance, and Voice in the Writing of Canadian Women's History," in *Writing Women's History: International Perspectives*, ed. Karen Offen, Ruth Roach Pierson, and Jane Rendall (Bloomington: Indiana University Press, 1991), 91.

16. Luba Lisun, interview by the author, 1 December 2014, transcript.

17. Mary Bochenko, interview by the author, 27 January 2015, transcript.

18. Lisun, interview.

19. Rita Moir, interview by the author, 13 December 2012, transcript.

20. Lisun, interview.

21. Terri Forbis, interview by the author, 24 January 2013, transcript.

22. Forbis, interview.

23. Ibid.

24. Founded at Simon Fraser University, the Vancouver Women's Caucus was the birthplace of the 1970 Abortion Caravan—a revolutionary campaign for better reproductive rights in Canada. The Student Society of McGill University *Birth Control Handbook* was first published in 1968, breaking Canadian criminal laws regarding distribution of birth control and abortion information. The book became very popular very quickly and was soon in demand at birth control centres, in sexual education programs, and on

university and college campuses across the country. As Christabelle Sethna explains, the *Birth Control Handbook* became an important tool for peer- and self-education on the topics of reproductive and sexual health. Sethna, "The Evolution of the *Birth Control Handbook*: From Student Peer-Education Manual to Feminist Self-Empowerment Text, 1968–1975," in *Rethinking Canada: The Promise of Women's History*, ed. Mona Gleason, Tamara Myers, and Adele Perry (Don Mills, ON: Oxford University Press, 2011), 89–118.

25. Moir, interview by the author, 13 December 2012, transcript.

26. Judy Burgess, interview by the author, 2 December 2012, transcript.

27. Ray Keitges to Lethbridge City Council, 2 April 1974. "Letters and Petitions Re: Funding of Birth Control Centre 1974," 2011.1085 069, in *Early City Record Collection* at the Galt Museum and Archives, Lethbridge.

28. [Name indiscernible] to Lethbridge City Council, ca. March–April 1974. "Letters and Petitions Re: Funding of Birth Control Centre 1974," 2011.1085 069, in *Early City Record Collection* at the Galt Museum and Archives, Lethbridge.

29. Burgess, interview, 8 December 2012.

30. Rita Moir, interview by the author, 7 October 2014, transcript.

31. Moir, interview, 13 December 2012.

32. Burgess, interview, 8 December 2012.

33. Ibid.

34. For editorials, see "No More Birth Control?" *The Meliorist*, 14 March 1974, 1; Beverly Johnson, "Support the Birth Control Centre," *The Meliorist*, 21 March 1974, 1; Moir, "Support for Centre," 4; "Viewpoints on Centre: Council Takes a Stand," *The Endeavour*, 25 March 1974, 2; "Birth Control Centre Opposes Panel Discussion," *The Endeavour*, 1 April 1974, 2. Letters to city council can be found in "Letters and Petitions Re: Funding of Birth Control Centre 1974," Early City Records Collection, 2011.1085 069, Galt Museum and Archives, Lethbridge.

35. Moir, interview, 7 October 2014.

36. Rosemary R. Edmunds to Lethbridge City Council, 2 April 1974, "Letters and Petitions Re: Funding of Birth Control Centre 1974," Early City Records Collection, 2011.1085 069, Galt Museum and Archives, Lethbridge.

37. Forbis interview.

38. Ibid.

7

"Ultra Activists" in a "Very Closeted Place"

The Early Years of Edmonton's Gay Alliance
Toward Equality, 1972–77

Erin Gallagher-Cohoon

"The gay scene in Edmonton is very quiet," wrote Ken King, secretary of
Gay Alliance Toward Equality (GATE), in a letter to the managing editor of
Australia's *Butch Magazine Monthly*, adding, "in the sense that it is hidden.
There is a great deal of paranoia in this city, caused in part by the basic
conservative nature of the province and general fears." King was writing in
November 1972, and his letter revealed that the Edmonton queer community
was in the middle of a transition in the early 1970s. His letter went on to say
that there were active gay organizations in the city and that they continued
to grow thanks to "the young gays who seem to be unwilling to remain in
their closets."[1] Despite being "quiet," Edmonton boasted a number of bars
where people went to meet and socialize, a gay club called Club 70, a new
social organization called Workshop '70, and, of course, GATE.

The growth of an increasingly visible queer community at this time was
due in part to legal changes. In 1969, amendments to the Canadian Criminal Code legalized sodomy and acts of "gross indecency" provided these
took place between two consenting adults in private. Although sometimes
remembered as the moment that Canada decriminalized homosexuality, this is at best only partially true. In fact, historian Tom Hooper has
argued that the 1969 Omnibus Bill recriminalized homosexuality.[2] Although
these amendments seemed to indicate a liberalization of attitudes towards

homosexuality, the policing of queer sex actually increased as a result of the bill. The age of consent for homosexual activity was set at twenty-one, higher than the age of consent for heterosexual activity. Additionally, the revised Criminal Code did not fully protect gay men, who were still harassed by the police not only in public spaces including parks, washrooms, and other cruising areas, but also by raids on private-membership bathhouses, where consensual sex might happen between more than two people.[3]

Although far from a radical celebration of homosexuality, the 1969 amendments did provide a small wedge which activists could then use to open up new possibilities, especially for gay men who were regularly targeted by police. The law specifically criminalized male homosexual activities. In Canada (as in many other places), lesbian women were historically ignored in criminal law; female same-sex eroticism has a distinct legal history.[4] After 1969, cities across Canada experienced a surge of organized activism as gay and lesbian groups advocated for increased legal protections, social acceptance, and sexual liberation.[5]

This chapter analyzes the early history of GATE Edmonton, an activist organization founded to advance gay rights in a politically conservative province. Perceptions of Alberta as a conservative hinterland obscure histories of activism. Telling Albertan histories of activism matters. These stories provide inspiration and insight that might otherwise be forgotten.

One of my Dads, who was a long-time Edmonton activist, believed that my research would not reveal any Edmonton queer activism prior to the AIDS crisis of the 1980s. In his understandings of the province, at least a decade of queer activism had been forgotten.

As historian Valerie Korinek notes in her seminal work on Prairie queer histories, "the stereotypes of an old, reactionary, largely rural Alberta continue to hold sway."[6] Korinek's research places GATE within the larger Prairie context, highlighting histories of queer presence, interregional mobility, and activism across Manitoba, Saskatchewan, and Alberta. Korinek argues that queer socializing, community-building and social service provision were political and politicizing actions. Although she questions Albertan exceptionalism,—she remarks, for example, that the idea that "Alberta was a more virulently homophobic province . . . is debatable"—Alberta stills stands out in her work as different from other provinces, even other Prairie provinces.[7] "Of the cities in this study," Korinek writes, "Edmonton was perhaps the most challenging in which to be queer."[8] Due to limited archival and oral history sources, Albertan history is completely missing from the first section of the book, which documents queer histories prior to 1969. By placing GATE's history within and alongside alternative Albertan histories more broadly, as this edited collection does, I can emphasize the ways in which Edmonton's early queer activists belonged in a province that has a long tradition of pushing back against conservativism despite the risks and challenges of doing so.

GATE, like many similar organizations at the time, was largely White and male. However, the role of lesbian women in GATE's development must be acknowledged and is discussed in more explicit detail later in the chapter. Given the distinct histories of gay men and lesbian women, and given the nature of the organization, I frequently distinguish between the two terms. Although, for a brief time, "gay" referred to both gay men and gay women, during the 1970s "lesbian" became the preferred term for homosexual women, and "gay" came to indicate homosexual men.[9] In this chapter, I also use the term "queer" in relation to a larger 2SLGBTQ+ community as an inclusive whole, although this is a reclamation of a word that in the 1970s was used pejoratively.

How to "Behave Like 'Civilized People'" and Other Debates: The Beginnings of GATE Edmonton

GATE Edmonton, the first self-described gay liberation organization in a province known for its "basic conservative nature," was formed in the years following Canada's partial decriminalization of homosexuality. Founded in 1972 by Michael Roberts, "Edmonton's first 'public' homosexual," GATE was initially a small group of university students who met at private residences.[10] Roberts, who had recently moved from Vancouver and drew inspiration from GATE Vancouver, was a driving force behind this initial impetus to organize.

GATE Edmonton started as a "semi-campus organization," an unofficial university club composed initially of several male students, rather than a broad-based grassroots organization drawn from diverse segments of the queer community. In 1984, Rick Hurlbut, a student at the time, described the problems then facing GATE's executive committee. He noted that, historically, "leadership, as was typical of the Gay Rights Movement of the time, was charismatic and somewhat autocratic. Key individuals, not necessarily elected, formed GATE's policy, acted as spokespersons, and generally decided the direction the group would move."[11] Another critic, who signed his letter to the editor of the alternative newspaper *Poundmaker* simply as Ramon, agreed with this assessment. Without explicitly naming Roberts, Ramon argued that GATE developed in the way that it did because of one dominant personality who did not accurately represent the diversity of opinions and lifestyles in the gay community. "Although searching out acceptance by 'straights,' he frequently showed little tolerance for gays experiencing or practicing a different homosexual lifestyle," Ramon wrote, adding that very few people within the gay community saw GATE as a "militant" group.[12]

Ramon describes GATE as a sexually staid organization that was not well-known nor accepted in the larger Edmonton gay community. Ramon's letter to the editor was a direct response to an earlier article on GATE written by *Poundmaker* staff member, Eugene (Devil inside) Plawiuk.[13] In contrast to Ramon, Plawiuk attributed GATE's lack of popularity within the gay community to the fact that "many gays don't want to go marching in the streets."[14] So which was it? Was GATE too political and activist or too interested in presenting an image of respectable and restrained sexuality? Too radical or not radical enough?

In part, this difference of opinion was the result of a diversity of perspectives among the people making these judgments within and outside the queer community. The question was what constitutes an effective activist strategy and should that strategy focus on changing laws, raising social consciousness, or providing social services. Some commentators may have perceived GATE differently because of the group's adaptability and wide range of interests. GATE members were astute enough to emphasize different aspects of their activism depending on the audience. In 1974, when a member of GATE spoke at Club '70's Annual General Meeting to encourage others to attend a drop-in, the member explained "that G.A.T.E. has changed radically and is no longer the aggressive band of former days."[15] This may have been attempt by the GATE member to reassure Club 70 members who were otherwise ill-inclined to get involved. However, according to M. L. Mumert, one of the charter members of GATE, late 1974 was a time when the group became more radical, not less:

> At that time, many of the people involved in GATE were ultra activists
> who regularly wanted to organize parades with banners around the
> city, most especially if there was a political campaign or some homo-
> phobic celebrity in town. While I pass no judgements on this type of

activity, other than to applaud it from the safety of my closet, the high level of visibility of these activities caused a lot of people to leave or not to join GATE in the first place.[16]

Throughout the 1970s, GATE Edmonton engaged in a diversity of actions, including mounting education campaigns and letter-writing campaigns, lobbying the Alberta Human Rights Commission, protesting Canadian immigration policy, and providing social services. The minutes of the 2 November 1977 general meeting, for example, show evidence of multiple simultaneous actions, some of which were more radical than others, ranging from social dances at Club 70 and Flashback to picketing a civic election forum where mayoral candidates were questioned about their position on gay rights.[17]

In later years, GATE increasingly emphasized peer counselling and other social services. After some of the more politically active GATE members helped form the Alberta Lesbian and Gay Rights Association (ALGRA) in 1979, GATE voted to refrain from any political affiliation.[18] This does not mean that it abstained from all political activity, however, because it became a group member of ALGRA.[19] As another example, GATE polled political candidates in the 1982 provincial election to determine their stance on civil rights protections for sexual minorities.[20]

At the same time, no clear boundaries existed among radical gay liberation, the reform of civil rights' legislation, and service-oriented efforts to support individual and community well-being. These ambiguities were discussed at a general meeting on 8 January 1975, when GATE members debated the position of gay activists within society. The hand-written meeting notes contain an incomplete reference to gay activists as: "reformist, revolutionary, or political change agents?" Crossed-out in the same note was a final possibility—"radicals."[21] In the 1970s, as GATE was evolving as an organization, members were questioning how best they could support and strengthen their community. At times this meant becoming politically active. However, the provision of social services was equally important and can be seen as an extension of, rather than a departure from, the organization's activist principles.

The debate over whether GATE was revolutionary or reform-oriented also reflected something of the character of the early organization. Plawiuk's 1973 article in *Poundmaker* captured both GATE's "political militancy" (which the group was supposedly "getting over") and its pursuit of a politics of respectability in an effort to gain social acceptance.[22] "One thing GATE does," Plawiuk explained, "is try to de-emphasize the sex angle of gayness. . . . When people phone up the first time the person answering usually tries to dissuade the caller from the idea that they have orgies, or that by coming over to the house they are going to find a bed partner."[23] In this way, GATE was attempting to dissociate itself from a common stereotype of gay men as promiscuous and emotionally uncommitted, a stereotype that ultimately labelled them as sexual deviants and cast them as potentially dangerous to the moral foundations of society.

Some gay men saw this emphasis on sexual respectability as counterproductive. They were not interested in following monogamous heterosexual norms. In response to Plawiuk's article, for example, Ramon explained that, although some gay folk obviously benefited from GATE's existence, the group promoted a very limited vision of "gay life" that did not serve the needs of a more diverse community. In particular, Ramon argued, GATE members attempted to represent themselves as respectable queers by downplaying and depoliticizing their own sexuality. "It is unfortunate, in my opinion," wrote Ramon,

that they want to be understood as humans and not "faggots" for faggots is what they are. . . . The self-confident homosexual will not be set back by faggot, fairy, gearbox, and so on. It is the writer's opinion that these are colorful explicit terms far more meaningful than homosexual and not derogatory if one is self-assured in one's own homosexual role.[24]

In other words, some segments of the gay community saw GATE as attempting to assimilate homosexuality into a largely heteronormative culture.

The debate around sexual liberation was happening not only outside the organization but internally as well. A meeting on 17 August 1972 included a discussion about whether "cruising" should be allowed at GATE. Cruising here referred to the practice of looking to meet people, often in public places, to have casual sex. The meeting ended with the Chairperson "suggesting that everyone just behave like 'civilized people.'"[25] In other words, from the beginning of its existence as an organization, GATE Edmonton was implicated in debates over how to act as a gay man among other gay men and, more broadly, in public spaces in the city. Being "civilized" or "respectable" was often a practical tactic used by activists to gain the respect and support of the larger, mainstream society. It has also been described as a selling out of radical principles. If respectability politics are thought of as one end of a spectrum of queer activism, the other end would likely be liberation ideologies. However, as GATE demonstrated, distinctions between respectability politics and gay liberation may seem clear-cut in theory but are often messy in practice.

Under the banner of liberation politics, GATE collaborated with a wide range of organizations, not only gay rights organizations across Canada but also other social justice groups. On 17 November 1972, for example, GATE issued a message in support of a rally by the University of Alberta Vietnam Action Committee, stating that "*all* people must have the freedom to determine their way of life. Whether one wishes to choose one's sexual orientation or one's government, one must be free—free from both internal and external pressures—free from both internal and external oppression." GATE ended this statement by declaring, "The oppressed peoples of the world demand freedom—and demand it NOW!"[26]

Gay liberation was a radical activist stance that rejected the status quo and encouraged "coming out" as a political tactic. Gay liberationists deliberately built a visible movement that was meant to liberate gays and lesbians from the discrimination of a heterosexist society and from their own internal prejudices.[27] One of their primary tactics was to organize protest marches to challenge the social isolation of the closet and to change social norms. In the United States, the gay liberation movement rejected civil rights activism. After all, "why petition to be let into a social system so deeply riven by racism, sexism, militarism, and heterosexism?"[28]

In Canada, however, civil rights were linked to liberation activism. Organizing around a human rights paradigm allowed GATE Edmonton and other Canadian gay liberation organizations to build a visible community and to create a political identity.[29] They did not see these goals as contrary to the values of gay liberation.

Community building was linked to GATE's lobbying for civil rights because without legal protections, people would not join the gay liberation movement. In 1974, for example, one GATE member noted that "people are afraid of involvement because of fear of exposure."[30] GATE blurred the line between radical high-profile activism and immediate on-the-ground services. Early on, GATE Edmonton implemented a drop-in evening and a phone line, initially in a private residence and then later at its office.[31] The organization also hosted dances and provided peer counselling. In a city with few openly gay residents, community building was an essential function of the group. So, although some accused GATE members of being radical activists who were too quick to hold a protest march, one of their first impulses was to provide a structure for community building. Indeed, such an action was a necessary part of achieving social, political, and sexual liberation.

Struggles to Build "Active Gay Solidarity in Edmonton"[32]

In a July 1983 interview, Walter Cavalieri—GATE's director of social services at the time—emphasized the solidarity felt by the gay and lesbian communities:

> I think, in spite of all of the bitchiness that is ascribed to gay men and the butchness ascribed to gay women, we are an extraordinarily loving and caring community. I think we all experience so much oppression that we have discovered within ourselves a capacity to reach out and share—not only the capacity, but the understanding that we *must*, if we are to survive, treat each other with some degree of tenderness and love and sharing.[33]

Despite Cavalieri's optimistic portrayal of "an extraordinarily loving and caring community," and despite the gay liberationist challenge to heteronormativity, GATE Edmonton—like many gay liberation organizations at the time—was a predominantly male space.[34] Its organizing members, who were initially all men, had to work to develop a more inclusive space for its increasing female membership. By 1976, according to the *Calgary Herald*, about a third of GATE Edmonton's members were women.[35]

Female representation in the organization and male-female collaboration were important discussion points early on. On 16 February 1973, GATE held a drop-in "long anticipated by the all male membership of GATE," which "brought out several Edmonton gay women for the purpose of finding areas of mutual interest and involvement." The conversation went on to acknowledge that the men and women had "areas of mutual interest and concern" but also "that lesbians have problem areas that no male organization can really handle." As a result, there was some debate over whether GATE should be restructured to accommodate both lesbian women and gay men or whether a separate lesbian organization should be created that could collaborate with, while remaining separate from, GATE Edmonton.[36]

"It is encouraging to note that male or female sexism didn't seem to establish itself as a valid reason for not becoming affiliated with a gay liberation organization," wrote Don Musbach, GATE's regional co-ordinator, in his summary of the drop-in meeting.[37] Women did subsequently become more involved in GATE; key women went on to work on various committees, to be counted among those present at meetings, and to take on other duties, including volunteering to answer the crisis phone line. Women were present at the annual meeting held in March 1974 and the minutes suggest that they discussed volunteering as female phone counsellors due to the increase in the number of women calling for "information and assistance."[38] However, relationships between women and men in the organization were not always positive. A separate lesbian organization, Womonspace, was founded in 1982 by women who had left GATE because "they were doing all the work but the men made all the decisions."[39] One Womonspace member recalled "that if we had something to say, it was either ignored, interrupted or we were being patronized."[40] GATE did not always succeed in creating an inclusive environment and remained an organization dominated by male leadership.

CONCERN: Anita Bryant Comes to Town

Another way that GATE attempted to build community was by organizing and participating in coalitions with other social justice groups. In 1978, for example, GATE was simultaneously involved in two coalitions that tackled the same issue using very different tactics. Both organized in protest against "some homophobic celebrity in town."[41] One of these coalitions—a collaboration with, among others, the Metropolitan Community Church, Boyle Street Meeting of the Religious Society of Friends, Club 70, Jasper Avenue Social Club, Gay Youth of Alberta, and the Alberta Human Rights and Civil Liberties Association—was called CONCERN. The other was named the Coalition to Answer Anita Bryant. Both organized against Anita Bryant's visit to Edmonton. Bryant's Canadian speaking tour was a matter of concern and protest by gay and lesbian activists across the country.[42] Bryant was known for her anti-gay organizing in Dade County, Florida, where, because of her memorable campaign to "Save the Children," a county ordinance that protected homosexuals from discrimination was overturned.[43]

CONCERN initially proposed to organize a public debate, because "the moral strength lay with CONCERN and not with Miss Bryant." They preferred the format of a debate or a forum rather than a demonstration, arguing that Bryant "had been confronted too few times by reason and argument rather than emotional outbursts."[44] To indicate their disagreement with this tactic, the Edmonton Women's Coalition responded by forming the Coalition to Answer Anita Bryant, which organized a cleverly named "unwelcoming committee" that would demonstrate against Bryant's stop in Edmonton.[45]

GATE members debated what tactics the organization should endorse. During the 17 April 1978 regular general meeting, a proposed motion to limit GATE's participation to only those activities organized by CONCERN was defeated. Instead, the majority voted to endorse and participate in both CONCERN and the Coalition to Answer Anita Bryant, and to inform GATE members of all the actions being organized.[46] In this way, GATE simultaneously took a reformist and a revolutionary stance by helping to organize a reasoned debate on the issues raised by Bryant's visit while also joining a protest of over three hundred people.[47]

Surviving the Bible Belt

Finally, GATE's community extended outside the province. GATE Edmonton shared many of the strategies, and tactics of other organizations, such as GATE Vancouver and Gays of Ottawa. It also often shared similar challenges. This is in part because all were confronting the same heterosexist political structures and cultural norms. They also deliberately built coalitions and were supportive of activists and causes in other Canadian cities. Edmonton activists, for example, raised money in support of John Damien, a jockey who was fired by the Ontario Racing Commission because of his sexual orientation.[48]

However, Alberta is known as the conservative backwoods of Canada. Gay activists themselves described the province's conservativism and the oppressive prejudices they faced. In 1983, Cavalieri, an American ex-pat who lived in Toronto and Lennoxville before moving to Edmonton, described Alberta as a "Bible belt. Terrifyingly so at times. It's a very closeted place. Probably the most closeted place I've lived." He explained that it was difficult to get Edmontonians to turn out to show support, often because of the dangers of being exposed publicly.[49] In contrast to larger metropolitan centres such as Toronto or Vancouver, activist communities in Edmonton remained relatively small. The size of the network of activists in Edmonton had a real effect on the types of actions that could be taken. In 1972, for example, GATE attempted to hold a demonstration in connection with Gay Pride Week but had to cancel. "The possibility, actually the probability," wrote Michael Roberts regretfully, "of only one or two people participating in a 'demonstration' seemed ludicrous."[50] The small size of Edmonton's activist community challenged GATE's attempts at organizing.

At the same time, Edmonton was not unique in its social environment. In the 1970s, blatant homophobia was prevalent throughout Canada. A 1975 article from the *Edmonton Journal* noted, "If you're a homosexual there are better places to be than Edmonton, Alberta, or Canada, for that matter." Comparing queer activism in Canada to activism in the United States, the journalist declared that "gay power in Canada is at a crawl."[51] Edmonton was regionally different from Toronto and Vancouver, two cities that would quickly become hubs of activism, but in the early 1970s, discrimination in the media and political backlash were not exceptional. Nowhere in Canada, for example, was it illegal to discriminate in housing or employment based on someone's sexual orientation until Québec amended its Charter of Human Rights and Freedoms in 1977.[52]

Who Will Protect You Now?

Like other provinces in Canada, Alberta had no civil rights legislation that explicitly protected gays and lesbians. However, the political context of the province was changing in the early 1970s and this change allowed a moment of possibility for gay and lesbian activists. In 1971, the Social Credit Party, which had dominated Albertan politics for thirty-six years, was defeated by the Progressive Conservatives. On 1 January 1973, under the Progressive Conservatives, two important pieces of legislation came into effect: the Alberta Bill of Rights and the Individual's Rights Protection Act (IRPA). When it was initially enacted, IRPA protected individuals from discrimination based on "race, religious beliefs, color, sex, age, ancestry or place of origin."[53] People who experienced discrimination could file a complaint with the Alberta Human Rights Commission. The complaint would then be investigated and, if deemed necessary, some form of mediation would be attempted. The Alberta Human Rights Commission was the first gatekeeper in a process that might see a case of discrimination being argued at the Supreme Court of Alberta.[54]

IRPA did not include sexual orientation in its list of protected categories, but it did give GATE activists a legislative framework within which to advance their cause. It also gave the organization a target: the Alberta Human Rights Commission. In 1976, GATE presented a brief titled "Homosexuals: A Minority Without Rights" to the commission. In it, GATE argued that homophobia existed in the province and had a demonstrable effect on the lives of gay and lesbian Albertans. The brief cited specific examples of discrimination, including the 1975 vandalism of GATE's office, the refusal of certain newspapers to print advertisements from GATE, and firings of gay teachers. GATE recognized that because sexual orientation was not included as a specific category under either IRPA or the Alberta Bill of Rights, gay and lesbian residents were not legally protected from discrimination.[55]

GATE also recognized that public education and legal changes went hand in hand. "The Alberta Human Rights Commission is given a mandate to promote the principle that every person is equal in dignity and rights," the brief stated, "and to research, develop and conduct programmes of public education to combat discrimination."[56] Inclusion of sexual orientation in civil rights legislation was seen as a first step. Education would then be needed to combat prejudice and ignorance.[57] The brief itself was a form of education; GATE attempted to raise awareness of the challenges faced by gay and lesbian Albertans through briefs, presentations, and letter-writing campaigns to politicians and commission members.[58]

In part as a result of GATE's activism, in 1976 the Alberta Human Rights Commission recommended that "sexual preference" be protected under IRPA. Unfortunately, this suggestion was not taken up by the Progressive Conservative government. In 1978, the commission released a statement to the media that explained:

> While neither condoning nor condemning the many life styles that now may be legally practiced . . . the Commission is unequivocal in its belief that society should not, in the fields of employment, housing and services, discriminate against people because of the life styles they choose to live, providing the practice of those styles of life does not contravene the law. During the past four years several groups have approached the Commission and the Government seeking protection under the Individual's Rights Protection Act. The Commission believes

that some of these groups should now receive that protection and has recommended it on grounds of physical characteristics, marital status, source of income and sexual preference.[59]

The commission, after some changes in leadership, did not reiterate this recommendation in their 1979 submission to the provincial government.[60] GATE continued to submit briefs and to present its case to the commission, although to little effect.[61] Sexual minorities were not protected by Alberta human rights legislation until 1998, when the Supreme Court of Canada ruled, in *Vriend v. Alberta*, that this exclusion violated the Canadian Charter of Rights and Freedoms. The phrase "sexual orientation" was still not explicitly included until 2009, when the divisive Bill-44 was passed—a bill that simultaneously protected the rights of sexual minorities while also limiting teachers' ability to discuss "controversial" topics, including homosexuality.[62]

The lack of explicit legal protections for sexual minorities had a very real on-the-ground effect. As GATE mentioned in its briefs, cases of discrimination often went unreported for several reasons, including fears of being outed. Being publicly known as a homosexual could lead to instances of further discrimination in employment, housing, and even in family law cases such as child custody determinations. Without the inclusion of "sexual orientation" in IRPA, it was very unlikely that the Alberta Human Rights Commission would investigate and mediate instances of discrimination against gay men and lesbian women. Undaunted, GATE Edmonton pushed on.

When Your Life Is a Caricature: Confronting the Media

At the same time that GATE was taking a civil rights approach, its members were also confronting other forms of discrimination, including negative or stereotyped portrayals in the media. On 28 November 1976, for example, Bob Radke and Rosemary Ray wrote to the University of Alberta's paper *The Gateway* regarding a cartoon that conflated homosexuality with a lack of masculinity. In their letter, they explicitly linked a willingness to "treat the subject with humour" and to laugh at "cardboard stereotypes" with a society that ignored the "mental and physical abuse" suffered by gays and lesbians. "The plight of the homosexual in today's society is no laughing matter," Radke and Ray reminded the paper. "This does not mean that we, the homosexuals, have lost our sense of humour. It merely emphasizes the fact that we do not consider our situation to be all that amusing."[63]

In another case, the University of Alberta's Business Administration and Commerce Undergraduate Society's newsletter felt it necessary to reassure readers that the Ambassador Tavern, a popular meeting spot for both gay folk and Commerce students, was "not a haven for Fags or etc."[64] Prior to this notice in the student paper, the Ambassador had begun to refuse service to its gay clientele.[65] Michael Roberts, insulted by the newsletter's use of a derogatory term, wrote to the editor: "I would like to agree with you, the Ambassador is not a haven for fags, however I and many of my *homosexual* student friends do go there to enjoy our drinks."[66] This prompted the editor to write a retraction, which was published alongside Roberts's letter of complaint.[67]

Alongside these stereotyped and demeaning portrayals of gay men, GATE also confronted a deliberate attempt by media outlets to silence the organization. In 1976, GATE went head to head with the *Edmonton Journal* for the paper's refusal "to print ads for our counselling service on the grounds that it is a 'family newspaper.'"[68] The *Edmonton Journal* was not the only newspaper that refused advertisements from GATE; others included the *Grande Prairie Daily Herald-Tribune*, the *Calgary Herald*, and the *Red Deer Advocate*.[69] Although the *Edmonton Journal* defended its practice as "sensitivity towards the feeling of the general public" rather than discrimination, and although "sexual orientation" was still not a protected category under IRPA, GATE decided to submit a complaint on 3 March 1976 to the Alberta Human Rights Commission.[70]

GATE Edmonton's strategy in this case was no doubt inspired by GATE Vancouver, which had filed a complaint of discrimination against the *Vancouver Sun* for refusing to publish an advertisement for the newspaper *Gay Tide*.[71] GATE Vancouver's complaint was eventually debated before the Supreme Court of Canada in *GATE v. Vancouver Sun*, the first Supreme Court case of its kind.[72] The *Sun*'s refusal to publish an advertisement submitted to the paper by GATE Vancouver was initially deemed discriminatory by the board of inquiry appointed to review the case. After multiple appeals to the Supreme Court of British Columbia and the BC Court of Appeal, the case made its way to the Supreme Court of Canada, which "ruled that freedom of expression and freedom of the press—in this case, the freedom not to print something—trumped minority civil rights."[73] The outcome of the GATE Edmonton complaint is less clear. Very little is mentioned about it in subsequent meeting minutes. It is possible that after "sexual orientation" was not ultimately included in IRPA, GATE decided to pursue other actions, including continued lobbying of the Alberta Human Rights Commission.

The Legacy

Edmonton's first gay liberation organization was a hodgepodge creation, built of the hopes and ambitions of a core group of activists. Throughout the 1970s, GATE Edmonton spoke out against discrimination in the media, lobbied the government for human rights protections, built coalitions with other groups regionally and nationally, and provided services necessary for people's social and emotional survival. Many of the group's initiatives were not ultimately successful. For example, the Alberta government did not institute the legislative changes that GATE had pursued. However, GATE was successful in building an active and visible queer community. As Cavalieri observed in 1983, "Almost every one of the groups in this city spun off from GATE. We parented them through the years, giving them some financial help and some moral support."[74]

As the first gay activist group in the city, GATE provided the template for other organizations that would soon follow. It was also successful, despite its supposed radical beginnings in a politically conservative province, in being recognized by the government six years after its formation. The informal organization started by a small group of university students, and accused of being run by "ultra activists," would by 1977 be officially incorporated as a society under Alberta's Societies Act.[75] However, by 1987 GATE lost its society status and, forever adaptable, rebranded itself as the Gay and Lesbian Community Centre of Edmonton, a predecessor of Pride Centre of Edmonton.[76] At different points throughout its first decade, GATE emphasized different actions depending on what its members saw as the immediate needs of their community, but at no point did the organization completely abandon its gay liberation principles, and it often attempted several strategies at once. A change of tactics did not equal an abandonment of GATE's vision.

Acknowledgements

For their advice and for taking the time to discuss this paper with me, I would like to particularly thank Michael Phair, Valerie Korinek, and Karissa Patton. I would also like to acknowledge the important work of the activists and archivists who continue to preserve this important history. The City of Edmonton Archives houses the Gay and Lesbian Archives of Edmonton, which was created to collect and safeguard records related to the history of the Edmonton queer community.

NOTES

1. Ken King to Bill Munro, 3 November 1972, MS. 595, series 1, file 5, Gay and Lesbian Archives of Edmonton, City of Edmonton Archives (hereafter GLA Edmonton).
2. Tom Hooper, "Queering '69: The Recriminalization of Homosexuality in Canada," *The Canadian Historical Review* 100, no. 2 (2019): 257–73.
3. Tom Warner, *Never Going Back: A History of Queer Activism in Canada* (Toronto: University of Toronto Press, 2002), 100; Thomas Hooper, "'More Than Two Is a Crowd': Mononormativity and Gross Indecency in the *Criminal Code*, 1981–82," *Journal of Canadian Studies* 48, no. 1 (2014): 68.
4. Katherine Arnup, "'Mothers Just Like Others': Lesbians, Divorce, and Child Custody in Canada," *Canadian Journal of Women and the Law* 3, no. 1 (1989): 19n4; David Kimmel and Daniel J. Robinson, "Sex, Crime, Pathology: Homosexuality and Criminal Code Reform in Canada, 1949–1969," *Canadian Journal of Law and Society* 16, no. 1 (2001): 163. For more on the history of lesbianism and the law, see Karen Pearlston, "Avoiding the Vulva: Judicial Interpretations of Lesbian Sex Under the *Divorce Act*, 1968," *Canadian Journal of Law and Society* 32, no. 2 (2017): 37–53.
5. Laura L. Bonnett, "Transgressing the Public/Private Divide: Gay, Lesbian, Bisexual and Transgender Citizenship Claims in Alberta, 1968–1998" (PhD diss., University of Alberta, 2006), 64.
6. Valerie J. Korinek, *Prairie Fairies: A History of Queer Communities and People in Western Canada, 1930–1985* (Toronto: University of Toronto Press, 2018), 219.
7. Korinek, *Prairie Fairies*, 365.
8. Ibid., 395.
9. Warner, *Never Going Back*, 4. See also Marc Stein, *Rethinking the Gay and Lesbian Movement* (New York: Routledge, 2012), 92.

10. E. Plawiuk, "GATE: Fighting for Gay Equality," newspaper clipping, *Poundmaker*, 9 October 1973, pp. 12–13, MS. 595, series 1, file 18, GLA Edmonton.

11. Rick Hurlbut, "The Executive Committee of the Gay Alliance Toward Equality: Problems and Solutions," 16 April 1984, p. 1, MS. 595, series 1, file 18, GLA Edmonton.

12. Ramon, "Whither GATE?" letter to the editor of *Poundmaker*, 19 October 1973, MS. 595, series 1, file 18, GLA Edmonton.

13. E. Plawiuk was probably the "Eugene (Devil inside) Plawiuk" listed as staff.

14. Plawiuk, "GATE: Fighting for Gay Equality."

15. Minutes of annual general meeting, Club 70, 20 January 1974, p. 8, MS. 595, series 11, file 6, GLA Edmonton.

16. M. L. Mumert, "Background on G.A.T.E.," n.d., MS. 595, series 1, file 18, GLA Edmonton.

17. Minutes of general meeting, GATE, 2 November 1977, pp. 1, 7, MS. 595, series 1, file 29, GLA Edmonton.

18. Mumert, "Background on G.A.T.E."

19. Minutes of general meeting, GATE, 2 May 1979, p. 2, MS. 595, series 1, file 31, GLA Edmonton.

20. GATE, "Election '82," 30 October 1982, MS. 595, series 9, file 54, GLA Edmonton.

21. Minutes of meeting, GATE, 8 January 1975, p. 2, MS. 595, series 1, file 27, GLA Edmonton. For one scholar's analysis of the distinctions among various forms of queer activism, see Stein, *Rethinking*, chap. 3, "Gay Liberation, Lesbian Feminism, and Gay and Lesbian Liberalism, 1969–73."

22. The term "politics of respectability" (or "respectability politics") refers to the embrace of normative values on the part of upwardly mobile marginalized groups who are seeking to prove themselves worthy of inclusion in the social mainstream. In its origins, the term described "a philosophy promulgated by black elites to 'uplift the race' by correcting the 'bad' traits of the black poor." Fredrick S. Harris, "The Rise of Respectability Politics," *Dissent* 61, no. 1 (2014): 33. More recently, the term has been used with reference to organizations that "attempt to assimilate lesbian and gay relationships into mainstream marriage rather than attempt to garner societal acceptance for difference and deviation." Jes L. Matsick and Terri D. Conley, "Maybe 'I Do,' Maybe I Don't: Respectability Politics in the Same-Sex Marriage Ruling," *Analyses of Social Issues and Public Policy* 15, no. 1 (2015): 411. Although a politics of respectability is often presented as antithetical to more radical ideologies, such as gay liberation, as this chapter shows, activists and

organizations may use a variety of tactics that transgress this theoretical distinction.

23. Plawiuk, "GATE: Fighting for Gay Equality."

24. Ramon, "Whither GATE?"

25. Minutes of regular meeting, GATE, 17 August 1972, p. 2, MS. 595, series 1, file 24, GLA Edmonton.

26. Gay Alliance Toward Equality, statement of support, 17 November 1972, MS 595, series 1, file 48, GLA Edmonton.

27. Stein, *Rethinking*, 84.

28. Miriam Smith, "Social Movements and Equality Seeking: The Case of Gay Liberation in Canada," *Canadian Journal of Political Science / Revue canadienne de science politique* 31, no. 2 (1998): 290.

29. For another analysis of gay and lesbian activism in relation to human rights legislation, see Valerie J. Korinek, "Activism = Public Education: The History of Public Discourses of Homosexuality in Saskatchewan, 1971–1993," in *I Could Not Speak My Heart: Education and Social Justice for Gay and Lesbian Youth*, ed. James McNinch and Mary Cronin (Regina: Canadian Plains Research Center, 2004), 109–37.

30. Minutes of annual meeting, GATE, 7 March 1974, p. 1, MS. 595, series 1, file 26, GLA Edmonton.

31. Don Meen to John [surname unknown], 12 May 1983, pp. 1–2, MS. 595, series 1, file 18, GLA Edmonton.

32. Don Musbach, "Summary of GATE Drop-in of Saturday, Feb. 16," p. 2, MS. 595, series 1, file 26, GLA Edmonton.

33. Walter Cavalieri, interview by Shirley Shea, 3 July 1983, transcript, p. 10, MS. 595, series 1, file 5, GLA Edmonton.

34. Smith, "Social Movements," 291.

35. "Edmonton Alliance: Homosexuals Making Their Position Known," *Calgary Herald*, 3 January 1976, p. 44, MS. 595, series 1, file 18, GLA Edmonton.

36. Musbach, "Summary of GATE Drop-in," 1–2.

37. Ibid., 2.

38. Minutes of annual meeting, GATE, 7 March 1974, MS. 595, series 1, file 26, GLA Edmonton.>

39. Warner, *Never Going Back*, 181.

40. Noelle Lucas, "Womonspace: Building a Lesbian Community in Edmonton, Alberta, 1970–1990" (MA thesis, University of Saskatchewan, 2002), 37.

41. Mumert, "Background on G.A.T.E."

42. See Julia Pyryeskina, "'A Remarkably Dense Historical and Political Juncture': Anita Bryant, *The Body Politic*, and the Canadian Gay and Lesbian

Community in January 1978," *Canadian Journal of History* 53, no, 1 (2018): 58–85.

43. Bonnett, "Transgressing the Public/Private Divide," 73.

44. Minutes of meeting, CONCERN, 9 March 1978, MS. 595, series 1, file 30, GLA Edmonton.

45. Minutes of regular general meeting, GATE, 17 April 1978, MS. 595, series 1, file 30, GLA Edmonton.

46. Ibid.

47. Bonnett, "Transgressing the Public/Private Divide," 74.

48. Minutes of the regular monthly general meeting, GATE, 15 September 1976, p. 4, MS. 595, series 1, file 28, GLA Edmonton; minutes of general meeting, GATE, 3 November 1976, p. 2, MS. 595, series 1, file 28, GLA Edmonton; "Benefit Dance for John Damien Defence Fund," 14 October 1976, MS. 595, series 1, file 28, GLA Edmonton.

49. Cavalieri, interview, 1.

50. Michael Roberts, form letter to unknown recipient, 21 August 1972, MS. 595, series 1, file 48, GLA Edmonton. See also, Michael Roberts, form letter to unknown recipient, 10 August 1972, MS. 595, series 1, file 48, GLA Edmonton.

51. "'Gay Power' Low-Geared Here; Gets Cold Shoulder from Lawyers," *Edmonton Journal*, 9 May 1975, p. 13, MS. 595, series 1, file 18, GLA Edmonton.

52. Gloria Filax, *Queer Youth in the Province of the "Severely Normal"* (Vancouver: University of British Columbia Press, 2006), 75.

53. Michael Roberts, "A Brief Requesting an Amendment to Bill #2, 'The Individual's Rights Protection Act,' so as to Give Equal Protection Before the Law to Homosexuals," 28 September 1972, p. 1, MS. 595, series 9, file 61, GLA Edmonton.

54. "The Individual's Rights Protection Act of Alberta," pamphlet, n.d., MS. 595, series 9, file 61, GLA Edmonton.

55. For more on GATE's submissions to IRPA, see Korinek, *Prairie Fairies*, 358–65.

56. Gay Alliance Toward Equality (Edmonton), "Homosexuals: A Minority Without Rights," 1 March 1976, p. 16, MS. 595, series 9, file 10, GLA Edmonton.

57. Ibid., 17.

58. For a similar analysis of the links between activism and public education, see Korinek, "Activism = Public Education."

59. "Background Information," media release, 10 May 1978, p. 2, MS. 595, series 9, file 10, GLA Edmonton.

60. Bonnett, "Transgressing the Public/Private Divide," 70, 226–27, 233.

61. See, for example, "Human Rights and Affectional and Sexual Preference," January 1980, MS. 595, series 9, file 63, GLA Edmonton.

62. Lise Gotel, "Queering Law: Not by *Vriend*," *Canadian Journal of Law and Society* 17, no. 1 (2002): 90; "Alberta Passes Law Allowing Parents to Pull Kids Out of Class," *CBC News*, 2 June 2009, http://www.cbc.ca/news/canada/alberta-passes-law-allowing-parents-to-pull-kids-out-of-class-1.777604; Trish Audette, "Bill 44 Passes After Long Debate," *Edmonton Journal*, 2 June 2009.

63. Bob Radke and Rosemary Ray to *The Gateway*, 28 November 1976, MS. 595, series 1, file 5, GLA Edmonton.

64. Our Drunken Downtown Correspondent, "The Ambassador," *Occasionally from BACUS*, no. 5 (January 1973), MS. 595, series 1, file 5, GLA Edmonton.

65. Korinek, *Prairie Fairies*, 225; Ken King to Bill Munro, 3 November 1972, MS. 595, series 1, file 5, GLA Edmonton; Minutes of the executive meeting, 20 January 1973, MS. 595, series 1, file 25, GLA Edmonton.

66. Michael Roberts to Keray Henke, letter to the editor, *Occasionally from BACUS*, p. 6, 25 January 1973, MS. 595, series 1, file 5, GLA Edmonton.

67. Keray Henke to Michael Roberts, 29 January 1973, MS. 595, series 1, file 5, GLA Edmonton; Keray Henke, retraction, *Occasionally from BACUS*, p. 2, MS. 595, series 1, file 5, GLA Edmonton.

68. GATE Civil Rights Committee Report, 7 January 1976, MS. 595, series 1, file 28, GLA Edmonton.

69. GATE Civil Rights Committee Report, 4 February 1976, MS. 595, series 1, file 28, GLA Edmonton.

70. Bryson W. Stone to R. E. Radke, 25 February 1976, p. 2, MS. 595, series 1, file 22, GLA Edmonton; GATE Civil Rights Committee Report, 3 March 1976, MS. 595, series 1, file 28, GLA Edmonton.

71. GATE, "Homosexuals," 10.

72. Smith, "Social Movements," 294.

73. Ibid., 302.

74. Cavalieri interview, 4.

75. Certificate of Incorporation, 12 August 1977, MS. 595, series 1, file 4, GLA Edmonton.

76. "Our History," Pride Centre of Edmonton, accessed July 16, 2021, https://pridecentreofedmonton.ca/about/our-history/; Korinek, *Prairie Fairies*, 246.

PART III

Doing Politics in a New Way

Protesters defy the War Measures Act, Calgary 16 October 1970. Courtesy of Calgary Herald Photograph Collection, Glenbow Archives, Calgary, NA-2864-6745-CS3-9a-10.

Ernest Manning on Medicare and Socialism

Canada is dangerously close to setting her feet on a path that can lead to but one ultimate end. That end will be a nation turned into a regimented socialist welfare state. [. . .]

To those who want to see a free society preserved in Canada, the proposed compulsory federal medical care program is a direct challenge to individual liberty and responsibility.

Ernest Manning, "National Medicare—Let's Look Before We Leap," speech to the Alberta Division of the Canadian Medical Association, 8 September 1965

Introduction

Alberta barely surfaces in the histories of dissident political activism in Canada in the 1960s and 1970s. Montréal, Toronto, and, of course, Vancouver take pride of place, augmented by a few accounts of radicalism among draft dodgers or community organizers in smaller locales.[1] Historians of that time seem to regard Alberta as having missed the tumult of these decades, with the one substantial political change being the replacement, in 1971, of one conservative dynasty (which had ruled the province for thirty-six years) with another conservative one (which would rule it for nearly forty-four).

Many decades of conservative ascendancy in the province, coupled with a unique Alberta self-righteousness about the role of its conservatism in the country, have spawned an Alberta Angel Complex.[2] Ernest Manning's sermon to Alberta doctors in 1965, quoted in the opening to this section, illustrates that while liberal Canadians might pride themselves on their superiority when compared with Alberta's reactionary persistence, ideologues in this province have also taken pleasure in striding to the pulpit to issue their own warning, this one about the country's liberal sins. Manning was warning Albertans about the "direct challenge to individual liberty and responsibility" represented by the implementation of compulsory state health insurance. Alberta, he maintained, was single-handedly erecting a barrier to prevent the country from a dangerous slide into a tyrannical modernist trap.

Manning's habit of preaching against progressives outside the province is a practice taken up by more recent premiers, including Rachel Notley and Jason Kenney. In both cases, they directed their thunder against perceived enemies of Alberta's bitumen economy. In her 2015 election night victory speech and again at her first news conference the next morning, Notley reassured her "partners in the energy industry" that "they can count on us to work collaboratively with them."[3] This "Alberta Inc." approach was reiterated the next year, when she issued a full-throated attack on federal NDP representatives. When the federal NDP descended on Edmonton for a national convention, their agenda included a proposal that might be seen as a twenty-first century form of bucking conservatism, the Leap Manifesto. The manifesto was, as its subtitle declared, "A Call for a Canada Based on Caring for the Earth and One Another." Along with wide-ranging social reforms, it proposed to swiftly phase out the production of fossil fuels and halt the pipeline projects intended to facilitate export of them. The document suggested a shift towards clean energy and "energy democracy."[4] Notley dismissed the manifesto as "naïve," and "ill-considered" and "very tone-deaf" to Alberta's "economic realities."[5] In this and other attacks, she reverted to a trope that goes back at least to William Aberhart in the 1930s. She portrayed herself as a defender of a province misunderstood and unjustly damned by outsiders who have little grasp of Alberta's uniqueness.

For his part, Kenney has energetically taken up Notley's lead in his expressed contempt for environmentalists, whom he claims are determined to sabotage the development and export of petroleum from Alberta. In announcing a public inquiry in 2019 into what he condemned as "foreign meddling," largely by foundations based in the US, Kenney took pains to emphasize that Alberta was waging this necessary war on behalf of the entire country. These enemies of development, he warned, "focused on Canada because they saw us as the easy target, as the pushover, as the kid in the schoolyard most easy to bully."[6] Virtuous angel though it is, Alberta will not be a bullied one. Canadians, he implied should adopt some of this province's conservative grit.

Alberta's conservatism is nothing if not tenacious, but the articles in this section illustrate that dissent was simmering in the province in the 1960s and 1970s, even if it didn't always register on the national consciousness or in the minds of subsequent historians. The political unruliness in Alberta is illustrated by a series of clashes between students and the administration at the University of Alberta in the mid-1960s. The events were separated in time by no more than months. But that brief interval witnessed a transformation in political thinking and practice.

On 12 February 1964, Premier Ernest Manning brusquely reminded U of A students of their political impotence when, with a single phone call, he stifled a protest planned for the opening of the legislature the next day. The

U of A Residence Committee for Lower Rents had organized a march across the High Level Bridge to the legislature to make their case against rising dormitory fees. Learning of that plan, Manning telephoned U of A president Walter Johns on the afternoon before the march with a simple message. The action would "prejudice the students' chance of getting government cooperation in the future," reported the U of A student paper, *The Gateway*. By evening, the protest had been cancelled.[7] Seven months later, Johns would reassert his fundamental rejection of the entire notion of academic activism when, in response to a faculty-student demonstration at city hall against the return to power of the corrupt Mayor William Hawrelak, Johns declared, "I don't agree with the idea that the academic community should be a centre of vocal protest."[8]

Yet in December 1965, the first New Left group at the university put Johns on notice that they intended to turn U of A into precisely what he rejected. A confrontation flared up when the board of governors and the deans' council refused to allow what has been described as Canada's first New Left organization, the Student Union for Peace Action (SUPA), to use a booth on campus to distribute information against the US war on Vietnam because it violated the university's rule against solicitation and canvassing. (In its fundamental causes, the standoff was remarkably like the University of California, Berkeley campus free-speech fight, which students had won a year earlier after they occupied the administration building, leading to eight hundred arrests.) SUPA representative Peter Boothroyd defied the administration. He declared that he intended "to keep this booth open until it is physically removed or until we are physically removed."[9] SUPA's determination rallied supporters from campus and outside, forcing the U of A administration to back down.[10]

Matters rapidly escalated. In the summer of 1968, with the world in turmoil, Johns felt it necessary to warn publicly that the university was "not an instrument for direct social or revolutionary action."[11] The university was preparing to take "prompt and decisive action" against any student who acted outside of "the due process of the law."[12] The message was reinforced that fall when forty members of the Students for a Democratic University (SDU) subjected the dean of arts to an assertive questioning about the lack of student representation on university decision-making bodies. He responded by cautioning them that the university had files on every one of them.[13]

The moment of intensity would pass. By 1972, Boothroyd would lament that the campus was "apolitical."[14] Yet the capacity of the premier to short-circuit a student demonstration with a phone call—to say nothing of the premier's conviction that suppression was appropriate and necessary—had dissolved. Over a remarkably short period, youthful activists had mounted a democratic challenge to at least some of the coercive authority vested in politicians and university administrators.

Doing politics in a new way, Anthony Hyde asserts, was the primary legacy of the New Left. Indeed, in that blissful dawn, youthful activists redefined politics—its content, who could do it, and how it was practised. In particular, he argues, the New Left "attacked the stasis of the Cold War"—static thinking and conceptualization that had so stultified political discussion and practice in the West for two decades prior.[15] Nothing was more shocking to me than, in 1967, at age seventeen, walking into *The Gauntlet* office at the University of Calgary and having George Russell (yes, that George Russell, later editor-at-large at Fox News) pin a red armband on me to commemorate the fiftieth anniversary of the Bolshevik Revolution. "Was this possible?" I marvelled. To say openly that an event in the Soviet Union, which I rather imagined as a mirror image of Alberta—a sclerotic blob of political conformity—had changed the world for the better? The same amazement came when I heard Bob Cruise, standing in the students' union building behind a table of Internationalist pamphlets praising China, deride a heckler as a "mouthy anti-communist." Here were people who actually defended communism. And in Calgary! The notion was not in my ken before I encountered the new politics. Soon I was doing the unimaginable myself: standing in the snow on a Christmas Eve condemning the US empire's assault on the Vietnamese people as a crime, dismissing as a fraud its claim to be defending me from communism.

In some New Left circles, the formation of the New Democratic Party (NDP) in 1961 was more of the same old zombie politics featuring dead White men calling voters to resurrect them from the grave. But as Myrna Kostash has correctly observed, "the Canadian new left as a whole was never as alienated as the American from its socialist antecedents."[16] In Alberta, the creation of what was optimistically called the New Party had both positive and negative impacts, as Ken Novakowski and Mack Penner document in this section. For those youths tempted by adults' political organizations, the NDP offered a drive to the legislature down an avenue of dreams.

The youthful Novakowski enthusiastically hopped into the car and, from the back seat, urged the old man to put the pedal to the metal. Alas, the NDP proved to be an Edsel, a debility that, Penner points out, was probably secretly predicted and even cheered by the socialists who remained old-guard Co-operative Commonwealth Federation (CCF) stalwarts. They much preferred the trolley in any case. Meanwhile, for Alberta conservatives, the fact that a CCF/NDP government ruled Saskatchewan from 1944 to 1964 provided a near-to-hand bogeyman to warn Albertans of the dangers of the left-liberal welfare state and all its abominations. Those included, as Manning told the Alberta Division of the Canadian Medical Association in 1965, the "direct challenge to individual liberty and responsibility" represented by compulsory state health insurance.[17] Medicare made Manning's skin creep, as it should ours, he insisted.

But ultimately, for a variety of reasons, the NDP in Alberta would not be a home to most of the energetic New Leftists in the province in the 1960s and early 1970s. Instead, as PearlAnn and Baldwin Reichwein and Larry Hannant illustrate, non-party dissidents acted on their own initiative to address issues they saw as pressing. These included the need to accommodate thousands of indigent young people—some Canadian, others seeking refuge from the US war machine—who took to the roads in the late 1960s. Other actions initiated by the left in the 1960s and 1970s included University of Calgary student ventures into the community to challenge repressive and corrupt government schemes and the courageous stand of churchgoers, unionists, students, and internationals who acted locally to oppose the global scourge of racist authoritarianism represented by South African apartheid. Never the wasteland that it was too often seen to be, Alberta in that decade proved it had more than a little of the right stuff to hold its leftist head high.

Larry Hannant

NOTES

1. The Canadian literature on the New Left and the sixties is growing. Bryan Palmer's *Canada's 1960s: The Ironies of Identity in a Rebellious Era* (Toronto: University of Toronto Press, 2009), with its declared focus on Canadian identity, ranges over many topics beyond the New Left, although one lengthy chapter is a detailed survey of the early years of youth-led political

organizing. His chapter is updated and included in M. Athena Palaeologu, ed., *The Sixties in Canada: A Turbulent and Creative Decade* (Montréal: Black Rose Books, 2009). Karen Dubinsky, Catherine Krull, Susan Lord, Sean Mills and Scott Rutherford's edited volume *New World Coming: The Sixties and the Shaping of Global Consciousness* (Toronto: Between the Lines, 2009) has a global reach. And although the volume includes Canadian content, and one chapter descends into Sarnia's "Chemical Valley," there is no mention of Alberta. Jessica Squires explores Canadian activists' assistance to one important source of radical activists, the United States, in *Building Sanctuary: The Movement to Support Vietnam War Resisters in Canada, 1965–73* (Vancouver: University of British Columbia Press, 2014). Sean Mills's *The Empire Within: Postcolonial Thought and Political Activism in Sixties Montreal* (Montréal and Kingston: McGill-Queen's University Press, 2010) and James M. Pitsula's *New World Dawning: The Sixties at Regina Campus* (Regina: Canadian Plains Research Center, 2008) are outstanding assessments of radical politics in an individual city or campus. Roberta Lexier's very brief "To Struggle Together or Fracture Apart: The Sixties Student Movements at English-Canadian Universities," in *Debating Dissent: Canada and the Sixties*, ed. Lara Campbell, Dominque Clément, and Gregory S. Kealey (Toronto: University of Toronto Press, 2012), doesn't mention Alberta. Neither does Cyril Levitt's *Children of Privilege: Student Revolt in the Sixties: A Study of Student Movements in Canada, the United States, and West Germany* (Toronto: University of Toronto Press, 1984). Although he taught at and served in the administration of the University of Alberta for thirteen years, Doug Owram appears to have taken almost nothing from the university to add to *Born at the Right Time: A History of the Baby Boom Generation* (Toronto: University of Toronto Press, 1996). The histories that do devote some attention to the province are those produced relatively early in the Long Sixties or immediately after. In the former category is Dimitrios J. Roussopoulos, ed., *The New Left in Canada* (Montréal: Our Generation Press and Black Rose Books, 1970), which includes one substantial chapter on Alberta written by Richard Price, the president of the U of A student council in 1965–66. Myrna Kostash's early survey of Canada's youth movement in the 1960s, *Long Way from Home: The Story of the Sixties Generation in Canada* (Toronto: James Lorimer, 1980), is the exception to the rule that Alberta is left out of the histories of the time, no doubt because of her roots in the province.

2. The concept of the Angel Complex has been applied primarily to Canadians' attitudes towards racist and illiberal views in the United States. Denise Balkisson says liberal Canadians "use the United States to our advantage

when we don't want to face our own problems, and that includes the problems that we have with race and racism." Hana Sung and Denise Balkisson, "The Angel Complex." *Colour Code: A Podcast about Race in Canada*, 27 September 2016. Podcast, website, 28:15. https://www. theglobeandmail.com/news/national/colour-code-podcast-race-in-canada/ article31494658/. But there are two sides to the political coin of angelic sentiments. Alberta shows that angels can be devilishly conservative, too. I thank Mack Penner and Karissa Robyn Patton for drawing my attention to the Canadian Angel Complex.

3. Cited in Kevin Taft, *Oil's Deep State: How the Petroleum Industry Undermines Democracy and Stops Action on Global Warming – in Alberta, and in Ottawa* (Toronto: James Lorimer, 2017), 181.

4. The Leap Manifesto: A Call for a Canada Based on Caring for the Earth and One Another, http://leapmanifesto.org/en/the-leap-manifesto/#manifesto-content.

5. "NDP Leap Manifesto Naïve, Ill-Considered, Tone-Deaf: Notley," *Global News*, 17 April 2016, https://globalnews.ca/news/2644036/ndp-leap-manifesto-naive-ill-considered-and-tone-deaf-rachel-notley/. Government officials and Alberta NDP insiders joined Notley in condemning Leap. Notley also thought it was "tone deaf" for the University of Alberta to award David Suzuki an honorary degree in 2018. A truly angelic Alberta would be celebrating a distinguished scientist who began both his academic and his broadcasting careers at U of A. Dean Bennett, "Notley Disagrees with University of Alberta Honorary Degree for David Suzuki," *Globe and Mail*, 25 April 2018, https://www.theglobeandmail.com/canada/article-notley-disagrees-with-university-of-alberta-honorary-degree-for-david/.

6. Sammy Hudes, "'Follow the Money Trail': Kenney Launches $2.5M Inquiry into Foreign Funding of Environmental Groups," *Calgary Herald*, 5 July 2019, https://calgaryherald.com/news/politics/kenney-government-launches-inquiry-into-foreign-funded-meddling-in-albertas-energy-sector. The persistence of oil-industry chauvinism in Alberta is systemic, and not restricted to political personalities. As former Alberta Liberal leader Taft points out, "the governing party, the opposition party, universities, regulators, key parts of the civil service, and maybe even the courts are all partially or substantially captured by the fossil fuel industry" (*Oil's Deep State*, 114).

7. "Manning Phones Dr. Johns; Major Demonstration Killed," *The Gateway*, 14 February 1964, 1.

8. Ruth Worth, "Alberta's Professor, Poet, Editor, and Heel-Fly," *Globe and Mail*, 2 September 1964, 7.

9. Don Sellar, "SUPA 'Viet' Booth Stays, Despite Deans' Verdict," *The Gateway*, 1 December 1965, 1.

10. Richard Price, "The New Left in Alberta," in Roussopoulos, *New Left in Canada*, 43.

11. Price, "New Left in Alberta," 43.

12. "And if you do not behave (i.e., conform) this term . . . ," *The Gateway*, 11 September 1968, 5.

13. Price, "New Left in Alberta," 49.

14. "Boothroyd's Lament: 'Campus Apolitical,'" *The Gateway*, 23 November 1972, 3. At the same time, feminist activist Delores Russell could see a silver lining in the demise of the SDU. The death of the male-dominated radical student movement opened space for the birth of the women's movement as an independent sociopolitical entity, she told the same forum Boothroyd addressed.

15. Anthony Hyde, "The Legacy of the New Left," in *The New Left: Legacy and Continuity*, ed. Dimitrios Roussopoulos (Montréal: Black Rose Books, 2007), 53, 54.

16. Kostash, *Long Way from Home*, 182.

17. Ernest C. Manning, "National Medicare—Let's Look Before We Leap," speech to Canadian Medical Association (Alberta Division), 8 September 1965, GR77.173, box 22, file 241b, Ernest C. Manning fonds, Premiers' Papers, Provincial Archives of Alberta.

8 Daring to Be Left in Social Credit Alberta

Recollections of a Young New Democratic Party Activist in the 1960s

Ken Novakowski

As I sat in my Vancouver home and watched the Alberta provincial election results roll in on the evening of 5 May 2015, I suddenly felt tears passing over my cheeks. They were tears of joy. A short time later, my phone began to ring and person after person who knew of my involvement in the Alberta New Democratic Party in the 1960s called to chat and seek out my thoughts on what was happening in my home province. When the evening ended, I realized Alberta would now have an NDP premier whom I had only met as a toddler whenever I dropped in to meet with her father at their family home in the Garneau area of Edmonton.

Even though I had not lived in Alberta since 1971, I still followed political developments in the province with interest. That election led me to think back to my youth, to those years spent on the left in Alberta, tracing my activism to the period from 1965, when I first became politically involved, until 1971, when I moved to British Columbia. I had kept extensive files about all of my arenas of activism, so when the editors of *Bucking Conservatism* invited me to share my memories of being on the left in Alberta during that time, I quickly agreed.

I can identify three areas of political work that characterized my activism: building an informed and active left-wing youth movement, influencing the Alberta NDP to move left, and working to build a broad, issue-based left in the province. And even though much of my activism involved provincial and even national forums and events, most of my story will reflect events in Edmonton.

First, my involvement at the University of Alberta campus and in the Alberta New Democratic Youth (NDY) provided me with an opportunity to learn more about the political left. It also allowed me to play a key role in helping to build a broad, active, and progressive youth movement. This eventually extended to my doing so on a national scale.

Second, I was committed to the view that the political vehicle for change in Canada was the NDP, the party of labour. I thought the party should offer more progressive solutions to the problems facing Albertans, so I set out to mobilize people inside the party to make that change. I found myself doing that primarily through the NDY and later the left-wing group within the NDP called the Waffle.

Third, I believed in the value of coalitions on the left, bringing together a range of organizations committed to a common cause. I found myself doing that in the anti-war movement, either through the NDY/NDP or the Edmonton Committee to End the War in Vietnam. Similarly, the battles around civic issues lent themselves to bringing different groups together in common cause.

I was born in Alberta and lived there for twenty-seven years, every one of them with a Social Credit government in office. And as a red-diaper baby (my father was a communist) I learned early some of the problems this presented to those wanting to improve the work lives and social amenities of most Albertans.

I grew up in the small and, by 1950s standards, thriving farming community of Mundare, about an hour's drive east of Edmonton. The town not only was a commercial centre for farmers but also provided educational, cultural, religious, and recreational outlets for people of all ages. Culturally mostly Ukrainian, the town was also a significant centre for the Greek Catholic faith.

I was the eighth of ten children in the family, raised by a very busy full-time mother and a father who operated a small business, an automotive sales and repair garage that included selling and servicing farm implements. I grew up with stories of my dad's political history—from his arrest and trial as an organizer of the December 1932 Edmonton Hunger March, to his second-place showing running for the legislative assembly as a Communist in 1935, to his significant role in the founding of the Mundare Co-op Store and in the provincial cooperative movement. As I grew older I spent long hours talking politics with my father and began to shape my own political thinking. At some point, I decided I was very much a socialist but did not share my father's view that the Communist Party was the appropriate vehicle for change in Canada.

I had a lot of respect for my dad's beliefs and his political activities during the Depression. In 1956, when I was twelve, I read *The Scalpel, the Sword*, Ted Allan and Sydney Gordon's biography of Norman Bethune, and was very impressed by the life of this Canadian communist. That same year, Khrushchev's revelations of Stalin's horrific disposal of dissenters and others suggested that the Communist Party of the Soviet Union no longer possessed the moral authority or credibility to provide leadership to Communist parties around the world. During the Cold War, the increasing reality for the vast majority of working-class Canadians was that the Communist Party was not even considered as a political option. My Grade 7 social studies teacher, Stanley Ruzycki, was one of two sitting Co-operative Commonwealth Federation (CCF) MLAs and we spent some time after hours talking about the socialism represented by his party. And when the CCF merged with labour in 1961 to create the NDP, I watched the whole event on television and was inspired by the possibilities this new party represented.

I enrolled at U of A in the fall of 1962. But not until two years later, when I switched from majoring in the sciences to political science and philosophy, did I meet others who shared my political inclinations and drew me into political involvement. Since 1947, Social Credit governments had continued to sell out our oil resources to giant corporations, usually American. Oil royalties buoyed the economy, but successive Social Credit governments made no effort to diversify the economy. In the sixties, family farms were beginning to disappear, again in favour of corporate enterprises. And Social Credit ministers and MLAs, often citing Christian values, created an aura of paternalism that pervaded not only government but other public institutions in Alberta.

But I had learned a bit of Alberta history that went beyond the oil politics of E. C. Manning and the ruling Social Credit Party. I knew there was a strong progressive tradition in the province that was expressed not only in the militant mine unions of the Crowsnest Pass and other Alberta communities but also in the actions of farmers. They had taken on the large grain companies and the banks, held grain strikes, and even formed their own co-ops. Alberta was also part of the broad progressive brushfire that swept through the West after the First World War, helping to elect a large Progressive Party caucus in Ottawa and progressives in several provincial governments. In Alberta, the United Farmers of Alberta (UFA) was elected in 1921. In 1935, the UFA was swept out by the populist Social Credit Party, promising relief from the Depression. The 1932 Edmonton Hunger March was a landmark event of political protest during the Depression, and the founding meeting of Canada's first national socialist party, the CCF, was held in Calgary that same year. This all added to my belief that Albertans had a progressive tradition; it needed only to be reawakened.

In the spring of 1965, Wayne Coulter signed me up as a member of the Alberta NDY and with that I also became a member of the Alberta NDP. I made numerous friends and immediately engaged in animated discussions about left-wing ideas and movements and about everything that was wrong with the world. I found many in the NDY who shared my political thoughts and who were struggling with finding the best vehicle to bring about the changes we sought. This was university in the sixties, when student radicalism was in the ascendancy across North America and students were demanding a greater say in their education.

While I could understand the appeal that the New Left had to students, I did not agree with their total cynicism about the electoral process. I had made a conscious decision to join the NDP because it had the potential to present a political alternative and because it was the party of organized labour. Historically, the labour movement has been the largest and most successful endeavour of the working class to improve their lives and livelihoods. I did not believe that student rebellion by itself could ever materialize into a lasting movement for societal change. But I did see the demand for democratization of our universities and opposition to the war in Vietnam as catalysts for young people, drawing them into the political process.

In the fall of 1965, at its annual convention, the Alberta Young New Democrats (AYND) passed numerous resolutions calling for a more activist youth movement to take on issues like the war in Vietnam. The majority view was that we needed to be more than an electoral appendage to the senior party. We needed to raise issues important to young people and to publicly lead on those issues. That same convention elected me president of the NDY to help forge this new direction.

Responding to a motion from the council of the AYND, the federal NDY called on its provincial organizations across Canada to organize protest demonstrations on 26 March 1966 in opposition to the war in Vietnam. These turned out to be the largest peace demonstrations ever before held in Canada, drawing thousands in Vancouver and Ottawa. Over three hundred marched in Edmonton from city hall down Jasper Avenue to the legislature, where speakers included Alberta Federation of Labour president Doug Murdoch and Ed Nelson from the Alberta Farmers' Union.

A week before the demonstration, the U of A campus NDY club sponsored a large public meeting at convocation hall, drawing over three hundred people to hear Yale professor Staughton Lynd accuse his government of lying to Americans again and again about its intentions in Vietnam. He emphatically stated that the American war on Vietnam was "illegal, immoral and undemocratic." John Burke, a political science graduate student and vice-president of the NDY club, said that Canada had "completely lost her sense of objectivity" in its continued complicity with American involvement in the war.[1] As the anti-war movement grew, so did the number of young people participating in NDY activities.

In January of 1967, the NDY club scheduled a public meeting on campus featuring Donald Duncan, a former master sergeant with the US Army who was critical of American aims and methods in the war. U of A president Dr. Walter Johns objected to the meeting and the use of university facilities "by any political party to attack the foreign policy of a friendly power." Johns backed down when his position was widely criticized. An editorial in the conservative *Edmonton Journal* asked, "Why the fuss?" It went on to state, "We were not aware that the students of our university are accountable to the government of the United States for their choice of political speakers."[2] The meeting went ahead, drawing over six hundred people.

But NDY activities were not confined to anti-war actions. One of the reasons we believed the NDY had broad potential was because it reached beyond the campus and its students. We could also organize and mobilize high school students and young workers involved in the union movement.

As part of growing the NDY, we set out to establish clubs in the city high schools in Edmonton and Calgary. In Edmonton, we leafleted high school students on their way to school with specially designed brochures and with the NDY publication *Confrontations*. Published by the federal NDY, the newspaper highlighted actions by young people across the country and internationally. Much like the administrative opposition we had found on campus, we soon faced criticism from the Edmonton superintendent of schools, Dr. Roland Jones. He said that "schools should not be used for partisan politics in any form." [3] Once again we were surprised by the response of the *Edmonton Journal*. In an editorial titled "School and politics," it took school officials to task, stating emphatically, "The response of the public school system to the 'threat' of political literature in our high schools is absurd." [4]

The Edmonton City Young New Democrats took on organizing support pickets for striking unions. When the United Packinghouse Workers' of America, Local 243, went on strike against Canada Packers in the summer of 1966, the NDY joined the picket lines. We obtained additional publicity for the strikers and helped to identify the NDP as the party for working people. Two years later, the Alberta NDY joined striking postal workers in 1968 when they struck across the country for higher wages, better working conditions, and job security. On 19 July, Edmonton NDYers walked the picket lines and drew media attention to the issues in the strike.

One of the significant developments in building a strong and active NDY presence on the U of A campus was the establishment of NDY House at 11137 89th Avenue in the 1966–67 year. A very short distance from campus, NDY House quickly became an important political action centre where meetings and seminars were organized. It gave the NDY a presence on campus that no other student political organization could claim. Additionally, it had a significant agitprop capability located in the basement: silkscreening equipment and a Gestetner printing press to turn out materials for a whole range of campaigns. NDY volunteer labour produced leaflets and posters that were distributed all over the campus, highlighting meetings, seminars, events, and protests. NDY House rent was covered by those of us who lived there.

In early 1966, the Alberta YND joined with the Saskatchewan NDY in the printing and distribution of the newspaper *Candor*. The SNDY, a much larger organization, had begun producing the paper in the fall of 1965 and welcomed the AYND's participation. The AYND also initiated the organization of an annual conference in early May at the Banff School of Fine Arts. It was co-sponsored by the SNDY and the British Columbia YND, but the Alberta organization carried virtually all of the planning and organizing of the event.

The first conference, held on 7, 8, and 9 May 1966, drew 60 participants from the three provinces; they heard speakers address the overall theme "Political Action and Direct Action." The conferences provided an excellent opportunity for young leftists from all of the provinces not only to broaden their knowledge and understanding of issues but also to share and learn from their mutual experiences. Three subsequent conferences were held in 1967, 1968, and 1969, on topics including economic nationalism and worker-student alliances. The conference grew in attendance over the years, the last one involving over 150 participants. While each conference contributed to a broadened understanding of issues, it was the time spent interacting on the Banff School's lawns during breaks and subsequent social events that proved most invaluable. This is where new initiatives were hatched and ongoing alliances built. Overall, it was an experience in movement building.

By 1967, the AYND had functioning clubs in Grande Prairie, Red Deer, and Lethbridge, in addition to two clubs each in Calgary and Edmonton—and those four clubs had grown significantly in size as well. But in addition to its work in the youth movement, the Alberta NDY also played a significant role in attempting to move the politics of the Alberta NDP in a more progressive direction.

As young people, we were not oblivious to the political climate that was created by years of Social Credit government in the province with little effective opposition. Indeed, we recognized that it was clearly an act of courage in 1960s Alberta to even proclaim one's support for the NDP. In seeking to move the Alberta NDP left, we were trying to make the party more appealing to young people. And we firmly believed Albertans would be open to a genuinely progressive choice.

When the NDP was formed in Alberta in 1962, the key organizers of the new party ensured that the more left-leaning elements of the old CCF leadership would have little influence in the NDP. As a result, many of these leaders chose instead to put their energy into the newly created Woodsworth-Irvine Socialist Fellowship, a separate group committed to conducting socialist education programs. And so it was the youth activists in the Alberta NDP who ended up providing leadership within the party for more progressive positions on policy issues and in public statements.

By virtue of being president of the Alberta NDY, I had a seat on the provincial party executive and soon began engaging in the discussions and debates that occurred there. Much of the party's direction was formulated by the executive. The leader, president, treasurer, and secretary for most of this period were, respectively, Neil Reimer, Ivor Dent, Roy Jahma, and Grant Notley. They were a powerful group of people, and their strategy for electoral success was to focus on trying to discredit the Social Credit government rather than on emphasizing NDP policies and ideas. When we began to criticize this negative approach in favour of a strategy that would focus on progressive changes in Alberta, we often found more significant support for these ideas at the council meetings and conventions of the party.

For example, at the March 1967 party convention, a resolution put forward by the Alberta NDY and adopted by the convention resulted in a major story in the 20 March *Edmonton Journal*, headlined "Sweeping mental health reforms urged by Alberta NDP convention." The government's approach to mental health had come under broad criticism. The resolution called for the decentralization of mental health services, with the construction of cottage-type facilities throughout the province to facilitate greater attention to the health of the patients. Our initiative had an impact. Eight months later, the Social Credit government announced the creation of a comprehensive study of mental health treatment methods and facilities in the province, led by W. R. N. Blair, head of the U of A psychology department.

And the NDY also felt it had an important role in elections, helping NDP candidates get elected. In the Pincher Creek–Crowsnest by-election in the fall of 1966, carloads of NDYers drove from Calgary and Edmonton to engage in door-to-door canvassing every weekend of the campaign. As we listened to the results on election night, 6 October, we were ecstatic. Our candidate, Garth Turcott, had won and would sit in the legislature as the first elected NDP MLA. Later that night I walked from NDY House across the High Level Bridge to the provincial legislature and touched it. I firmly believed it was the beginning of change in Alberta. As did the *Edmonton Journal*, which ran a cartoon the next day showing a very sad Premier Manning as a tree trunk, woefully watching a leaf labelled "Pincher Creek" falling from his well-laden tree.

Success, however, was short lived. Turcott took his cues from the NDP leadership and focused in the legislature almost entirely on making allegations of impropriety against government ministers. That became an important theme the NDP carried into the May 1967 general election. However, as a new party, we failed to emphasize to Albertans all the positive changes we would introduce if elected. Into the vacuum moved Progressive

Conservative leader Peter Lougheed with his comprehensive platform "Blue-print for the Seventies." On election night, 23 May 1967, we lost the only seat we had and were blanked again. Lougheed's Conservatives won six seats, formed the official opposition, setting the stage for the next election. The high point of the Pincher Creek–Crowsnest by-election now seemed a long time back.

The 1967 election campaign had been noteworthy for Young New Democrats because for many it was their first taste of electoral politics. We served as canvassers in many city ridings and, in particular, a large number of us worked hard to try get Notley elected in Edmonton-Norwood. The NDY House silkscreens were going full time. We turned out the election signs for virtually all sixty-five ridings in the province. No one could accuse us of not doing our part in that election. Our impact on the party continued. I was elected a vice-president of the provincial NDP in 1967.

Following the 1967 election, I wrote a seven-page document titled "Critique of the Alberta NDP." Written primarily to stimulate inner-party discussion, it took the leadership to task for the "bland negativity of the entire campaign" and its failure to "present a coherent, progressive platform that would completely distinguish it from the other three parties." And I held the leader, Neil Reimer, responsible for the tone and nature of the campaign.

When stepping down as Alberta NDY president at its convention in December 1967, I sounded a warning to the senior party that was reported in the 11 December issue of the *Calgary Herald*: it needed "to come up with some constructive answers to the criticisms levelled at it" by the NDY, or the youth organization would have no other alternative but to look for a new provincial leader.

A year after the election, Reimer stepped down as leader. The tone of his parting comments to the 1968 convention were captured in a page three *Edmonton Journal* headline on 11 November: "Retiring leader warns against leftward swing."

In the ensuing leadership race, most of the youth movement threw its votes and support behind Gordon Wright. He was the main challenger to Notley, who, perhaps unfairly, was viewed as too close to the outgoing leadership; we wanted a change, a progressive change. Notley not only won but began to advance the policies of the NDP in public forums around the province. He went on to become a much-respected politician in the province, for many years the NDP's lone voice in the legislature.

The Edmonton NDY's political involvement was not confined to provincial politics. We had established a second NDY House in 1968, at 10042 118th Street, a half block off Jasper Avenue. Again, the basement housed multiple silkscreens but also a small printing press, compliments of an Edmonton firefighter and union activist. In the fall of 1968, Barrie Chivers, an active NDYer, became manager of Ivor Dent's bid to become mayor of Edmonton. Virtually all of the campaign posters and materials were produced at NDY House, and Dent went on to win the election. A known New Democrat, he was not the first of those with such leanings to occupy the mayor's chair in Edmonton. Elmer Roper—Alberta CCF leader from 1942 to 1955 and a CCF MLA for Edmonton from 1944 to 1955—also served as Edmonton mayor, from 1959 to 1963.

The NDY also got involved in civic issues. Another major story, "Delegation to protest council ban," made the front page of the *Edmonton Journal* on 9 January 1969. The NDY was opposed to the city council's decision to allow a representative of the Edmonton Chamber of Commerce to attend and participate in closed-door city council planning sessions. The publicity from our ensuing protest against this act of favouritism caused the chamber to withdraw its representative, a complete victory for our position.

From 29 June to 2 July 1967, I attended my first federal NDY convention, held at the Royal York Hotel in Toronto, preceding the fourth federal NDP convention. It was a fascinating experience for me, twenty-three years old, meeting young socialists and political activists from across Canada, engaging in intense political discussions and debates on the convention floor. I was soon drafted to run for federal NDY president on a left-wing platform, challenging the hold that the youth movement's more conservative elements had had on the NDY since it was formed six years earlier. In an upset election, I won on the second ballot. A front-page story in the 3 July *Globe and Mail* said it all: "New Democrat Youth revolts, moves left."

I soon found myself in the thick of federal NDP politics. Because of all the media attention generated by my election, I was asked to speak to the party convention, and I drew significant applause when I stated that nationalization should remain an important instrument of NDP policy. Immediately following the convention, I participated in a national television program with NDP leader Tommy Douglas discussing the war in Vietnam, an issue that had been prominent in both the youth and party conventions. I greatly admired Douglas and was awestruck by the experience.

In December 1967, the federal NDY launched the newspaper *Confrontations*. It covered regional, national, and international events of interest to the young left across the country. Our slogan, for both the NDY and *Confrontations*, had become "For an independent, socialist Canada." In Alberta, we established Confrontations Publications and, using NDY House facilities, began producing pamphlets, posters, and reading materials, making them all available to NDYers and others across Canada. We staffed tables at all progressive events in Edmonton, selling our literature and handing out copies of *Candor* and *Confrontations*.

Earlier I recounted the Alberta NDY's involvement in mobilizing against the war in Vietnam. The anti-war movement in Edmonton had grown from early initiatives, and in addition to the NDY, the Students' Union for Peace Action, the Voice of Women, and many church and labour groups spoke out against the war. The Edmonton Committee to End the War in Vietnam (ECEWV) emerged as an umbrella coordinating structure to bring together these groups and others to focus on reaching out to people and educating them about what was going on in Vietnam. And the ECEWV took on the role of organizing demonstrations in Edmonton to coincide with the International Days of Protest—usually twice a year. Our 27 April 1968 demonstration was the front-page story the following Monday in the *Edmonton Journal*. Each demonstration was larger than the last one, and this one was endorsed by fifteen separate organizations.

The anti-war movement was focused on public protest, and opposition was growing significantly in the United States and around the world. We held teach-ins and distributed leaflets, and our 5 April 1969 demonstration drew a thousand participants with twenty supporting organizations, with the NDY continuing to play an important role in these protests.

By July of 1969, when I stepped down as federal NDY president, the youth movement had grown considerably across the country. The convention was more united than previous ones had been and clearly reflected the more left-wing politics first adopted two years earlier. In my president's report to the convention, I identified capitalism as the challenge we faced and argued that we would never achieve a just society unless it included economic justice for all. I called upon the youth movement to make a greater effort in having its voice heard in the councils of the federal NDP.

The Waffle movement was now emerging across Canada as a strong force in the NDP. The Waffle was initiated as a caucus within the NDP that pledged to fight "for an independent, socialist Canada." It advanced strongly progressive positions on issues such as nationalization, women's rights, Québec sovereignty, labour, and democracy. The Waffle had the potential to change the party into more of a socialist party, a direction that NDYers had sought for years. Provincial Waffle branches were established in every province. In Alberta, we formed a steering committee that included not only youth activists but also a broad spectrum of party members from across the province.

Edmonton Waffle members had begun to revitalize the NDP's metro council—a city-wide council representing all the city's NDP ridings. Led by its new president, Tom Pocklington, the metro council began to coordinate efforts on a number of civic issues. It publicly campaigned to defeat three civic monetary bylaws in the fall of 1970 that would have built an omniplex, a huge civic facility that would house all professional sports at considerable cost to taxpayers. This money would be much better spent on community facilities in all parts of the city. Metro council distributed fifty thousand leaflets that urged people to "Vote No to Omniplex." Voters rejected the project.

Metro council concerned itself with a myriad of issues important to people, including the problems of high rents and inadequate public housing. It advocated for improved public daycare facilities and increased public transportation. The council also advocated that the NDP become active in civic politics, a position again surprisingly endorsed by the *Edmonton Journal*, in a 4 September 1970 editorial. Under the heading "Welcome step," it stated that the "possibility that the New Democratic Party would run a slate of candidates in the next civic election is good news for all those interested in better civic government."

The Alberta Waffle organized a Western Regional NDP Waffle Conference at the Banff School of Fine Arts, to be held 25 and 26 April 1970. The conference brought together activists from the three westernmost provinces. We held sessions to develop positions on issues from labour and industrial democracy to regionalism and Québec nationalism. The conference was a precursor to the National Waffle Conference held in Toronto later that summer and to the NDP's leadership convention in Ottawa in April 1971.

The Alberta Waffle organized to influence the February 1971 provincial NDP convention. Our work had already resulted in the executive producing a far more progressive energy statement than it might otherwise have done. It called for nationalization of privately owned natural gas, electrical, and water utilities, pipelines, the McIntyre-Porcupine and other large coal-exporting interests, and development of the Athabasca oil sands as a Crown corporation. We introduced a motion "that an Alberta NDP government would establish immediately a public corporation whose prime purpose will be to explore for, develop, produce and direct the usage of all sources of energy within the province." After a ninety-minute debate, the Waffle motion, although defeated, garnered support from 40 percent of the delegates.

From 21 to 24 April 1971, we were at the NDP National Leadership Convention in Ottawa. Half the Alberta NDP delegation attended Waffle caucus meetings, where I served as one of the chairpersons. I had played a significant role on the Waffle's national steering committee and chaired the Waffle floor committee during the convention. We had a significant impact on policy debates and in the actual leadership contest; our candidate, Jim Laxer, went through to the final ballot before being defeated by David Lewis. Although Lewis had won the leadership, we saw the convention as a high point because we had succeeded in engendering significant debate and discussion and broad support on key issues important to Canada's future.

In Alberta, Social Credit premier Harry Strom called a general election for 30 August 1971, the first election with Notley as NDP leader. Notley had chosen to run in Spirit River–Fairview in the Peace River country, a riding he was to win and represent until his untimely death in 1984. I campaigned for Barrie Chivers in Edmonton-Beverley. On election night, the Social Credit dynasty ended. The Progressive Conservatives under Lougheed had won. Alberta New Democrats would have to wait another forty-four years before they would form a government. Two days after the 1971 election, I was on my way to British Columbia.

It was clear that young people were turning away from many of the policies of the Manning and Strom governments. Campus politics indicated that, but young workers were also increasingly looking for alternatives to both the social conservatism and the narrow economic strategies of Social Credit. One might believe we hardly made a dent in the conservative armour that covered the province, but we mobilized people and found ways of challenging what had been a homogenous right wing. Small dents in the armour, perhaps, but that is almost always how progressives have moved forward.

When I reflect upon those seven years spent on the left in Alberta, I realize how fortunate I was to be part of a young left that learned how to organize and communicate with the tools we had available to us at the time. And we engaged in the political process. As Stephen Langdon, then a member of the parliamentary press gallery, wrote in the July 1971 issue of *Maclean's* magazine,

> Among the young in this country, especially the students, the dominant political mood is cynicism, a belief that all political parties are similarly uncaring and irrelevant. [. . .] This is the constituency in which Waffle supporters live. They are constantly being told [by these young people] that the NDP is too moderate, too similar to the old-line parties. It's natural then, that the Waffle should be trying to make the NDP more radical, more aggressive, to differentiate it from other parties, to make it more appealing to the young.

Although Langdon's comments referred to the Waffle following the 1971 federal NDP convention, they capture well what motivated NDYers in Alberta to push the NDP left.

When I look at young people today, I sense their frustration with issues such as inequality, poverty, and the climate crisis, all products of capitalism. But I often see that frustration leads them to opt out of the political process. It is equally essential today that the NDP offer clear, progressive policies and strategies for these and other critical issues in its election campaigns.

I mentioned earlier my feelings when the NDP government was elected in Alberta in May 2015. Later that summer I visited Edmonton and had another emotional moment: once again I walked to and touched the Alberta legislature as I had done the night of the Pincher Creek–Crowsnest by-election forty-nine years earlier. It took a long time, but this time it was for real.

NOTES

1. "U.S. Peace Offensive 'A Big Lie' Rebel Yale Professor Maintains," *Edmonton Journal*, 21 March 1966, 21.
2. Walter Johns, quoted in editorial, "Why the Fuss?" *Edmonton Journal*, 11 January 1967, 4.
3. Roland Jones, "NDY Steps Up Newspaper Distribution," *Edmonton Journal*, 24 September 1968.
4. "School and Politics," editorial, *Edmonton Journal*, 30 September 1968, 4.

Socialist Survival

The Woodsworth-Irvine Socialist Fellowship and the Preservation of Radical Thought in Alberta

Mack Penner

For three decades, from 1932 to 1962, the Co-operative Commonwealth Federation (CCF) provided political representation for the socialist movement in Alberta. The party's popular support peaked around the provincial election of 1944, when it won approximately one-quarter of the popular vote but just two seats in the legislature. From that point, Cold War anti-communism combined with rising prosperity to undermine the CCF's electoral appeal. In this way, the 1944 election simultaneously marked both a high point and a missed opportunity that, in the words of historian Alvin Finkel, "proved a crushing blow."[1] By the outset of the 1960s, the CCF had ceased to be an effective player in the province's electoral politics. The dissolution of the CCF in 1962 and its replacement by the New Democratic Party (NDP), then, represented a new beginning for left politics in the province. But this new beginning raised concerns for many socialists, who feared that the creation of the NDP would entail significant dilution of the socialist ideology that had been the foundation for the CCF's political activity.[2]

For some CCF stalwarts who believed that the 1950s had already seen a lamentable retreat from unabashed socialism in favour of "an antiseptic version of Keynesian 'planning,'" the direction of the NDP only exacerbated those worries.[3] Especially in Alberta, socialists were eager to see the new party continue to define itself in explicitly socialist terms—something that seemed improbable given the elevated status of pragmatic labour bureaucrats within it. The anti-communist political climate of the Cold War had resulted in the purging of communists and the general de-radicalization of most unions in Alberta, as elsewhere, which led in turn to the perception that a labour party like the NDP would be an unlikely champion for a genuinely socialist message.[4] In accordance with these concerns, the final convention of the Alberta CCF adopted a resolution that held that upon the dissolution of the federation, provision would be made for the creation of an organization devoted to socialist education and study in the province. Such an organization, it was hoped, would "salvage as much as possible of what [socialists] considered to be important in the CCF."[5] Members of the CCF coordinating committee in Edmonton took responsibility for establishing the organization and began the process of creating what would become, in 1962, the Woodsworth-Irvine Socialist Fellowship (WISF), named for CCF founder J. S. Woodsworth and veteran Alberta socialist William Irvine. Irvine, for his part, openly protested the name to no avail at the fellowship's first meeting. Membership in WISF was initially available for an annual fee of $1.50, and the fellowship quickly became home to more than a hundred members, mostly from the area around Edmonton, with some sympathizers from intellectual circles in Calgary.[6] Among the best known of these were socialist activists such as Betty Mardiros, Nellie Peterson, and Floyd Johnson, as well as academics like Tony Mardiros and Ed Shaffer.[7]

For the first decade of its existence, until 1972, WISF had no formal association with the NDP. Many of the most principled and experienced socialist activists from the CCF chose to embrace WISF rather than the NDP, thus creating a situation in which there was no significant socialist caucus within the provincial party structure. Political scientist and historian Larry Pratt has described this period of WISF's non-affiliation as "a retreat into political irrelevance."[8] But assessing WISF as politically irrelevant in the decade beginning in 1962 is troublesome in at least two senses. First, the suggestion that WISF retreated from the NDP ignores the reality that the fellowship applied for affiliation to the Alberta NDP in 1963. The WISF appeal was denied by the national party executive on the grounds that affiliated memberships were not intended to apply to groups composed of party members whose central aim was the promotion of particular viewpoints on policy matters.[9] The party elite was actively trying to avoid the formation of a left-wing faction within its ranks, an issue that would arise again with the emergence of the Waffle movement in the early 1970s. If there was a retreat at all it was a forced one, and at any rate, a majority of individual WISF members were also, however reluctantly, individual members of the NDP.[10] So WISF members did continue to participate in electoral politics, at least to some degree.

Second, and more importantly, to argue that the non-affiliated WISF was politically irrelevant requires assuming a rather narrow view of what can constitute politically important activity. While it is true that WISF spent the 1960s and early 1970s operating outside of the immediate terrain of electoral politics, it provided a platform from which socialist thought was promoted, studied, and refined in Alberta. Come 1972, when WISF finally became affiliated with the NDP, it was a group with a decade's worth of development behind it and with rigorously developed perspectives on socialist theory and its societal applications. Over the first decade of its existence, then, WISF functioned in the politically essential task of preserving socialist thought in Alberta. Indeed, WISF's determination to keep alive a socialist alternative posed an ongoing challenge to the NDP leadership. Noting this, the leader of the Alberta section of the Communist Party of Canada, Bill Tuomi, privately mentioned to a fellow communist in 1965 that the NDP was struggling to garner financial support from its extensive contacts in the province. While the NDP attracted little public support, WISF "was growing in membership and obtaining all of the left-wing element out of the N.D.P."[11] A vacuum to the left of the NDP made room for a quasi-party, which is what WISF became. Perhaps the key factor curbing WISF's influence was the limited ambition of its members, who typically remained loyal to the NDP.

Preserving socialist thought, independent of direct participation in electoral politics, was important in 1960s Alberta because economic conditions in the province were such that there was little general appetite for any form of counterhegemonic movement. Since the 1940s, the reactionary Social Credit government led by Premier Ernest Manning had overseen a stunning recovery from the economic doldrums of the 1930s, and most Albertans had experienced a material improvement in their lives as a result. In particular, after 1947, the government used windfall revenues from the rapid private development of the provincial oil industry to finance robust expenditure programs in health care, education, and other areas important to ordinary people.[12] Perhaps the best example of this was a five-year spending program commenced in 1959 that, in a televised address to the province, Manning described as "a gigantic five-year anti-recession development program that will be the boldest, most aggressive, and far-reaching program of its kind ever attempted by a provincial government in Canada."[13] The features of Manning's program included fifty seniors' homes that would house 4,100 people; community improvements like swimming pools, recreation centres, and camping facilities; the construction of the Foothills Hospital in Calgary; the renovation of the (now very controversial) Mitchener Centre for "mental defectives" in Red Deer; and the construction of a provincial museum and archives in Edmonton.[14] This spending, coupled with the vehemently anti-communist politico-cultural environment of the Cold War, made the government very popular and seriously undermined the appeal of socialist politics in Alberta.

A growing awareness that socialism was no longer particularly appealing to Canadians, including Albertans, was the immediate impetus behind the creation of the NDP. Accordingly, the draft program adopted at the party's 1961 national founding convention bore little resemblance to the CCF's founding document, the Regina Manifesto. Gone were enthusiastic calls for the eradication of capitalism in Canada, abandoned in favour of advocating moderate welfare-state goals such as increased employment, national health insurance, sick benefits, free education, and a progressive taxation system to accommodate egalitarian redistribution of wealth.[15] In Alberta, the NDP leadership was particularly willing to embrace moderate politics, combining with them the search for a personal scandal that might do political harm to Manning and Social Credit. Political scientist Howard Leeson describes the leadership of the NDP during the early 1960s, especially Grant Notley and then party leader Neil Reimer: "Their interests were organizational, their approach competitive, and their focus provincial. There was little time for philosophical debate about policies and issues. [. . .] Instead there was a deliberate concentration on short-term tactics, the advantage of position on immediate issues, and a new policy of direct attack on Manning and Social Credit."[16] In other words, the NDP did not appear to be a party well suited to socialists for whom politics was inseparable from an ideological appeal to a fundamentally different kind of political economy.

In this way, socialists in Alberta found themselves up against a powerful conservatism in two senses. One was the broadly popular conservative government of Social Credit, underpinned by a flourishing economic order, which rendered the practice of mass socialist politics all but impossible.

At the same time, because of the stability of this conservative order, the NDP—ostensibly the proper home for Alberta socialists—turned its back on ideological politics altogether in an attempt to pose a more immediate electoral challenge to Social Credit. The NDP became a conservative social-democratic party. The relative conservatism of the NDP, then, was a primary point of conflict between the party and socialists, especially those who had come out of the CCF tradition, which represented a committed leftist alternative within Alberta's political landscape. This antagonistic relationship was manifested in a final decision made by the CCF to transfer all of its assets to WISF and not to the NDP. This decision cemented a degree of acrimony between socialists and social democrats in the province and led directly to WISF's formal isolation from the NDP until 1972.[17]

The asset transfer came about as a direct result of the decision made at the final provincial CCF convention to both dissolve the party and create the educational group that would become WISF. In other provinces, the CCF had dissolved and transferred its assets to the new party. But Alberta socialists' suspicion of the NDP's political character made them dubious about a simple asset transfer. The main item of value was Woodsworth House in Edmonton, which had been bought in 1949 through unsecured loans from CCF members and was owned by the Alberta Woodsworth House Association. For thirteen years, it had served as the headquarters of the provincial party.[18] After the acrimonious parting from the NDP, WISF retained Woodsworth House, and it became the site of many of WISF's regular meetings.

Even though the financial prize was far from enormous, NDP leaders saw losing it as a serious slight. Reimer, who assumed the NDP presidency, was particularly offended and opposed WISF's 1963 application for affiliation with the NDP.[19] Leeson, a friend, assistant, and, later, biographer of Notley, described the asset transfer as a "last act of defiance" made by "'armchair socialists.'"[20] A fairer analysis might identify an act of preservation determined not so much to spite the NDP as to ensure, in some form, the perpetuation of a vehicle for socialism in Alberta. But at any rate, organizational isolation appeared to be the price of socialist preservation, and WISF embarked upon its first decade removed from direct participation in electoral politics. In this way, WISF functioned almost as an Albertan iteration of the New Left, emerging as a political force without formal ties to conventional political parties and espousing an unapologetic brand of socialism. While it lacked the youthfulness of the prototypical

New Leftist formation, it certainly functioned as a prominent critical voice to the left of the NDP.

Separated as it was from the institutional activity of the NDP, WISF embraced its orientation as an educational group devoted to the study and promotion of socialism. Initially, WISF's educational mandate was met mostly by holding regular meetings for members and for the general public, as well as by its creation of a book club that made recommendations for texts on politics, philosophy, and history. Later, WISF would begin publishing a monthly newsletter, *The Nutcracker*, the name of which harkened back to the tradition of prairie radicalism and a publication of the same title that Irvine, along with J. H. Ford, had established in Calgary in 1916.[21] *The Nutcracker* served as both a tool to circulate relevant organizational updates and a forum for short, lively essays on issues ranging from public ownership of the provincial oil industry to the fallout from the military coup against Salvador Allende's Chilean government in 1973. In 1965, these activities began to be supplemented with annual "summer seminars" designed to allow "socialists of all kinds, together with interested non-socialists, to engage in discussion and reasonable debate of questions concerning the thought and practice of socialism."[22]

The seminars—ultimately ten of them in all—were held at the School of Fine Arts in Banff on all but a few occasions until 1974 and were arguably the most significant undertaking of WISF each year. Indeed, the seminars were sufficiently important socialist gatherings that the RCMP maintained surveillance on attendees and linked them to other activities in their home communities.[23] The fellowship devoted significant time and effort to advertising the seminars, both to members and non-members, and while it may be difficult to assess the degree of influence of these events in any concrete way, their orientation was clear. Examining the nature of the summer seminars—the speakers who were invited and their topics—reveals much about WISF's socialist outlook. Contrasting this with the main priorities of the NDP at the time reveals the degree to which the two organizations differed and makes clear that WISF did indeed function to perpetuate socialist thought in Alberta.

The summer seminar of 1966, titled "The Real World of Democracy," was based on the 1964 Massey Lectures of C. B. Macpherson. A political scientist from the University of Toronto, Macpherson was well known at the time for his theory of "possessive individualism" as well as his 1953 book, *Democracy in Alberta.*[24] Alvin Finkel, while not wholly taken with Macpherson's argument, has deemed *Democracy in Alberta* "a brilliant work of political theory" that situates Social Credit ideas "in the context of debates on the larger meaning of democracy in the western world"; until the release of Finkel's *The Social Credit Phenomenon in Alberta* in 1989, it was the most significant text on the Social Credit era in the province.[25] Macpherson's scholarship on Alberta has come under sustained criticism in the decades since its publication, mostly for socio-demographic errors, but because he injected the issue of social class into the debate about the province's political makeup, Macpherson was well suited to address the seminar.[26]

The focus of Macpherson's address to the seminar was not merely provincial in scope. Rather, as the title of his Massey Lectures suggests, Macpherson was concerned with democracy at a global level. He considered the state of democracy in three distinct contexts—illiberal communist countries, illiberal underdeveloped countries, and liberal capitalist countries—in order to reach certain conclusions about the probable outcome of the global struggle between communist and capitalist nations that was then the defining geopolitical issue in the world. Macpherson argued that because communist and underdeveloped countries had by the 1960s shown definitively that "market behaviour is no longer the sole source of power," the balance of power between nations would have to be determined according to "the degree to which their economic and political systems satisfy the desires of all their people."[27] In light of this conclusion, he anticipated that the relative global power of capitalist liberal democracies in the West would depend on their ability, or willingness, to abandon a moral order based on acquisitive market principles.[28] For socialists in Western countries, like members of WISF, the implications of Macpherson's lectures would have been obvious: the continued existence of capitalist markets as the fundamental economic structure in any country threatened the moral authority of that society.[29] Given the Cold War political environment in which such ideas were deemed to be subversive, it is little surprise that the RCMP monitored the seminars.

Other speakers at the 1966 summer seminar included Guyanese politician and writer Cheddi Jagan, as well as former president of the Saskatchewan New Democratic Youth James Harding.[30] Pursuing further the themes of Macpherson's lectures, both Jagan and Harding advanced radical visions of the future, calling for a renewed commitment to socialist politics. Speaking in particular about developing countries, Jagan advocated a robust and simultaneous struggle against all forms of imperialism and colonialism, a struggle that would include

> nationalization of the commanding heights of the economy—factories, mines, plantations, banks, insurance companies, import-export trade; monetary and fiscal reforms aimed at preventing the outflow of capital and the redistribution of wealth; land reform for the development of agriculture and laying the basis for industrialization; and democratization of all social and governmental institutions so as to involve the mass of the people more intimately in the process of government and development.[31]

Jagan's presentation—reminiscent of the CCF's 1933 Regina Manifesto—suggests an interest on the part of WISF in socialism not just as a domestic struggle but as an international ideal. And indeed, socialist internationalism, an enduring focus on countries throughout the world, was a central interest of WISF throughout its existence. The WISF publications list includes numerous works on nations in Asia, Latin America, and Africa, for example.[32]

Where Jagan emphasized developing countries, Harding's address to the seminar—"Liberalism, Social Democracy, and the Danger of Totalitarianism"—took a more domestic perspective. He put forward a noteworthy critique of social democracy and suggested a strategic political model for what he termed "relevant radicalism."[33] Regarding social democracy of the sort that the NDP was practising at the time, Harding concluded that it had become largely indistinguishable from welfare-state liberalism and that it therefore offered no genuine hope for the transformation of society. He stressed the pressing necessity to oppose the liberal welfarism of the NDP and instead to develop a mode of politics that would begin with the inculcation of a political consciousness based on "freedom and brotherhood."[34] For Harding, politics of this kind involved looking directly to the legacies of WISF's namesakes, Woodsworth and Irvine, and retaining their foundational political ethos, despite the enormous historical changes that confronted socialists in the 1960s.[35]

The distance between the concerns of WISF and the NDP in 1966 was arguably the greatest that it would ever be. While WISF was concerned with the wide-ranging and internationally significant issues raised by speakers at that year's summer seminar, the NDP had adopted a relatively narrow attitude, concerning itself with little more than the most immediate exigencies of Alberta politics. The NDP's focus in the years prior to the provincial election of 1967 was on negative, sometimes personal, attacks on Manning and other members of the Social Credit government. The provincial economy, still riding a seemingly endless wave of growth propelled mostly by an oil industry that by then directly or indirectly employed about half of all workers in the province, did not provide good fodder for material criticism of the government.[36] So the NDP concentrated its efforts on episodes like the so-called Turcott Affair. Garth Turcott was a lawyer from Pincher Creek who, in a 1966 by-election, became the first elected NDP MLA in Alberta. In his short stint as an elected legislator, Turcott became famous as a muckraker who, first upon his entry to the legislature and later in his reply to the 1967 Speech from the Throne, relentlessly highlighted allegations of corruption against two prominent Social Credit insiders. He accused minister of municipal affairs A. J. Hooke and former treasurer E. W. Hinman of engaging in "business and land dealings which were in conflict with their public duties," and, at the direction of Reimer and Notley, Turcott devoted his every energy to steering public attention toward these accusations.[37] Manning's response was politically shrewd. He forced a censure vote against Turcott in the legislature and called the election of 1967, which did not unfold well for the NDP. The Turcott Affair illustrates the NDP's political approach at the time. It ignored fundamental questions of the sort that WISF was concerned with and concentrated on seeking to gain any sort of political edge on Social Credit.

The ethos that drove the Turcott Affair also drove the NDP's provincial election campaign in 1967. The campaign was an overwhelmingly negative one, oriented around the issue of governmental corruption. Ideological matters were avoided but so were issues like the consequences of farm mechanization on rural families, land prices, urbanization, and the provincial industrial strategy.[38] This approach resulted in a resounding defeat. The NDP did not win a seat—not even Turcott's—and Social Credit won another enormous legislative majority. Indeed, the one substantial development of the election was a significant increase in the vote share for the reorganized Progressive Conservative Party, which won six seats.[39] Ken Novakowski, a socialist and leader of the New Democratic Youth at the time, attributed the failure of the election to the fact that NDP leader Reimer "neglected to tell the people of Alberta just what he proposed to do in Mr. Manning's place and how the election of an NDP government would bring changes to the economic situation of the province."[40]

Novakowski's critique prefigured a schism that would emerge within the NDP after the election, as an increasingly vocal and youthful socialist minority in the party began to question its moderate, non-ideological character. This schism later resulted in the emergence of the Alberta Waffle caucus, which pressed for "an independent socialist Canada."[41] More immediately, left-criticism within the party seemed to present a new opening for WISF to exert influence inside the NDP. Some of the socialists in the party at the time were WISF members—though Novakowski was not—and the fellowship began to orient its educational activities, especially the summer seminar, around questions of how young socialists, increasingly evident in society in the late 1960s, might play a role in the radicalization of Canadian politics.[42]

The 1968 WISF summer seminar was organized around the theme "Radical Reshaping of Canadian Society: Ways and Means." Among the issues considered were the role of political parties in fomenting transformative social change, the prospects for socialism in Canada, and the significance of youth in radical social movements. This last issue was addressed by Novakowski in a speech entitled "Radical Youth and the Reshaping of Society."[43] Novakowski was likely the best-known socialist in the Alberta NDP at the time, and inviting him demonstrates WISF's excitement with the shift in the political tone of the moment. There seemed to be new potential for the NDP, both nationally and provincially, to accommodate genuinely socialist politics after having resisted it since the party's inception. The NDP might, it seemed after all, be a viable political vehicle for socialists. In subsequent years, as Novakowski and the Waffle caucus became increasingly prominent influences in the party, WISF's enthusiasm would be confirmed and increased.[44]

The Waffle played a small but significant role in the Alberta NDP from 1969 to 1971. And while it is difficult to precisely set out the degree to which the Waffle caucus influenced the provincial NDP leadership to become more amenable to socialist politics, there can be no denying that the party leadership had become so by the early 1970s. Notley, who had replaced Reimer as party leader in 1968, was no longer quite as convinced of the primacy of non-ideological politics—though he certainly remained more moderate than people like Novakowski—and consequently a new place for socialists opened up in the NDP.[45] By 1971, WISF had become openly supportive of the party, believing that it was the only viable political organization to further the cause of democratic socialism in Canada. A contingent from WISF attended the 1971 provincial convention of the NDP, and an article in *The Nutcracker* recapped the experience in highly optimistic terms. Jointly written by members of the convention contingent, it noted a palpable change in "both direction and emphasis," remarking with particular approval upon the party's newfound preference for the terminology of "democratic socialism" rather than "social democracy." Referring to youth-led criticism of the Canadian capitalist system and the injustices it created, the article praised the NDP for "responding as a 'people's party' should . . . to the 'winds of change' that are blowing from many directions."[46] The article concluded with expressions of hope that Notley would be elected as an MLA in that year's election and that even if he were to fail to win election, the NDP would continue to serve as an ally in the movement for socialism. The animosity that had characterized WISF's early relationship to the party had all but disappeared, and the ideological chasm between the organizations that had existed throughout most of the 1960s had shrunken considerably.[47]

Given this support, it was no great surprise that by early 1972 WISF had begun to anticipate becoming an official affiliate to the party. In the January 1972 issue of *The Nutcracker*, Nellie Peterson, a former CCFer and well-known WISF member, predicted imminent affiliation, and within a month her prediction proved correct.[48] By February 1972, at the urging of a "great majority" of members, WISF applied for and was granted affiliation to the NDP.[49] Over the following months, the fellowship held a number of meetings at which members discussed their new role within the framework of the party. At one meeting, NDP party secretary Bill Dryden was invited to answer members' questions about the various ways in which WISF could participate in and influence the party.[50] By the middle of 1972, WISF had settled into its new role, capping a decade during which the fellowship had gone from being resolutely at odds with the provincial NDP to becoming an affiliate and supporter.

WISF's affiliation came at an important time, given that it followed closely on the heels of the disintegration of the Waffle's organization and influence within the NDP. At a national level, the Waffle became embroiled in sectarian conflicts after the party conventions of 1970 and 1971; provincially, the Waffle movement declined after Novakowski, its leader, left for British Columbia in 1971.[51] The decline of the Waffle left WISF as the primary socialist influence on the Alberta NDP, elevating the political significance of the group. The main avenue by which WISF could play this new role was to encourage the NDP to adopt socialist policies at both provincial and federal conventions, where WISF delegates put forth resolutions and proposals. At the 1973 federal NDP convention, for example, WISF submitted eighteen separate resolutions, which advocated a more critical political stance vis-à-vis the federal Liberals, wholesale nationalization of public transport and commercial banks, and a guaranteed annual income, among other things.[52] It certainly was not true that WISF's proposals were always or even usually embraced by the party—for example, Notley fought stridently against a policy of widespread nationalization that WISF put forward at the 1973 provincial party convention—but the fellowship had become a socialist fixture within the party apparatus.[53]

WISF lasted into the twenty-first century, its operations ceasing around 2007 because its membership was aging and shrinking and increasingly lacked the energy to keep the fellowship afloat.[54] It was certainly not the only socialist organization to suffer a decline in the late twentieth and early twenty-first centuries. In the 1960s and early 1970s, though, WISF was a vibrant organization that functioned as a tool of survival for a small group of socialists in Alberta. In 1962, when WISF was established, the Social Credit government had successfully quelled any broad popular impulse for transformative social change, and to cope with this reality, the NDP accordingly abandoned any open support for such change. The result was that socialists were left politically isolated in the province without an obvious electoral ally in their ideological struggle.

In this context, WISF appears not as an organization defined by political insignificance but as one that redoubled a commitment to socialism in the most active way it could, given prevailing historical conditions. While it would be an exaggeration to suggest that WISF posed a serious threat to conservative hegemony in Alberta, it no doubt functioned to hold back the willingness within the NDP to shift increasingly to the right in order to operate within a seemingly entrenched reactionary political culture. Had WISF not carried out "political education as a means of enquiry into and spreading awareness of socialist solutions to Canada's problems," the NDP might have been poised to disavow its socialist lineage.[55] It turned out that WISF offered both an intellectual community oriented around the theory and practice of socialism and an institutional platform from which a group of more than a hundred Alberta socialists could maintain a critical position vis-à-vis the NDP's conservative tendencies in the 1960s. Far from irrelevant, WISF's contribution to ensuring the endurance of socialist thought was of real political and intellectual significance.

NOTES

1. Alvin Finkel, *The Social Credit Phenomenon in Alberta* (Toronto: University of Toronto Press, 1989), 92–95.
2. Robin Hunter, "Social Democracy in Alberta: From the CCF to the NDP," in *Socialism and Democracy in Alberta: Essays in Honour of Grant Notley*, ed. Larry Pratt (Edmonton: NeWest Press, 1986), 67.
3. Ibid.
4. For an account of the role played by anti-communism in the postwar labour movement, see James Muir, "Alberta Labour and Working Class Life, 1940–1959," in *Working People in Alberta: A History*, ed. Alvin Finkel (Edmonton: Athabasca University Press, 2012), 135–39.
5. Anthony Mardiros, *William Irvine: The Life of a Prairie Radical* (Toronto: Lorimer, 1979), 223–24, 252.
6. RCMP Security Service, Calgary, Communist Party of Canada (Southern Alberta Special Club), 5 November 1964, Library and Archives Canada (hereafter LAC) Access to Information Act (hereafter ATIP) A2016-00880, vol. 1, p. 97.
7. Mardiros, *William Irvine*, 253.
8. Larry Pratt, "Grant Notley: Politics as Calling," in Pratt, *Socialism and Democracy*, 12.
9. See correspondence between Betty Mardiros, Terence Grier, and Grant Notley, file: Woodsworth-Irvine Socialist Fellowship—Affiliated Organizations, PR1984.178/689, Provincial Archives of Alberta, Edmonton (hereafter PAA).
10. Betty Mardiros, "The Woodsworth-Irvine Socialist Fellowship," newspaper clipping, file: *The Commonwealth*, vol. 32, no. 21, vol. 33, no. 1, and Clippings Related to the Woodsworth-Irvine Socialist Fellowship, PR2010.0139/0003, PAA.
11. RCMP Security Service, Edmonton, Communist Activities in Political Parties – Alberta, 8 June 1965, LAC ATIP A2016-00880, vol. 1, pp. 84–85.
12. Ed Shaffer, "The Political Economy of Oil in Alberta," in *Essays on the Political Economy of Alberta*, ed. David Leadbeater (Toronto: New Hogtown Press, 1984), 182.

13. Ernest Manning, quoted in Brian Brennan, *The Good Steward: The Ernest C. Manning Story* (Calgary: Fifth House, 2008), 135.

14. Brennan, *Good Steward*, 135–37.

15. Desmond Morton, *The New Democrats, 1961–1986: The Politics of Change* (Toronto: Copp Clark Pitman, 1986), 19–24.

16. Howard Leeson, *Grant Notley: The Social Conscience of Alberta*, 2nd ed. (Edmonton: University of Alberta Press, 2015), 63.

17. The split is described in Leeson, *Grant Notley*, 55–58.

18. Mardiros, *William Irvine*, 252.

19. Leeson, *Grant Notley*, 58.

20. Ibid., 57.

21. For more on the first iteration of *The Nutcracker* and William Irvine's contributions to it, see Mardiros, *William Irvine*, 41–52. Copies of WISF's *Nutcracker* can be found in the Betty Mardiros fonds, PR97.488, at the Provincial Archives of Alberta.

22. Anthony Mardiros, unpublished history of WISF, n.d., Betty Mardiros fonds, PR97.488, PAA. An initial "seminar" was held shortly after the creation of WISF, but it was largely a recreational event at which attendees enjoyed summertime activities rather than debating socialist theory. The first formal seminar took place in 1965.

23. RCMP Security Service, Calgary, Communist Party of Canada (Southern Alberta Special Club), 16 November 1965, LAC ATIP A2016-00880, vol. 1, pp. 92–92.

24. C. B. Macpherson, *Democracy in Alberta: Social Credit and the Party System*, 3rd ed. (1953; Toronto: University of Toronto Press, 2013).

25. Finkel, *Social Credit Phenomenon*, 6.

26. For a summary of the various critiques that have been levelled at Macpherson's study of Alberta, see Finkel, *Social Credit Phenomenon*, 6–8.

27. C. B. Macpherson, *The Real World of Democracy: The Massey Lectures Fourth Series* (Toronto: Canadian Broadcasting Corporation, 1966), 65.

28. Macpherson, *Real World*, 66.

29. It should be noted here that while his insights could certainly be received as favouring a socialist outlook, Macpherson was not necessarily a socialist in any obvious sense. Indeed, while he has often been described as a Marxist, or at least a Marxian, recent work has shown that Macpherson's ideological position can equally be understood as a critical one within the liberal tradition. See Ian McKay, "Challenging the Common Sense of Neoliberalism: Gramsci, Macpherson, and the Next Left," *Socialist Register* 54 (2018): 275–97.

30. Program for "The Real World of Democracy," the third summer seminar sponsored by the Woodsworth-Irvine Socialist Fellowship, 1966, file: Woodsworth-Irvine Socialist Fellowship summer seminars, PR2010.0139/0002, PAA.

31. Cheddi Jagan, quoted in "The Real World of Democracy," newspaper clipping, file: *The Commonwealth*, vol. 32, no. 21, vol. 33, no. 1, and Clippings Related to the Woodsworth-Irvine Socialist Fellowship, PR2010.0139/0003, PAA.

32. See, for example, various copies of *The Nutcracker* in the Betty Mardiros fonds, PR97.488, PAA.

33. James Harding, "Liberalism, Social Democracy, and the Danger of Totalitarianism: Paper Presented at the Third Summer Seminar (1966) of the Woodsworth Irvine Socialist Fellowship," 2, file: Woodsworth-Irvine Socialist Fellowship summer seminars, PR2010.0139/0002, PAA.

34. Harding, "Liberalism," 22.

35. Ibid.

36. Brennan, *Good Steward*, 141.

37. Pratt, "Grant Notley," 27.

38. Ibid., 27–28.

39. Elections Alberta, "Candidate Summary of Results: General Election Results—Tuesday, May 23, 1967," http://web.archive.org/web/20080625054137/http://www.elections.ab.ca/pastelections.html#1967.

40. Ken Novakowski, quoted in Pratt, "Grant Notley," 28.

41. "The Waffle Manifesto: For an Independent Socialist Canada (1969)," Socialist History Project, http://www.socialisthistory.ca/Docs/Waffle/WaffleManifesto.htm.

42. Program for "The Radical Reshaping of Canadian Society: Ways and Means," the fifth summer seminar sponsored by the Woodsworth-Irvine Socialist Fellowship, 1968, file: Woodsworth-Irvine Socialist Fellowship summer seminars, PR2010.0139/0002, PAA.

43. Ibid.

44. "The Alberta NDP Convention," author unknown, *The Nutcracker*, vol. 2, no. 3, 2 February 1971, Betty Mardiros fonds, PR97.488, PAA.

45. Pratt, "Grant Notley," 35.

46. "The Alberta NDP Convention," author unknown, *The Nutcracker*, vol. 2, no. 3, 2 February 1971, Betty Mardiros fonds, PR97.488, PAA.

47. Ibid.

48. Nellie Peterson, "Some Thoughts About '71," *The Nutcracker*, vol. 3, no. 1, 1 January 1972, file: Affiliated Organizations—Woodsworth-Irvine Socialist Fellowship publications, *The Nutcracker*, PR1984.178/690, PAA.

49. "Affiliation to the New Democratic Party," author unknown, *The Nutcracker*, vol. 3, no. 2, 1 February 1972, file: Affiliated Organizations—Woodsworth-Irvine Socialist Fellowship publications, *The Nutcracker*, PR1984.178/690, PAA.

50. "Next Meeting of Fellowship," author unknown, *The Nutcracker*, vol. 3, no. 4, 1 April 1972, file: Affiliated Organizations—Woodsworth-Irvine Socialist Fellowship publications, *The Nutcracker*, PR1984.178/690, PAA.

51. Pratt, "Grant Notley," 35.

52. "Resolutions Submitted by the Woodsworth-Irvine Socialist Fellowship for the Seventh Federal Convention of the New Democratic Party—Vancouver, B.C., 1973," Betty Mardiros fonds, PR97.488, PAA.

53. Allan Tupper, "Opportunity and Constraint: Grant Notley and the Modern State," in Pratt, *Socialism and Democracy in Alberta*, 93.

54. "Brief History of the Woodsworth-Irvine Socialist Fellowship" (author unknown), n.d., William Irvine fonds, M-9554-95, Glenbow Archives, Calgary.

55. "What is the Woodsworth-Irvine Socialist Fellowship?," author unknown, *The Nutcracker*, vol. 1, no. 6, p. 1, n.d., file: Betty Mardiros fonds, PR97.488, PAA.

10 Learning Marxism from Tom Flanagan

Left-Wing Activism at the University of Calgary in the Late 1960s and Early 1970s

Larry Hannant

Guerrilla theatre galvanized the city of Calgary in the spring of 1967, inadvertently revealing the depth of the city's conservatism. The visiting San Francisco Mime Troupe had earned a reputation in the United States for biting political theatre. *The Minstrel Show—or Civil Rights in a Cracker Barrel* was its 1967 satire about state repression of the civil rights campaign. The activist-actors had clashed with police often enough in San Francisco and had seen cracker justice in the American South. Invited to Canada by the U of C students' council and the student newspaper, *The Gauntlet*, the troupe got a taste of cracker justice northern style. And Stampede City gave them the bum's rush.

Arriving on 14 March, the actors landed in trouble even before they spoke their first lines. At the U of C campus, someone called city police to report a member of the troupe using marijuana. Orlin Vaughn was arrested and charged with possession of the drug. Two fellow mime troupe members were arrested the next day and, unlike Vaughn, were denied bail. Citing the first arrest, the U of C administration banned the performance planned for the evening of 15 March. The students' council—Good Uncle Ernies—dutifully seconded the closure.[1] When the troupe strode into the U of C dining hall at noon on 15 March to give an impromptu show promoting an off-campus production of the play, campus and city police were called to eject them. Police applied the same force the next day to a meeting that brought together two hundred students and faculty to condemn the ban. A philosophy professor, Zeno Vendler, was manhandled by a campus cop who thought he was one of the actors. "What are you doing?" Vendler demanded. "I lecture here." "Sure, sure," was the reply. "I've heard that one before. Get your instruments and let's go."[2] He and five other professors were taken into custody when they did not obey quickly enough.[3]

Authorities in Calgary clearly did not regard protest as a sacred right. Indeed, the contempt for freedom of assembly by powerful authorities across the province was brutally spelled out in April 1969 by Alberta Supreme Court Chief Justice J. V. H. Milvain. Speaking at a ceremony marking, ironically, Respect for Law Week in Calgary, Milvain condemned the "noisy clamorers after what they call civil rights." Weighing in on the issue, he continued: "The clamorer after civil rights wants the freedom to break your head with his stick. But it is your duty not to go on freedom marches, camp outside legislatures or preach insurrection." A citizen's responsibility, Milvain insisted, was not to protest, and media were negligent when they "played up" complaints about police abuse of human rights.[4]

Calgary had not always been bereft of open demonstrations by dissidents. In the 1930s, like many cities in the West, the city had been the site of frequent and spirited public actions. Usually they were led by the Communist Party of Canada or its various popular-front organizations of married and single men, ex-servicemen, and women. A strike of city relief recipients in the fall of 1934, for instance, was described in the Communist Party's newspaper, *The Worker*, as "the biggest strike of unemployed ever to take place in Canada."[5] But post–World War II prosperity based on oil exploitation and the Cold War suppression of the Communist Party, among other factors, made public demonstrations a relic of the dirty thirties. Scanning Calgary newspapers in the 1950s and early 1960s yields no sign of citizens acting on their right of public assembly. The centuries-old customary right had fallen into abeyance.

A conservative trend also prevailed at U of C, which had gained its autonomy from the University of Alberta only in 1966. In August 1973, as part of an assessment of all university campuses in Canada that was requested by the Royal Canadian Mounted Police Security Service, two Calgary RCMP intelligence officers offered this trenchant summary of the U of C political environment: "As a whole it is reasonable to state that the U. of C. campus is probably the least radical campus in Canada."[6] Those RCMP officers had clearly never visited campuses in the Atlantic region and small Ontario cities, where they would have encountered even less sympathy for progressive causes.[7] Nonetheless, their judgment of U of C seems to be an early affirmation of what has come to be the standard tale about the conservatism that reigned at the campus.

Student conservatism was one thing. Yet by the 1990s, students' right-wing political orientation appeared to have been eclipsed by the ultra-conservative views of a handful of faculty members, who came to be called the Calgary School. Today, the Calgary School has faded from media prominence, so perhaps a word of background is in order. Those who were fortunate enough to sleep through the nasty partisanship of Prime Minister Stephen Harper, which was perhaps the heyday of the Calgary School, will need to be reminded that the unofficial group is composed of like-minded U of C professors who have been remarkably successful in injecting US-style conservatism into politics in Alberta and Canada. Harper, their most eminent protégé, was in on the ground floor at the construction of the Reform Party, was instrumental in merging it with the Progressive Conservative Party of Canada to create a new entity, the Conservative Party, and led that party to a minority and then majority government in Ottawa between 2006 and 2015. Throughout that era, Calgary School co-founder and U of C political science professor Tom Flanagan was the Harper-whisperer. Right-wing commentator Ezra Levant called Flanagan "Don Tomaso," Harper's "master strategist, the godfather."[8]

Now here's the confession that is implicit in the title of this paper. I attended U of C from 1967 to 1974, with the exception of 1969–70 and 1971–72, when I was working and travelling away from Calgary. I completed a Bachelor of Arts in history in 1973 and began the first year of post-graduate work under Calgary School partisan David Bercuson, before leaving the program without completing it. So I was shaped intellectually by two members of the Calgary School. Just not the way Stephen Harper was.

Call it early-onset dementia or advanced nostalgia, but my recollection of the university differs from that of the RCMP. During the time I attended the university, conservatism undeniably was an influential political sentiment among its students. With two exceptions, in 1967–68 and 1969–70, successful candidates for student union elections were invariably youthful conservatives, some of whom would go on to political careers with provincial and national Conservative Parties.

Yet the campus was also marked by two contrary trends. One was a thriving, if small, progressive academic community with a healthy optimism about making change for the better. The second was leftist activism that challenged the status quo and promoted the ideas and practices that we believed would lead to a more just, democratic, and equal world. And that hardy band of U of C activists was engaged not only in trying to change the political views of students. We also set out to sway the political sentiments of the people of Calgary. Seeing ourselves as pretty well red, we were intent on wiping a different streak of red from the back of Calgary's neck.

In his comprehensive history of the generation who came of age in the post–World War II years, Doug Owram contends that university students were the "most privileged of this privileged generation."[9] His generalization is an accurate description of university students in the country and the province at the time. In Alberta in 1966, full-time university student numbers totalled only 16,000, making up 1 percent of the population of 1.5 million. So we did enjoy some advantages not shared by most of the people of the province.

But if we were among the 1 percent, New Leftists at U of C were very different from today's elite. Like me, most leftists came from modest family backgrounds. My family was poor. We survived only thanks to extraordinary labour on the part of my mother. She cooked, cleaned up, and did the laundry for sometimes as many as five male boarders in addition to five kids, did child care for neighbours, and in her spare time sold Regal cards door to door. This supplemented—in fact, probably exceeded—my stepdad's severely constrained income as a lower-level manager in the post office. My fellow leftists at U of C often came from families who also struggled financially. Tom was the son of a widowed rural schoolteacher; Bill a recent immigrant who still retained a slight accent from his childhood in Holland; George, Jim, and Margaret, as well as Bob and Mary Lee, from large families of modest incomes; Pat a former worker in a grocery store who was raising a toddler. Just two or three of some thirty *Gauntlet* staffers owned cars. We walked or bused to school and social events.

Another significant characteristic of the New Left in Calgary was that we were overwhelmingly local; we had sprung from a Calgary upbringing. U of C could not be accused of being a hotbed of "foreign agitators"—radical international students from dangerous places such as Berlin, Birmingham, or Brooklyn whom the media, politicians, and even university administrators like U of A president Walter Johns persisted in blaming for activism.[10] Having grown up in politically conservative Calgary, our radicalism was all the more remarkable. We were children of our times, not of our parents. And we were fortunate that in the half-decade before we graduated from high school the province had created a bona fide—if small—university in the city. The fact that we could walk or bus to classes, faced no dormitory or significant transportation fees, and could live at home (or in improvised co-ops of three to five like-minded folks) made university education possible for children of less-than-prosperous backgrounds.

The university showed some signs of being in tune with the broader progressive academic environment of the day. A scan of the U of C academic calendar from 1967 to 1974 reveals a rising presence of courses with an alternative focus. Beginning from the late '60s, the academic calendar lists courses in the departments of history, political science, philosophy, economics, and sociology and anthropology, among other departments, that reflect the worldwide intellectual shift of the day toward the political left. New history courses in 1970–71, for instance, included "Movements of Social and Economic Protest in Canada," taught by David Bercuson (before he donned, intellectually, a military uniform). Another course dealt with the English Revolution of the seventeenth century and was taught by the Briton David Whitefield, whom the RCMP identified in a 1975 report as a Communist Party of Canada member and "definitely a leading light within the subversive element at the U. of C." (It seemed a surprise to the reporting Mounties that Whitefield's openly communist status—he had run for the party in three elections by 1975—"has not apparently affected his employment.")[11]

Courses in the philosophy department in the 1972–73 calendar included "Marx and Engels" and "The Marxist Tradition." In the Department of Political Science, the course that students had long relied on to let them catch up on lost sleep, "Canadian Political Institutions," was augmented in 1970–71 by new ones guaranteed to catapult them directly to the barricades: "Socialist Theory," "Revolution and Reform," and "Politics, War and Revolution," the last of which included a component on Mao Zedong and the Chinese revolution. The times they were a-changin'.

The socialist theory course was introduced by—and, in 1970–71, co-taught by—a political science professor who, from 1968 to 1976, was intellectually and politically inclined toward the progressive side of the political spectrum. This youthful firebrand was Tom Flanagan. He was, at age twenty-six, four years younger than Berkeley Free Speech leader Jack Weinberg, who coined the phrase "Don't trust anyone over thirty." In class, Flanagan wore a button proclaiming "Stop at Two," announcing that he had heard of the population time bomb. So we thought he might just be a fellow traveller on the road down Highway 61.

In a 2004 *Walrus* magazine article titled "The Man Behind Stephen Harper," Marci McDonald writes that unlike other members of the Calgary School, Flanagan "appears never to have strayed from a conservative path."[12] Flanagan, like me, remembers things differently. About socialism, he recalled in an interview, "I was very intensely interested in the topic [and] read quite widely on it." His leftist book collection of "hundreds of volumes" included the collected works of Mao Zedong. Moreover, while this was, in his words, "partly just an intellectual interest," progressive politics "was also a personal political orientation for a few years."[13] Indeed, the period that for Flanagan ended around 1976 included at least one active foray into Alberta provincial politics. In the March 1975 provincial election, Flanagan helped to distribute campaign literature for the NDP candidate in the Calgary Foothills riding. Alas, Flanagan's assistance did not help Ken Gee much. Taking just 8 percent of the vote, he was decisively beaten by a Conservative.

In 1970–71, I took "Socialist Theory," a political science class co-taught by Flanagan and Bob Ware, a Marxist philosophy professor. Significantly, Ware recalls that Flanagan suggested, perhaps in 1969, that they teach it together, reflecting Flanagan's left-curiosity.[14] I began the year-long course when I was twenty, having had before then only a rudimentary introduction to alternative political theory. Like several other budding leftists at U of C, some of my early introduction to socialist ideas came from one of the founders of the Calgary School.

Now, I'm hardly a brilliant Marxist. Still, you can imagine my shock recently when I checked my U of C transcript. I got a C in "Socialist Theory"! (There are some, I admit, who would consider that to be a pretty accurate assessment of my grasp of Marxism.) And that grade might actually have exaggerated my knowledge of socialism. We'll never know, because Flanagan and Ware took to heart one of the then-current challenges to academic convention. This related to the always-sensitive question of grading. On the first day of classes, they set out the conditions of the course. The deal was that the entire grade for the course would be determined by an essay—but even if you didn't submit one, you'd be guaranteed a C. You could do more work and improve your grade. Of course, only keeners would do that. I was no capitalist-lackey keener. I militantly submitted no essay and got a C. It pulled down my grade point average, but I knew revolution would erupt before any of us graduated anyway.

But let's probe into what lay beneath that grading innovation. It was a concession to leftist criticism of one of the fundamentals of the education system. We viewed the grading structure in universities as a perverse reflection of the inequities of the capitalist system. It pays workers according to a class-biased hierarchy. The hidebound university grading system that distributed marbles according to an A+-to-F pattern mimicked capitalist wage inequity. It had to go. In "Socialist Theory," it did go. In a small way, both students and professors in the class saw themselves as raising a little hell.

At this point you are probably thinking that the introduction at U of C of courses in Marxism, protest, and revolution sprang from the same phenomenon that allowed the Calgary Stampeders to get to the Grey Cup game in 1968 after an absence of two decades—that's right: imports. Like many universities in the late 1960s and early 1970s, U of C was hiring professors as fast as cash could make its way down the highway from Edmonton. In Calgary's case, the need to acquire new faculty was made even more intense by the fact that in 1960 the campus had just two buildings perched out on what one graduate of 1962 described as "a blasted plain" where "whenever you opened your mouth outside you got grit in your teeth."[15] From that hapless start, U of C expanded energetically (and also laid down a lot of sod to cut the grit). Enrolment at U of C almost doubled from 1968 to 1971 (5,000 to 9,200). Acquiring faculty was urgent, and there were not many to be had in Canada. By the early 1970s, 45 percent of all U of C profs were born outside of Canada. Some 46 percent of the full professors were either American or British. Inevitably, those profs brought with them cutting-edge political perspectives and theories from the world. They used those ideas to assault what the radical U of C sociology professor Clement Blakeslee described as "the rigid fundamentalist mentality of the Bible belt" that still prevailed in Alberta.[16] So although the troublemaking students who stirred things up in Calgary were rarely "outside agitators," some faculty members were.

Certainly the RCMP intelligence officers who wrote the comprehensive 1973 report thought that foreigners were the source of radicalism at U of C. They argued that "the main instigators of radicalism are usually 'import' to this locale." The authors added, "Whenever any activity becomes apparent it usually involves basically one of the same individuals."[17] They then named Ware, the American-born philosophy prof who had co-taught "Socialist Theory."

It might be tempting to conclude that while at least some U of C profs— many of them foreigners—were radicals, the U of C students themselves were conservative. The idea has some merit. In the spring of 1973, U of C students elected a born-again Christian student union president who assembled a slate of candidates for executive positions based entirely on students who had Found Jesus. Yet, radical candidates were at times successful in student politics. Pat Pattison, who describes himself now as "one of the long-haired guys that talked about things that were off campus and . . . international," was elected student president in 1969.[18] Partly because of Pattison's influence, U of C students remained within the Canadian Union of Students (CUS), the national student organization that was damned by authorities in 1968–69 as a hotbed of anti-war and Marxist-inspired student agitators. U of C's membership in CUS ended only with the organization itself, in late 1969.

It should also be noted that by the time the RCMP issued its comprehensive report on the U of C campus in August 1973, much of the heat was gone from the youth revolution everywhere. Owram's *Born at the Right Time* argues that already "by the beginning of 1970, the great national movements were either gone or on their way out." By 1973, when the RCMP conducted its national survey of student radicalism, Owram adds, "the number of incidents of protest occupations [on university campuses had] sank into insignificance."[19] Little wonder that a Christian fundamentalist could become student president at U of C that year.

Given the conservative bent of so many elected student politicians, the organizational home of most radical students at U of C was *The Gauntlet*. Newspaper radicalism represented a pattern duplicated at many campuses across the country.[20] The RCMP understood and made use of that tendency, keeping files on student newspapers, rating them according to their political tendency—"moderately radical" for the University of Toronto *Varsity*; "Maoist" for the *McGill Daily*—and using them as a key source of information to keep tabs on activists.[21] New Left–inspired students dominated the U of C paper from 1967, when the leftist Kevin Peterson became editor, through to 1975, with a break of part of one year when the student union closed the paper and brought in a temporary replacement edited by a council member who set out to correct what council claimed to be the paper's inflammatory leftist content. That brief moment aside, through the late 1960s and early 1970s *The Gauntlet* was the U of C headquarters of both oppositional journalism and oppositional politics. That political influence was felt on the campus, into the city, and even nationally. *Gauntlet* writers were well regarded for their competence and leftism by other student papers, who elected Peterson as Canadian University Press president in 1967, George Russell as national bureau chief in 1969, and Mick Lowe as Ontario regional fieldworker in 1973. Indeed, it was Russell who stamped CUP's radicalism on the minds of a wider public in February 1970, when he delivered the organization's statement to the Special Senate Committee on Mass Media. A *Globe and Mail* reporter disparaged it as "a long Marxist-toned dissertation" that annoyed the senators.[22]

As one of those activist-journalists, I recall two cases that illustrate the nature of the political engagement that either was rooted at *The Gauntlet* or was initiated by *Gauntlet* staffers. One occurred on 16 October 1970, when U of C students spearheaded one of the very few protests in the country against the government of Canada's use of the War Measures Act (WMA) to suppress Québec nationalism. Early on that morning, the federal government had declared the WMA in effect and outlawed the Front de libération du Québec (FLQ). In Calgary, agitation against that decision began at Speaker's Corner in the U of C Students' Union Building. By mid-morning, just hours after learning the news, students were engaged in a spirited debate about the justice or injustice of invoking the WMA. The government claimed it was necessary to prevent an "apprehended insurrection" by the FLQ, aimed at the takeover of the governments of Québec and Canada. But many students weren't buying it, and an intense debate over the WMA and Québec nationalism erupted. The animated discussion raged, at times with pushing and shoving over control of the microphone; one former student went so far as to call them "fistfights," but argument rather than violence was the norm.[23] Students on campus sent competing telegrams to politicians and authorities in Ottawa that alternatively deplored and praised the use of the WMA.[24]

The democratic roughhousing went on until early afternoon, when several of us took over the desks and copy tables at the *Gauntlet* office to prepare signs slamming the use of the WMA and commenting on politics in Québec and the country. Our signs were direct, often blunt, maybe a bit over the top. One displayed the demand for "Québec Libre." Others read "Ho Ho Ho Chi Minh, The FLQ Is Gonna Win"; "The FLQ Are the Outlaws, but Trudeau Is the Bad Guy"; "We Support the FLQ"; "Welcome to Canada, the Friendly Police State." We set out to take our outrage over the use of this extraordinary legislation into the city streets.

At that time, students could borrow megaphones from the audiovisual office of the university, and I signed one out. We spread the word at the university and beyond, piled into cars about 2:30 p.m., and arrived at the centre of Calgary, the Eighth Avenue Mall, for a demonstration. The *Calgary Herald* had been alerted, as had the police. Under the conditions of martial law, which applied across Canada, we expected that police would suppress our demonstration. Expressing agreement with the FLQ was illegal. Arrest was possible, and as we made our way downtown, when one of us mentioned that she had a bag of marijuana in her pocket, we urged her to dump it. Sure enough, plainclothes and uniformed police were already in place when we arrived on the mall.

About thirty students had set out from the campus. For a few moments we milled about indecisively. Finally, armed with the megaphone, I stood up on a cement planter and declared myself in support of the FLQ. (My reckless assertion was based on little knowledge, but I had heard the FLQ Manifesto read on CBC radio a couple of days before, and the sheer anti-capitalist bravado of it was utterly exhilarating.) Remarkably, the expected police shutdown did not happen. What had begun as a small demonstration quickly flared into a spontaneous mass democracy event that, according to the *Calgary Herald* report, included three hundred people. Among the crowd were youth and high school students who happened to be on the mall on a Friday afternoon and who took up our rambunctious anti-authoritarian impudence. Bob Mercer spoke about political activists Pierre Vallières and Charles Gagnon, jailed Felquistes who had been joined by the many lawyers, academics, poets, singers, labour leaders, and other Québec activists arrested early that morning. (Mercer, born and raised in Calgary, lived at that time in Vancouver, where he was one of the radicals with the New West Co-op, a founder of the FART Party [Front for Anarchist Revolutionary Terrorism—slogan "FART Now"] and co-founder of the Vancouver Street Theatre Company.) After more than an hour on the street, and with darkness approaching, on Bob's suggestion we concluded with what he called a Yippie Parade Drill. We formed a circle and, on the order "Forward march," proceeded to advance on one another, laughing uproariously.

Rough as it was, with elements of simplistic analysis, emotional excess, and *opéra bouffe*, the anti-WMA demonstration in Calgary was a singular event in Canada. Looking at newspaper accounts, there appear to have been only two other anti-WMA demonstrations on 16 October: one at the University of Ottawa, and the other at York University in Toronto. But only in Calgary did university students take their anger at the use of the WMA from the campus to the heart of their city. In a small way, U of C students engaged the city of Calgary in a mass democratic exercise that dared to take on repressive government power.

The demonstration was remarkable also because it took place in a city where the right of public assembly was, in 1970, still rarely used and where police power was arbitrarily exercised in public and private. In 1967, for instance, I was sitting in a downtown coffee house with a fellow longhair, trying to look as cool as possible drinking rank coffee from a Styrofoam cup, when plainclothes police swept through the place, demanding identification from everyone. When they came to me, I refused, saying I did not have to provide it. A cop lifted me by the front of my jacket, marched me outside to a waiting patrol car, and took me to police headquarters, where I was searched and interrogated for an hour before being released. No charge, of course.

In 1968, journalist-activists at *The Gauntlet* were involved in another public act of oppositional journalism and civic political involvement. Calgary in the 1960s was growing rapidly, and development was particularly intense in the downtown core, where high-rise office towers and apartments were increasingly pushing out the single-family homes of relatively poor people in core districts such as Eau Claire, Victoria Park, and Beltline. Taking on the issue, *The Gauntlet* published a special edition to expose a cozy arrangement, with the land-owning corporation Eau Claire Estates Ltd. at the heart of it, working in conjunction with the city to carve out an exclusive park for the rich.

As part of their journalistic investigations, several reporters at the *Calgary Herald*, some of whom had been student journalists at *The Gauntlet*, had come across a disturbing plan to reshape the downtown core. The proposal by developers was to get official approval from the city to create a multi-lane freeway-style road on the north side of the downtown, cutting through the long-established neighbourhood of Eau Claire and separating Prince's Island in the Bow River from the city. (At that time there was no pedestrian overpass across the Bow on the north side of the island, so the island could not be accessed from that direction.) The developers would then build luxury accommodation on the park edge of the new freeway. Wealthy residents would enjoy exclusive access to the park, the riff-raff kept isolated on the south side of the freeway. The scheme would generate huge profits for land-owning corporations, especially Eau Claire Estates Ltd. What was being called urban renewal, *The Gauntlet* editorial in the supplement charged, "is nothing less than rape."[25] Rape of the poor, that is, by both private developers and the city.

The *Herald* refused to publish the material, so it was brought to *The Gauntlet*, and with additions and photos by *Gauntlet* staffers, the paper printed an eight-page "Urban Renewal" supplement. More than that, in order to maximize its effect in the city, we published several thousand extra copies of the supplement and took it to the streets at the Eighth Avenue Mall, where staffers handed it out free to passersby to bring the issue to the attention of citizens. In the supplement, *The Gauntlet* appealed to Calgarians to support "a broad public examination of urban renewal." At least for the fourteen named directors of Eau Claire Estates Ltd.—including Max Bell, publisher of the Calgary *Albertan*, the city's second daily newspaper—it was a wake-up call about the power of the press. Even if this press was run by students.

While assembling in the *Gauntlet* office before setting out for downtown with our bundles, the staffers who had volunteered for the public distribution felt more than a little apprehension. Was it legal to gather on the mall and hand out provocative material such as this? Should we be ready for arrest? We were the most engaged activists in the city, yet few of us had put ourselves on the line in this way before. And most of us had never seen anyone else using public space to advance a political cause. Calgary was happy once a year to have the Stampede parade take over the streets but not keen on seeing oppositional political ideas voiced there.

Initiatives by young people and students in the late 1960s broke that taboo. This is one of the overlooked legacies of the New Left in Calgary. Those demonstrations and public actions of 1968 and 1970, coupled with events such as the twice-yearly anti–Vietnam War marches that began in late 1967, helped to advance a popular right to take to the streets. In the era before the Charter of Rights and Freedoms, the 1960s Bill of Rights had proclaimed that "freedom of assembly and association" existed in Canada.[26] But authorities and police in the city cared little for legislated rights. Indeed, the chief justice of the Alberta Supreme Court believed that a dutiful citizen shunned demonstrations, parades, marches. In challenging this official contempt for a long-held customary right, young people reminded Calgary of its own militant history and reaffirmed a right that had been neglected for over twenty-five years.

NOTES

1. "'Frisco Mime Troupe Runs into Difficulty,'" *Calgary Herald*, 15 March 1967, 33.
2. "Students Protest Police Action," *Globe and Mail*, 17 March 1967, 29.
3. "Mimers Cause Campus Turmoil," and Lynn Rach, "U. of C. Students Protest Paternalism," *Calgary Herald*, 16 March 1967, 1–2.
4. J. V. H. Milvain, quoted in "The Real Threat to Order," *Globe and Mail*, 10 April 1969, 6.
5. *The Worker*, 17 November 1934, 1.
6. RCMP Security Service, Calgary, "University of Calgary," 28 August 1973, Library and Archives Canada (hereafter LAC), Access to Information Act (hereafter ATIP), A2016-00880, vol. 5, p 560.
7. For instance, Steve Hewitt reports that, in 1969, the RCMP believed there was not a single individual at Waterloo Lutheran University who merited being considered a subversive. Hewitt, *Spying 101: The RCMP's Secret Activities at Canadian Universities, 1917–1997* (Toronto: University of Toronto Press, 2002), 140.
8. Marci McDonald, "The Man Behind Stephen Harper," *The Walrus*, 12 October 2004, updated 28 July 2016, https://thewalrus.ca/the-man-behind-stephen-harper/.
9. Doug Owram, *Born at the Right Time: A History of the Baby-Boom Generation* (Toronto: University of Toronto Press, 1997), 175.
10. Murray Williamsen, "A Letter About Dr. Walter Johns," *The Gateway*, 11 February 1969, 5.
11. RCMP Security Service, Calgary, "University of Calgary," 17 November 1975, LAC ATIP A2016-00880, p. 523, vol. 5.
12. McDonald, "Man Behind Stephen Harper."
13. Tom Flanagan, interview by the author, 22 May 2016, telephone.
14. Bob Ware, interview by the author, 9 May 2016, telephone.
15. Alan Arthur, quoted in Valerie Berenyi, "A Campus Transformation," *UCalgary Alumni Magazine*, Spring 2016, 24.

16. Clement Blakeslee, "Alberta—the Not So Quiet Revolution," *The Gauntlet*, 26 October 1966, 4.
17. RCMP Security Service, Calgary, "University of Calgary," 28 August 1973, 561.
18. Pat Pattison, interview by the author, 20 May 2016, telephone.
19. Owram, *Born at the Right Time*, 298–99.
20. At the University of Regina in 1969, for instance, the board of governors authorized the university administration to halt the collection of fees to the student council over the latter's refusal to muzzle the student newspaper, *The Carillon*. "Coercion Applied in Regina," *The Gauntlet*, 15 January 1969, 1.
21. Hewitt, *Spying 101*, 178.
22. Farrell Crook, "Marxist Jargon Used by Student Press Editors Baffles Senate Committee," *Globe and Mail*, 11 February 1970, 8.
23. George Fetherling, "Man of a Hundred Thousand Books," *Geist*, Spring 2011, 61.
24. Bunny Wright, "Speaker's Corner," *Calgary Herald*, 17 October 1970, 51. The *Herald* relegated the protest to its Family Living section, a recent renaming of what for decades had been called the Women's Section. Presumably protest was an important family value to cultivate.
25. "Editorial, Special Housing Supplement," *The Gauntlet*, 11 December 1968, H1.
26. *Canadian Bill of Rights*, SC 1960, c. 44, Government of Canada Justice Laws Website, http://laws-lois.justice.gc.ca/eng/acts/C-12.3/page-1.html.

11

Drop In, Hang Out, and Crash

Outreach Programs for Transient Youth and War Resisters in Edmonton

Baldwin Reichwein and PearlAnn Reichwein

Our family crossed the country in a Volkswagen bus in 1967 and in 1968. Many young hitchhikers flashed us the peace sign on our moves between Edmonton and Halifax. In 1969, I (Baldwin) returned from graduate studies to work for Alberta's Department of Public Welfare, managing the delivery of social services in South Edmonton. The office was located in an old bowling alley near the Calgary Trail, and I enjoyed walking home for lunch with my wife and family near the University of Alberta (U of A). We lived in the neighbourhood of Garneau, next door to Alberta-born Vernon ("Vern") Wishart, his American wife, Johanna ("Jo") Wishart, and their children.[1] The Wisharts had recently returned from living in India for several years. Reverend Vern Wishart was the minister at Garneau United Church and wore a not-so-conservative leather jacket even as I reverted back to shirt-and-tie after grad school. The pastor and the public servant soon discovered that they had something in common, namely, the welfare of young people. The public servant and his family soon saw—and to an extent shared in—the street ministry work by the pastor at Garneau United Church.

In the summertime, I (PearlAnn) liked walking with my friend and neighbour Karen Wishart to 7-Eleven for Slurpees and then to Garneau United Church to hang out in the basement with musicians playing guitars. My family often went to nearby St. Joseph's College chapel on campus, where everyone sat cross-legged on the carpet for Sunday mass, and I played in a children's tambourine band led by a nun. Afterward, we would pass university students and other folks as they sat outside drinking locally roasted Java Jive coffee or smoked in the new Students' Union Building (SUB). And it was not unusual for our neighbour Mrs. Wishart to call, asking us to have one or two young Americans join us at our dinner table. This was the beat of everyday neighbourhood life in Garneau, a distinctive university community of people and ideas.

Wandering the world was a passion of youth in the late 1960s and early 1970s. Tens of thousands of hitchhikers and travellers hit the road to cross Canada. At the same time, well over one hundred thousand young Americans crossed the border north, compelled by the politics of the Vietnam War. Historian Linda Mahood describes fifty thousand hitchhikers passing through Calgary in 1971, and historian Ben Bradley points to Banff preparing for more than twenty thousand transient youth in 1970, many traveling on the Trans-Canada Highway.[2] Canada had not seen such numbers of youth on the move since the Great Depression. Travelling far from home was part of the sixties' generation for many reasons, as author Myrna Kostash makes clear:

> I turned twenty-one, and threw myself into the great learning about camaraderie, war, imperialism, rock n' roll, the Godhead, vagabonding, lust, appetite and woman power; and I consider myself to have been young in a period when the vision of the good and the true was up for grabs. In seeking our re-vision, thousands and thousands of us wandered very far from "home, from our families, our communities, the values with which we were bred, the ideals with which we were entrusted, the country we were to inherit."[3]

Travellers from both sides of the border converged in mass migration across Canada. Many arrived in Edmonton lacking accommodation, community, and livelihood. A member of city council was openly hostile to young transients even as certain churches and civic employees demonstrated leadership and made efforts to serve them. In August 1968, at a council meeting considering support for a teen drop-in centre, alderman Julia Kiniski did more than just reject the idea. Casting her eye over the seventy-five youths who had packed the council chamber to back the plan, she stated "Why have a centre for the dirty devils we see around here? They're not like me, at least I wash myself."[4]

This study focuses on Garneau as a neighbourhood microcosm of community support services offered to transient hitchhikers and war resisters in 1969.[5] Garneau United Church and St. George's Anglican Church joined forces in ecumenical spirit to initiate a grassroots church-funded project that responded to multiple needs arising from the tide of young people flooding into Edmonton. They opened a drop-in centre in Garneau United that was visited by approximately five thousand young people from Canada, the United States, and offshore. Visitors were described as "by and large intelligent, middle or upper class kids and usually close to the drug scene or 'hippy' scene."[6] In this way, two relatively traditional church communities came face to face with highly untraditional, unique groups of strangers. Community outreach was also joined by more public welfare supports. Together the two churches challenged conventions and raised the bar for compassion and inclusive social services.

Varsity Neighbourhoods and Churches

At the turn of the twentieth century, many arrivals to the city of Strathcona (which later merged with Edmonton) came by the Calgary Trail and the Canadian Pacific Railway's spur line. Strathcona and Garneau were among the earliest residential neighbourhoods south of the North Saskatchewan River. Their craftsman-style houses and neighbourhood churches on elm-lined streets accented a varsity character around the U of A campus from the early 1900s.

Garneau United (established 1938) and St. George's Anglican (1955) were, and still are, neighbourhood churches close to the university.[7] Their congregations customarily interacted with the neighbourhood and varsity populations, both formally and informally. In the 1960s, the university began to expropriate homes in North Garneau for campus expansion. The city rezoned Garneau for high rises and approved new outlying suburbs, which had, according to a Garneau history, "a profound effect on the community and the life of the congregation. Many church families moved. The community began to change from a more permanent family residential area to rented residences, student dwellings, and high rise apartments. . . . Garneau would need to see itself in a different role than as a residential congregation."[8] Older neighbourhoods like Garneau were shifting with demographics and urban changes in a city that, in 1969, had a population of 422,418.[9] Garneau

United considered folding as its congregation aged and waned but decided instead to seek new ways of going forward.[10]

Before Reverend Wishart arrived in 1968, the Edmonton Presbytery of the United Church had determined that Garneau United, located at 11148 84th Avenue, was set in "a rapidly changing community" and had a vital role to play there. Three areas were chosen as a focus for its ministry: "1) serving the pastoral needs of the congregation, 2) serving the university in cooperation with the chaplains and 3) an experimental ministry to the surrounding community with particular concern for apartment dwellers. It was further suggested that relations with St. George's Anglican be encouraged." Garneau United, despite declining church membership, was attracting "people who [were] desirous of Christian fellowship within a community of believers who see God's mission primarily in relation to the world."[11] In earlier decades, outreach undertaken by such Protestant church congregations was considered part of the Social Gospel that applied Christian ethics to social problems in the community.

The Reverend Bern (Harry Bernard) Barrett was the minister of nearby St. George's Anglican Church, at 11733 87th Avenue, which by 1968 was also in flux. A history of the district written in 1971 noted that the previous two years had seen a decisive repositioning of the church from a traditional orientation to a focus on "understanding our mission in relation to the community around us. One example of this has been the pioneering work of Garneau, in cooperation with St. George's, among transient youth, this counterculture, and the drug scene. The Coffee House in Ramsay Hall is another example of seeing our mission in relation to the community."[12] Both ministers and their congregations near the U of A campus were also aware of the anti–Vietnam War movement and welcomed war resisters in their midst.

Specific church communities engaged with transient youth and war resisters. By doing so, they bucked conservative attitudes in their respective church bureaucracies, government ranks, and the community at large. The new drop-in project unexpectedly put congregations in the vanguard to serve the unique, sometimes overlapping, populations of transient youth and war resisters in 1969.

The Drop-In Program and Its Spinoffs

The two church communities developed a summer program for young people that operated out of Garneau United Church, hiring twenty-two-year-old Evelyn Battell, a second-year theology student at St. Stephen's College, to manage it with volunteer help.[13] At a September 1969 meeting of the Official Board of Garneau United, she reported that the drop-in program had started up in May and was initially attended by about one hundred young people. During June and July, another influx arrived, a large number of them "close to the drug scene," she said. "Numerous emergency situations were encountered," she added—typically related to drug use, sexual activity, and money.[14] "Churches on the Southside were contacted, and as a result a 'plug-in' was set up to facilitate access to professional services such as legal and medical services."[15] Asked for help by Garneau United, Metropolitan United Church, located four blocks away, sent a staff member to the Garneau Drop-In to coordinate a "crash-pad" service that provided overnight shelter in private homes because "often some of the young people who came to the Drop-In had no place to sleep except the streets."[16] Garneau United and the University Hospital Emergency Ward, across the street, collaborated closely to assist youth who were "coming down" from drug use.[17] In total, the Garneau Drop-In had five thousand youth from Canada, the United States, and a few from overseas pass through its doors from mid May to August 1969.[18]

Activities at the drop-in were largely youth driven, by kids who "seemed or felt alienated from society," Battell wrote, adding,

> The kids at Drop-In spent their time talking, dancing, listening to music and meeting new people. Sometimes projects happened such as seminars with doctors, lawyers, teachers and police. Every weekend there were dances with a live band, or a folksinger. Once a fellow read some poetry and one weekend we sponsored a rock festival at Mayfair Park (it got rained out). The staff, Dr. C. F. Johnston—Church history professor and interested member of Garneau congregation—and myself and the ministers of the two churches, spent their time talking to kids who had various problems or just needed to talk.[19]

The U of A student newspaper reported that Mi'kmaq singer Willie Dunn was giving a concert, singing "Indian protest songs" at the Garneau drop-in on 21 November 1969, with proceeds from the fifty-cent admission to go to the Native People's Defence Fund.[20]

Edmonton police on the scene were not always open or tolerant. The churches noted that "hip kids" and transients were "hassled" by the police at the Garneau drop-in on at least one occasion during its first summer.[21] In August, Battell saw fourteen-year-old "delinquents" and older motorcycle gang members, between 19 and 25 years old, converge on the drop-in, as she later reported to the church's board meeting. It was not a loving spoonful: "The 'Hippie' group did not want to be associated with the newcomers and left."[22] Battell indicated that the newcomers were "somewhat rougher, and the staff felt they did not have the resources or insight to deal with this group and this led to closure of the project about a week ahead of time."[23] Yet the drop-in program was deemed to be a success, and the joint committee of the two congregations recommended that it continue through the winter months, on weekends only.[24]

Garneau's drop-in project had several spinoffs. One was Metropolitan United's "crash-pad" program, which arranged for overnight "bed and breakfast" accommodations in private family homes for one to three nights. A total of thirty-six homes provided space for 232 young people to "crash" for a total occupation of 481 overnight stays from May to August of 1969.[25] According to a May 1970 proposal for a crisis centre, the crash-pad program "brought 'hip kids' and 'straights' into contact. For the most part this was a positive experience and overcame some of the apprehensions on both sides."[26] Crash pads later led to hostels with names such as "The White House," "The Kremlin," and "Fallen Arches." Hostels were operated by young people with minimum interference by establishment types. The "Heads-Up, Plug-In" referral project focused on legal, medical, psychiatric, and job counselling advice and resources for youth who found regular channels to be closed or difficult to deal with. It was sponsored by Knox United, Holy Trinity Anglican, the Moravian Church, and Strathcona Baptist Church congregations, as well as the YMCA, to extend responsive community-driven services.[27]

Responding to some Edmontonians' uncertainty about the transients and the drop-in services, in July 1969 the *Edmonton Journal* carried a feature about both Garneau's drop-in and the work being carried out by several Southside churches and the YMCA. "People were equating long hair and sandals with hideous diseases of the body and mind," it reported. "Nothing could be farther from the truth." The youth, ranging in age from thirteen to twenty-three, were often students, although "some are drop-outs, others are transients, a few are young people on a cheap trip and others are draft dodgers from the U.S., who usually need jobs and friends." It was a generation, pointed out one crash-pad coordinator, often viewed "with suspicion and animosity" and whose members "feel they don't wish to fit into our society."[28] The *Journal* also wrote about an initiative that summer by Edmonton's YMCA to help shed its "square image" and offer community services to youth.[29]

Occasional letters to the editor illustrated the controversy surrounding these efforts to work with street youth. One letter writer saw hippies as drug addicts and deviants. In contrast, a response from Dawson Creek, British Columbia, asked,

> Is 'Hippie' just a convenient term to call any individual under 30 whom you neither like nor understand? Many so called hippies are merely young and uncertain teenaged children who turn to the trappings and mannerisms of hippiedom, because it's something new and different from the routine of school and home life. [. . .] In other words, it's a fad for many which they will outgrow.[30]

Meanwhile, the province of Alberta was also stepping up its public service role. In 1966, the Social Credit government had passed a new Child Welfare Act and the Preventive Social Service (PSS) Act. The province's Department of Public Welfare then took over child welfare functions from the municipalities, while the latter focused on administering or enabling the delivery of preventive social services such as supports to youth. In the final decade of the Social Credit era, Alberta was flush with revenue from natural resources and also began to benefit from new fifty-fifty cost-sharing under the Canada Assistance Plan (CAP) that existed from 1966 to 1996. With strong public revenues and progressive deputy ministers, the provincial government was reforming itself and changes with cost-sharing.[31] In 1969, the province supported the City of Edmonton's social services department as it broke ground in a number of areas. Mayor Ivor Dent referred to the city's "total welfare package," an integrated approach to delivering social services and a community-based project later known as West 10.[32] Consequently, Garneau United Church became aware of grant funding the city had available for projects concerning youth.[33]

In preparation for an expected influx of young travellers in 1970, the Joint Committee of Garneau United and St. George's Anglican, supported by city centre churches, developed plans for a crisis centre. At a May meeting, the board of Garneau United decided that the city should be approached with a request for financial assistance, in an effort "to secure the necessary funds to carry out the project to fulfillment."[34] The proposal for the crisis centre mentioned that some five thousand young people had "passed through" the door of Garneau's drop-in program in 1969. In addition, it identified several existing services for youths, such as the Downtown Teen Centre, overnight accommodation at the YMCA and YWCA, crashing and crisis places, and ways for medical, legal, and drug emergency services to maintain contact with one another.[35] The city received the proposal and allocated financial assistance for crisis services in 1970 to be offered through the existing downtown teen centre, Inner Spirit. Given her earlier work at Garneau United, Battell was hired as director of the centre. Ties to the church communities, especially Garneau, were maintained. Several individual congregation members still continued to take in and work with young people following referral from the crisis line.[36]

Garneau United's role shifted compared to its first summer in 1969. The church's annual report for 1970 noted that its "concern for dialogue and bridge building between the generations can now be taken up with real seriousness. The Barricade Coffee House in Ramsay Hall which opened in December is we hope a move in that direction."[37] The intent was to create a space where youth were accepted. Garneau's drop-in project also served as a catalyst for other church communities and private and public services to become involved with the transient movement.

In the midst of both transient youth and war resister migrations, the Alberta government's social programs also transformed during the 1960s. Municipal and senior levels of government became more amenable to extending funding and services to young people, as the role of the province expanded. The province had a mandate to respond under legislation to children and youth deemed at risk and in need of protection and, by the late 1960s, was the sole authority for child protection services. For a few summers, one or two provincial social workers functioned on special assignment to assist transient youth at the street level, until youth transiency trends slowed toward the mid-1970s. Regionally, a new Alberta Department of Youth deployed staff to reach out to youth in the late 1960s. This department's wide focus on conventional recreation and leadership development (e.g., 4H Clubs, Outward Bound) was more for local youth than for transients, but "drug misuse" was also an emphasis, as were drop-in centres, seen as a new approach to "dealing with the problems of youth."[38]

Nationally, the issue of transient youth stirred enough concern that the Pierre Trudeau government commissioned the Transient Youth Inquiry in 1969, to investigate why thousands of young people were hitchhiking across the country. It heard a range of submissions, from those in support of youth travellers seeing Canada to those condemning them as moral and social deviants. Temporary youth hostels were recommended as a solution and subsequently received federal funding. Trudeau also saw youth travel as a means to build national unity. But transiency also spurred action by those keen to stamp it out. "Canada's youth hitchhiking 'craze' declined in the mid-1970s," according to Mahood, "because anti-hitchhiking groups put pressure on the police and RCMP to levy fines and enforce by-laws banning hitchhiking in towns and cities."[39] Yet certain church, non-government, and government services in Alberta had provided substantial support to meet basic needs for a sizable cohort of transient youth and developed a system of community-driven support programs.

Taking in Young Americans

Prominent among the transients were American war resisters, who had refused to serve in the US war on Vietnam and moved to Canada. The Vietnam War and war resisters were controversial for governments and church organizations. Canada initially took an ambiguous position on war resisters entering the country, distinguishing between draft resisters and deserters. Draft resisters were welcomed, because, according to David Churchill, they were "the very type of immigrant—young, middle-class and educated—that the government wanted." Beginning in May 1969, the government also allowed deserters to enter Canada, as any other potential immigrant. In so doing, Canada "went against the common practice of its military allies." However, African Americans, working class, or less educated deserters had more difficulty seeking entry and were often denied at the border.[40]

In the summer of 1969, the *Edmonton Journal* reported that five hundred "draft dodgers" lived in the city, and the number of arrivals picked up as Canadian immigration officials no longer questioned the draft status of landed immigrant applicants. It was "easier to get into the country" with Edmonton as a destination, compared to some other places in Canada, and the city had good job opportunities. "Getting jobs is no problem and people are sympathetic," said a young Californian man resisting the draft. "Here people actually say they would do it too if they were Americans." The Alexander Ross Society, composed primarily of university students, had taken up the task of providing "temporary assistance and lodging as well as advice to draft dodgers who come here." U of A's Students for a Democratic University noted that its Vancouver counterpart was "swamped" with war resisters and wanted to contact more in Edmonton "who might be able to help others moving into the city."[41]

In the United Church of Canada, the call to help war resisters created controversy, with clergy and congregation members coming out on opposite sides.[42] Locally, members of the board of Garneau United Church in November 1969 expressed concern about "the matter of draft dodgers and our responsibility as a congregation."[43] The decision was made to reach out to take in Americans. The crash-pad, drop-in, and plug-in programs enabled congregations and other local residents to put compassionate principles into action. Nearby neighbours such as Mary and Fred Engelmann—a social worker and political science professor, respectively, both from the United States—also opened their doors to shelter war resisters.[44]

The U of A campus and the neighbouring Garneau district were a local hub for anti-war protest and the peace movement as well. For example, in 1969, a Vietnam War "Moratorium Rally" was held on campus and drew a capacity crowd to a film and panel discussion at the theatre in the Students' Union Building. The next day, 15 November, a crowd of six hundred gathered at the Alberta legislature for a worldwide peace rally and march to City Hall held in conjunction with the historic anti-Vietnam war demonstration of as many as half a million protesters in Washington, D.C. Reverend David Crawley, of All Saints' Anglican Cathedral in downtown Edmonton, spoke at the rally and indicated that, as a Christian, he could not support the war in Vietnam, which he felt was unjust.[45]

Although city residents showed considerable readiness to help war resisters and support peace activism, critics were also present. Those who wanted the newcomers gone saw an opportunity in October 1970, when the government of Canada imposed the War Measures Act (WMA) and suspended civil liberties during the Front de libération du Québec crisis; the

Edmonton chief of police, for instance, indicated that "he might use the act to run the draft-dodgers out of town." The effect on war resisters and their allies, Kostash observes, "was not a little paranoia; people huddled in their houses, too frightened even to talk politics on the phone."[46] The mayors of Toronto and Vancouver also considered the WMA as a potential tool to clear out draft dodgers and hippies in their respective cities. Additionally, RCMP surveillance of Canadian university campuses and local communities included collecting information on resisters and sharing it with the FBI.[47]

Church congregations and others understood that powerful conservative figures did not look favourably on aiding war resisters and transient youth. However, despite the controversy and debate in Canada, the board of Garneau United Church was clear in encouraging its congregation members to open their doors and welcome them: "We commend the work of those in our congregation who have taken young American immigrants into their homes and helped them to adjust to Canadian life."[48]

Conclusion

Garneau United Church and St. George's Anglican Church communities in conservative Alberta became involved, by choice and intent, with controversial mass migrations of transient youth hitchhikers and American war resisters in the late 1960s and early in the next decade. Garneau's drop-in program operated in a grey area of ambiguous laws, policies, and practices concerning the two movements. Moreover, it exhibited compassionate leadership in a volatile political climate. The program was a catalyst and had many spinoffs that involved public and private services. The ministers, board members, staff, volunteers, and congregations of the two churches acted with strong support from an extensive church and community network. The two congregations came to understand that the community around them had local and regional, national, and transnational dimensions. Certain churches led the way with responsive grassroots community service outreach, and governments followed with public welfare supports to take in transient youth in need. As a result, young people found more places open where they could drop in, hang out, and crash, co-creating these social spaces as active participants in their own conversations, music, and lifestyles in coffee houses and on the road. In Edmonton, as elsewhere, some moved on, but others stayed and put down roots, contributing in many ways to the political, cultural, and social fabric of the city and larger civil society. In 1969, the churches that responded to mass youth migrations demonstrated a capacity to initiate and mobilize a flexible and effective response for youth support, later assisted and emulated in the public sector by progressive social services in Alberta. At a time of challenging questions and restless politics, a kind welcome to wayfarers and war resisters was possible, indeed, intentional, as demonstrated in these interactions of transient youth, communities, and the state.

NOTES

1. For biographical background on Vernon Roy William Wishart (1927–2019), see Vernon R. Wishart, *What Lies Behind the Picture? A Personal Journey into Cree Ancestry* (Red Deer: Central Alberta Historical Society, 2006); "Vernon Wishart," *Edmonton Journal*, 7 May 2019, https://edmontonjournal. remembering.ca/obituary/vernon-wishart-1074510445.

2. Linda Mahood, "Hitchin' a Ride in the 1970s: Canadian Youth Culture and the Romance with Mobility," *Histoire sociale / Social history* 47, no. 93 (2014): 219; also see Linda Mahood, "Thumb Wars: Hitchhiking, Canadian Youth Rituals and Risk in the Twentieth Century," *Journal of Social History* 49, Issue 3 (2016): 647–70; Ben Bradley, "Illicit Encampments, 'Hippie Architecture,' and Banff's High Tourist Season," *NiCHE*, 25 May 2018, https://niche-canada. org/2018/05/25/illicit-encampments-hippie-architecture-and-banffs-high-tourist-season/.

3. Myrna Kostash, *Long Way from Home: The Story of the Sixties Generation in Canada* (Toronto: James Lorimer, 1980), xiii.

4. Frank Burgess, "Teen-agers Cheer, Julia Snarls as Aldermen Back Teen Centre," *Edmonton Journal*, 20 August 1968, 3.

5. This chapter uses the term "war resister." The term "draft dodger" reflects primary sources and attitudes of the era. For background, see David S. Churchill, "An Ambiguous Welcome: Vietnam Draft Resistance, the Canadian State, and Cold War Containment," *Histoirie sociale /Social History* 37, no. 73 (2004): 1–26.

6. For the report on the drop-in, see Evelyn Battell, "Report on Drop-In," *Annual Report, 1969*, p. 1, file 2, box 1, acc. no. 1993.0377, United Church Collection, Provincial Archives of Alberta (hereafter PAA).

7. Provincial Archives of Alberta (PAA), Garneau United Church fonds, https://hermis.alberta.ca/paa/Details.aspx?st=edmonton&cp=1740&Return Url=%2Fpaa%2FSearch.aspx%3Fst%3Dedmonton%26cp%3D1740&dv=True &DeptID=1&ObjectID=PR3441; "St. George's Anglican Church," *Edmonton*

Maps Heritage, https://www.edmontonmapsheritage.ca/location/st-georges-anglican-church/.

8. "The Garneau Story," Heritage Sunday, bulletin insert, 31 January 1971, p. 1, file 6, box 1, acc. no. 1993.0377, PAA.

9. "Population History," City of Edmonton website, https://www.edmonton.ca/city_government/facts_figures/population-history.aspx.

10. "The Garneau Story," 1.

11. Ibid., 2.

12. Ibid.

13. Art Sorensen, "Churches, YMCA Provide 'Crash Pads' for Youth," *Edmonton Journal*, 12 July 1969, 21.

14. Evelyn Battell, quoted in Garneau United Church, minutes of meeting, Official Board, 3 September 1969, file 6, box 1, acc. no. 1993.0377, PAA.

15. Garneau United Church, minutes of meeting, Official Board, 3 September 1969, pp. 1–2, acc. no. 1993.0377, file 2, box 1, PAA.

16. Ibid.; also see Joint Committee of Garneau United and St. George's, "Garneau United and St. George's Anglican, Proposal for a Crisis Centre—Summer of 1970, Brief to the City of Edmonton Re: Proposed Contact and Referral Centre," 6 May 1970, pp. 1–5, file 6, box 1, acc. no. 1993.0377, PAA.

17. Garneau United was described as "strategically located for health services. The director of the Emergency Ward at the University Hospital is anxious to work with closely with us." Joint Committee of Garneau United and St. George's, "Proposal for a Crisis Centre."

18. Ibid.

19. Battell, "Report on Drop-In," 1.

20. "Willie Dunn Sings Protest Songs," *The Gateway*, 20 November 1969, 2. Willie Dunn was a singer-songwriter and also a film director in the innovative NFB Indian Film Crew; see his famed work, *The Ballad of Crowfoot*, NFB, 1968, https://www.nfb.ca/film/ballad_of_crowfoot/.

21. "Garneau United and St. George's Anglican, "Proposal for a Crisis Centre," 1.

22. Battell, "Report on Drop-In," 1.

23. Ibid.

24. Garneau United Church, minutes of meeting, Official Board, 3 September 1969, 1.

25. Garneau United Church, minutes of meeting, Official Board, 3 September 1969, 1; also see Joint Committee of Garneau United and St. George's, "Proposal for a Crisis Centre," 1.

26. Garneau United and St. George's Anglican, "Proposal for a Crisis Centre," 1.

27. Garneau United Church, "Report on Drop-In," 1.

28. Sorensen, "Churches, YMCA," 21.

29. "Reorganization Helps Y Shed 'Square' Image," *Edmonton Journal*, 19 July 1969, 19.

30. R. M. Rosie, "Hippies Defined," letter to the editor, *Edmonton Journal*, 7 May 1969, 4.

31. For background on needs-based programs and social policy in Alberta, see PearlAnn Reichwein and Baldwin Reichwein, "Architects of Human Services: The Senior Policy Makers of Alberta's Department of Public Welfare, 1957–1971," *Canadian Social Worker/ Travail Sociale Canadien* 20, 2 (2019): 49–63.

32. Paul Bennett, "New Welfare Operation Within Year," *Edmonton Journal*, 3 July 1969, 21.

33. Garneau United Church, minutes of meeting, Official Board, 21 May 1970, p. 1, file 6, box 1, acc. no. 1993.0377, PAA.

34. Garneau United Church, minutes of meeting, Official Board, 21 May 1970, 1.

35. Garneau United and St. George's Anglican, "Proposal for a Crisis Centre," 1–5.

36. Garneau United Church, "The Church and the Community," Annual Report 1970, p. 1, file 2, box 2, acc. no. 1993.0377, PAA.

37. Garneau United Church, "The Church and the Community," 1. Also see Kathryn A. Ivany, *Bridging Downtown and Inner City: The First 30 Years of Edmonton City Centre Church Corporation* (Edmonton: Edmonton City Centre Church Corporation, 2000), 21.

38. Province of Alberta, *Fourth Annual Report of Youth 1969*, 6–11, 12.

39. Mahood, "Hitchin' a Ride," 219–21, 227.

40. David Churchill, "An Ambiguous Welcome: Vietnam Draft Resistance, the Canadian State, and Cold War Containment," *Histoirie sociale /Social History* 37, no. 73 (2004): 2, 19, 22.

41. Alexander MacDonald, "City Treats Us Well Say Draft-Dodgers," *Edmonton Journal*, 23 July 1969, 2.

42. Mara Alexandra Apostol, "Speaking Truth to Power: How the *United Church Observer* and *The Canadian Mennonite* Helped Their Denominations Navigate a New Church-State Dynamic During the Vietnam War" (MA thesis, McMaster Divinity College, 2010).

43. Garneau United Church, minutes of meeting, Official Board, 5 November 1969, 1.

44. Observation shared in eulogy for Mary Engelmann (1927–2017) by her son Peter Engelmann at Garneau United Church, Edmonton, 9 September 2017. She was a Quaker, born in New York state, and her husband was Jewish, born in Vienna.

45. Dale Rogers, "Vietnam Moratorium Returns to City," *The Gateway*, 18 November 1969, 1; "Nov. 15, 1969: Anti-Vietnam War Demonstration Held," *The New York Times*, 15 November 2011, https://learning.blogs.nytimes. com/2011/11/15/nov-15-1969-anti-vietnam-war-demonstration-held/.
46. Kostash, *Long Way from Home*, 232.
47. Kostash, *Long Way from Home*, 229, 266–67; Churchill, "Ambiguous Welcome," 2.
48. Garneau United Church, "Report of Session," Annual Report 1970, p. 2, file 2, box 1, acc. no. 1993.0377, PAA.

12 Solidarity on the Cricket Pitch

Confronting South African Apartheid in Edmonton

Larry Hannant

Landlocked, peaceful, and distant from the front lines of world conflicts raging in the 1960s and 1970s, Alberta could well have allowed a vast field of aloofness to define its attitude toward world affairs. But some Albertans put their hearts and arms into campaigns of international solidarity that linked them with peoples far removed from the province. The US war on Vietnam, for instance, spawned early and energetic resistance. The first teach-in at the University of Alberta to raise awareness about it was held in October 1965, just six months after the University of Michigan had introduced that new tool of education and political engagement. In December 1965, the community-based Edmonton Committee to End the War in Vietnam travelled to Calgary to present a petition against the war to the US consulate there.[1] Demonstrations against the war were held regularly in both Edmonton and Calgary beginning the next year. Other acts of solidarity in the early 1970s took the form of picketers at Alberta supermarkets urging consumers to boycott California grapes to support farm workers there and calls for consumers to avoid coffee produced in Angola, to help end the slave-like treatment of workers in that colony.[2]

One of the most spectacular cases of international solidarity saw the Free Southern Africa Committee (FSAC) unite a broad array of people in Edmonton and organize a sit-in and mass arrest to protest a scandalous perversion of justice internationally. In September 1976, sixty-one women and men in the city went to jail to take a stand against South Africa's apartheid system.

The arrests were a local contribution to a decades-long world effort to bring an end to that systemic racism and exploitation.

Although well established in the nineteenth century, the South African system of racism known as apartheid became official policy in 1948. Under apartheid, people of South Africa were arbitrarily placed into one racial category—"white," "black," or "coloured." People of mostly European ancestry, defined as White, made up about 10 percent of the population but held virtually all political power. Systemic discriminatory laws were applied against Indigenous Africans ("blacks") and those of South Asian background who had come as enslaved people or had immigrated through the eighteenth and nineteenth centuries ("coloureds"). People slotted into those groups who lived in areas not designated for them were forcibly removed, the Blacks to impoverished ghettos known as "townships."

Apartheid sparked significant internal resistance. The White minority government dealt with the frequent strikes, protests, and acts of rebellion by banning opposition groups and killing or imprisoning anti-apartheid leaders. African National Congress military leader Nelson Mandela, who was also a member of the Communist Party of South Africa, was jailed for twenty-seven years, along with other leaders. Activists who fled abroad were pursued, harassed, and sometimes assassinated.

Apartheid violated every human rights standard so blatantly that the world community condemned it early and often. The UN General Assembly criticized it as contrary to the charter of the United Nations every year from 1952 until 1990. The more exclusive Security Council joined in the censure after 1960. In 1966, the General Assembly labelled apartheid as a crime against humanity, and in 1984 the Security Council endorsed that statement. The 1973 Convention on the Suppression and Punishment of the Crime of Apartheid was written to extend the definition beyond South Africa, to include other states that practised racial discrimination, such as Israel, with its systemic discrimination against Palestinians.[3]

Despite the rhetorical condemnation of apartheid by the UN and other international organizations, the systemic violation of human rights in South African was long tolerated—indeed, informally supported—by Western governments because apartheid in South Africa served a useful purpose in the Cold War. South Africa advertised itself as a bastion of anti-communism. It promoted itself to Western countries as a barrier to national liberation movements in Africa that were inspired or led by communists and assisted by the USSR or China. Moreover, southern Africa is blessed with abundant and valuable resources—gold, diamonds, and base metals—from which international corporations profit handsomely. South Africa sheltered and perpetuated that exploitation. Thus, racist South Africa benefited from the ongoing support of many Western governments and companies.

With regard to South African apartheid, Canada has taken to seeing itself through a heroic lens. A 2013 *Toronto Star* article captured that self-congratulatory sentiment, proclaiming that "Canada truly stood tall. It spearheaded a key international committee leading the fight against apartheid."[4] But as Yves Engler, the author of *Canada in Africa: 300 Years of Aid and Exploitation*, has pointed out, Canada took half measures at best, following a policy motivated by pragmatism, not principle. Prime Minister John Diefenbaker did adopt a progressive stand in 1961, calling for South Africa to be expelled from the Commonwealth. (His initiative, notes John S. Saul, "found only relatively muted echoes within the broader society" in the country.)[5] Moreover, writes Engler, Diefenbaker was motivated primarily to head off a boycott by Black African nations that threatened to tear apart the Commonwealth. In the 1970s and 1980s, prime ministers Joe Clark and Brian Mulroney gained reputations as being at the forefront of the campaign against apartheid, taking credit for the isolation of South Africa that contributed to apartheid's collapse in 1990. Yet both prime ministers—along with apparent progressives such as Pierre Trudeau—continued to allow Canadian mining companies to exploit the resources and Black people of the country.[6]

In Canada's case, popular opposition to South African apartheid from United Church, union, and university activists predated attention by politicians. Diefenbaker, for instance, had received petitions in 1960 from students and union members urging him to act against South Africa.[7] Grassroots activists would persist in their efforts for another three decades in the face of opposition and apathy from the Canadian government and, at times, mainstream organizations such as the Canadian Labour Congress. Businesspeople and some union leaders persisted in seeing communists lurking behind the freedom struggle in southern Africa.

Early grassroots work was done by Garth Legge at the Africa Desk of the United Church of Canada and Cranford Pratt at the University of Toronto, who took up their solidarity work in the 1960s. In 1970, they and two other activists wrote "The Black Paper: An Alternative Policy for Canada Towards Southern Africa," a response to a recently released Trudeau government white paper on the issue.[8] And beginning in the 1960s, in Canada and abroad, grassroots activists took up a long-standing device of the weak to bring to heel powerful criminals, cheats, and scoundrels—the boycott. Boycotting consumer products, along with shunning South Africa economically, culturally, academically, and in sports, became a weapon in the hands of principled activists to isolate and weaken the country's unyielding White-supremacist regime.

By the early 1970s, social justice advocates in several places in Canada were stepping up their involvement, and in 1976 in Edmonton dozens of people took a stand not just against racial discrimination in South Africa but also against the Canadian businesses that were profiting from the system of racial segregation and attempting to disguise its noxious reality.

The spirit of protest was strengthened in Alberta and across the country as a result of the South African state suppression in 1976 of student protests against the government's requirement that most education be taught in Afrikaans, the language of the White minority. A mass march of fifteen thousand students on 16 June at Soweto, a Black township attached to Johannesburg, was met by a barrage of police bullets that immediately killed two boys. Continued protest that day and the next saw the death toll climb, by some estimates to seven hundred, in Soweto and nationally. The killing of schoolchildren confirmed for the world that the South African government had no compunctions about using utter savagery in its bid to suppress popular opposition.

In Edmonton, what heightened the stakes further still was a rising concern among the elite about the fate of the Commonwealth Games, scheduled to be held in the city in August 1978. After almost two decades of international activism aimed at South African apartheid, sports had taken a front-row place in the campaign. Those who wanted to undermine the ban on recognizing and doing business with a racist regime used sports as a wedge. What harm could come from playing games with South African athletes? White South Africans might even learn tolerance by competing with international Black athletes. But principled activists were having none of it, and both individuals and countries kept up the pressure through institutions such as the International Olympic Committee and the Commonwealth.

During the July 1976 Olympic Games in Montréal, sports was almost overtaken by politics as the chief preoccupation of politicians and the media. A South African team was not in Montréal, since the International Olympic

Committee had disbarred the country in 1970. But twenty-nine African countries (along with Iraq and Guyana) boycotted the games as a statement against the fact that participating nation New Zealand retained sporting ties with South Africa. Yet Edmonton Commonwealth Games president Dr. Maury Van Vliet continued to exude confidence that the 1978 games would proceed smoothly. However, a *Globe and Mail* headline that fall pointed to danger: "Edmonton's games next target of Ganga's boycott plans?" Complete with a photo of a glowering Jean-Claude Ganga—the secretary general of the Supreme Council for Sport in Africa, which had organized the Montréal boycott—the article foresaw headaches stemming from the South Africa issue.[9] At a city hall rally in early September 1976, Cecil Abrahams, vice-president of the Canadian branch of the South African Non-Racial Olympic Games Committee, laid out the issue bluntly: if New Zealand was not barred, Edmonton's Commonwealth Games would not go on.[10]

To raise the stakes further, in the spring and summer of 1976, what was promoted as a multiracial cricket team from South Africa was scheduled to tour Canada. The Edmonton Cricket League, led by president Geoff Williams, invited the team to play in Edmonton. The team was sponsored by South African industrialist Harry Oppenheimer, whose Anglo American/Consolidated Diamond Mines was the largest employer of Black labour in the country. He and other members of the family were keen cricket enthusiasts, funding South African teams and cricket pitches. An Edmontonian with close ties to the city's cricket community wrote to the *Edmonton Journal* to assert that the match should proceed because it was an effort by Oppenheimer to undermine South African apartheid. Oppenheimer "is undoubtedly a thorn in the side of the [South African] government. By sponsoring multi-racial sporting teams, he is demonstrating, albeit in a small way, that the different ethnic groups in South Africa can work together harmoniously and on an equal footing."[11] Seeing the impending match as a precursor to what could become a major battle over the 1978 games, Edmontonians suddenly found themselves paying new attention to a sport that almost none of them had ever played or watched.

Activism in Edmonton in support of the anti-apartheid struggle had already begun to emerge in November 1973, when Ralph Mason of the Calgary Angola Boycott Committee visited to describe the history of the colonization of southern Africa and outline the growing military effort by South Africa to suppress the national liberation struggles determined to free people in the region from Portuguese control.[12] (Angola and Mozambique were Portuguese colonies until 1975.) The public meeting concluded with a call for further organizational work among "anyone interested in helping to end Albertan and Canadian support for the apartheid policies practiced in Southern African countries."[13] By March 1974, the Edmonton FSAC was formed and had begun to engage in work to help raise awareness of the problem and end it.

When the Oppenheimer cricket team tour was announced, teams in several Canadian cities refused to take the bait, but Williams, president of the Edmonton Cricket League, rejected the boycott, saying "politics and sports shouldn't mix."[14] The 3 July match would go ahead, he vowed. But together with the African Association of Alberta, the FSAC mounted a concerted campaign to halt the event. The FSAC conducted research into Oppenheimer's fortune, showing that his profits "are used to subsidize these tours abroad, [while] at home in South Africa he and others with similar interests are supporting a regime which systematically exploits and oppresses the Black majority." The cricket team was nothing but a "private showcase acting as a publicity agent" for the South African government.[15]

City council was divided on the issue, with Mayor Terry Cavanaugh opting to shift attention to the federal government, saying that it had a responsibility to determine if the team could visit. Councillor David Leadbeater put forward a motion to block the team from using city facilities, but a majority on council defeated it. Edmontonians, and particularly cricket players, eagerly took up the issue. The city's police superintendent, W. H. Stewart, advised his superior on 28 June that a "number of blacks, the names of whom I shall have in a day or two, who play for the Victoria Cricket Club [in Edmonton], are opposing the visit and are believed collaborating with the Free Southern Africa Committee."[16] In fact, the game was rejected by eight local cricket teams, as well as by Commonwealth Games president Van Vliet and at least two *Edmonton Journal* columnists. Members and supporters of the FSAC vowed to hold a sit-in on the pitch. On 30 June, Williams conceded. The South African team would tour eastern Canada instead.[17] In a victory demonstration, the FSAC thanked the people of Edmonton for "a fantastic public reaction" and vowed to continue their solidary actions. The committee's resolve would soon be tested.

Late in the summer, the contest was ramped up again, with a new cricket team sent on a tour of Canada. This time there was a significant difference—the team included no South Africans. It was a creation of Derrick Robins, an English multimillionaire and sports promoter who lived part time in South Africa. Robins sponsored cricket tours of a number of countries using teams made up of international players but not South Africans. Called the Derrick Robins' XI teams, they comprised mostly English cricketers who toured South Africa and other countries several times through the early and mid-1970s. In the early fall of 1976, a Robins' XI team was slated to tour Canada.

The fact that this Robins' XI squad included both Blacks and Whites, none of them South Africans, complicated the issue in the minds of some people. The public was never informed as to whether any team members had ever played in South Africa, although the FSAC said that several had. Internal police reports confirmed the number as five of the fifteen players.[18]

In advance of the cricket match on 18 September, police worked out elaborate plans to stymie protest. Plainclothes detectives attended a 15 September FSAC rally, where civil disobedience was discussed, and the next day the force plotted its moves. The deputy chief of police and four other senior officers were briefed by members of a Royal Canadian Mounted Police intelligence unit about demonstrations against the South African cricket team held in Toronto the previous July. "We were also advised as to the usual modus operandi of the F.S.A.C. members and informed of their willingness to use violent means to achieve their ends," noted Staff Sergeant F. Topp.[19] Police leaders also called together Robins and the cricket team, with Robins expressing frustration at "why his group has been singled out by the F.S.A.C. and particularly on their Edmonton stop." Topp went on to say that Robins "was then informed of the possible value of the Edmonton demonstration to the F.S.A.C. in light of the upcoming Commonwealth Games." Finally, on the morning of the match, the police squads slated to make the arrests were assembled and advised of "the absolute necessity of proper and lawful behavior in the face of the anticipated professional baiting." Police clearly anticipated a violent clash with hardened agitators on the cricket pitch.

What they got was an energetic but moderate demonstration by a fair cross-section of Edmonton society—university professors and students, church members, young political activists, and members of the international community, particularly Guyanese who were both active cricket players and strongly anti-apartheid. When the match began at 11:00 a.m., about seventy protesters circled the field carrying signs and shouting slogans against racist

South Africa and urging the local Edmonton team to leave the pitch. "Let Robins play with himself!" they called out. Some protesters carried signs covered with aluminum foil, which was used to redirect sunlight into the faces of the players.

Shortly after 2:00 p.m., as was customary, the cricketers took a tea break. The demonstrators promptly occupied the empty pitch, sat, and had a tea break of their own. Police recorded the presence of Councillor Leadbeater in the crowd. When the players returned, it was evident that no game was going to occur. Police called on Williams to advise the protesters to vacate the field. The city's cricket league president was happy to oblige because, as he told the media, the protest was "absolutely ridiculous."[20]

With arrest imminent, a few demonstrators chose to leave the field, but over sixty remained. The police began their arrests, in some cases harshly pulling people away from the linked-arms group. Photos in the *Edmonton Journal* reveal both some rough handling, about which the demonstrators complained, and relatively benign arrests in which demonstrators were carefully carried to police vans.

In less than an hour, sixty-one people—twenty-two of them women— were charged with assault by trespass and obstructing police officers. Criminal records were checked. Ironically, none of the "professionals" who were said to be ready to "use violent means to achieve their ends" had police records. They were told their bail conditions included not returning to picket the next day's rematch. The group, who quickly became known as the Edmonton 61, were processed only slowly, released through the night and into the early morning. Almost certainly without being conscious of its significance, police opted to make the last person to be freed a Communist Party activist with an iconic name—Joe Hill. So as the night wore on, the Edmonton 61 choir joyously serenaded their former jailors with the famous song that begins "I dreamed I saw Joe Hill last night."[21]

Some of the arrested protesters were clearly new at this game. One produced as proof of identification a Texaco credit card, with a number that the police dutifully recorded.[22] But despite their elaborate plans for the operation, police were not well prepared for a mass arrest. Kimball Cariou, one of the arrestees, recalls that the prisoners, having been taken into custody about mid-afternoon, were hungry by evening. Frequent calls for food produced nothing; only well into the evening were they given some cold hot dogs. Yet police were ready to oblige when asked for cigarettes—and, oddly, given that the cells were filled with what were regarded as violent agitators, police nonetheless supplied matches.[23] Entering not guilty pleas, the arrested sixty-one were barred from appearing the next day at Victoria Park. Still, some one hundred demonstrators arrived to oppose the process; there were no further arrests.

In total, ninety-two police officers were devoted to anti-protest duty over the course of four days, and the city spent almost twelve thousand dollars on the operation, not including the cost of later court appearances.[24] In their accounts, police went to great lengths to challenge the media reports, including national television images, that the demonstrators had been manhandled and that Black people arrested had suffered particular abuse. (For example, FSAC member Andra Thakur, of Guyanese origin, charged that police had told him he should go home if he wanted to protest apartheid.)[25] Police also made efforts to contend that the demonstrators had been given adequate warning about the consequences of remaining on the pitch, an issue that would figure prominently in the subsequent trials.[26]

A number of individuals and organizations—among them the Alberta Federation of Labour president, Reg Basken, as well as the Edmonton Labour Council, the Alberta New Democratic Party, and the provincial branch of the Communist Party—called for the charges to be dropped. Police received some public complaints about the arrests alongside messages in support of their actions. One business owner, for example, in a letter to police, wrote, "More power to you. Don't let the criticism of the fickle public deter you."[27]

Just a week after the arrests, trials of the Edmonton 61 began. Considering its political foundation, the elaborate process, and significant costs of the police operation, the trials hinged on a legal technicality rather than politics. Had police given adequate warning to protesters about the consequences of remaining on the pitch and sufficient opportunity for them to leave before making the arrests? In December, assessing the case against the first eighteen brought to trial, Judge James Dimos found them not guilty because, he ruled, police had not adequately warned the protesters to clear the field before they were arrested. On 11 January, charges against the others were dropped.[28]

Beating the charges was an encouraging victory that generated much attention to the issue of South African apartheid and spurred on the FSAC's other activity. In 1976, the committee, with considerable work by Ken Luckhardt and Brenda Wall, produced a groundbreaking study of the important business links between Canada and both South Africa and the former

Portuguese colonies in southern Africa that lived under the thumb of South Africa. The main connection, the FSAC revealed, was mining corporations that drew great profit from their operations in the region and wanted to maintain their advantageous business connections. The FSAC published a booklet called *Millions Against Millions* that documented the business links. These included companies originating in Canada, such as farm implement manufacturer Massey-Ferguson, Alcan Aluminum, and Falconbridge, and those with roots in South Africa, such as Oppenheimer's Anglo American/ Consolidated Diamond Mines, which, in the 1960s, had bought a stake in Canada's oil, gas, and mining sector.[29] "We were the first in Canada to look at Canadian investment in South Africa," recalls Luckhardt.[30] Following up on this initiative, Luckhardt and Wall, his partner, moved in 1977 to London, where they worked full time on the issue of apartheid in South Africa. In 1980, they published *Organize or Starve! A History of the South African Congress of Trade Unions*, the official history of SACTU.

The FSAC, meanwhile, turned its attention to boycotts on the U of A campus and in the city. The group focused on two products made by a company with South African ownership: Carling O'Keefe beer and Rothmans tobacco. But its bid to convince the U of A student council to refuse to sell the two products failed in March 1977, although council did pass a motion urging individual students to act with conscience when it came to South African products. This snub to international solidarity by the student council reflected its decision the previous September not to support those arrested at the Victoria Park cricket pitch. The FSAC, however, kept up the campaign by encouraging individual students and consumers in the city to boycott those and other products associated with apartheid.[31]

The FSAC also engaged in guerrilla theatre actions in shopping centres, as part of the campaign to alert consumers to conditions in South Africa and help them identify South African products to shun. One protest, against a De Beers diamond display, involved a fashionably dressed woman, secretly part of the action, approaching a group of boycott picketers. She then took out a chain, looped it around a Black male protester, and demanded that he fall to his knees and start working, digging diamonds. Police arrived and made an arrest—not of the woman but of the Black man.[32]

The Edmonton protest and the prospect of a boycott of the Edmonton Commonwealth Games helped to intensify the pressure on South Africa. A potential games boycott was avoided when Commonwealth members agreed in June 1977 "to discourage contact or competition by their nationals" with South Africa. Effectively, the main holdout to that point, New Zealand, had been brought into the growing international boycott.[33]

By the 1980s, international pressure from activists was combining with mass protest and insurgent strikes inside South Africa's government to exert intense pressure on the White racist state. A six-month military battle in Angola pitting Cuban forces and allied southern African liberation forces against the South Africa army and its proxies in 1987–88 stymied the South African military bid to dominate its northern neighbours and impose its system on the wider region. Dramatic change in the Soviet Union and Eastern Europe beginning in 1989 also had repercussions in southern Africa. With the speedy unravelling of the Soviet bloc of states, the Western preoccupation with communism as a world threat began to fade. Western leaders now found it expedient to scorn their former friend, racist South Africa. In 1989, newly elected US president George H. W. Bush announced a commitment to fully enforce US sanctions against South Africa, which his predecessor, Ronald Reagan, had refused to do. The next year, South African president F. W. de Klerk released Nelson Mandela from prison, launching the process of introducing democracy and dismantling apartheid.

Activism aimed at overturning apartheid in South Africa was one of the most sustained examples of worldwide solidarity in defence of human rights in the twentieth century. The fact that Albertans, located fifteen thousand kilometres from the site of the injustice, worked for many years and suffered privation and arrest to support human rights principles illustrates the strength and commitment to international solidarity within the province. International solidarity affirmed itself in Alberta and showed not just its relevance but also its capacity to help create enduring and positive change in the world.

Examining the legacy of what has come to be called the New Left, this Alberta example of international solidarity points to a broader pattern characteristic of that time and cohort. One of the enduring impacts of the New Left was its engagement in struggle in support of distant people who were fighting to change their lives. It is true that New Leftists took up causes as a result of being inspired by the determination and dedication of those international militants—the Vietnamese and South Africans being only two of many courageous peoples. But that response was a new phenomenon in the 1960s and 1970s. National liberation struggles also raged in the 1950s, and although people in Alberta and beyond were alert and sympathetic to them, the prevailing reaction was at best charity. Laudable as it is, charity differs profoundly from international solidarity activism. Each involves some sacrifice, but solidarity—as Edmontonians showed in 1976—means, at key moments, incurring the wrath of the powerful, putting one's own body on the line, defying the law, going to jail. That dedication to someone else's condition—which had first been taken up a decade earlier as Albertans acted in support of the resistance to US imperialism in Vietnam—revealed the principled face of international solidarity in the province.

Acknowledgements

My sincere thanks to Ken Luckhardt and Kimball Cariou for their assistance and suggestions during the research and writing of this chapter.

NOTES

1. "Year-End Review," *The Gateway*, 17 March 1966, 14–15.
2. Albertans were also on the receiving end of gestures of international solidarity. In July 1970, Cree people on the Saddle Lake reserve near St. Paul occupied the Blue Quills school, demanding the right to control their own education. In support of this act of civil resistance, César Chávez, leader of the California farm workers union, sent a crate of grapes to the reserve. "Native Awakening: Alberta Indians Occupy a Rural Residential School and Signal a New Era in Native Activism," Canada: A People's History, CBC Learning, http://www.cbc.ca/history/EPISCONTENTSE1EP16CH2PA3LE. html. See also the chapter by Tarisa Dawn Little in this volume.
3. John Dugard, introductory note, "Convention on the Suppression and Punishment of the Crime of Apartheid," Audiovisual Library of International Law, United Nations, http://legal.un.org/avl/ha/cspca/cspca.html.
4. Bill Schiller, "Nelson Mandela: Canada Helped Lead International Fight Against Apartheid," *Toronto Star*, 6 December 2013.
5. John S. Saul, "Liberation Support and Anti-Apartheid Work as Seeds of Global Consciousness: The Birth of Solidarity with Southern African Struggles," in *New World Coming: The Sixties and the Shaping of Global Consciousness*, ed. Karen Dubinsky, Catherine Krull, Susan Lord, Sean Mills, and Scott Rutherford (Toronto: Between the Lines, 2009), 135.

6. Yves Engler, "Our Shame: Canada Supported Apartheid South Africa," Yves Engler (blog), 10 December 2013, https://yvesengler.com/2013/12/10/our-shame-canada-supported-apartheid-south-africa/.

7. Haroon Siddiqui, "The Real Canadian Heroes of the Anti-apartheid Struggle," opinion, *Toronto Star*, 14 December 2013.

8. Chris Webb, "Hidden Histories and Political Legacies of the Canadian Anti-apartheid Movement," *Canadian Dimension*, 30 April 2014; Garth Legge, Cranford Pratt, Richard Williams, and Hugh Winsor, "The Black Paper: An Alternative Policy for Canada Towards Southern Africa," *Canadian Journal of African Studies* 4, no. 3 (1970): 363–94.

9. "Edmonton Games Next Target of Ganga's Boycott Plans?" *Globe and Mail*, 14 October 1976, 53.

10. Tom Baker, "Rally Slams Apartheid," *The Gateway*, 16 September 1976, 1.

11. Dorian G. W. Smith, "How Long Shall We Give In to Blackmail?" *Edmonton Journal*, 2 July 1976, 5.

12. "Southern African Actions Planned," *Poundmaker*, 12 November 1973, 7. On 22 November 1972, the alternative newspaper *Poundmaker* had reprinted a *Manchester Guardian* article exposing the South African regime's sex- and racially segregated hostels for women and men in a Johannesburg-area slum. *Poundmaker*, 22 November 1972, 14.

13. Ibid.

14. K. Cariou, "Protests Stop Cricket Match," *Canadian Tribune*, 12 July 1976, 1.

15. Cariou, "Protests."

16. Superintendent W. Stewart to Inspector F. Pollock, 28 June 1976, FOIPP (Freedom of Information and Protection of Privacy Act) file 2017-G-313, Edmonton Police Service (hereafter EPS).

17. Cariou, "Protests." The South African team's tour in eastern Canada was similarly controversial. In Toronto on 10 July, thirty-three solidarity activists were arrested as they occupied the pitch at the private Toronto Cricket, Skating and Curling Club. Protest forced a halt to the matches that were planned for Ottawa and Montréal. "Toronto Club Picketed," *Canadian Tribune*, 19 July 1976, 1, 2; "Montreal Match Stopped," *Canadian Tribune*, 26 July 1976, 5.

18. Staff Sergeant Andrew report, 28 September 1976, FOIPP file 2017-G-313, EPS. Reports on policing of the protests were made by members of Edmonton Police Service.

19. Staff Sergeant F. Topp report, 19 September 1976, FOIPP file 2017-G-313, EPS.

20. "Protest Isn't Cricket," *Edmonton Journal*, 20 September 1976, 1, 13, 17; Chris Zdeb, "Sept. 18, 1976: Apartheid Protest Wasn't Cricket," *Edmonton Journal*, 18 September 2014.

21. Kimball Cariou, interview by the author, 31 May 2017, telephone.
22. Constable Goodrich report, 25 September 1976, FOIPP file 2017-G-313, EPS.
23. Cariou, interview.
24. EPS response to request from Ald. Kennedy, 29 November 1976, FOIPP file 2017-G-313, EPS.
25. "Protesters Accuse Police of Racism," *Edmonton Journal*, 21 September 1976, 20.
26. Constable G. Burkett report, 26 September 1976, FOIPP file 2017-G-313, EPS.
27. [Name redacted] to Chief of Police, 29 September 1976, FOIPP file 2017-G-313, EPS.
28. "Court Drops Charges Against Demonstrators," *Canadian Tribune*, 24 January 1977, 8.
29. Susan Hurlich, "Canadian Transnational Corporations in Namibia: An Economic and Political Overview," in *Allies in Apartheid: Western Capitalism in Occupied Namibia*, ed. Allan D Cooper (London: Macmillan, 1988), 49.
30. Ken Luckhardt, interview by the author, 19 April 2017, telephone.
31. "Boycott Motion Pulled," and Allen Young, "S. Africa Boycott Continues," *The Gateway*, 22 March 1977, 1.
32. Cariou, interview.
33. "Accord Ends Threat of Games Boycott," *Globe and Mail*, 15 June 1977, 31.

PART IV

Countercultural and Environmental Radicalism

The face of the counterculture: hoisting the peace symbol at the Festival Express rock concert, Calgary, 5 July 1970. Photographer David Cunningham. Courtesy of Glenbow Archives, Calgary, NA-5689-6-7a.

Letters from Andy Russell to Alberta Premier Ernest Manning and His Response

October 4, 1963

Dear Mr. Manning;
Recently I accepted an appointment as prairie province editor of a new publication, "The Sportsman's Handbook," which will be published from Cambridge, Mass., and circulated internationally. [. . .]

I tackle the job of reporting on my home province with some awareness of a country that has been misused and neglected. [. . .] Country that was once second to none for fishing and hunting and wilderness camping is now a torn up wasted hell of slashing, oil prospect lines and roads. Much of the so-called industrial exploration has been carried out completely contrary to the law. Fire hazards and soil erosion along the eastern watershed of the Rockies are such, that it amounts to a criminal scandal. [. . .]

Sincerely,
Andy Russell

November 19, 1963

Dear Mr. Manning:
I take this opportunity to urge you to create a new Ministry of Recreation and Conservation in this Province. In view of increasing tourism, usage of crown lands for industrial and recreational development and the vital need for better wildlife administration, the formation of such a Ministry is of the greatest importance. [. . .]

It is of vital importance to us and to future generations to educate the people against the abuse of the land as a community to which they belong. So that they will use it with love and respect. There is no other way for land to survive the weight of mechanized man. [. . .]

Sincerely,
Andy Russell

Office of the Premier
Edmonton
December 4, 1963

Dear Mr. Russell,
[...] Concerning your suggestion that a Ministry of Recreation and Conservation be established, I would advise that I fully appreciate the importance of these matters but I do feel that there is sufficient provision already to attend to these matters through the existing government structure and channels. [...]

I am sure you can appreciate how unwise it would be to establish new Ministries, Boards and Branches when ample provision has been made to assure that these resources are properly administered and protected. [...]

Yours very truly,
Ernest Manning
Premier

Andy Russell to Ernest Manning and response, correspondence from July to December of 1963, M153/40-41, Archives and Library, Whyte Museum of the Canadian Rockies.

Introduction

Few words were tossed around more often yet understood less precisely in the Long Sixties than counterculture. It was something to be lived, not to be defined. Even asking for a meaning made you akin to the square who dared to inquire of trumpet master Louis Armstrong "What is jazz?" Armstrong scoffed: "If you have to ask, you'll never know"[1] Hip folks got it; straights never would.

Protected by the shield of several decades' distance from the 1960s and 1970s, historians have recently dared to venture into the battlefield of culture and counterculture and come up with a description that, to no one's surprise, confirms the comprehensive nature of the two concepts. The venerable British chronicler of the twentieth century Arthur Marwick defines culture as "the network or totality of attitudes, values and practices of a particular group of human beings."[2] In other words, just about everything we think and do. Looking closely at counterculture, Judith I. McKenzie characterizes it as "a deliberate attempt to live according to norms that are different from, and to some extent contradictory to, those institutionally enforced by society."[3] To paraphrase, culture is everything; counterculture is a challenge to everything. Although it was an expression of the early 1950s, Marlon Brando's growling response in *The Wild One* to the question of what he was rebelling against said it all for sixties radicals: "Waddya got?"[4] The abundant signs in Western society of militarism, inequality, sexism, racism, environmental destruction, and stultifying conformity provided plenty of targets for youthful activists' rage. Rock musicians, who were the most acclaimed poets of the age, echoed the theme. Thus the aggressive US war on Vietnam and its visceral racial divides would provoke The Guess Who to snarl, in "American Woman," that "I don't need your war machines. I don't need your ghetto scenes."[5] A generalized fear that, as a manifesto from one commune in rural British Columbia put it, "Time is rapidly running out for Mother Earth," led the Animals to call out "We gotta get out of this place! If it's the last thing we ever do" and Barry McGuire to intone about society being on "the eve of destruction."[6]

If the counterculture was comprehensive, it also never lost its focus on politics. Indeed, politics and culture were one. Nothing showed that more bluntly than the aggressive guitar licks that catapulted Mick Jagger's raw voice—"Everywhere I hear the sound of marching, charging feet"—into the Rolling Stones' anthem to the worldwide rebellions of 1968, "Street Fighting Man."[7] This was decidedly not Roy Rogers and Dale Evans intoning "Happy trails to you. . . ." But it was not only music that was political. Everything was—all culture, art, sex, relationships, education, even football. The standard line used by one leftist Canadian football fan to lord it over another was "Our Americans beat your Americans," combining in a phrase both fan loyalty and a politically conscious contempt for yet another sign of Canada's subordination to its southern neighbour.

The progressive movements in the 1960s and 1970s held up every issue to be examined in the light of political values. They asked how a person should live consciously, conscientiously, and, as Mario Savio would declare on the steps of Sproul Hall at the University of California at Berkeley in 1964, free "from the operation of the machine." His famous command would resonate with many: "You've got to put your bodies upon the gears and upon the wheels, upon the levers, upon all the apparatus, and you've got to make it stop!"[8] True, only a minority of people fully acted on Savio's advice, but millions more made public expressions of their dissenting values by adopting one or several of the myriad options that counterculture provided them.

One common factor in the spread of countercultural forms across so many Western countries was the presence of the significant baby boomer population, which Alberta had in abundance. But in the 1960s, the province was marked by a singular feature that spurred the development of a cultural form of rebellion. Ironically, it was the stolid Social Credit government headed by Ernest Manning. The running joke in the province—or at least in its cities—was that nobody ever admitted to voting for Social Credit, yet the party handily won every election until 1971. Manning was respected but not loved. The straitlaced Christianity that made him an incorruptible politician also made him the public face of a puritanical government that many Albertans resented. This was evident, for example, in the grumbling over the government's 1963–64 banning or censorship of the films *Irma la Douce* and *Tom Jones*, based on their allegedly libidinous themes.[9] Not for nothing was Manning popularly known as Uncle Ernie. The countercultural trend of the late 1960s let Albertans vote Social Credit but also convince the world that they never did, with evidence for the latter being their far-out bell-bottoms. For the adventurous among them, bell-bottoms would lead to long hair, beads, marijuana, and rock festivals. Within a remarkably short time, a Beatles-look hairstyle that in 1965 would get a man harassed on Calgary streets was being adopted by enough freaks to make it safe. And so for other cultural forms of rebellion. While subversive political action was relatively rare in the province, more than a few Albertans took up one aspect or another of the alternative cultural flowering of the era, even if it was as modest as women who might once have strictly kept to wearing dresses and skirts in public now deciding that pantsuits were perfectly proper.

This was the moment of the birth of an environmental movement world-wide, and, like millions of others, Albertans were stirred by the sentiment. A rare and vocal few, like the far-sighted Andy Russell, took up the cause years before it was widely adopted. The environmentalism of the later sixties would add anti-capitalism to Russell's compassion for nature, weaving in political and countercultural strands. The new ecological thinking demanded that society live, reconfigure its economy, and embrace humanity and nature in a fundamentally different way. This new regard for the fate of the earth required a cultural revolution, a break with established ways of thinking and acting. Albertans were not slow to take up the task. Indeed, Alberta estab-lished a pioneering Ecology Corps in 1971 and that same year also created the first provincial department of the environment—events that activists like Russell and Edmonton's Save Tomorrow, Oppose Pollution, as well as the mildly reformist post-Manning Social Credit administration of 1969–71, could take credit for.[10]

Environmentalism and the counterculture also led more than a few Albertans to a growing respect for Indigenous peoples, whose way of life and outlook on the world had previously been dismissed as backward and doomed. Aboriginal traditions began to acquire a new respect from people who felt a rising distrust of the aggressive modernity that had prevailed since the dawn of the capitalist era. One of the Albertans to act on this new interest in Indigenous peoples was an unlikely radical, businessman-turned-book publisher Mel Hurtig. He had begun his career in the early 1950s managing his uncle's fur business in Edmonton but in 1956 took up selling books and then, beginning in 1967, publishing them.[11] His press was a rarity in Canada, just one of three trade book publishers outside of Toronto in the 1960s. Hurtig was both a nationalist and an iconoclast. One of his first successes was to publish, in 1969, Harold Cardinal's *The Unjust Society: The Tragedy of Canada's Indians*, a stirring condemnation of the Canadian government's "thinly disguised programme of extermination through assimilation."[12]

Labelled "The Alberta Bad Boy" by Toronto's *Globe and Mail*, Hurtig was not alone in being a homegrown firebrand. As the contributions to this section make clear, Albertans were perfectly capable of bucking the cultural and environmental conservatism of their province. As Jennifer Salahub and PearlAnn Reichwein document, visual artists Marion Nicoll and Sid Marty were both raised in Alberta and were wrapped in the same cultural swaddling clothes as their cohorts. Yet each was already at least embryonically dissident before brief experiences in larger cosmopolitan centres struck sparks in what was already oppositional tinder. Tom Radford was also a child of the province, moved to document the resistance of Indigenous people in Northern Alberta to the devastation of their livelihood and homes caused by modernist megaprojects outside the province.

Albertans who had grown up elsewhere quickly sank roots into their adopted soil. Louise Swift had been weaned on union and civic activism in British Columbia's Kootenay region. Transplanted to Edmonton as a young woman, she made common cause with other women who were aghast at global environmental depredations such as radioactivity from nuclear weapons testing, the first of many steps along her lifelong path of environmental and peace engagement. And as Jan Olson and PearlAnn Reichwein show, Americans fleeing militarism south of the 49th parallel had seen battles against the destruction that went under the guise of urban progress. In Edmonton, they donned their civic activist capes to take on the northern manifestation of it.

Yet, like the broader movement, the environmental counterculture of grassroots Albertans such as Sid Marty, Andy Russell, Frank Ladouceur, and Ian Tyson would remain a minority trend in a province where the oil industry's already-mighty influence only grew after the accession to power of a Conservative government in 1971. As George Melnyk notes in his magisterial history of Alberta literature, the "dissenting voices" who for a decade had given a "new edge" to writing about Alberta's environment, culture, and politics were not able to ascend to a prominent place in the popular imagination. Instead, writing that "glorified Alberta's past and its natural environment"—which, Melnyk argues, sprang from "the need for mythology"—would reclaim the greatest attention.[13] Still, a countervailing mythology persevered, nurturing the many-splendoured cultural flowers that continue to bloom alongside the province's wild rose.

Larry Hannant

NOTES

1. Armstrong's statement is rendered in various ways and is said to apply to different musical forms, but the sentiment behind the reply is so genuine as to be irrefutable. See John F. Szwed, *Jazz 101: A Complete Guide to Learning and Loving Jazz* (New York: Hyperion, 2000), 18.

2. Arthur Marwick, *The Sixties: Cultural Revolution in Britain, France, Italy, and the United States, c.1958–c.1974* (New York: Oxford University Press, 1998), 11.

3. Judith I. McKenzie, *Environmental Politics in Canada: Managing the Commons into the Twenty-First Century* (Toronto: Oxford University Press, 2002), 57.

4. *The Wild One*, directed by László Benedek (Los Angeles: Columbia Pictures, 1953).

5. Randy Bachman, Burton Cummings, Jim Kale, and Garry Peterson, "American Woman," 1970, *American Woman*, RCA Victor, recording.

6. Mann Cynthia Weil, "We Gotta Get Out of This Place," 1965, *The Animals, We Gotta Get Out of This Place*, Columbia Graphophone, recording; P. F. Sloan, "Eve of Destruction," 1965, *Barry McGuire, Eve of Destruction*, Dunhill Records, recording; Ochiltree Commune manifesto, quoted in *Canadian Countercultures and the Environment*, ed. Colin M. Coates (Calgary: University of Calgary Press, 2016), 6.

7. Mick Jagger and Keith Richards, "Street Fighting Man," track 1 on the Rolling Stones, *Beggars Banquet*, London Records, 1968.

8. Mario Savio, "The Machine Speech," 2 December 1964, YouTube video, 0:27, https://www.youtube.com/watch?v=KJKbDz4EZio.

9. Bruce Ferrier, "On Social Credit: Reactionary Medieval Irrationalism," *The Gateway*, 23 February 1965, 2.

10. Alvin Finkel, *The Social Credit Phenomenon in Alberta* (Toronto: University of Toronto Press, 1989), 186; George Koch, "A New Political Star Blazes

Up, Terminating the Third Great Cycle," in *Alberta in the 20th Century: A Journalistic History of the Province*, vol. 10, *The Sixties Revolution and the Fall of Social Credit*, ed. Paul Bunner (Edmonton: United Western Communications, 2002), 290.

11. George Russell, "The Alberta Bad Boy," *Globe and Mail*, 15 June 1974, A20.

12. George Melnyk, *The Literary History of Alberta*, vol. 2, *From the End of the War to the End of the Century* (Edmonton: University of Alberta Press, 1999), 169–70; Harold Cardinal, *The Unjust Society: The Tragedy of Canada's Indians* (Edmonton: M. E. Hurtig, 1969), 1.

13. Melnyk, *Literary History of Alberta*, vol. 2, 136.

13 From Nuclear Disarmament to Raging Granny

A Recollection of Peace Activism and Environmental Advocacy in the 1960s and 1970s

Louise Swift

Louise Swift is a mother, grandmother, and activist who lives in Edmonton. What follows are some of the stories of her activism during the 1960s and 1970s. These stories shed light on the energy and innovative methods of anti-nuclear and anti-pollution activists in Edmonton and Canada during these decades. Her stories highlight her determination to make change throughout the 1960s and 1970s. What's more, Swift's stories dispel myths about what and who is an activist.

Although Swift writes mostly about the history of the organizations she was part of, as well as the roles of other people in those organizations, her words are an autobiography of sorts. This recounting of her involvement in several campaigns adds to the historical literature on activism in Canada, as well as to this book's study of oppositional trends in Alberta. Importantly, her words highlight themes of determination, making change, and the importance of alliances. The stories Swift shares in this article highlight local, regional, and national histories of anti-war, anti-nuclear, and anti-pollution movements in the 1960s and 1970s.

Modest as they are, Swift's stories underplay her own leadership role and presence in significant organizations like Save Tomorrow,

Oppose Pollution (STOP). Created in 1970, STOP joined a handful of pioneering environmental activist groups across the country that sprang up in 1969 and 1970 to tackle some of the most obvious of the by-products of industrial profiteering—pesticides and air and water pollution, for example.[1]

The histories Swift shares also challenge myths about age and the trajectory of activism after the 1960s and 1970s. Writing about the 1960s generation, Doug Owram says their engagement in causes faded as they faced "the realities of the adult world—marriage, jobs, children."[2] But Swift points out that activism was her job, while motherhood was also entwined with it.[3] Her family is what inspired her activism from the start, and it remained an ongoing source of inspiration. (I met her in her home in Edmonton, where she lives with one of her children and some of her grandchildren, and her continued commitment both to social change and to her family is still apparent.) In fact, Swift is still an activist today: a force within the Edmonton chapter of the Raging Grannies movement.

Karissa Robyn Patton

On a Path to Activism

Growing up in Rossland, British Columbia, in the 1930s and 1940s, I was no stranger to activism. Rossland was a beautiful mountainous place fuelled by a mining economy but far from quiet and apolitical. My father was a staunch supporter of the Co-operative Commonwealth Federation, was a strong union member, and became involved in the local Co-operative Transportation Society (CTS). The CTS provided transportation for anyone in Rossland employed by the Consolidated Mining and Smelting Company (now known as Teck Resources) in neighbouring Trail. In 1947, some of the local teenagers, myself included, looked to our parents' example and went on strike at our high school. Although I cannot recall all of the details about the strike now, I remember it as an exciting event in which we missed about a week of school.[4] That strike was only the beginning of my activism, and in 1960, as I packed my bags and moved to the big city, I knew there would be much more excitement to come. I moved to Edmonton, where I was married, had children, and still live with my children and grandchildren.

In the early 1960s, with my new journey as a parent came a growing concern about the future of our world. I remember thinking, "How can a person of good conscience bring children into a world that might not last very long? And what if I bring a child into a life of poor health and/or serious sickness caused by pollution?" I was not the only one who felt this way. Of particular concern at the time was above-ground nuclear weapons testing, which was recognized as a danger even by the president of the United States, John Kennedy, who expressed concern for the future of his own children. Most of my Edmonton friends were also young mothers, and many of us belonged to the same anti-nuclear and anti-war groups that sprang up during those years.

These popular fears led, in the early 1960s, to the creation of anti-nuclear organizations in Edmonton and, more broadly, Canada. The year 1960 saw the formation of the Edmonton Committee for the Control of Radiation Hazards and of the Combined Universities Campaign for Nuclear Disarmament (CUCND) active among students at the University of Alberta. Other groups, like the Voice of Women (VOW) and the Canadian Committee for Control of Radiation Hazards (CCCRH), emerged to promote nuclear disarmament and peace.

Scary Times: The Cold War and Canadian Nuclear Politics

It is important to remember that the Cold War years were scary times for me and many others. At the time, nuclear war felt like a real possibility.[5] These feelings were intensified by events such as the Cuban Missile Crisis of 1962 and the ongoing US war on Vietnam. Being in the activist community made us all feel as though we were doing something useful or productive in the face of something so terrible. We had a strong community in Edmonton, and many other activist communities existed all over Canada and the United States.

During the Cuban Missile Crisis, Canadians were shocked into a new awareness of the possibility of nuclear war, and nuclear disarmament became one of the hot issues during the next year's federal election. Anti-nuclear sentiment arose in the federal cabinet, with Defence Minister Douglas Harkness resigning in February 1963 when Prime Minister John Diefenbaker refused to place US nuclear warheads in Canada. In the April 1963 federal election, Lester Pearson's Liberals won a minority government partly on the strength of their promise that, if elected, they would not accept nuclear warheads from the United States.

After the election, many anti-nuclear and peace activist groups kept a close eye on the Liberal government. One prominent peace activist group, VOW (formed in 1960), was convinced that Pearson would keep his word, because his wife, Maryon Pearson, was a VOW member. When, just five months later, Pearson and the Liberals went back on their word, anti-nuclear and peace activist groups were appalled and felt that they had been betrayed. However, VOW, the Edmonton Peace Council, CCCRH, and CUCND continued to protest Canada's acquisition of nuclear warheads, and Edmonton remained a significant place of anti-nuclear organizing in Canada.

Edmonton Beginnings and Edmonton Alliances

Thinking back to activism in Edmonton during the 1960s and 1970s, one name stands out: Mary Van Stolk. Van Stolk and her husband started the CCCRH in Edmonton in 1958 to inform the public about the dangers of nuclear fallout from the above-ground testing of nuclear devices.[6] Fashioned after Bertrand Russell's Campaign for Nuclear Disarmament in the United Kingdom, CCCRH played a huge role in organizing anti-nuclear protests and campaigns in Edmonton and indeed across Canada. Previously Mary Brown, she met her husband, Jan Van Stolk, while she was modelling in the United States. After their wedding, the couple moved to Edmonton, where they started their lives together as an activist power couple. She was a very beautiful woman and had a fascinating personality. She threw many parties and loved to cook and entertain. She also loved to learn. When she was interested in any subject she would read everything she could get her hands on in order to educate herself. So, when she started the anti-nuclear movement in the late 1950s, she was convinced that above-ground nuclear testing was wrong and dangerous to the continuation of life on earth. She worked tirelessly on that campaign.

When the head office of CCCRH moved from Edmonton to Toronto in 1961, Mary Van Stolk was excited and willing to travel between the two cities in order to keep her role as executive director. However, shortly after the move, she was replaced by F. C. Hunnius as executive director and the CCCRH became the Canadian Campaign for Nuclear Disarmament (CCND). She was devastated. Hunnius and his backers were excellent organizers and had simply sold memberships to people who would swing the vote his way in the election. This did not deter Van Stolk's activism, though; she continued to urge people across Canada to sign a national petition against nuclear weapons. She worked with church groups, teachers, politicians, and many other Canadians. During those years, she even set up a booth at the very popular Strathcona farmers' market every Saturday so people could sign copies of her petition. Normally, to get a booth at the farmers' market, one had to be a vendor with a product to sell. But Van Stolk was able to bypass the rule by convincing the market's organizers of the importance of activism against above-ground nuclear testing. She was never alone at the booth, because she was always joined by like-minded volunteers.

The Edmonton chapter of CCND allied itself with other peace and nuclear disarmament groups, like VOW, during the early 1960s. VOW was a national peace group that advocated for peace and protested against nuclear weapons and testing as well as the Vietnam War. CCND partnered with VOW to bring attention to the possibility of nuclear war and the health hazards of nuclear testing in the atmosphere and underwater. We saw it as a victory when, in August 1963, the governments of the Soviet Union, the United States, and Britain agreed to the Limited Nuclear Test Ban Treaty that put all nuclear tests underground.

However, our activism did not end with the 1963 treaty. There was still much work to do on exposing the lasting effects of nuclear testing. So, following the lead of the national VOW, our local VOW chapter joined women from many countries in collecting baby teeth for testing of strontium-90, a cancer-causing element that was one of the airborne elements distributed by above-ground nuclear testing. VOW and CCND worked together with researchers at U of A, and we depended heavily on the advice of the researchers there to teach us how strontium-90 was produced and its potential effects on the body. Strontium-90 has a similar makeup to calcium, and bones and teeth absorb it easily. So, baby teeth were ideal for testing for traces of the element. The campaign culminated in 1965 when the renowned peace activist and scientist Dr. Ursula Franklin received over forty-five thousand Canadian baby teeth for testing at her University of Toronto lab. The effort alerted tens of thousands of Canadian women to an international hazard.

The Edmonton chapters of VOW and CCND continued to work together in their peace and nuclear disarmament goals, and from 1965 to 1970 they organized Mother's Day marches along with the Edmonton Peace Council.

We used these marches to bring awareness to important peace issues, particularly opposition to the Vietnam War and nuclear weapons. Each year, the Mother's Day March brought between a hundred and three hundred people together, with women pushing strollers full of young children marching twenty-seven blocks along Jasper Avenue.

STOP: Influencing Change Locally, Provincially, and Nationally

As the 1960s came to an end and the 1970s began, my children grew, and so did my concern about the world around me. Pollution became a significant anxiety for me and others in Edmonton and across Canada. In May of 1970, Save Tomorrow, Oppose Pollution (STOP) was born, and it burst into the activist circles of Edmonton with a bang. Van Stolk, one of its founding members, was adamant that members of the group should not have to pay a fee to join the group; instead, they should pay with time and commitment to the causes STOP took up. In the first year, hundreds of volunteers appeared out of the woodwork to join the organization. The first campaign we organized through STOP was a door-knocking and on-the-street initiative in which we asked citizens of Edmonton to sign four postcards—one to their MLA, one to their MP, one to the premier of the province, and one to the prime minister of Canada. The postcards said, "I demand strict enforcement of existing pollution controls and immediate legislation to stop further pollution." At the bottom, it read, "Please Reply."

There was free parking on Jasper Avenue after 6:00 p.m., so every night about twenty-five teams of STOP members, armed with postcards and maps, would park their cars and talk to passersby, asking them to sign the postcards. Many people signed, and some even joined the ranks. They would come back the next night to help us get more and more Edmontonians to sign. In what seemed like no time at all, we had sent 150,000 postcards signed by citizens of Edmonton to the Alberta legislature and federal representatives.

The provincial and federal representatives did respond, but their replies soon became quite controversial. Some of the signatures were illegible; one MLA assumed that a particular signer was a young schoolboy, and, astonishingly, in his response, the MLA advised the citizen to improve his writing and discuss the issue with his parents. In fact, the signer was a professor at

U of A, who then contacted the media. The next day, the story was on the front page of the *Edmonton Journal*, which began a very fruitful relationship between STOP and the media in Edmonton.

STOP was not the only environmentally conscious activist group in Edmonton at the time. The city was abuzz with anti-pollution activism; in the spring of 1970, the Edmonton Anti-Pollution Group and the Interdisciplinary Committee for Environmental Quality (ICEQ) joined STOP in its battles. The three groups worked together to distribute activist tasks and responsibilities so that they would not step on one another's toes. In the end, the three groups agreed that the Edmonton Anti-Pollution Group would write and distribute environmental reports based on the scientific research produced by ICEQ and that STOP would continue with its more radical and outreach-based activities. Inadvertently, these activities grew as we sought to solve the problem of office space.

For a year, STOP had space in the offices of the Anglican Diocese. After that, we were able to get into the Students' Union Building on the U of A campus. Many students volunteered to work for STOP, so the move proved to be doubly advantageous. Active young university students could hardly wait to finish a class or their assignments so they could go to the STOP office, talk to Mary Van Stolk, and volunteer for the organization.

One campaign the U of A students were particularly excited about was STOP's Dirty Pictures campaign. Launched as a photo contest in the fall of 1970, the Dirty Pictures campaign asked citizens to provide us with pictorial evidence of pollution in Alberta. Hundreds upon hundreds of photos were sent to us, and a panel of judges chose the best evidence of the worst pollution. Our goal was to embarrass the person or company producing the pollution, in hopes that they would think twice about their practices. The Dirty Pictures campaign continued for four years.

In the early 1970s, STOP was especially involved in consciousness raising and outreach education. For example, we established a speakers bureau, through which we gathered volunteers to travel to schools and community groups and teach about pollution. Eventually we had over thirty volunteer speakers. Indeed, in 1973 alone, twenty-eight speakers reached 121 classrooms, 21 radio shows, 2 television programs, and 78 other community groups. We also developed a puppet theatre program for younger children. We held puppet shows at playgrounds, schools, and children's theatres, performing for over twenty thousand children in the first three years.

The puppet shows were such a success that in 1973 STOP produced two ten-minute puppet films, titled "The Saga of Smokestack Charlie" and "Les Adventures de Jean Boucane." The films, both about why we should recycle, were shared across the country, reaching nearly forty-six thousand children by the end of 1974.

The outreach education initiatives by STOP did not end with the speakers bureau and puppet shows; we continued to produce and distribute information pamphlets and reports. In the organization's first five years, STOP produced and distributed 46,800 copies of twenty-three different pamphlets and reports. These publications addressed a variety of environmental topics, including the dangers of asbestos, the environmental impact of a new car, what was really in your cosmetics, and the environmental impact of the province selling water to the United States. We also produced a monthly newsletter, which was not always easy without today's computers and copiers. We cranked out reports and newsletters by hand on a Gestetner mimeograph, and we used to say, "If we had one cent for every turn of this Gestetner, we'd be rich!" But all the hard work was worth it because our pamphlets and newsletters drew attention to important environmental issues, often inspiring change in Edmonton and Alberta. Through our work in raising awareness about asbestos, we were able to stop asbestos-laced playdough from making its way into our city kindergartens and preschools. Also, our report *The University of Alberta as a Polluter* directly influenced the university's decision to institute controls on electricity and incineration, develop a paper and newspaper recycling program on campus, and establish a pollution-control committee.

When pamphlets were not enough, we took on provincial and federal policy and legislation. For example, during the summer of 1970, STOP initiated a city-wide collection of the carcinogenic insecticide DDT. During the process, we discovered that the City of Edmonton was trying to destroy the DDT by burning it in its incinerator, right in the middle of the city; however, the incinerator did not have the capacity to destroy the DDT because it did not burn at a high enough temperature. Unbelievably, this meant that chemicals from the DDT were being spread all over the city. One of the city employees who had been told to burn the DDT came to STOP and informed us of the blunder. Once STOP got involved, the city halted the incineration and sought a better way to destroy the remaining DDT.

The employee who came to STOP about the DDT issue told us about other inner workings of the regulation of his job. He explained that workers who reported safety issues could be fired for doing so, because the supervisors thought it made them look bad. So, STOP not only took on the issue of DDT but also began a new campaign geared toward provincial worker protection legislation. In 1973, STOP convinced an opposition member of the legislature to introduce a bill that would protect workers who reported pollution by their employers. Even though the bill was defeated, it brought attention to the unfair labour practice.

Many other STOP campaigns for political change had positive results, however. One of our most exciting political victories was the creation of a provincial environment department. STOP was one of the activist groups that influenced the province to create the department. Prior to 1971, the responsibility of environmental protection came under the jurisdiction of the Alberta Department of Health. But, in 1971, the provincial government was persuaded to create a specific department, which in turn made our goal of influencing legislative change much more attainable. For example, our 1971 bottle recycling campaign was a prime force in the enactment of Alberta's Beverage Container Act.

Similarly, after we discovered that the paint used in the production of pencils contained lead, we lobbied the federal government to regulate what chemicals and substances could be used in the production of such materials. Our lobbying influenced federal legislation that protects children by regulating these chemicals and substances.

STOP campaigned locally to raise awareness about the damaging amount of phosphates in washing detergents in an effort to change legislation at the federal level. After a company distributed free samples of phosphorus detergent in Edmonton through the mail, we used the opportunity to highlight the issue of phosphates in Canadian waterways. We collected hundreds of the free samples with the plan to mail each MP a sample with a letter explaining how phosphates in the detergent promoted weed growth and spoiled Canadian waterways. Unfortunately, the sample boxes were a few ounces over the limit for free postage to MPs, so we had to open each box, empty some detergent out, seal the boxes back up, readdress them, and send them off. The extra amount we salvaged from each box we amalgamated into a huge container and deposited it on the steps of the Alberta legislature. Even though the legislation governing the detergent was a federal responsibility, we asked the provincial government to use its influence with the federal government to change the law governing the amount of phosphates in detergents. Over time the law was changed.

STOP eventually moved its office from the Students' Union Building to my basement and continued operating from there until about 1976, when the group moved to the Environmental Resource Centre on Saskatchewan Drive. The Environmental Resource Centre soon took on the job of advocating for the environment, mainly because the people who had been active for so many years had moved on to better-paying jobs or other parts of the country.

Slowed Down but Never Stopped

By 1976, the activities of STOP had slowed down; the Environmental Resource Centre took over the lobbying and advocacy initiatives, and activists moved on. But the spirit of our activism and our devotion to environmental issues continued to circulate in various forms. One was a song composed by STOP's water pollution team and sung to the tune of "My Bonnie Lies over the Ocean":

> The Codfish lie dead in the ocean,
> The Bluefish lie dead in the sea,
> They all died from water pollution,
> Caused by the oil company.
> Don't swim, don't swim,
> Remember the bluefish and cod, and cod,
> It's not our sea and—
> Texaco leased it from God!!!

The song was taken up in 1992 by the Edmonton Raging Grannies, a group of women over the age of sixty who voice their political messages through songs. I'm one of them, and we are still singing. Some things continue to thrive, in spite of all odds.

NOTES

1. Ryan O'Connor identifies just six environmental organizations throughout Canada in 1970. O'Connor, *The First Green Wave: Pollution Probe and the Origins of Environmental Activism in Ontario* (Vancouver: University of British Columbia Press, 2015), 180n2.

2. Doug Owram, *Born at the Right Time: A History of the Baby-Boom Generation* (Toronto: University of Toronto Press, 1996), 306.

3. Indeed, Owram's presentation of marriage and children as stifling activism ignores the politicization of marriage, child rearing, and domestic divisions of labour that have been taken up by women activists in a variety of ways throughout the twentieth century. Women did not have the luxury of separating their family life and political life. After all, this is the time period when the famous slogan "the personal is political" was coined. Swift's story indicates that, at least for some, activism did not end in 1980 but continued on as a significant part of life.

4. There was a dispute between the senior students and the teachers in 1947. I'm not sure of all the details but I think it had to do with authoritarianism and the way students were treated by some, but not all, of the teachers. In fact, some of the more progressive teachers were sympathetic to the students' concerns. But these were the days when the strap was still used in schools. The confrontation was finally settled after lots of meetings—some of which included family members of the students—and eventually we all went back to classes. As far as I can remember there were no penalties for the main organizers of the strike.

5. See Patricia McMahon, *Essence of Indecision: Diefenbaker's Nuclear Policy, 1957–1963* (Montréal and Kingston: McGill-Queen's University Press, 2014), 66–67.

6. See McMahon, *Essence of Indecision*, 66.

14 The Mill Creek Park Movement and Citizen Activism in Edmonton, 1964–75

PearlAnn Reichwein and Jan Olson

Even on a warm summer day, the Mill Creek Ravine stays cool. Running six kilometres toward the river, the creek meanders through rural, industrial, and neighbourhood spaces. Sunlight filters through aspen leaves and spruce trees growing on terraced benchlands of wild roses and long grass, as the creek makes its way to meet the North Saskatchewan River in the heart of Edmonton. Cyclists stream by on an asphalt path that follows the grade of an old railway bed. The forest ends where side streets begin.

A similar tranquility was suddenly disturbed in 1975, when a bulldozer rolled up, ready to transform the ravine. The driver faced an unexpected standoff, as two women with children, joined by other neighbours, placed themselves in front of the bulldozer. That day, construction was postponed by their peaceful act of civil resistance. Residents of Mill Creek would continue to face off against city hall and resort to many more strategies to preserve the ravine and their neighbourhoods. They fought city hall and won the day. This community action gave a grassroots expression to citizen rights, environmental values, and belief in a democratic civic process, influenced by insights both local and transnational.

Like many North American cities in the 1960s and 1970s, Edmonton proposed a master freeway plan to reshape an early urban settlement into a modern automobile city. The Metropolitan Edmonton Transportation Study (METS) aimed to build many freeways for modern and efficient automobility. The older urban footprint of the former city of Strathcona, on the south side of the river, complete with its turn-of-the-century Whyte Avenue main street and neighbourhoods, was in the way of these plans. METS aimed to re-engineer Mill Creek Ravine as a futuristic automobile corridor to link suburbs and downtown, with Old Strathcona yielding to the new route. Land speculators—then termed "block busters" by many neighbours—also saw potential in an urban remake that would level both houses and pioneer brick-and-mortar commercial blocks to generate profits as a benefit of freeway development. These were exciting times for urban growth and business in Alberta's capital city. But what of the neighbours and existing assets?

More recently Canadian historians and geographers have begun to focus on freeway opposition and the politics surrounding the construction of urban expressways.[1] The story of Mill Creek adds to this literature and understanding of the politics of freeway proposals in Edmonton. MacKinnon Ravine has been analyzed as a landscape of possibility that became parkland following freeway fights focused on northwest Edmonton.[2] The contested case of Mill Creek Ravine, across the river, offers insights from a district formed by the earlier city of Strathcona and its settlement patterns on the south side of the river. The case also suggests that this neighbourhood's civic activism had local and transnational influences.

Mobilization of civic pushback to freeways created urban activism in many North American cities.[3] Local proponents of Mill Creek engaged effective counterstrategies of urban activism informed by contemporary concepts of community development, environmentalism, and a people's park. They also drew on examples of California freeway debates. Urban reform philosophies, such as those put forth by Jane Jacobs and San Francisco activists, often positioned parks for the people as a bulkhead of civil-resistance tactics and public space, to assert the value of the commons.[4] But parks, too, were a contested space of design and privilege.[5] In Edmonton, Mill Creek became a focal point for the concept of building a park as an expression of the commons and of a larger civic sense of public space as home. Debates over the ravine and its district manifested an ongoing struggle to maintain both public space and the public's role in municipal governance and change.

Landscape and Place

Today, the downstream reach of Mill Creek is urban parkland, achieved through the work of citizens who mobilized to halt a freeway and conserve a neighbourhood. From Indigenous camps and river lots to a German working-class district on an early railway, and then to current pressures for high-density redevelopment, the Mill Creek Ravine area has, over the years, exemplified a multi-layered social and cultural landscape with its own politics of land use and activism.

The origins of urban Edmonton lie in twin cities north and south of the North Saskatchewan River. The pressures of city life were a significant challenge as early as 1907. Movement from rural to urban life at the turn of the century was difficult in many cities and was exacerbated by rapid growth in the Canadian West. Town planners advised Edmonton council in 1907 to set aside deep ravines that were valued as community public resources and parks. Planner Frederick Todd was recruited to offer his insights as a Canadian landscape architect from Montréal. Trained in the firm of Frederick Law Olmsted—renowned creator of New York's Central Park and Montréal's Mount Royal Park—and familiar with the Garden Cities and the City Beautiful movements, Todd recommended protection of Edmonton's river valley lands and emphasized the importance of nature in urban life and health.[6] Public parks were seen as the green lungs of the city. As he put it, "a crowded population, if they are to live in health and happiness, must have space for the enjoyment of that peaceful beauty of nature—which because it is the opposite of all that is sordid and artificial in our city lives—is so wonderfully refreshing to the tired souls of city dwellers."[7]

Before Mill Creek took shape as a park, its ravine spiralled through various land-use cycles. First Nations' occupation, colonial settlement, industry, and recreation all shaped the historical landscape. The ravine was home to wildlife: elk, deer, moose, rabbits, coyotes, woodpeckers, bats, frogs, and a multitude of roaming species. Fish swam in the lower reaches of the creek, and, later, Chinese pheasants were introduced. The ravine was also home to many early industries, including the Edmonton, Yukon and Pacific Railway (EY&P), which crossed the North Saskatchewan River, and meat packers like Gainers Meats. Proximity to water, graded elevations, and a train line contributed to such land use and developments. By the early 1900s, meat packers, brick makers, coal mines, lumberyards, and dairies dotted the ravine landscape, as did miners' shacks and dumping grounds.[8] A residential street grid extended to the top of the bank. The ravine was neglected as a recreational space by all but free-range children. Between 1940 and the 1970s, Mill Creek Ravine was a dumping ground for polychlorinated biphenyl (PCB) products, old transformers, and reeking garbage. A city dump existed where today people and dogs play in a well-used meadow, but, at that time, children were forbidden to play there.[9] Indigenous, industrial, agricultural, residential, and itinerant uses of the ravine overlapped and coexisted for many decades.

Local neighbourhoods experienced hardships during the Great Depression and World War II. Jobs were scarce and paid little, and many families depended on government relief, charity, food handouts, and the generosity of neighbours and strangers. People built makeshift shacks to dwell in ravines. Mill Creek Ravine near Connor's Road became the community of Ross's Acreage.[10] Twenty-five families and bachelors lived there, which was seen as a problem in 1934, when the city declared the ravine to be parkland; by 1950, all had been evicted except for one elderly resident. After World War II, the Mill Creek area was known as a district of German postwar immigrants. Many local Lutheran and Moravian churches and businesses reflected these cultural associations, as did the prevalence of backyard beekeeping, apple trees, and gardens.[11] Two German immigrant brothers dug the excavation for Mill Creek Outdoor Swimming Pool using shovels and wheelbarrows in the 1950s. Despite the men's labour there and in the nearby meat-packing plants, considerable anti-German prejudice persisted. Land prices here were also among the lowest in the city. The neighbourhood east of the creek, by contrast, was an Alberta francophone district and Catholic. By the 1960s, established communities had grown on the footprint of an earlier city.

The City of Edmonton was eager to build freeways in the 1960s, especially ones enabling access to downtown. The METS proposal called for expropriation of the "German Area" to build a four-lane automobile freeway that would run for three-and-a-half miles through Mill Creek Ravine, with the aim of connecting new suburbs in Millwoods to the downtown. In 1964, three thousand citizens objected to this controversial proposal.[12] Still, the city began to prepare for a freeway by re-engineering Mill Creek. In 1966, the creek's upstream reach was buried fifteen metres deep in a four-and-a-half-metre-high bypass sewer, near 75th Street and Whitemud Freeway, going north to Argyle Road. The lower reach was buried at 93rd Avenue and flowed underground in a pipe until it met an outflow with a fifty-foot drop into the North Saskatchewan River.[13] Upstream movement of fish and spawning was obstructed. The creek was enjoyed between Argyle and 93rd Avenue as a water runoff system. Because flooding of the creek was common, city engineers built a water control system near 80th Avenue in 1970.

The demographic composition of the Mill Creek area—diverse workers, professionals, women at home with children, and seniors—was a defining neighbourhood characteristic. Residents found housing in Mill Creek affordable to rent or buy. Older housing stock in Old Strathcona resembled the homes and streets in older parts of Canada and the United States. Four-square two-storey homes, bungalows, and old miners' shacks sat on long, narrow, 33-foot frontage lots, and some lots left open for vegetable gardens. German-Canadian worker families, often Lutheran Church members, and Moravians had established apple trees, bees, and gardens as well as a social culture that valued nature and healthy fresh air. What Mill Creek offered was much like country living complete with rough edgelands and industry in the middle of the city. As an affordable working-class district with heritage elements, it attracted a mix of old and new residents.[14]

Mill Creek Fights a Freeway

The University of Alberta (U of A) expanded in the late 1960s. Because the Mill Creek district was inexpensive and not far from campus, many new academics and families moved in. The community benefited, as educated and activist citizens were part of this influx. Ideas of civil rights, urban reform, land ethics, and civic politics moved with the young newcomers—especially those coming from larger cities like Toronto, San Francisco, and New York—who were also shaped by baby-boom demographics, the Cold War, and the Vietnam War.

Carolyn (née Binks) Nutter and Richard ("Butch") Nutter moved from California to Edmonton in the 1960s for graduate studies at U of A. Carolyn was a Queen's University BA graduate born in Kingston, Ontario, who had studied at Stanford for a year and worked while her husband Butch, from Shelby, Montana, was in the US Army near San Francisco. They purchased a small house on the Mill Creek Ravine from a German widow in the summer of 1968 and later added a basement. Living an idyllic life, they went to graduate school and cared for four children. Soon, they started new jobs in social work and were active citizens. Much was at risk when they learned that a four-lane freeway would obliterate the neighbourhood and destroy their home.[15] Along with others, they pushed back.

Opposition from nearby neighbours, homeowners, and community leagues was immediate. The head of the City of Edmonton parks and recreation department was also opposed to incursions. Other ravine and valley communities—Riverdale, Cloverdale, and Centretown—were also jeopardized by the METS proposal. The neighbourhoods on the Southside, inspired by the success of Riverdale in halting large transportation projects, also became politicized. The Nutters had lived in California and watched new freeways, like the San Francisco Embarcadero Freeway, wreck communities. American activists also knew that freeways were not a solution to urban traffic congestion. Even in Edmonton, an early freeway proposed for Mill Creek, in 1957, had been opposed—a petition written by the Reverend D.J. Elson of nearby Holy Trinity Anglican Church was signed by seven hundred citizens. "As our population grows, we are going to need more, not less, parkland. I am pleading for those who are silent. I am pleading for our children," argued Elson.[16]

To drum up opposition to the Mill Creek freeway plan in the 1960s, the Nutters composed a brief petition against the Mill Creek Ravine Freeway.[17] In the petition's preface, they described the importance of the ravine for recreation and conservation: "By virtue of Mill Creek Ravine's unique elongated shape it has served, not only the year-round recreational needs in a large area otherwise without such facilities, but has also provided a natural wildlife sanctuary."[18] The activists went door-to-door and were able to collect signatures from seventy-two of the seventy-five households. Comments from the three households that chose not to sign the petition recorded and shared in a neighbourhood newsletter: "I work for a contractor who does business with the city. If I sign this petition the city may stop doing business with my boss"; "The freeway is needed. I'll move to a different part of town"; "The ravine is so messy and dirty. The freeway will clean it up."[19]

Butch Nutter presented the signed petition to city council in September 1968. He also spoke of the California example as a case against intra-city freeways. Councillors were surprised by the overwhelming opposition to a Mill Creek freeway; they also knew a civic election was coming. Many city dwellers had never known a farm or campground; urban recreational experiences in the wooded ravines and river valley provided residents access to nature in the city's own backyard. Citizens began to pressure the city to connect the system of ravines in the river valley, to develop walking and biking paths along both banks of the North Saskatchewan River. The community activists also presented alternative solutions to a freeway, including a proposal called "UNI" that called for one-way streets.[20]

The Nutters, Joe Weinberger, and other activists persisted in organizing opposition to the Mill Creek freeway. The final community meeting, in 1972, was held in the gym at Rutherford School, on the east side of the Mill Creek Ravine. The janitor set chairs on the stage for the city councillors and asked organizers how many to set on the floor for residents. Butch and Joe expected forty to attend. Almost three hundred packed the hall. After the meeting, Alderman Cec Purvis asked Joe and Butch to help organize his campaign to replace MLA J. Donovan Ross as the Social Credit candidate for Strathcona Centre. They agreed that if the Mill Creek Ravine Freeway was stopped, they could probably do some work relevant to the Social Credit nomination meeting. Purvis lost the nomination, but the election of Peter Lougheed's Progressive Conservatives soon followed.[21] On 26 May 1972, the Mill Creek freeway came before Edmonton City Council; six voted against the freeway, and Purvis cast the crucial seventh vote to reject it. He was later elected Edmonton's mayor, in 1977.

Renewal/Dislocation: Mega Recplex Park or People's Park?

The district east of the CPR tracks on Edmonton's Southside developed without planned parks but had the wooded Mill Creek Ravine. As the population of the area increased, residents argued that they had contributed tax revenue to the city, over a longer period of time than other areas, without an adequate return in terms of recreational areas. In 1972, city councillors agreed that a rejuvenation of the area was warranted. At this point, Mill Creek Ravine was a dumping ground for the city's winter road sand, used cars, old clothes, and effluence from the Gainers Meat plant and city incinerator. The creek was almost an open sewer, as city storm sewers emptied directly into it.[22] The city had neglected to enforce bylaws and environmental protection here near the low-cost district. The ravine had some picnic areas and the public's favourite Mill Creek Outdoor Swimming Pool. Recreational activities such as skidooing and motorbiking were enjoyed but also damaged the area.

In 1974, the city hired Butler Krebes & Associates, a local landscape architecture firm, which released a $2 million site-development master plan the following year.[23] It proposed the construction of two artificial ice arenas and a new recreational facility complex with volleyball and tennis courts, plus an information centre, and the enclosure of Mill Creek Outdoor Swimming Pool for year-round use. The plan also included large ponds, a new playground, and a working replica of the old Birds Mill at 87th Avenue. The proposed mega-park threatened to remove more than four hundred homes and dislocate residents. The "urban renewal" it also promised would require the removal of an existing community, and, in effect, was an expropriation proposal comparable in scale to the clearance of Africville in Halifax during the 1960s.[24] As it was, forty houses ended up being transferred out of the Mill Creek Ravine.

Later, the city told the community that no park would be built in the area at all, because the ravine *was* the park. The community accepted this resolution but was uneasy. Mill Creek Ravine communities voiced many objections to the proposed master plan; for example, they stated that residents had not been adequately consulted before Butler Krebes designed its plan. By April 1975, residents had organized a group called "Build A Park," led by neighbours Gurston Dacks, Butch Nutter, and Roger Deegan. The new group was supported by a large coalition of community members who supported a variety of neighbourhood initiatives: Save Tomorrow, Oppose Pollution (STOP), Opportunities for Youth, community leagues, schools, and others, along with a local park committee of Mill Creek residents. It was also sponsored by the city's parks and recreation department, suggesting a nascent collaboration. The objectives of Build A Park were articulated as a community-based cooperative effort that elevated ecosystem protection to value natural areas and incorporated elements of a people's park for environmental education and adventure:

1. To help develop ravines as natural areas valuable for environmental education. The ecosystem should be disturbed as little as possible and in fact should be considerably protected.

2. To help parents in the community develop "adventure play grounds" with the cooperation of Edmonton Parks and Recreation.

3. To demonstrate by doing it, that citizens can help short cut the bureaucratic process, build a people's adventure park in cooperation with the city, and do it quicker and less expensively than the city doing it alone; and have fun, to boot.

4. To help form a strong group of community action volunteers who will carry on the Mill Creek Build A Park.[25]

Build A Park's committee members thought that Butler Krebes had underestimated costs. They also criticized the master plan, pointing out that the city would need to obtain 421 lots and almost as many houses for demolition, plus a meat-packing plant, and reroute local motorized traffic. The plan would also affect the local ecology by removing many trees, adding cement-pad parking lots, and increasing pollutants in the creek.[26]

Build A Park responded to the Butler Krebes plan with an urban environmental counterstrategy. Deegan, a local music composer trained at UCLA, was on Build A Park's board of directors. He recommended that the city's planning model address ten specific criteria in a pro-nature and pro-neighbourhood scheme:

1. That the park be a pedestrian park for the over 30,000 citizens who live within walking distance of the park.

2. That mobility issues of the very old, young and handicapped be addressed.

3. That it be a water based park.

4. That the boundaries of the park will not extend to remove present residences.

5. That education be emphasized through signs and displays.

6. That a historic theme be emphasized.

7. That it will include the Gainers building to become the southside parks and recreation department's headquarters, a community centre and or education centre.

8. That pedestrian and bike connections are made to the River Valley.

9. That it be a community school park.

10. That they do not develop beyond the necessary to reach the above 9 aims.[27]

Still, the city invoked its own park plan, and tree removal began without notice to the community. One September morning, writer Barbara Dacks, a resident and parent who lived on 87th Avenue, phoned Carolyn Nutter and other neighbourhood women. She said that a large truck had stopped at the end of her block and a bulldozer was being driven off the truck. "What can we do?" was her question. Nutter responded, "We can stop the bulldozer.

Get your kids. We'll bring ours. And we will stop the bulldozer." They hurried over and ran in front of the bulldozer and asked the workers, "What do you intend to do?" They said, "We were sent to 'smooth' out a 'dangerous' cutbank on the west side of the ravine." The women said "No way!" The city employees asked them to move and to let them work. Dacks refused. Finally, the workers asked what they should do and she told them to go back to the shop. The driver got in the truck and drove away. About thirty minutes later, the truck returned and its driver told the bulldozer operator, "Okay, load 'er up. We're finished here for today." They drove the Caterpillar D8 bulldozer onto the flatbed and left.[28]

Arguments between city and community went on for years. In the late 1970s, nearby communities came together again to push the city to retain Mill Creek Ravine Park for its natural characteristics. Gurston Dacks brought forty-five residents together for a meeting convened at Ritchie Community Hall. A Princeton University–trained political scientist, Dacks was hired as a U of A professor in 1971. He suggested that residents ensure that only pathways, walking trails, bike paths, bridges, and picnic sites be constructed as recreation amenities in Mill Creek Ravine. The counterproposal was strategic and helped to refocus on a modest plan. The city welcomed it, given budgetary realities, and designed a ravine park with benches, picnic tables, paths, and eighteen footbridges crossing the creek at intervals—three of these were original EY&P trestle bridges retained for heritage value, and fifteen were newly built Glulam bridges. Still, some nearby residents were dismayed by the wide paved bike paths and the number of bridges.[29] Many questioned why the city had even sought community consultation and involvement. Local newspaper journalist and bicycle-guide writer Gail Helgason wrote that "the 18 monstrosities which criss-cross little Mill Creek might be more appropriate over the Nile."[30]

The residents questioned why the city repeatedly proposed grand schemes for the ravine. Designs to build parks and recreation facilities in Mill Creek mirrored the top-down freeway engineering of METS. This plan ran against the public's expressed desire for a park with nature appreciation, play, and outdoor education as an essential focus. To them, the creek and woods were the invaluable amenity. Over the years, the public engaged in tactics such as petitions, a peaceful blockade, and mobilization of local stakeholder groups, which culminated in a civic political process that proved worthwhile. Community stakeholder groups generated a counterproposal for a park and backed it up by writing a nature education curriculum for schools, a curriculum implemented by some teachers but never officially adopted). Neighbours invested in the commons as their own public asset.

Drawing on environmental and urban reform movements of the 1960s and 1970s, and other local and far-reaching influences, the Mill Creek movement adopted a distinctive mix of tactics and ideas centred on the environmental and social benefits of Mill Creek as a ravine ecosystem and a people's park for enjoyment as a public amenity. In choosing a nature park as their form of resistance to the auto-centric city planning outgrowth of postwar urban capitalism, local citizens grounded a counterhegemonic critique in everyday practice and advocacy, introducing elements of grass-roots activism and democratic civil debate to city administration and city hall. The freeway and mega-park plans were pushed back, and, as a result, the demolition of hundreds of homes and a mass dislocation of residents were avoided and the forested ravine lands were conserved as a naturalized urban park.

Conclusion

Multi-layered stories entwine in Mill Creek as a cultural landscape with a social and ecological history. Changing and overlapping social groups have occupied the area, where people and other species have lived together. Today it forms an ecological backbone for biodiversity, habitat, water drainage, and air as well as for social needs: dwelling, recreation, health, and spiritual rest. During the pandemic, the need for urban parks was all the more evident and, in the years to come, as cities seek to address issues of climate change, natural areas within city limits like Mill Creek will only grow in importance to a city's population.

Neighbours and a grassroots coalition of interests and creative thinkers turned the tide of freeway development and public park making. They dared to take on city hall, and they won. This action was a philosophical expression of environmental values and faith in democratic civic process, contemporaneous with influences that were both local and transnational. The spirit and strategies of grassroots urbanists were much in evidence, as neighbours became activists together in efforts to save their homes and the local woods. A closer look at the Mill Creek Park movement sheds light on Edmonton's culture of civic activism in the 1970s and the people who helped to shape it.

As current plans for Edmonton-area parks push extravagant engineering schemes that intensify recreational and even industrial uses of the river valley, it is worth remembering the Mill Creek movement of the 1970s and how it played out to reassert the foremost value of ecosystems both in everyday practices and in civic politics. Today, the story remains relevant: current neighbourhood resistance to development of the public commons owes much to efforts first put forward to stop a freeway and build a community-driven park instead of an expropriated recreational landscape of urban displacement.

Prospects have turned to "daylighting" Mill Creek's outflow with intent to surface a buried drainage and restore its river mouth and fish habitat, but infill politics continue to challenge mature neighbourhoods at the same time as local neighbours continue to confront them. Today, the City of Edmonton manages "nature" in Mill Creek while the River Valley Alliance engineers the river valley with paved trails and pedestrian bridges, and EpCor constructs a new power plant on the valley floor.[31] Key questions first raised over forty years ago remain: Who has the right to the city as an ongoing negotiation and creation of space and social life?[32] How are the values of conserving complex natural and cultural landscapes weighted, compared with the aims of urban redevelopment? Local people and residents can assert their active rights to imagine and shape the city, even in the face of state planners and capital.

The fight against the freeway and the battle of the bulldozer in Edmonton were emblematic of the environmental movement across Canada and elsewhere in the era. Mill Creek represents one of many civic efforts to stand up and speak out for the neighbourhood and the local woods. Its significance today speaks to a wellspring of conservation values and the power of the public to push back against the market and the state's rationalistic urban design order. This movement insists on a bottom-up civics and modernity, one that values and embraces the environment and the neighbourhood as a shared commons and home.

Acknowledgements

The authors gratefully acknowledge the citizens who took part in the Mill Creek Park movement, many of whom still live in the neighbourhood, and those currently working to ensure mature neighbourhoods and public parks as heritage legacies for the future.

NOTES

1. See, for example, Valérie Poirier, "'L'autoroute est-ouest, c'est pas le progrès!': Environnement et mobilisation citoyenne en opposition au projet d'autoroute est-ouest à Montréal en 1971," *Bulletin d'histoire politique* 23, no. 2 (2015): 66–91; Daniel Ross, "'Vive la vélorution!': Le Monde à bicyclette and the Origins of Cycling Advocacy in Montreal," in *Canadian Countercultures and the Environment*, ed. Colin M. Coates (Calgary: University of Calgary Press, 2016), 127–50; Danielle Robinson, "Modernism at a Crossroad: The Spadina Expressway Controversy in Toronto, Ontario, ca. 1960–1971," *Canadian Historical Review* 92, no. 2 (2011): 295–322; Robinson, "The Streets Belong to the People: Expressway Disputes in Canada, c. 1960–1975" (PhD diss., McMaster University, 2012); Robinson, "'Must Everything Give Way to the Automobile?' The Ancaster and Dundas Expressway Proposals in Ontario, 1967–1968," *Ontario History* 100 (2008): 57–79; Ian Milligan, "'This Board Has a Duty to Intervene': Challenging the Spadina Expressway Through the Ontario Municipal Board, 1963–1971," *Urban History Review* 39, no. 2 (2011): 25–39; Richard White, *Planning Toronto: The Planners, the Plans, Their Legacies, 1940–80* (Vancouver: University of British Columbia Press, 2016).

2. Shannon Stunden Bower, "The Affordances of MacKinnon Ravine: Fighting Freeways and Pursuing Government Reform in Edmonton, Alberta," *Urban History Review* 44, no. 1–2 (2015): 59.

3. For American examples, see Raymond A. Mohl, "Stop the Road: Freeway Revolts in American Cities," *Journal of Urban History* 30, no. 5 (2004): 674–706; Katherine M. Johnson, "Captain Blake Versus the Highwaymen: Or, How San Francisco Won the Freeway Revolt," *Journal of Planning History* 8, no. 1 (2009): 56–83.

4. Jane Jacobs, *The Death and Life of Great American Cities* (New York: Random House, 1961); Peter Allen, "The End of Modernism? People's Park, Urban Renewal, and Community Design," *Journal of the Society of Architectural Historians* 70, no. 3 (2011): 354.

5. Jennifer J. Nelson, "The Space of Africville: Creating, Regulating and Remembering the Urban 'Slum,'" *Canadian Journal of Law and Society* 15, no. 2 (2000): 163–85; *Canadian Encyclopedia*, s.v. "Africville," by Jon Tattrie, 20 January 2021, http://www.thecanadianencyclopedia.ca/en/article/africville/.

6. Nancy Pollock-Ellwand, "The Prolific Interpreter of the Olmsted Vision: Frederick G. Todd, Canada's First Landscape Architect," *Planning Perspectives*, 34:2 (2019): 191–214; Peter Jacobs, "Frederick G. Todd and the Creation of Canada's Urban Landscape," *Bulletin of the Association for*

Preservation Technology 15, no. 4 (1983): 27–35; Walter Van Nus, "The Fate of City Beautiful Thought in Canada, 1893–1930," *Historical Papers* 10, no. 1 (1975): 191–210; H. V. Nelles, "How Did Calgary Get Its River Parks?" *Urban History Review/Revue d'histoire urbaine* 34, no. 1 (2005): 28–45.

7. Frederick Todd, quoted in "Council Minutes," 1907, RG 8.14, City of Edmonton Archives (hereafter EA). Todd made similar comments related to the Ottawa capital region, see Pollock-Ellwand, 18.

8. Jan Olson, *Scona Lives: A History of Riverlots 13, 15, and 17* (Edmonton: Missy Publishing, 2016), 96–111.

9. Terry Romaniuk, interview by Jan Olson, 12 October 2014.

10. "Report of Dr. T. H. Whitelaw, Medical Health Officer," 15 March 1929, folder EA-31, EA.

11. Gordon Kent, "Germans Found the Taste of Old Country on Whyte," *Edmonton Journal*, 9 April 2009.

12. "Over 3000 Citizens Object to Freeway at Mill Creek," *Edmonton Journal*, 25 July 1964, Clipping file 5, Mill Creek, EA.

13. Elise Stolte, "Bringing Mill Creek Above Ground Tied to LRT Expansion," *Edmonton Journal*, 18 September 2014. When the water levels are normal, the creek runs through a set of small pipes, but when water levels are much higher, the flow of water is restricted and backs up into the large bypass sewer. Thus, Mill Creek is a highly engineered drainage that passes in common parlance as nature, but is also a constructed landscape of hybridized nature-culture.

14. Olson, *Scona Lives*, 107–10.

15. Butch Nutter and Carolyn Nutter, interview by Jan Olson, 15 February 2012.

16. "Dr. D. J. Elson: 700 Oppose Road Through Mill Creek," *Edmonton Journal*, 21 February 1957, Clipping file, Mill Creek, EA.

17. Olson, *Scona Lives*, 141–45.

18. "Over 3000 Citizens Object."

19. Mill Creek Build A Park newsletter, n.d., MS-348, file 37, EA.

20. Butch and Carolyn Nutter, interview by Jan Olson, 15 February 2012.

21. Ibid.

22. "The Integration of the Mill Creek Ravine into the Extended Park System of the City of Edmonton," June 1974, MS-348, file 41, EA.

23. "Planning Criteria Submission," 28 April 1975, MS-348, file 39, EA.

24. For background on the state-driven removal and clearance of Africville in Halifax, Nova Scotia, see Tina Loo, "Africville: The Dynamics of State Power in Postwar Canada," *Acadiensis* 39, 2 (2010): 23–47; Tina Loo, *Moved by the State: Forced Relocation and Making a Good Life in Postwar Canada* (Vancouver: University of British Columbia Press, 2019), 121–56. Seaview

Park, renamed Africville Park, was established by the city of Halifax and Africville was later designated a national historic site, see Parks Canada, Directory of Federal Heritage Designations, "Africville National Historic Site of Canada," https://www.pc.gc.ca/apps/dfhd/page_nhs_eng.aspx?id=1763.

25. Mill Creek Build A Park newsletter, n.d., MS-348, file 37, EA.

26. "Integration of the Mill Creek Ravine."

27. "Critique of Draft of Mill Creek Ravine Site Development Master Plan Butler-Krebes Associated Ltd., by Paul McGaffey for Mill Creek Build A Park," n.d. [ca. 1970], MS-348, file 40, EA.

28. Carolyn Nutter, interview by Jan Olson , 14 March 2012. The cutbank is still intact on the west side of the ravine.

29. "Integration of the Mill Creek Ravine."

30. Gail Helgason, "What Did We Do to Deserve This?" *Edmonton Journal*, 31 August 1984, Clipping file, Mill Creek, EA. Helgason was a Carleton University journalism graduate and author of guidebooks for cycling tours and mountain tours of Alberta.

31. For recent projects and debates, see "River Valley Alliance Projects," City of Edmonton website, https://www.edmonton.ca/projects_plans/parks_recreation/river-valley-alliance-projects.aspx; "Mill Creek Daylighting," City of Edmonton website, https://www.edmonton.ca/city_government/environmental_stewardship/mill-creek-study.aspx; Citizens for Responsible Development website, http://c4rd.ca/(accessed 1 June 2017); Elise Stolte, "'This Is Not the Place': Sixteen Speakers Line Up to Appeal Mill Creek House Approval," 15 February 2018; Dustin Cook, "Epcor's River Valley Solar Farm Proposal Back Before City Council Tuesday," *Edmonton Journal*, 5 October 2020, https://edmontonjournal.com/news/local-news/epcors-contentious-river-valley-solar-farm-proposal-back-before-city-council-tuesday.

32. David Harvey states that the right to the city "is not merely a right of access to what the property speculators and state planners define, but an active right to make the city different, to shape it more in accord with our heart's desire, and to re-make ourselves thereby in a different image." Harvey, "The Right to the City," *International Journal of Urban and Regional Research* 27, no. 4 (2003): 941.

"A Lot of Heifer Dust"

Alberta Maverick Marion Nicoll and Abstract Art

Jennifer E. Salahub

Madam, you insult me. That thing you described—the pink, blanc mange with the brutal black slash is "abstract expressionism" which is anathema to a "classical abstractionist" such as myself. I start with something—the model—the street we live in and struggle with the thing, drawing it, trying to find the skeleton that is there. I do this 24 hrs. a day. I dream it, eat it and agonize over it. Usually it is damned hard work with mistakes barring the way. You have to fight your way through the underbrush with every painting.[1]

Upon being called an abstract expressionist by her good friend Jean Johnson, Marion Nicoll's response was immediate and passionate. Nicoll's letter, written from New York City in 1959, reads—in part jest, part sober rant—as an indication of just how seriously she approached her art and the hurdles that marked her creative process. What this letter also reveals is that Nicoll saw herself as a bushwhacker: she was not *following* a path—she was forging one of her own. Nicoll's identity as an abstract artist in the 1960s was informed by the better part of a lifetime of experience. This chapter considers the strategies that allowed her to navigate through a time and place where women and abstract art had yet to be liberated.[2]

According to the counterculture ethos that informed the mythology of the 1960s, Nicoll, who had turned fifty-one on 11 April 1960, was of the wrong age to "turn on, tune in, and drop out." By all rights, she should have

Figure 1. Nicoll's *Prophet* is considered to be one of Canada's finest examples of classical abstraction. Marion Nicoll, *Prophet*, 1960, oil on canvas, Glenbow Museum; a gift from Shirley and Peter Savage, 1990.

been considered persona non grata by the generation that coined the phrase "Don't trust anyone over thirty." And yet Nicoll had more in common with this youthful generation than she had with her own, for she was in the habit of challenging the status quo—studying abroad, marrying late, not having children, pursuing an unconventional career. In fact, it would be Nicoll's batiks, jewellery, and especially her abstract paintings and prints that would exemplify modernity to Alberta's avant-garde throughout the 1960s. As she vigorously pointed out to Johnson, she was *not* an abstract expressionist but rather worked in the "classical" tradition of abstract art, in which images are inspired by nature or by concrete objects rather than being entirely non-representational (see figure 1).

Today, Nicoll is recognized as one of the earliest abstract painters in Alberta, as well as the first female artist from the Prairies to be elected to the Canadian Royal Academy (1976). She is fondly remembered by her former students as having a remarkable presence—as a big-boned woman who smoked cigarillos and, when asked how it felt to be the only female instructor at "the Tech" (that is, the Provincial Institute of Technology and Art), is said to have replied "almost outnumbered."[3] Stan Perrott, a former student and, from 1967 to 1974, head of the Alberta College of Art (ACA), would describe Nicoll as "loveable, crusty and affirmative."[4] She was, he said, "the rock upon which everybody stood when they were starting out to make art."[5] Of course, to some of those starting out she was formidable. "She scared the hell out of everybody," two students recalled.[6] Like most women pushing the boundaries, Nicoll set out to exceed expectations—and she did so. When she retired in 1966, it took four men to replace her.[7]

Nevertheless, throughout her life as an artist, Nicoll was viewed with suspicion by those outside of the art community, and she was summarily dismissed by many of her male colleagues. She worked in a variety of modern styles and media, for which she was repeatedly castigated. In mid-century Alberta, it was presumed that any middle-aged, middle-class woman would have assuredly donned the dressings of respectability—complete with white gloves and a cloak of invisibility. But propriety was not Nicoll's goal; her life was her art, and her style her own. Contemporary photographs show her resplendent in batik-patterned muumuus and chunky silver jewellery, all of which she designed and made (see figure 2). And in the words of one former ACA student, "Marion was a woman who wore scarves and muumuus well."[8]

Figure 2. Marion Nicoll in her studio in the 1960s. Consistent with her outlook that art and life are one, she wears a distinctive muumuu with a batik pattern of her own design. Photographer unknown. Photo courtesy of the Collection of the Alberta Foundation of the Arts, 1982-003-007.

In spite of her triumphs—as an educator, a craftsperson, a crafts advocate, a professional artist—the mainstream press continually attempted to reframe her. Nicoll was described not as a professional artist but rather as an "art and craft teacher" and "a wife, housekeeper, full-time and night school teacher" or, simply, an eccentric.[9] That she had an extensive formal art education and would hold a permanent faculty position at the Tech for more than three decades, or that she was an active member of the art community, teaching at the Banff summer school and participating in the Emma Lake Artists' Workshops—or that she had been funded several times by the Canada Council, or even that her jewellery was exhibited as examples of modern Canadian metalwork at the 1958 Brussels World's Fair—was seldom accorded any significance. During the swinging sixties, when one might have believed that society had finally caught up with Nicoll's lifestyle, she was still being judged by the outdated mores of her conservative contemporaries.

Perhaps nothing is more indicative of Canada's cultural dynamism in the 1960s than Expo '67, the world exhibition in Montréal that is often regarded as this country's coming out party. At Expo, and across Canada, art was everywhere on display—including work by Nicoll's students. However, it should be remembered that even in the 1960s the definition of Canadian art had yet to be articulated, with many still arguing that historically it was merely a derivation of European or American art. Across the country, contemporary artists would take up the challenge: to define and shape Canadian art and identity.

Alberta was also in search of a cultural identity; however, the province was looking inward to its history for affirmation of its uniqueness and was suspicious of changes wrought by outsiders. There was a strong sense of belonging to a community of settlers and pioneers. (Calgary's Heritage Park Historical Village was established in 1963.) Many Albertans of a certain age were survivors of the Great Depression and had witnessed first-hand the effects of the dirty thirties. Theirs was an insular view—one that celebrated wheat, cattle, oil, the prairie landscape, the Calgary Stampede, and western music. There was a genuine respect for hard work and rural traditions that, in the visual arts, would translate as a strong preference for craftsmanship over concept.

The conviction that modern art in Alberta was a homegrown phenomenon was promoted by Alberta artists and described as the creative coming together of local makers, local materials, and local inspiration. Nicoll would credit her former teacher, Alfred Crocker (A. C.) Leighton, a British academic landscape artist who directed the art department at the Tech from 1929 to 1936, for envisioning the seminal role that Alberta-born artists would someday play: "He said that this country would be painted by people who were born here; [. . .] that he came here as a stranger and would never be as close to it as the people who were born in this place, and it would never be painted until somebody here did it."[10] One of Nicoll's students, Luke Lindoe, who later became head of ACA's ceramics department, would affirm that "we were able to be isolated and independent. Consequently, ceramics in Alberta grew as a thing separate, not tied to any apron strings."[11]

Reinforcing this insular reading was a general distrust of the federal government and urbanized central Canada. In provincial politics, this identity was given form by the Alberta Social Credit Party (in power from 1935 to 1971), which had been founded on conservative Christian values by William ("Bible Bill") Aberhart. Under his successor, Ernest Manning, the Socreds became known as the most conservative provincial government in Canada.

Alberta's government took pains to set boundaries. At one point, airlines were forbidden to serve alcohol over the province's air space. Alberta artists saw themselves benefiting from this isolation. George Wood, a student at the Tech in the 1950s and an instructor there in the 1960s, would remark that people in Alberta were "in some ways fortunate that we lie well off the much-traveled cultural routes. We are left alone to weave our own aesthetic thread."[12]

The cultural climate in Calgary was, by tradition, conservative. In the visual arts, the art community was primarily made up of naturalistic painters, who would continue to remain popular with the public, while the much smaller cohort of modern painters was looked upon with disbelief and disdain. Nicoll would state that "any time modern art stuck its head up though, it got smacked down."[13] In 1926, two art students at the Tech, Maxwell Bates and W. L. (Roy) Stevenson, were banned from exhibiting with the Calgary Sketch Club because their work was seen as too modern.[14] A decade later, Leighton was forced to surreptitiously take his art students into a locked storeroom to show them an Emily Carr exhibition, which had been banned by the head of the Tech as being "too modern."[15] And, in the late 1940s, upon discovering Nicoll's growing obsession with abstraction, Leighton, her former teacher, is said to have walked the floor for three days, unable to sleep.[16]

Considering how energetically Nicoll bucked Alberta's cultural conservatism, it is surprising to discover that she had been born and raised in this milieu. Marion Florence Mackay was the daughter of Florence Gingras, an American-born schoolteacher, and Robert Mackay, a Scottish immigrant. She was born in Calgary in 1909 into middle-class respectability. From Marion's earliest years, art was an integral part of her life, with her father supporting her aspirations. She would later confide that he could have been an artist, "but I don't think that men in Canada at that time ever did that sort of thing, not in western Canada."[17]

From an early age she challenged conventions, recalling that in Grade 1 her version of what might have been a simple geometric rendering—a drawing of the Union Jack—was distinguished by having a ripple in it. Upon completing Grade 11, she announced that there was no purpose in her returning to high school because she intended to go to art school. And her parents yielded. In 1927, Marion travelled to Toronto to attend the Ontario College of Art (OCA), where she studied landscape painting under the tutelage of J. E. H. MacDonald, a member of the Group of Seven, as well as taking classes in craft and design. While a love for painting and the prairie landscape was a driving force throughout her life, her academic career was underpinned by craft. Ironically, her later fame as a painter would mean that her advocacy of craft and her cutting-edge work in textiles and jewellery have gone unremarked.[18]

Poor health and her mother's insistence kept Marion in Calgary after completing only two years of the four-year OCA diploma. Marion enrolled, somewhat reluctantly, at the Tech, where she came under the eye of Leighton, the school's new director. After graduation, "Miss M. F. S. Mackay" worked alongside Leighton as a teaching assistant and, from 1935, as a full-time "instructress" in Crafts and Design. In 1937, she travelled to England to study at the London County Council School of Art and Crafts (now Central St. Martins), where she continued to hone her skills, not only in painting but in weaving, textile printing, pottery, bookbinding, architectural decorations, and mosaics, even adding a course in glaze chemistry.

Marion returned to Calgary in 1938, to the Tech and to James "Jim" McLaren Nicoll, whom she had met at the Calgary Sketch Club in the early 1930s. They married in 1940 and she took on his name and a new identity—that of a wife. For the duration of World War II, she accompanied her husband, who was supervising construction jobs for the Commonwealth Air Training Program, across the country. During this period, she continued to paint academic landscapes in the style she had been taught and that her much older husband admired. In 1945, the Nicolls returned to Calgary, and the following year, Marion resumed teaching at the Tech.

By the 1950s, the fascination with modernism was being felt in Alberta and a small community of like-minded individuals was finding a forum. The nuclei existed where one might expect the ideologies of the counterculture and modern art to be nurtured: in the universities and post-secondary institutions where art was being taught and discussed. In Calgary, the flame shone brightest within the art department of the Tech (established in 1916) where the entrenched British-influenced academic conservatism was slowly eroding. In 1960, the art department took its first step toward autonomy and was renamed the Alberta College of Art.

Being housed within a technical institution was no small burden. Throughout the '60s, the arts students had to run a gauntlet of teasing and ogling by Tech-side students—with young women taking the brunt of the chauvinism. One of them remembered Nicoll as "a wonderful role model" at a time "when there weren't many women teaching in art schools."[19] Others were even more impressed when Nicoll, finally fed up with the harassment, turned a water hose on the Tech men.[20]

Whereas it had been virtually impossible even to consider being a self-sustaining artist in Alberta during the early 1950s, by the end of the decade it was possible—and students were graduating with that very intention. By the early 1960s, the persona of the modern artist in Alberta was beginning to come together. It was young, defiant, and primarily male. As Bill Duma, who attended ACA from 1958 to 1962, described it, "This was the time of the beatniks, Jack Kerouac, bongo drums, poetry, coffee houses . . . and dark smoky basement Jazz clubs such as the Foggy Manor." He went on to remember his instructor Perrott telling him, "'Once you attend art school for a couple of years you will never look at things in the same way and probably not fit into main stream society again.' How right he was and how lucky we were."[21] If some change was stirring at ACA, much conservatism remained, even among the instructors themselves, for the world of fine art would remain very much a male bastion. Commenting on the demographic shift that would by 1960 see women art students in the majority, H. G. Glyde, chief instructor of the art department, condescendingly observed that "in spite of this preponderance of femininity the quality and vigor of the work produced is exceptional and promises interesting developments in the art world."[22] While women might have been filling the classrooms, the faculty would remain predominantly male—Nicoll being the exception. Illingworth "Buck" Kerr, who headed the art department from 1947 to 1967, saw her as primarily valuable for her "feminine mind and temperament" and her "good work in support of crafts," rather than for her "creative work as a painter."[23] In short, her value as a teacher was put forward as proof of a woman's innate ability to nurture rather than inspire. Little wonder that Nicoll, facing a return to Calgary after spending the 1958–59 academic year in New York City, wrote to a friend saying that the prejudice against her in her home city—"I'm considered a craftsman and a woman [rather than] a real painter"—would cause Kerr to put "me right back to what he considers normal and fitting of my lowly position in ten minutes.[24]

Despite the rampant chauvinism, Nicoll would use her skills and reputation as an abstract artist and designer to bring art into Calgary through public commissions, including children's playgrounds: "I've always wanted to do a playground, [. . .] probably because they are always so dull and uninteresting places."[25] And, on a grander scale, in 1967 she was commissioned by the provincial government to design a cast concrete wall for a tourist camp on the Trans-Canada Highway.

Yet the press remained cautious. In a 1967 article headlined "Abstract art with a cigarillo," *Albertan* columnist Eva Reid subjects both the abstract art and the cigarillo-wielding artist to scrutiny, while at the same time attempting to make both palatable to Calgarians:

> Using abstract, for which she is so very well known, the artist tells the story of a temporary home. The triangle symbol in the Indian language indicates the passage of time, the beadlike symbols speak of day and night, while the morning star indicates people on the move, Mrs. Nicoll explained.
>
> A native daughter [Nicoll] who has distinguished herself in the arts has judged paintings at the Calgary exhibition and Stampede art show for many years. Her father, Robert Mackay, an associate director [of the Stampede], was the first superintendent of the city's electric light and power. Her husband was also an associate director, so this family's collection of Stampede badges competes with a museum.[26]

In 1945, while teaching at the Banff summer school, Nicoll met J. W. G. (Jock) Macdonald and his wife, Barbara. Macdonald's tenure as head of the art department at the Tech would last only one year before he moved on to the OCA and central Canada, but they remained fast friends. Macdonald had graduated with a diploma in design and an art specialist teacher's certificate from the Edinburgh College of Art in 1922 and worked in textile design before being hired in 1926 to direct the design department at the Vancouver School of Art, where he taught design and craft classes. Like Nicoll, he is remembered as a painter—the first to exhibit abstract art in Vancouver, an active member of the Painters Eleven, and one of the first to proselytize abstract art in Canada. In Macdonald, Nicoll found not only a kindred spirit but, when he introduced her to the intricacies of automatic drawing, a mentor.

At the time, Nicoll was already a well-educated professional, familiar with the current trends in modern art, who knew that the European surrealists had developed automatics as a way of bypassing the rational. She had read about Paul-Émile Borduas and Québec's *Les Automatistes* in

Canadian Art and would recall, "To me the best painting done in Canada is done in the province of Quebec."[27] Under Macdonald's guidance, she began to experiment with automatic drawing: "you take a pencil and in a quiet place you put the pencil on the paper and you sit there and wait until your hand moves of its own accord. You do that every day, [. . .] It will happen without any effort on your part."[28] Here was a totally different approach to art making, and Nicoll was smitten—and sustained by Macdonald's continued enthusiasm.

Given the critical success of the abstract paintings she made during the 1960s, curators and historians have continued to look for ties between her automatic drawings and her abstract paintings. While recognizing that there are few formal similarities, most are in agreement. As Brooks Joyner suggested, "The quasi-abstract space in these watercolours replaces her disciplined composition; and the careful colour structures she learned from Leighton give way to painterly, fluid, colour washes."[29] A decade later, Christopher Jackson would conclude, "There is no doubt that automatics broke down her academic prejudices and allowed her to make use of abstract forms."[30] Nicoll herself would state, "I don't think I would have become an abstract painter if I had not done the automatic for eleven years."[31] This influence of the automatic shows up in Nicoll's dream-like imagery of dripping amoeba and cellular shapes within her batiks and jewellery. In fact, upon seeing the batiks, one might assume they were automatic drawings done using a pen-like *tjanting* tool and hot wax on fabric instead of pen and ink on paper.

Nicoll's craft remains an important, if overlooked, signifier of modernity in Alberta in the 1950s and 1960s. Not only was her work in craft media being shown and purchased locally, it was being exhibited nationally and internationally—she marketed her jewellery as "sculpture to wear."[32] "Plateau," a sterling silver brooch by Nicoll, was featured in the National Gallery of Canada's *First National Fine Crafts Exhibition* (1957) and was selected to represent Canadian contemporary metalwork at the Universal and International Exhibition in Brussels in 1958.

In 1957, when her modern jewellery was being shown in Ottawa and she was organizing and adjudicating the provincial exhibition *Alberta Craft*, Nicoll took part in what is generally regarded as the tipping point of her painting career—the Emma Lake Workshop in northern Saskatchewan. The annual summer workshop brought together professional artists and critics from across North America, and that summer it was conducted by Will Barnet, a much-admired American abstract painter and printmaker. It was Barnet who introduced Nicoll to a new formal vocabulary—one that would move her from naturalism to abstraction and generate her most prolific period of painting. Nicoll would later recall that "this sudden abstraction was the most astounding experience I have ever had. I knew then. No question whatsoever in my mind. This was for me. Believe you me, it was for me. I felt as if someone had cut off one hundred pounds and given me wings."[33]

Inspired by Barnet and abstraction, the Nicolls spent the 1958–59 academic year in New York City. There she set up a tight and productive regime, attending classes and critiques at the Art Students League in the morning and painting the rest of the day (interspersed with visits to public and private galleries and studios, where she had access to both historic and contemporary art.) She felt challenged, productive, and confident about her work and herself. In New York, there was no doubt she was an artist and a respected one—she would even receive an offer of a teaching position at the prestigious Cooper Union for the Advancement of Science and Art. In November, Nicoll reported that her paintings were "showing a big change—better color and much simpler imagery."[34] In later interviews, she would recount her experiences as the workaday life of an artist: "I worked eight hours a day, seven days a week, and did 60 canvases. [. . .] It was absolute heaven."[35] Jim was taking a course in existentialism at Hunter College and, as always, was willing to engage in heated philosophical discussions. But by the spring Jim was yearning to return to Alberta. Fortunately, Nicoll was awarded a Canada Council fellowship, which eased the financial strain of living in the Big Apple and allowed the couple to travel to Europe for several months before returning home. It was just as well, because, as she confided to a friend, without this break, she doubted she would survive the transition from New York to Calgary: "If I had to return to Calgary straight from here . . . I would slit my throat and bleed messily from here to Times Square."[36]

Nicoll knew it would be an uphill battle against the conservative tendencies of her home province and the prejudices she faced at the Tech. It must have been an added aggravation to know she would once again be back under the jaundiced eye of Kerr, whom, she noted, "didn't approve too much of women in positions of any responsibility."[37] So antagonistic was he that the mild-mannered Perrott would write to another colleague, "There seems to be a streak in this man, growing yearly, that makes him sadistically 'torture' those to whom he is committed to render the decencies of civilized behaviour."[38]

Nicoll's return to Calgary would indeed be marked by culture shock. She had left the very definition of modernity—the Big Apple and the energy of the virile New York school of art—to return to a parochial Prairie community. Adding insult to injury, she would, according to popular opinion, be working in a cultural void. As Archibald Key, curator of *Alberta Artists 1961*, indignantly reminded his audience, it had recently been stated in *Canadian Art*, the nation's premier art journal, that "there exists, between Ontario and British Columbia, something close to an artistic wasteland."[39]

While the greater Canadian art community would have understood the direction that Nicoll's work was taking—and would even have recognized her voice as unique to the Prairies—to her detractors, she was "selling out," dismissed as simply a follower of an American school of art. For the uninitiated conservative Albertan, Nicoll remained an enigma—a middle-aged woman making unseemly, if not unsightly, paintings. Was it even art? This question would remain under discussion in Alberta for much of the decade. In 1963, an article in the University of Alberta's student paper begins as follows:

> More and more these days we are being confronted by something called "Modern Art." [. . .] Many people, when they come face to face with an abstract painting or read a so-called "beat" poem, call it rubbish. [. . .] Is modern art true art? Or are these supposed artists trying to pull the canvas over the public's eyes? Is there any set of rules to which we can refer to judge whether or not a piece of work is art? Can we trust the critics in their judgments? Can we trust the artists?[40]

The mainstream press responded to this puzzle not by engaging in a critical art conversation but by reframing the artist to meet ongoing social expectations. Nicoll was identified not as a professional—a cutting-edge abstract artist with a long-standing reputation—but instead as a middle-aged wife (Mrs. James Nicoll), a teacher of crafts, a good neighbour and community supporter (designing playgrounds). At best she was an eccentric, at worst a rank amateur. In the words of a chatty article published in 1958, "Batik, [...] takes on meaning when seen through the eyes of Calgary's—and possibly western Canada's—only teacher and hobbyist of the art."[41]

Nicoll was troubled by the reception (or lack thereof) that she and her abstract paintings met upon her return to Alberta, but she continued to be championed by Barnet and her friends, who empathized with the resistance and lack of engagement that she encountered in Calgary. Barnet urged her to be courageous and to continue painting "as she must."[42] Still, the titles of the work created immediately after her return are revealing. Her bold painting *Prophet* (1960) is perhaps a not-so-subtle nod to her feeling of rejection and alienation—"for a prophet is not without honour, but in his own country, and among his own kin, and in his own house" (Mark 6:4). The titles of two other paintings, *Ugly City* (1964) and *Hostile Place* (1965), likewise speak volumes about her state of mind at the time.

Nicoll had returned to a full teaching schedule at the Tech and, notwith-standing her misgivings about being again in Calgary, her students remember her enthusiasm for abstraction feeding her craft and design classes. The hectic pace she had set in New York continued with an exhibition of twenty oils shown at the Tech in December. A reviewer for *The Albertan* was not antagonistic, but he was certainly vague—attempting to define, rather than critique, the art, calling it "a resolute adherence to a classical concept of form and structure."[43]

Within the year, we begin to see a shift toward a greater acceptance of Nicoll's art, at least within the art community. The *Edmonton Journal* would describe her as a "well known western Canadian artist," while in Calgary the art critic Robin Neesham proffered that "Mrs. Nicoll, [. . .] at one time overly influenced by New Yorker Will Barnet, [is] now refining her own imagery to a point where she is making an original contribution."[44] In Winnipeg, Ken Winters, reviewing an exhibition of "Miss" Nicoll's work at the Yellow Door Gallery, proposed that hers was not simply a Prairie but a Canadian voice, and one whose "hard-won, hard-painted, distilled observations of life and the world are enormously worth our attention and respect."[45]

By the mid-sixties, even the local "reviews" were no longer hostile; instead, they were curious, focusing on the artist and her domestic, rather than professional, life. Adeline Flaherty provided *Calgary Herald* readers with a masterly portrayal of the artist-teacher as a suburban Sunday painter: "The Nicolls' home in Bowness is comfortable, unpretentious [. . .] also home for three cats, two dogs" and distinguished by being "the only studio in Canada that you enter through the bedroom."[46]

Nicoll was by now exhibiting regularly in Canada and the United States, and Barnet would write that he was pleased: "All your exhibiting is going to add up one day and you will awake one morning as queen of the Canadian painting world. Of course, this is only the first step and there are many other thrones awaiting you."[47] In 1963, it appeared the throne had been unveiled, for the controversial but extremely influential American art critic Clement Greenberg wrote that of the Prairie artists he had seen, "among the best both in oil and in water colour was Marion Nicoll."[48] Greenberg's article touched on the work of a number of Calgary artists, and while gratified to be singled out by the quintessential modernist critic, Nicoll was irked by some of his sweeping statements. For instance, Greenberg identified timidity on the part of artists as characteristic of Prairie art. The following issue of *Canadian Art* featured a selection of letters to the editor, and they were anything but timid, including a twenty-nine-verse rebuttal by the historian and art curator Moncrieff Williamson, as well as Nicoll's own pithy response to what she felt were Greenberg's generalizations. Her comment—"It is a lot of heifer dust"—placed her firmly back on Alberta soil.[49]

Despite these successes, by the end of the 1960s Nicoll's career as an artist was ending. Hers had been a difficult path—besides the continual psychological battle to be accepted in what was predominantly a man's world, she had been suffering physically from debilitating arthritis, a condition that would compel her to retire from teaching in 1966 and force her to stop painting in 1971. This was followed by a flurry of interviews and retrospective exhibitions. In a 1975 exhibition catalogue, Barnet would describe her as "one of Canada's most powerful, imaginative and poetic painters. She has developed a painting language that expresses the imagery, the structure and the atmosphere of her everyday surroundings."[50]

The following year, the national art community elected Nicoll to the Royal Canadian Academy of Arts—the first woman in Alberta to be so honoured. By the early 1980s, she was described as a "living legend," "a pioneer," and "Canada's most overlooked modern."[51] At the time of her death, in 1985, Nicoll was well on her way to being rewritten into the history of modern painting in Canada and today is remembered not only as a remarkable artist but as a pioneer of abstract art in Alberta. Death even brought a measure of gratitude for her perseverance in the face of Alberta's indifference and disdain. As a former student observed, "Many of us thought Calgary wasn't quite the right place for her, but we are indebted to her for staying here."[52] Nicoll not only bucked tradition and redefined boundaries but moved beyond the enclosure and brought back what she had learned.

NOTES

1. Marion Nicoll to Jean Johnson, 25 January 1959, quoted in Nancy Townshend, *A History of Art in Alberta, 1905–1970* (Calgary: Bayeux Arts, 2005), 146.
2. Marion (née Mackay) Nicoll assumed her married name in 1940. I refer to her before her marriage as Marion and following her marriage as Nicoll— and to her husband, James McLaren Nicoll, as Jim.
3. Natasha Pashak, "Almost Outnumbered: The Role of Alberta in the Life and Work of Marion Nicoll" (master's thesis, Concordia University, 2010), 1.
4. Stanford Perrott, quoted in Maxwell L. Foran, *The Chalk and the Easel: The Life and Work of Stanford Perrott* (Calgary: University of Calgary Press, 2001), 28.
5. Stanford Perrott, quoted in Pashak, "Almost Outnumbered," 77.
6. Valerie Greenfield, *Founders of the Alberta College of Art* (Calgary: ACA Gallery, 1986), 22.
7. Marion Nicoll, "Crafts in Alberta," typed manuscript, 6 January 1966, M-6642-62, Marion and Jim Nicoll fonds (hereafter Nicoll fonds), Glenbow Archives, Calgary (hereafter GA).
8. Bill Austin, librarian, interview by the author, Alberta College of Art and Design, September 2011.
9. Adeleine Flaherty, "Life and Painting Synonymous for Calgary Artist-Teacher," *Calgary Herald*, 27 January 1965.
10. Marion Nicoll, quoted in Duck Ventures [Ron Moppett and John Hall], *Marion Nicoll: A Retrospective, 1959–1971* (Edmonton: Edmonton Art Gallery, 1975), n.p.
11. Alberta Art Foundation, *Studio Ceramics in Alberta, 1947–1952* (Edmonton: Alberta Art Foundation, 1981), 13.
12. Mary-Beth Laviolette and Christine Sammon, eds., *75 Years of Art: Alberta College of Art and Design, 1926–2001* (Calgary: Alberta College of Art and Design, 2001), 25.
13. Duck Ventures, *Marion Nicoll.*
14. Christopher Jackson, *Marion Nicoll: Art and Influences* (Calgary: Glenbow Museum, 1986), 20.
15. J. Brooks Joyner, *Marion Nicoll, R.C.A.* (Calgary: Masters Gallery, 1979), n.p.
16. Marion Nicoll, interview by Helen K. Wright and Ingrid Mercer, 29 January 1973, M-6642-78, GA.

17. Marion Nicoll, interview by Laurel Chrumka, 1982, Junior League Women's Oral History Project, recording no. RCT-403-1-5, GA.

18. For more information about Marion Nicoll and her craft, see Jennifer Salahub, "Mine Had a Ripple in It," in Ann Davis and Elizabeth Herbert, *Marion Nicoll: Silence and Alchemy* (Calgary: University of Calgary Press, 2013), 69–103.

19. Carol Lindoe, quoted in Nancy Tousley, "Pioneering Local Artist Dies After Long Illness," *Calgary Herald*, 7 March 1985, 57.

20. Terry Baker, "Southern Alberta Institute of Technology: An Anecdotal History, 1905–1980" (unpublished manuscript, September 1980), 80.

21. Laviolette and Sammon, *75 Years of Art*, 23.

22. "Introduction to 'Art Department,'" *Art Tech Record, 1939–40* (Calgary: Provincial Institute of Technology and Art, 1940), 47.

23. Illingworth Kerr to Marion Nicoll, 14 February 1966, M-6642-117, Nicoll fonds, GA.

24. Nicoll to Johnson, 25 January 1959.

25. Linda Curtis, "A Child-Like Approach," *The Albertan*, 6 December 1969.

26. Eva Reid, "Abstract Art with a Cigarillo," *The Albertan*, 14 July 1967.

27. Duck Ventures, *Marion Nicoll*, n.p.

28. Duck Ventures, *Marion Nicoll*, n.p.

29. Joyner, *Marion Nicoll*, 75.

30. Jackson, *Marion Nicoll*, 16.

31. Nancy Townshend, *A History of Art in Alberta: 1905–1970* (Calgary: Bayeux Arts, 2005), 144.

32. In the Glenbow's collection there is an undated photograph of a display panel that reads, *M. Nicoll, Sculpture to Wear: Gold, Silver, Bronze*. GA S-91-(1-119).

33. Nicoll, interview by Wright and Mercer, 29 January 1973.

34. Marion Nicoll to Jean Johnson, 19 November 1958, quoted in Nancy Townshend, *A History of Art*, 144.

35. Jenni Morton, "Painter Teaches Craft Classes," *Calgary Herald*, 6 October 1963.

36. Nicoll to Johnson, 25 January 1959.

37. Marion Nicoll, interview by Joan Murray, 24 May 1979, 6, Nicoll fonds, GA.

38. Foran, *Chalk and Easel*, 71.

39. Calgary Allied Arts Countil, "Introduction," *The Calgary Allied Arts Council Presents: Alberta Artists 1961* (Calgary: Calgary Allied Arts Council, 1961), 1.

40. Don Wells, "The Shaming of the True: Pseudo Art or True?" *The Gateway*, 15 February 1963, 5.

41. Untitled article, *Amherstburg Echo* [Ont], 9 January 1958.

42. Will Barnet to Jim and Marion Nicoll, 15 July 1962, M-6642-1, Nicoll fonds, GA.

43. "Artist Shows Oil Paintings," *The Albertan*, 8 December 1959.

44. "Gallery Exhibition Thursday," *Edmonton Journal*, 25 January 1963; Robin Neesham, "Art Show Features Boldness of Nicoll's Abstract Works," *Calgary Herald*, 10 December 1963.

45. Ken Winters, "14 Monumental Gestures: A Review," *Winnipeg Free Press*, 30 January 1964.

46. Flaherty, "Life and Painting Synonymous."

47. Will Barnet to Marion Nicoll, 20 August 1961, M-6642-1, Nicoll fonds, GA.

48. Clement Greenberg, "Clement Greenberg's View of Art on the Prairies: Painting and Sculpture in Prairie Canada Today," *Canadian Art* 20, no. 2 (March–April 1963): 100.

49. Marion Nicoll, letter to the editor, and Moncrieff Williamson, "South of the Borduas—Down Tenth Street Way," *Canadian Art* 20, no. 3 (May–June 1963): 196.

50. Will Barnet, quoted in Duck Ventures, *Marion Nicoll*, n.p.

51. Patrick Tivy, "Living Legends Make Return for Tribute Exhibition," *Calgary Herald*, 21 January 1982; Ron Chalmers, "Show Outlines Art Pioneer's Career," *Edmonton Journal*, 30 August 1986; "Marion Nicoll" [Review of Exhibition], Masters Gallery, December 1978: 32–34, M-6642-134, GA.

52. Carol Lindoe, quoted in Tousley, "Pioneering Local Artist Dies."

16 Land and Love in the Rockies

The Poetic Politics of Sid Marty and *Headwaters*

PearlAnn Reichwein

A cowboy riding tall in the saddle is a quintessential figure of the Canadian West, evoking adventure and frontier masculinity. It is an image that Alberta writer Sid Marty set out to rewrite—even transform—in his first book of poetry. *Headwaters* drew from his time in the saddle as a national park warden in the Rocky Mountains.[1] Based on that experience, Marty's poems compelled readers to rethink the traditional man and his connection to the land, telling stories to invoke new themes of manhood, environment, and love that came to the fore in the 1960s and 1970s. His poems subverted the pattern of much mountain prose of the era and now. They revealed a complex and sensitive side to mountains and men, pointing toward a new, radical politics. Lyrically exploring themes of a cowboy's sense of belonging on the land and in love, Marty's poetry went miles beyond a conventional cowboy image and conservative ideas of the West; it was a key that opened up new ways to know the Rockies and the heart.

Marty was a working man in the warden service. Putting on a warden's Stetson also shaped his poems in *Headwaters*. Marty was able to speak for the land in the face of modernity and bureaucracy as well as against capitalist despoliation. As an outdoorsman, he also spoke of expressive and emotional masculinity. At the same time, he kept his sense of humour, beauty, and outrage. That, teamed with his epic western mountain themes—horses and rifles, bighorns and bears—was part of his poetry's appeal to many readers.

Born in England in 1944, son of a Canadian soldier and an English war bride, Marty grew up in Medicine Hat and Calgary. His paternal American great-grandparents had settled in southern Alberta and his forefathers were sheriffs. A talented writer and singer-songwriter, Marty went to university in Calgary and Montréal, pursuing graduate studies in English literature and publishing poems. He also sang and played guitar as a folk music performer from the early 1960s. Cities may have offered university education and a coffeehouse scene of singers, songwriters, and poets, but they did not fulfill those who longed for wild mountains. Marty left university to work as a full-time national park warden from 1968 to 1978, in Yoho, Jasper, Prince Albert, and Banff National Parks. It was here that his poetry and prose would find its stride. Riding horseback through the mountains, Marty composed much of his early poetry in the saddle, writing it down in warden cabins by night.[2] The Rockies were central to his writing, which in turn set a new standard for the genre of Canadian mountain literature.

Storm Warning: New Canadian Poets (1971), edited by Al Purdy, brought Marty's work to a new readership and situated him within a vanguard of writers. Marty's first complete book was *Headwaters* (1973), a volume comprising seventy-seven free verse poems. This early work introduced themes he would later explore in much of his prose and songwriting. *Men for the Mountains* (1978) was Marty's first prose book of western cowboy storytelling and remains one of the best-known Rocky Mountain tales by a contemporary Canadian writer. The book was twice highlighted by the Canadian Parks and Wilderness Society (CPAWS) as one of the most influential books in Canada's conservation movement, yet many of its themes were already emergent in the poetry Marty published in 1973. His later works include four highly acclaimed non-fiction books and three more books of poetry.[3]

Because it was an inspirational source that fed Marty's later writing, *Headwaters* calls for closer examination. In these poems the young warden is a new-generation cowboy—contemplative, articulate, and feeling—at work and at home in the mountains. The warden service, a traditionally male bastion, leads him to the backcountry; however, cowboy masculinity in Marty's text is far from a hypermasculine stereotype.[4] In short, the warden cowboy is a well-rounded man with humanity and strength of heart. His is a tough but kind, gentle, and passionate masculinity—one with the strength to speak for those without voices and to speak with his own inner voice, even if it violates conservative codes of silence and manhood. He is at once a quiet poet, an outspoken non-conformist, a conservative cowboy, and an erotic lover, all standpoints with multiple possibilities.

The *Globe and Mail*'s George Woodcock and other reviewers placed Marty among strong new poets in the West, but *Headwaters* was read not only in literary circles. It was also popular among diverse readers of nature and cowboy poetry.[5] George Melnyk's literary history of Alberta argues that in the 1960s and 1970s, writing by Albertans about themselves—which, in Melnyk's words, had "glorified Alberta's past and its natural environment"— began to see an "appearance of dissenting voices" and "a new edge."[6] Marty's work had exactly this new edge and dissident voice. A man's place both on the land and in love are two of the themes that stand out in his lyric cowboy poems.

The Land Poems

The poems in *Headwaters* often spoke of land ethics—defined by ecologist Aldo Leopold as caring and right relations between the land and people—as Marty exposed the ideals and struggles that wardens faced in parks.[7] Confronting contradictions in Canada's mountain parks also defined land use and management as problematic and political. At a time when the sixties' generation often proposed back-to-the-land alternatives, his poems asserted different ways to know the environment and ethics from a working warden's perspective.

At a time before myriad titles were published on mountain parks and by local people, Marty's work was unusual in being written by a park resident rather than a tourist. And not just an ordinary park resident but one who held the reins of a western bridle and wore a park warden's uniform. The national parks—areas of federal jurisdiction in the Rockies—became his arena in which to challenge abuses, affronts, and what he saw as a skewed political approach toward the land and to reassert land ethics.

In the land poems, Marty explores his philosophy of being and his place on the land. "Departure" focuses on the question of "What is true?" Like Wordsworth and Sartre, Marty seeks the meaning of life and existence. Looking for it in nature, he finds his answer in mountains:

> I tell you
> I have climbed mountains
> But what are they

What are they
but blue skies driven crazy cornered
sharpened
by the weight of heavy resolutions
in which we played no part

But they
are the headlong ships of my blood
sailing through a land
of animals and flowers
sailing through me
A man[8]

The mountains are as a bloodstream running through a man and a living land. Mountains rise above humans, but still the writer is part of the land. This is his place, his truth, and what he believes—a sense of being and a fundamental land ethic.

Even with the mountains in his blood, the power of the land looms large and cannot be underestimated. For example, in "Cairn Pass," a warden on horseback descends an alpine pass and races against winter on the southern boundary of Jasper Park. Chasing his stray pack pony, he nearly falls off his horse as "Earth claws for me/ come down young lover." Lightning sends rocks falling. Drizzle sets a dark mood; yesterday's "wild flowers are deserts of winter." To ward off the harsh elements, his mind finds comfort in the warmth of human love:

This the first storm of that season
broods on, freezes my intrusions
Its searching icy fingers nip my groin
wet and icy where the old chaps end

Wish I felt some warm hands now
woman bringing me coffee in
lazing in bed, and home with love[9]

The forces of nature animate the Earth and lovers alike. Even as he daydreams, the cowboy cannot escape being a mortal part of nature.

"Pushing the Boundary" reveals a land ethic and meanings behind the title of the collection. It positions the national park ideal and reality in tension:

> In here we declare
> only the animals
> may kill each other
> sometimes
> may even kill us.
>
> But it's hard to draw
> the boundary
> imaginary line
> that cuts the watersheds
> You got to know the ground
> climb the crumbling mountain walls
> to know which way the rivers run
> headwaters, where the world begins[10]

Principles and boundaries prove difficult to map and enforce on the land. Headwaters are a source of life to protect, and only animals are supposed to kill, yet the warden must terminate injured animals like bighorn rams, whom he observes "dragging their broken / hindquarters / over the finish line."[11] Even the warden is at risk inside the park. He rides the boundary with a thousand square miles to protect, keeping out hunters who riddle his markers with bullets fired from outside the park:

> And dressed all in green
> I float among the trees
> Staring out on the plains
> in September
> to hear the distant roll of guns
> draw near[12]

A competition plays out—hunters seeking game and a warden seeking hunters—that is reiterated in the poem "On the Boundary." The dangerous rivalry also makes clear the high stakes: "Last year a guide and his yankee hunters/

threatened a warden with loaded rifles." The warden on boundary patrol feels he grows horns and is a target for poachers from beyond the mountains, as if "I was a green pin" on their maps.[13]

In these poems, it is the warden who knows and makes the national park by riding the uneven land to enforce the rules on the ground. He becomes the boundary, predator, and prey in a place of shifting and dangerous contradictions. In this way, Marty places himself into the larger picture of the warden as a hunter of men who prey on territory designated as a public commons, where avaricious self-interest cannot be allowed to prevail, and he upholds land ethics and the law in precarious situations.

Underlying land ethics are further examined as a theme in poems that question the precarious existence of life and death on the land. Caring about death in the mountains figures prominently in these poems, but it is never simply death. Sometimes it is death caused by foreigners with the wealth to buy a trophy that claims to affirm the conquest of wilderness, a concern that comes up in "The Death of Mustahyh." Elegiac and political in tone, the poem recounts the killing of a silvertip grizzly and his future offspring:

> His terrible hide is a rag
> in a rich man's fist
> his lard sticks in the raven's craw
>
> He was shot out of season
> By a poaching guide
> for Yankee dollars
>
> He was sold to the highest bidder
> as a fixture in this sold out land
> His skeleton stinks
> an extant document of corruption[14]

Pointing to an absence of land ethics, the wrongful death of Mustahyh (the grizzly) poignantly illustrates another way that Canada sells itself out to the United States and how supine Canada is toward rapacious "Yankee dollars" in a capitalist culture that proclaims everything is for sale—even magnificent wild creatures in national parks—much as raw resources like oil and gas are.

Similarly "On Highway 16, Jasper" explores the pointless death of a moose struck on the Yellowhead Highway. Empathetic to the animal's three days of slow suffering, the point of view shifts to that of the moose and imagines its delirious pain—"for I had no voice"—evoking dignity and compassion.[15] Another fatal road accident surfaces in "Meat in Snow," this time involving a trucker run off the road and killed. Faced by futility, a first responder struggles to give meaning to a senseless scene and turns to making poetry "to ease a racing heart."[16] Accidental deaths, both non-human and human, are a painful loss in Marty's work that challenges indiscriminate violence on highways as another shortcoming of national parks in reality.

Pathos hangs in the air as a futile death once again confronts the warden in "Mercy." Chased by dogs, a doe has lost her fawn over the falls and is trapped. "Dogs and men have the world/ and they worry it to death," says the warden as he confronts "the masters of war." "I thought that life in this park/ should be holy/ and no killing/ would be at random," he reflects. Looking into the doe's eyes, he shoots.[17] Like the world beyond the park, nothing in it is safe from depredations; the war machine is endless. This poem also provoked contemporary reviewers to relate such pathos to the Vietnam War and anti-war protest.[18]

Another reminder of the volatile nature of life and death he witnesses is seen in "For Young Men." A climber has plummeted onto the glacier. The search and rescue team—a job for "young men and fools"—is "risking their necks/ to witness his adventure." The victim's brain was eaten by ravens. Someone jokes that the victim is "open minded," as a "way to numb the pain."[19] Pain, however, is a sign of humanity facing yet another trauma, and numbing it is a coping mechanism for some. Wardens experience situations beyond superficial assumptions of epic mountain adventure and masculine heroism. Duty calls, yet climbers put not only other men at risk but also their families. The warden is not a dauntless mountaineering machine or a solitary hero of westerns but a working man and mortal both in his apprehensions on the land and in caring for others.

An underlying gravity also arises in "Bright Morning." A speaker, presumably a warden and father, reaches for the baby's blue brush on top of "a box of bullets" on the windowsill. As he looks out the window to the mountaintops, he compares his brushing the baby's hair with the wind combing snow on the peaks.[20] Even as the man loves the mountains and nurtures a baby, he is armed with .308 calibre cartridges that can kill an elk or bear. Nuanced juxtaposition points to tensions in warden backcountry life for the caring cowboy and land steward. Duty is a two-sided coin with family on one face and wage labour on the other, even as the Rockies appear to be a beloved refuge for anti-modernists, they also exist in an undeniably bright and real modern world.

Finally, the poem "Invitation and Covenant" also explores right relations on the land as a possibility of living together. Nature is personified as a haunting and sensuous power that beckons the warden to come outdoors into the wild: "Yet you are alone with me/ even in the arms of my daughters," says the voice of Nature. "Come out/ from all that ordering geometry/ Unlatch the cabin door," the voice utters. "With the feel of my breath/ upon your loins/ like a glacier/ birthing in your blood" it persuades him to come outside as the snow begins.[21] The month of October gives way in Jasper's secluded Moosehorn Valley as to the approaching winter. As the final poem in the volume *Headwaters*, "Invitation and Covenant" offers an invitation to open doors and take hands with the wild on its own terms.

An invitation to such a covenant offers poetic potential for a radical politics that spurns human-built order and embraces loving the wild, implicitly destabilizing the culture/nature dichotomy in a move to integrate the two. To see humans wedded as one with the land emerges as an intrinsic land ethic and relationship. Embracing the wild, not taming or exploiting it, is a land ethic and radical politics. Taking hands with the wild circles back to being more human as part of the land in ecophilosophical terms, much as in the poem "Departure."

Ultimately, these poems call readers to know the land, respect life, and conserve the wild. They also assert the importance of law and governance in achieving such ends. The warden figure is symbolic of the rule of law in the Alberta Rockies and embodies the boundary lines of a national park, within which certain ethics prevail, even if ambiguous and flawed. In riding the Rockies, the warden draws a boundary on the land. The thin green line was paramount, and Marty understands the potential dire consequences of a land made vulnerable by a lack of protectors. His voice as a warden is a clarion call to action and a defence of boundaries, yet he is aware (painfully at times) of how illusory the dividing lines are for environmental protection in national parks and also for sovereignty in Canada. Ultimately, the boundary is a thin green line that fails to push back multifarious capitalist encroachments of poachers, tourists, and developers, not to mention government bureaucracy.

The warden thought that life would be holy within national parks and is appalled to find that it is not. The hard reality of life and death prevails in the mountains, with risks of many kinds. Life on the land touches him and makes him more aware and compassionate but also watchful. Contradictions abound as the poet finds the land a force of its own, but he also finds that the land can be defiled by those with sufficient means or inadequate understanding. He makes it clear that mortals are all predators or prey in one way or another, thereby seeing a world as ecological, but he also aspires to an ethical love of the land in a political world of ambiguities.

The Love Poems

In *Headwaters*, a cowboy's longing for a woman translates into a warm and tender language of love. And love is a way to know a man's true heart. Marty, the new and sensitive cowboy, understands that wild land alone will not sustain him. His poems often dwell on romantic thoughts of a lover far away or soon to be seen, much as a warden's life was a shift cycle of miles away. Many hours of intense physical work allow time for contemplation, memory, and imagination. Time does not stand still but works its way backward and forward in thoughts about love. The love poems navigate how a cowboy's heart that dares to reveal inner emotions can be strong and true—and where he finds himself in love.

First, "my love" is a figure present in many ways in these poems. Making coffee, splitting wood, and shoeing a gelding barely dull "the ache of love" and separation in the poem "The Work of Hands." The hands move in sundry cowboy tasks as the mind revisits "transitory flutterings of violet butterflies in green grass" and showers of flower petals in the sun. Distance is made worse by re-reading his lover's words while alone at Miette Cabin in Jasper.[22] The hands splicing rope falter as he struggles distractedly to bring mind and hands together. The distance between lovers is clear in the poem, but flashes of memory and fantasy pull him back to her. Meanwhile, memory and mood bring the lovers together across distance with fluttering impressions of light and landscape. The cowboy's hands are full, but the heart, too, is full of longing.

Making love is explored in the poem "Finding a Woman." It describes lovers "rocking in the night" as a man anchors sensations to finding a vessel, harbour, and home that is not his, but tenderly touched inside a woman.[23]

Finding a woman means finding his element and boundary with her. Without her, he is but a sailor adrift. Risks of opening his heart and feelings emerge as a young man finds his place in intimacy. Above all, a sensuous sexual encounter is expressed metaphorically in aesthetics of beauty and intimacy.

Mature love and expressive manliness are combined in "She Asks for a History." "It began as a stallion with a mare," the poet writes of the couple's early summer days and cold mountain nights together. The woman grew into a lover and summer blueberry-picking companion, with her "mouth my only berry." But she later departs for "the wild borealis," and the man recognizes he does not circumscribe her life. He is troubled by separation and agonizes in pain at the thought of being apart:

> I hold you too tightly now
> gaze too earnestly into your eyes
> in my selfishness, my unmanly fear
>
> We are so naked
> when the covers
> slip to the floor[24]

Shedding all, a feeling man is vulnerable and deeply in love. He reveals his fear and innermost sense that she is the centre of his life. In effect, the typical gender order is reversed, and he must await her return, knowing he is sensitive and fully exposed. He is not unafraid; he loves her and reveals an open heart that can be hurt or even rejected. The cowboy takes a new shape that challenges a conservative gender order by showing an emotional and caring man full of feelings for his woman.

Taking another lyrical direction toward love and sensuality as a way to a man's true heart, the abstract poem "Purple" leans to a figurative language of sensuous landscape. Its landscapes are abstracted to traverse boundaries and encode sexuality as a metaphorical way of seeing the land as "a shaft of snow/ married to rock/ where deep purple/ crowns the pole star."[25] Forms and colours are abstracted as a mood with a daydream feeling. The poem creates an impassioned circle of land and love enjoined as landscape imagery, calling out for an awakening—for "Love's giant life" to "shake me." Sensuous love is abstracted and understated lyrically as erotic landscape.

Marty's poems present alternatives for thinking about love and manhood. They also challenge the conservative gender order that expected men to be stoic and unemotional. The men in these poems are feeling and sensuous lovers, revealing emotion, vulnerability, and their innermost thoughts. Intimacy and sensuality fuses contact with the inner self. A man in love ultimately becomes more human. His lover is present in high country life. The land is also a figurative symbol of sensuality and life force, of moods and emotions. The poet shows sensitivity toward his lover and his own feelings, a sense of manliness and conventions different than a more typical taciturn and tough cowboy masculinity.

Knowing the Land and Heart

Marty translated the wild mountain backcountry into lyrical poetry—an expressive poetry of beauty and imagination—to rewrite the land and masculinity. Landscape lyricism and anti-modernism were joined as his poetry conveyed both the warden's way of life in the Rockies and a lost time in the West.[26] But his lyrical storytelling also expressed land ethics and love in poems with an irrefutable credence and appeal coming from a cowboy.[27]

Traditionally, Alberta writing rarely saw mountain prose and cowboy stories that were so revealing of open emotion and sensuousness. Marty challenged conservatism in a dissident voice that, although undeniably of the West, also ran counter to narratives of rugged cowboys and taming the land. Discovering himself in the land and in love, the poet portrays an unconventional cowboy and becomes the voice of a new kind of landman and lover.

In *Headwaters*, the cowboy warden is a man informed by reflexive ethics and practice in relations with the land and his mate. Exposed to the power of the land, man is touched by nature and a woman; he learns to listen. This creates a point of contact between the outer and inner world of man in Marty's poetry that alters boundaries and opens doors to be wild and to love. Man becomes aware and sensitized with compassion and strength. To be gentle with a grizzly and feel the pain of a dying moose beside the highway. To see a wild landscape as a lover and a lover's mouth as a blueberry. To love a woman tenderly and give away his whole heart. The warden is more fully a man because he feels and expresses emotions in lyrical complexity. Being wed to the land and to a strong woman is powerfully conveyed as love in poems that also rethink ecophilosophy and manhood. In this way, Marty's cowboy poetry conveys a radical potential for a new politics even as it revives elements of the Romantic and anti-modern imagery in conservative ideas of the West—cowboys on horseback and the Rockies as a colonial western frontier—in modern free form like the Beat poets.[28] Further, the work describes a sensuous landscape and intimate love that was unusual in Canada's mountain prose at the time but was made explicit in his poetry.

Marty's literary work in *Headwaters* documents a time and place at a major transition point. The district warden system in national parks ended with government changes in 1969, and wardens ceased to live year-round in the backcountry in 1972. In the Rockies, park wardens had once lived on the land, made backcountry cabins and warden stations their homes, married, raised families, and felt at home with pride of place and caring at the heart of a lived land ethic. Their presence on the land was part of tending parks and wildlife, knowing an ecosystem by dwelling within it.[29] Likewise, Marty and his wife, Myrna, were ultimately a warden family caring for the land and each other as they lived and worked together; the book's dedication to Myrna is also revealing. In many ways, Marty's poetry is a cultural landmark of flux and changing times between the backcountry traditions of a district warden system and emergent structures of government centralization. Positioned this way, it also becomes a form of lived resistance and poetic talking back to hegemonic state modernization trends in parks, much as it challenges conservative tropes of hypermasculine cowboys.

Just as he served as a public protector of Canada's national parks, Marty also stood up for Alberta's environment. National parks were a terrain spared from the hardest hits of resource extraction in Alberta in the 1960s and 1970s, because they were federal jurisdictions under law, but national parks still faced daily contradictions and incursions. Wildlife, highways, tourism, and escalating development were not an easy mix inside parks.[30] Moreover, oil and gas, recreation, and tourism were rapaciously eyeing the edges of the national parks with a view to open development. So Marty's poetic call for the wild acted as a rallying cry against callous violations and bureaucracy, advancing a more radical environmental politics for stronger land ethics to meet the ideal of national parks as protected by law.

The Great Divide headwaters, remotely situated in the Rockies range, are distal to life's modern intrusions, yet not so far away. Even as the warden rides away from modernity, it rides with him on patrols, enforcing wildlife regulations and searching for lost mountaineers as part of a modern administrative force and national park system. The long reach of the wardens is simultaneously a rationalist mechanism of the federal state. Here is the path typical of anti-modernists and Romantic poets: even in resisting modernity, all roads lead back to it. Yet even as Marty's employer the National Parks Branch—renamed Parks Canada in 1973—worked toward making the "wilderness" a managed space of master plans and bureaucracy, Marty tossed truth back to power and resisted from his vantage point of a western saddle, counting on Albertans and others to listen to him as a cowboy instead of a mere poet.

Nonetheless, certain local and regional park managers did not appreciate his literary politics, and after the publication in 1978 of *Men for the Mountains* they consigned him to a desk job that clipped his wings. His prose offered overt criticism of problems in Banff National Park, whereas his poetry had slid subversively under the radar. Despite it all, Marty would not be silenced or confined; he opted to resign from the warden service and move to southern Alberta, near Pincher Creek.[31] He turned his talents to freelance writing and to being a singer-songwriter, while raising a family and contributing to wilderness and conservation advocacy efforts in Alberta as a vocal advocate for the eastern slopes and the Old Man River. And he continued to ride and live in the foothills, close to his family roots, caring for the land.

The long-standing institution of Canada's national park warden service, served by Marty and many others, was forced to restructure under Pierre Trudeau's government and ultimately was broken up under Stephen Harper.[32] Continuing to advocate for the land, Marty stated in 2015, "I learned that asking people to do the right thing isn't good enough—you need to have people on the ground representing the government who are there to enforce the regulations for the benefit of the whole population."[33]

Like Thoreau, Marty writes of contact with nature and existence in pursuit of answers to the question of what is true.[34] His response is likewise an expression of politics and philosophy but from a working man: we are one with a living land. In *Headwaters,* the emphasis on a warden pushing physical boundaries of headwaters—"where the world begins"—is paralleled by the poet's imaginings that call out for "Love's giant life" to shake him but also to awaken readers. The sensuality of landscape also embodies sensuous love and passion. Existentialism and eroticism join forces, answering what it is to be alive. Imagination is a starting point for agency and change as poetry subtly offers readers the potential to see and feel the world anew—to "forget geometry"—and to step outside free and alive with a wilder nature.

The message of *Headwaters*—know the land and your own heart—is clear. Feeling can awaken insights and compassion. Marty's poetic politics of the Rockies convey that a sense of where we belong relies on listening for an intimate knowledge of caring and love.

NOTES

1. Sid Marty, *Headwaters* (Toronto: McClelland and Stewart, 1973).
2. For biographical information, see "Biography," Sid Marty website, http://www.sidmarty.com/biography; Sid Marty, *Leaning on the Wind: Under the Spell of the Great Chinook* (Toronto: HarperCollins, 1995), 2–4, 80–116; Lindsey Wallis, "Sid Marty: A Man for Alberta's Mountains," *Wild Lands Advocate* 23, no. 5 (2015): 25–27; Wikipedia, s.v. "Sid Marty," https://en.wikipedia.org/wiki/Sid_Marty.
3. Marty's published poetry also includes the volumes *Nobody Danced with Miss Rodeo* (1981), *Sky Humour* (1999), and *The Rider with Good Hands* (2012). His non-fiction books include: *Leaning on the Wind: Under the Spell of the Great Chinook* (1995), a finalist for the Governor General's Award for Literature and winner of the Mountain Environment and Culture Award at the Banff Mountain Book Festival; *Switchbacks* (1999), winner of the Jon Whyte Award at the Banff Mountain Book Festival; and *The Black Grizzly of Whiskey Creek* (2008), short-listed for a Governor General's Award. His literary and conservation efforts earned him the Banff Mountain Festivals Summit of Excellence Award in 2009 and the Alberta Wilderness Association's Wilderness Defender Award in 2015.
4. For related constructs and experiences of the cowboy, see Simon M. Evans, Sarah Carter, and W. B. Yeo, *Cowboys, Ranchers and the Cattle Business: Cross-Border Perspectives on Ranching History* (Calgary: Glenbow Museum and University of Calgary Press, 2000); Sheila J. Bannerman, "'Cowboys' of the Canadian West: Reorienting a Disoriented Mythology," *English Quarterly* 40, no. 1–2 (2008): 51–57.
5. George Woodcock, "The Songs Are Made of Soil," *Globe and Mail*, 5 October 1974, 35; George Woodcock, "The Strong New Voices of the West," *Globe and Mail*, 23 November 1981, L7; Kenneth Brewer, "*Headwaters*, by Sid Marty, and *Coyote Tantras*, by Barry Gifford (review)," *Western American Literature* 9, no. 1 (1974): 63–65; for similarities to Wordsworth and Emerson, see Clyde

Hosein, "Seeker on the Mountain," *Books In Canada* 3, no. 4 (1974): 31–32; William French, "Sharp and Clean as a Glacier Ridge," *Globe and Mail*, 26 January 1974, 32. French saw "great emphasis on nature in this poetry, but hardly any eroticism" in *Headwaters*; he also quotes an interview in which Marty said his Parks Canada colleagues "all bought the book."

6. George Melnyk, *The Literary History of Alberta*, vol. 2 (Edmonton: University of Alberta Press, 1999), 136.

7. Ecologist Aldo Leopold defined a land ethic as caring about the land and people to promote moral responsibility and belonging in a natural world. Ethics arise "in relation to something we can see, understand, feel, love, or otherwise have faith in." Leopold, *A Sand County Almanac and Sketches Here and There* (New York: Oxford University Press, 1987), 214.

8. Marty, "Departure," in *Headwaters*, 96.

9. Marty, "Cairn Pass," in *Headwaters*, 100–101.

10. Marty, "Pushing the Boundary," in *Headwaters*, 108–9.

11. Ibid.

12. Ibid.

13. Marty, "On the Boundary," in *Headwaters*, 85.

14. Marty, "The Death of Mustahyah," in *Headwaters*, 98.

15. Marty, "On Highway 16, Jasper," in *Headwaters*, 80.

16. Marty, "Meat in the Snow," in *Headwaters*, 36.

17. Marty, "Mercy," in *Headwaters*, 72–73.

18. Clyde Hosein, "Seeker on the Mountain," *Books in Canada* 3, no. 4 (1974): 31–32; French, "Sharp and Clean," 32.

19. Marty, "For Young Men," in *Headwaters*, 68.

20. Marty, "Bright Morning," in *Headwaters*, 69.

21. Marty, "Invitation and Covenant," in *Headwaters*, 110.

22. Marty, "The Work of Hands," in *Headwaters*, 42.

23. Marty, "Finding a Woman," in *Headwaters*, 92.

24. Marty, "She Asks for a History," in *Headwaters*, 94–95.

25. Marty, "Purple," in *Headwaters*, 101.

26. Louisa Mackenzie, *The Poetry of Place: Lyric, Landscape, and Ideology in Renaissance France* (Toronto: University of Toronto Press, 2011), 183; see also 3–16. Lyricism expresses an outflow of emotion. Poetic landscapes are socially and ideologically complex, carrying hope and "an acute awareness of their contingent relationship to the history they are trying to rewrite." Mackenzie, 183. See also John Kinsella, *Disclosed Poetics: Beyond Landscape and Lyricism* (Manchester: University of Manchester Press, 2007), xi–xii. On modernity, see T. J. Jackson Lears, *No Place for Grace: Antimodernism and the Transformation of American Culture, 1880–1920* (Chicago: University

of Chicago Press, 1994). Searching for a sense of pre-modern authenticity through intense physical, spiritual, or cultural means defines anti-modernism, itself produced by modernity.

27. W. H. New, "Tops and Tales: Mountain Anecdote and Mountain Metaphor," *Canadian Poetry: Studies, Documents, Reviews* 55 (Fall/Winter 2004): 8. Marty also engages storytelling as a strategy for teaching cautionary tales.

28. Melnyk, *Literary History*, 127–29; Hosein, "Seeker," 31–32.

29. See Nicole J. Eckert-Lyngstad, "The Backcountry as Home: Park Wardens, Families, and Jasper National Park's District Cabin System, 1952–1972" (MA thesis, University of Alberta, 2012), 84–85, 144–58; Robert J. Burns and Michael J. Schintz, *Guardians of the Wild: A History of the Warden Service of Canada's National Parks* (Calgary: University of Calgary Press, 2000), 249–65.

30. On the postwar context of national park use and development in the Rockies, see PearlAnn Reichwein, *Climber's Paradise: Making Canada's Mountain Parks, 1906–1974* (Edmonton: University of Alberta Press, 2014), 200–1, 206–8, 257–58. Banff National Park recorded more than 2.3 million tourists in 1969–70.

31. Marty, *Leaning on the Wind*, 3–4.

32. Dawn Walton, "Wardens Ordered to Stop Enforcement Duties," *Globe and Mail*, 11 May 2007.

33. Marty, quoted in Wallis, "Sid Marty," 27.

34. See Henry David Thoreau, *Walden: A Fully Annotated Edition*, ed. Jeffrey S. Cramer (New Haven: Yale University Press, 2004), xxiii–xxiv, 88; Thoreau, "Walking," in *Civil Disobedience and Other Essays* (New York: Dover, 1993), 61–69; Jack Turner, *A Political Companion to Henry David Thoreau* (Lexington: University Press of Kentucky, 2009), 1–12.

17   Death of a Delta

Tom Radford

There is a patience of the wild—dogged, tireless, persistent as life itself. —Jack London

Fort Chipewyan sits atop a granite bluff above Lake Athabasca, one hundred kilometres north of the Alberta oil sands. The view over the lake is one of the most dramatic in the North, the point where the jagged promontories of the Canadian Shield plunge into one of the largest freshwater lakes on the continent. Today home to a mixture of Cree, Chipewyan, and Métis peoples, for a time it was a fur trade post established by Alexander Mackenzie. His ill-fated expedition in search of a western ocean wintered here in 1788, making the improvised log buildings his men built the oldest European community in the province. First Nations had lived on the site for millennia, but history would come to know them only as Mackenzie's "guides."

As the party explored the Athabasca River, which Mackenzie mistakenly thought would lead him to the Pacific, he made note of a tar-like substance pouring from the ground in "bituminous fountains, into which a pole of twenty feet long may be inserted without the least resistance. The bitumen is in a fluid state, and when mixed with gum, or the resinous substance collected from the spruce fir, serves to gum the canoes."[1] If only the Europeans had been content with canoe repairs, as were the local inhabitants. Who could have guessed that the extraction of the sticky substance, later known as "tar sand," would one day drastically change the Athabasca wilderness and, for that matter, the very nature of Alberta itself?

When I worked in Fort Chipewyan in the summer of 1971, making my first film, the only access to the remote settlement—known to the locals simply as "Chip"—was by boat or the bush plane that once a week brought the mail, supplies, and the odd bootlegger. The streets were unpaved and the water, cold and clear, was still delivered door to door by a jocular old man in a horse-drawn wagon, who regimentally saluted each of his customers as if they were royalty. Only one tar sands operation, Great Canadian Oil Sands, financed by the Philadelphia capitalist J. Howard Pew, had been built upstream on the Athabasca. Its shining steel towers soared above the wilderness like a space station but had little impact on Indigenous culture. The people in Chip lived as if the massive refinery and strip mine did not exist, trapping and fishing in the tradition of their ancestors, a timeless rhythm that set them apart from the breakneck pace of the fossil fuel industry. The tiny community was perched on the edge of the sprawling Peace-Athabasca Delta, the largest boreal delta in the world. Largely uninhabited by humans, this 794,000-acre Garden of Eden was made a UNESCO World Heritage Site in 1983.[2]

My film, *Death of a Delta*, told the story of what set Indigenous communities like Chip apart from the rest of Alberta, focusing on their resistance to the massive extractive projects that politicians and engineers were imposing on northern Canada. Ironically, the construction of a dam on the Peace River near Hudson Hope, British Columbia, was to have an even greater impact on the residents of Fort Chipewyan than the oil sands. The Peace was the second great river that fed the delta, and its spring floodwaters were responsible for maintaining the ecosystem of lakes, channels, meadows, and marshes that made the local economy viable. But since the completion of the dam, across the BC border to the west, the delta had begun to dry up, and large populations of muskrats, beavers, waterfowl, fish, moose, caribou, and wood bison had become endangered. For the people of Chip, who had lived in a renewable relationship to the natural world for as long as anyone could remember, a way of life was coming to an end.

The massive dam was being built by BC Hydro to provide electric power for Vancouver and the Lower Mainland and was named after a long-time despoiler of northern wilderness, W. A. C. Bennett, the Social Credit premier. The dam was only the latest chapter in a "rush for spoils" that characterized BC history, the looting of natural resources with little regard for Indigenous peoples and their land. At least, that was our take as filmmakers. Young and intent on righting the wrongs of the past, to our mind even the old Hudson Bay Company trading post in Chip was a symbol of that plunder, closely tied to the British Empire and its American successor. We were outraged when we discovered Dow Chemical products on the shelves of the store. Dow had recently built a plant near Edmonton that was manufacturing napalm for the war in Vietnam.

The townspeople took our polemics in stride, curious and amused at how seriously we took ourselves, assuring us that Dow Chemical was the least of their problems. With years of resource development imposed on them from the South (the toxic mines of Uranium City had been built down the lake from them in Saskatchewan in 1952) they understood very well what was at stake with the dam. An unholy alliance of government and industry would have to be confronted if they were to save their town. Judging by the indifference of Social Credit administrations in both British Columbia and Alberta, it would be an uphill battle. The community was a crazy quilt of political factions—Métis, Cree, Chipewyan, Anglo—each subjected to the divide-and-conquer policies of the Department of Indian and Northern Affairs for generations. But the bureaucrats had failed to compromise the great strength of the village: its sense of kinship. Intermarriage among the various groups was the norm, and the resulting mixed-blood society was defiant in its defence of the distinctly northern way of life that the delta supported.

We had grown up in Edmonton in the shadow of Social Credit ourselves, a party that had been in power in Alberta for thirty-six years when our film crew arrived in the North. (Crew may be too strong a word—there were only two of us, cinematographer Bob Reece and me, doing sound.) Ernest Manning, the patriarch of conservatism in the province, had recently retired as premier, and although a progressive wing of the party was attempting to assert itself, an aura of "fundamental truth" remained. The established order derived from the Will of God, and "rocking the boat" was frowned upon. The universities were no exception, and it was rare for any controversial body of research to be made public. One outlier was a paper by Bill Fuller of the Department of Zoology at the University of Alberta titled "Death of a Delta," which became the inspiration for our film.[3] Fuller was alarmed at the ecological impact of the Bennett Dam on the Peace-Athabasca Delta. His research had traced a prolonged drought to the development of the project, which had constricted water flow to the region, especially the spring floods essential to trapping, the mainstay of life in Chip. Fuller's outspoken defence of the environment was decades ahead of its time, a thorn in the side of a government that—in deference to its BC Social Credit cousin—had turned its back on the downstream Alberta communities affected by low water levels. One of Fuller's supporters was a young David Suzuki, who began his career in genetics as an assistant professor at U of A. (Who could have imagined the controversy that Suzuki being awarded an honorary doctorate by the university in 2018 would stir up? Alberta had long since become "Oil's Deep State," as Kevin Taft, the Leader of the Opposition in the legislature from 2004 to 2008, calls it.)[4]

To inexperienced filmmakers, the Fuller paper was a godsend, focusing our random discontent on a well-researched and documented issue. The chance to investigate the abuses of corporate and political power and champion the rights of a small community fit perfectly with our intent to combine *cinema vérité* with community activism. Donald Brittain and Peter Pearson had recently produced a documentary with the National Film Board titled *Saul Alinsky Went to War*, which we admired greatly. The film recorded a political organizer's work with disenfranchised communities similar to Fort Chipewyan, challenging the conditions that keep the poor in poverty. Although we had no idea what we were doing—neither of us had even been to film school—we were determined to make a similar film. It was thus with some trepidation that we set foot in Chip for the first time, with a new camera and tape recorder fresh out of their shipping cases. We knew we were treading on thin ice.

The first day we shot nothing but interviews. Trapper Ernie Bourque: "I think someone should go up there with a ton of dynamite and blow that dam sky high. It isn't doing us any good. BC has enough water, they should stop taking our water." Fisherman Clement Mercredi: "You know how hard a guy has got to work on account of that bloody dam? I used to cross Lake Mamawi by boat, now I have to use a dog team to haul the boat across the mud. The water is only six inches deep." Frank Ladouceur, president of the local Métis association: "On the whole of Rat Island, the water's gone from the shore. One year we killed 17,000 muskrats in that lake, big rats. You get $2.85 for No. 1 rats in Regina. [. . .] [N]ow the fur's no good and the hide's so thin you're lucky to get sixty-five cents. If there was another one of those Riel Rebellions, I'd be one of them."

Ladouceur's trapline was at the mouth of the Athabasca, across the lake from Chip, where the river ended its long journey through the tar sands.[5] Myriad channels and sloughs formed a delta that defied navigation by any but the most seasoned boatman. But for Frank, shown the way by both father and grandfather for decades, the labyrinth had become second nature. The family had fled to the delta after their defeat at the Battle of Batoche in 1885, the end of the Riel Resistance. "Into the bush," Frank would say. "Those soldiers from Ontario were never going to find us." Short, broad shouldered, a fighter in the tradition of Gabriel Dumont, Frank once pulled the local Hudson Bay Company manager across the counter when the man tried to cheat him on his furs. "I was going to finish him good," Frank maintained, before a friend intervened.

In 1971, Ladouceur invited Peter Lougheed, the Leader of the Opposition in the Alberta legislature, to come north and see the damage the dam had caused to the delta. Lougheed, the first provincial leader to visit the isolated community, was shocked at the extent of the destruction and, with an election pending, brought the issue to the attention of southerners. There were many storylines in that election, not the least of which was the hunger for change in the province after thirty-six years of Social Credit rule, but for the first time in Alberta politics, the environment itself became an important issue and had a place in the downfall of the government.

One day, Frank and I were sitting in his outboard—drifting across what was left of Lake Mamawi, where the Peace River fed the delta from the west—drinking tea he had made on his tiny propane stove, which at that moment was balanced precariously on the boat's prow. White cumulus clouds rose in the heat, as an unseen current moved this vast waterland north toward the Rivière des Rocheurs and ultimately to the Slave and the Mackenzie, Canada's longest river system. Above us, the sky pulsed with the wings of migrating pelicans, ducks, and geese. As the sun sank low on the horizon, lake and sky became one, the colour of pearl. The moon rose to the east, Venus directly overhead, as the birds settled for the night. In the silence, the water turned to glass, reflecting the constellations that stretched above us. It was as if we were floating in a time and space as old as nature itself, far from the world of hydro dams and pipelines.

The scene reminded me of an old sepia photograph in the books that lined my grandfather's study back in Edmonton, depicting Ernest Thompson

Seton, the explorer and naturalist, crossing this same lake by canoe a hundred years ago. Seton marvelled at the bird life of the delta:

> The morning came with a strong north wind and rain that turned to snow, and with it great flocks of birds migrating from Athabasca Lake. Many rough legged Hawks, hundreds of small land birds, thousands of Snow-birds in flocks of 20 to 200 [. . .] passed over our heads going southward before the frost. About 8:30 the Geese began to pass in ever-increasing flocks; between 9:45 and 10, I counted 114 flocks averaging about 30 each [. . .] and they kept on at this rate until 2pm. This would give a total of nearly 100,000 Geese [. . .] so high they looked not like Geese, but threads across the sky. [. . .] I sketched and counted flock after flock with a sense of thankfulness.[6]

Today, wildlife biologist Kevin Timoney calls this same flyway a "mortality sink," as the parched delta funnels the birds south over the tar sands refineries and tailings ponds. Thousands disappear on the journey. The vast reservoirs that store the toxic residue of the refining process look like lakes from the air, and no matter how many deterrents the companies put in place, the birds keep trying to land on them. The vast migrations that so impressed Seton have disappeared. And as the pollution from the giant smokestacks spreads over the land, the songbirds of the boreal forest have gone silent.

Frank packs up the teapot and the bannock and we start for home. On the long journey across the delta, in the fashion of the country, the tall tales begin, each tied to a particular place and the memory it holds. *Ladouceur* means "sweetness" and, despite the dislocation of his people and their way of life, he always has a smile on his face and a story to tell. My favourite describes a summer's day years ago:

> In the middle of Lake Mamawi, I was digging for my lunch in the cardboard box at the bow of the boat, when I tripped over the fuel line to the outboard engine. My weight disconnected the line, and as the boat tipped, I knocked it overboard. The metal hose was heavy enough to sink to the bottom of the lake before I could grab it. Now it really was time for a cup of tea. It was a beautiful clear afternoon and I noticed a flock of whistling swans in the distance [. . .] such beautiful birds. As they circled to land I began to pay particular attention to their long slender necks. I wondered whether they would stretch the two feet required to connect the fuel tank to the engine? I was ready with my

rifle when the next flock approached the boat, and within an hour I had a new fuel line [. . .] at least one that would get me home.

We return to Chip by the light of the moon, Frank threading his way through the maze of channels. The delta is upwards of two hundred kilometres wide, yet often less than a foot deep. There are countless places to run aground. Well after dark, Frank's father, Modeste, greets us at the dock, armed with his fiddle and a bottle of whiskey. The Ladouceur kitchen is soon alive with the songs the Métis brought north from the uprisings of 1870 and 1885, when the federal government seized their lands: "The St. Anne's Reel," "Ciel du Manitoba," "Riel's Farewell." Each tune carries the memory of a Prairie republic won and lost. Gnarled fingers fly up and down the strings as feet tap out the tunes on the linoleum floor. The moose-skin moccasins are stitched with three intertwined Alberta roses, a traditional Cree design, and the multi-coloured beadwork sparkles in the light of a wood fire.

The music will follow me the rest of my life—a bridge back to this extraordinary community and its fierce battles with Big Hydro, and later Big Oil. Many of the films I make will carry the spirit of that fight: *Strange Empire*, the history of the Métis resistance in the nineteenth century; *I, Nuligak*, the first Inuit account of European colonization in the Arctic; *China Mission*, on Chester Ronning's fight to convince the Canadian government to recognize the People's Republic of China; *Tipping Point*, an investigation into the environmental impact of the tar sands. I will work with other western filmmakers to form the companies Film Frontiers, Filmwest, Great Plains, and Clearwater; I will seek out storytellers Anne Wheeler, Bob Reece, Reevan Dolgoy, and Gil Cardinal to develop a unique Alberta approach to documentary. Homegrown painters like Harry Savage and Sylvain Voyer, and composers like Roger Deegan, will work with us to develop a Prairie aesthetic, a language that evokes the beautiful land whose destruction we were witnessing. Like Frank's stories, narrative will be rooted in who we are, giving voice to the idea that a distinctive, deeply rooted culture is every bit as important as economic growth.

Death of a Delta was made for classroom use in Alberta's junior high schools. At first the Social Credit government, with an election approaching in 1971, considered the film too political and opted to delay its release. But when it won a prize the next year at the Festival dei Populi (The People's Festival) in Florence, Italy, the new Conservative government lifted the ban, and the film was shown in schools across the province. For a time, the documentary became part of a broader discussion on the future of resource development on a shrinking planet. Alberta's new premier, Peter Lougheed, demanded more royalties from the oil companies, instituted stronger regulations to protect the environment, and, true to his election promise, consulted with constituencies like Chip on proposed expansion of the fossil fuel industry. No one could do anything about the completed Bennett Dam, but at least similar mistakes could be avoided in the future. By the 1980s, as Lougheed was succeeded first by oilman Don Getty and then the "slash and burn" policies of Ralph Klein, any hope for a community-centred approach to northern development had disappeared. The protection of the environment was considered bad for business.

By the turn of the twenty-first century, the province had become one of the world's most powerful producers of fossil fuel—a major source of the greenhouse gases that were precipitating the crisis of climate change. The issue was mostly ignored in the province. Year by year, the grassroots democracy that had built Alberta was captured by immensely wealthy outside interests such as Exxon and Shell and the ultra-conservative brothers Charles and David Koch. The Conservatives who succeeded Lougheed welcomed these multinationals to what they called "the Alberta Advantage," a perfect place to do business, with a minimum of government to get in the way. Deregulation and privatization replaced what had been a robust public sector, the legacy of a frontier society where people had to pull together to get things done. Now, Big Oil in London and Houston, not the citizens of Fort Chip, would decide the province's future. Opposition would be tolerated in form but not substance. And for those who pushed back, there was the advice of Getty, the Edmonton Eskimo quarterback who had become premier: "You're either 'onside' or you're not." There would be no middle ground in a branch plant economy.

Northern lights dance across the sky above Fort Chipewyan. The furniture in the Ladouceur kitchen has been pushed aside and a party is underway. Modeste has thrown down the gauntlet—the walls are shaking with the Red River jigs of his ancestors. Sweat pouring from his brow, Frank dances with each of his twelve children. Among them is Raymond, "Big Ray," who towers over his dad but whose feet move like quicksilver. In the years ahead, while many of the Ladouceur kids will take jobs in the cities and boomtowns of the North, Ray will remain in Chip, like his father, eking out the living of a trapper in a destroyed landscape. When the Bennett Dam is a done deal, he will campaign against the pollution of air and water caused by the expansion of the tar sands. Working with "the two doctors," as he calls them—David Schindler in Edmonton and John O'Connor in Chip itself—he will search for a connection between toxins in the Athabasca River and the mysterious illnesses that have begun to beset the community. He will collect deformed fish from his nets and take them south for analysis. After extensive testing, Schindler and O'Connor begin to suspect the tar sands tailings ponds. Hastily constructed and porous, they leak poisons into the groundwater, which in turn seeps into the river. Could the deformities in the fish be connected to high incidences of cancer, lupus, and rheumatoid arthritis among the town's residents? Cholangiocarcinoma, cancer of the biliary tract, which normally occurs once among one hundred thousand people, has two confirmed and three suspected cases in Fort Chip, its population little more than a thousand.

At "the fork," near the place where Mackenzie came upon his "bitumenous fountains," a moose stands in water that barely reaches its ankles, its tracks crossing a vast mudflat where river channels used to run. Mackenzie described this place, where the currents of two mighty rivers, the Athabasca and the Clearwater, converge, as "forming one vast stream of moving water" a quarter mile from shore to shore. It was as if the ground trembled underfoot, the watershed of a vast wilderness sweeping by on its journey to a northern ocean.

Big Ray tells me that places where rivers meet hold great power for his people. Water is respected as a sacred gift. Yet recent measurements of the Athabasca show the lowest flow in the river's history. Schindler, winner of the Stockholm Water Prize, warns that global warming is melting the glaciers in the Columbia Icefield, from which the river flows, at an alarming rate, causing summer levels to drop as much as 40 percent. In addition, more than twenty new water licences have been issued for recent oil sands developments, allowing water withdrawal of up to 363,000,000 cubic metres from the river.

Big Ray knows he is tilting at windmills. Big Oil spends millions promoting what good community citizens they are. One of the local First Nations has gone into partnership with a tar sands company, as the citizens of Fort Chip watch their delta turn toxic. Once abundant fish and wildlife abandon the region or turn sick. The birds that remain continue to land on the deadly tailings ponds to the south, thinking they have discovered the lakes that have disappeared. Driven by winds that never seem to stop, the wildfires of a changing climate rage on the horizon. Strip mines leave the earth in turmoil. The silent Athabasca, its banks exposed down to the riverbed, winds through the devastation, nature's witness to the folly of man. Executive jets land on private runways built in the shadow of the giant refineries. Their passengers, managers from oil's deep state, carry out the daily bidding of the global economy, extracting enormous profit for investors outside the province. Exxon CEO Rex Tillerson (before he briefly became Donald Trump's secretary of state) made twenty-five million dollars a year. Big Ray is lucky to make twenty-five thousand.

The world we live in has changed drastically since that day in 1971 when I shared a cup of tea with Ray's dad, the family skiff floating across the still surface of Lake Mamawi. The delta, a microcosm of all life, stretched so far in every direction you thought you could feel the curve of the earth. One could not imagine that this great body of water, following the tilt of the continent to the Arctic Ocean, could ever disappear, or that the sheltering sky, so blue, so clear, was already home to a dangerous concentration of greenhouse gases. In the years that followed, as levels of carbon dioxide in the atmosphere increased, as Canada's boreal forest shrank, the natural reservoir that once allowed the earth to absorb much of the carbon in the atmosphere grew smaller.

Frank used to say that our northern history is the story of a succession of hinterlands, a geography of empire, where "hewers of wood and drawers of water" plied their trade for an economy controlled by "fat cats" far away. In the nineteenth and twentieth centuries, Montréal and Toronto, Vancouver and Calgary became profit centres for those same robber barons, each dedicated to expanding the resource frontier. Much of the rest of the country remained for all intents and purposes an outback, where environmental destruction could be rationalized as the price of progress. The fate of the Peace-Athabasca Delta is the classic example of such a surrender—troubling but soon forgotten. Out of sight, out of mind. But with climate change there will no longer be hinterlands. Humans will ignore damage to the natural world, wherever it be, at their own peril. The sustainability of the delta will be as critical to the planet's destiny as the Great Lakes or the Amazon. Frank knew this in his bones.

The old warrior's last years were spent with Big Ray, searching for new river channels to reach his stranded traplines. I would see him the odd time in Edmonton, where he still came to sell his furs. Each visit he seemed to be drinking more and his diabetes grew worse. When he died in 1989, it seemed as if the delta died with him. The construction of multiple upgraders in the tar sands, each with its own intake of water from the Athabasca, had rendered 80 percent of the delta's rivers and lakes inaccessible by boat. The promise in Treaty 8 to the Cree and Chipewyan peoples, to protect their life "as long as the rivers flow," had lost any meaning. Sacred places—the meadows where the elders once collected medicines, the graves where ancestors are buried—had all been left high and dry by the receding waters. And as if to mock all that had been lost, work began in British Columbia on a second giant hydro project on the Peace River, the Site C Dam. It was to cost over $11 billion.

Today, fewer than a thousand women, men, and children live in Fort Chipewyan. But many residents have not given up the struggle against the multinationals and the politicians who have been captured by the energy economy. Against the heaviest of odds, ordinary people still push back. The legacy of the ancestors has endured: Live renewably. Trust in your own distinct culture. Respect the land. Feel the flow of the river as it winds its way to that northern ocean.

I can still hear Frank's voice: "If there was another one of those Riel Rebellions, I'd be one of them." As global warming transforms the world around us, his fight to save a freshwater delta might well be the birthright we pass on to our own children. Their future may depend on it.

NOTES

1. Alexander Mackenzie, *Voyages from Montreal, on the River St. Laurence, Through the Continent of North America, to the Frozen and Pacific Oceans, in the Years 1789 and 1793* (London: Printed for T. Cadell, W. Davies, Corbett and Morgan, and W. Creech, 1801), lxxxvii, Peel's Prairie Provinces, University of Alberta Libraries, http://peel.library.ualberta.ca/bibliography/55.html.

2. Kevin Timoney, *The Peace-Athabasca Delta* (Edmonton: University of Alberta Press, 2013).

3. For more on Bill Fuller, see Ed Struzik, "Great Scientist Was at Home in the Muskeg," *Edmonton Journal*, 5 July 2009.

4. Kevin Taft, *Oil's Deep State* (Toronto: Lorimer, 2017).

5. For an extended portrait of Frank Ladouceur, see my 1975 film *Man Who Chooses the Bush*, available on the National Film Board of Canada website, https://www.nfb.ca/film/man_who_chooses_the_bush/.

6. Ernest Thompson Seaton, *The Arctic Prairies* (New York: Charles Scribner's Sons, 1911), 286–87.

Conclusion

Bucking Conservatism, Then and Now

Karissa Robyn Patton and Mack Penner

When Leon, Larry, and Karissa first proposed this collection, the Alberta New Democratic Party had held its position of government in the provincial legislature for just one year. Some hoped this collection could explain the NDP's uncharacteristic victory in 2015. Many wanted to know what had inspired this dramatic political shift and when Alberta "stopped being conservative." But as *Bucking Conservatism* hits the bookshelves, the province's reputation as Canada's conservative heartland has been seemingly reaffirmed. In April 2019, Alberta voters ended the brief reign of the NDP, electing instead a majority government of the United Conservative Party (UCP), with Jason Kenney as premier. The *National Observer* described the UCP's entry into the legislature as a "resounding victory."[1] Indeed, by Canadian electoral standards, the UCP's total of just more than half of the popular vote (54.9 percent) does represent a dominant electoral performance. Still, though, 54.9 percent is by no means a huge majority, and nearly a third of Albertans (32.7 percent) voted for the NDP.[2] Resounding as the UCP's victory may have been in 2019, it did not reveal anything actually resembling ideological unanimity in the province. The victory of the UCP, however, fits nicely into a broader narrative about Alberta politics and history. With Kenney at the helm, the myth of the province as a conservative monolith has returned in full force.

This image, while politically convenient, is obviously not accurate, as the introduction to this volume, along with each individual chapter, makes abundantly clear. However, insofar as the conservative myth continues to animate the general perception of the province, it is worth taking up. Even after the UCP's victory in 2019, for example, workers and activists mobilized against the imposition of a ruthlessly austere conservative budget and thousands of environmentalists marched for climate justice in Alberta's cities. Yet, an impression that political developments were going along in accordance with some conservative normality persisted. The prevailing narrative about conservatism in Alberta thus continues, as it has done historically, to erase and to obscure dissenting voices. This erasure of alternative stories in Alberta is lamentable. In the first place, it does a disservice to the historical study of Canada by exceptionalizing the history of the province and thus limiting its historiographical relevance. Rather more crucially, it hinders the ability of activists to understand themselves as furthering important historical traditions and forecloses upon possibilities for creating solidarity between Albertans and non-Albertans. Even further, the downplaying of Alberta's rich alternative history enables derisive talk about Alberta elsewhere in Canada. The province is singled out as the reference point against which the rest of the country, without altogether deserving it, can feel good about itself. The history rendered in *Bucking Conservatism* combats this trend in more ways than one.

In the aftermath of the 2019 provincial election, and the federal election later that year, Canadian media narratives were particularly interested in developments that adhered to existing stereotypes.[3] The 2019 provincial and federal elections both returned a near full slate of Conservatives to Alberta's legislative and parliamentary seats, fuelling rhetoric about western Canada as a bastion of conservatism. For an example of this phenomenon, one could look to media coverage of a number of "truck convoys" that made their way, on a couple of occasions, to Edmonton and Ottawa in order to convey support for the provincial oil industry and opposition to the work of environmentalists inside and outside of Alberta. On 18 October 2019, one of these convoys travelled from Red Deer to Edmonton in order to protest the visit paid by sixteen-year old Swedish climate activist Greta Thunberg to the legislature. Perhaps for the way they conveniently fit into an existing discourse about conservatism and petro-politics, the members of this convoy received no shortage of media attention. It is a little odd, however, that the truck drivers opposing Thunberg's visit even registered as important on a day that saw as many as four thousand mostly young climate strikers on the streets of Edmonton and in front of the legislature insisting on a livable future.[4] Climate strikers also protested that day in Alberta's other cities, including Calgary, Lethbridge, Red Deer, Medicine Hat, and Grande Prairie. But in a discursive context in which Alberta is assumed to be so thoroughly conservative, especially in its collective perspective on the fossil fuel industry, groups like the truck convoys easily come to represent Albertan political culture writ large.

In the case of the October 2019 climate strikes—a story that ought to have been about the obvious purchase of environmentalist politics in the province—far too much focus was placed on how Albertans, in supposedly typical form, showed up to express their displeasure with a young activist from another country. Or, from an equally erroneous perspective, the presence of a famous activist from Europe could be taken as evidence that environmentalist politics were being somehow foisted upon the province from elsewhere. In fact, dissent in Alberta is and has been "homegrown."[5]

Less than a year after the climate strikes, Albertans once again gathered en masse this time in solidarity with local and international Black Lives Matter activists who were protesting the killing of George Floyd in Minneapolis on 25 May 2020. Between June 4 and 7, stories of local acts of racism accompanied calls for defunding the police, while chants of "Black Lives Matter" and "Indigenous Lives Matter" rang out across the province. Over twenty thousand Albertans attended Black Lives Matter and Anti-Racism Rallies held in Calgary, Edmonton, Lethbridge, Red Deer, Grande Prairie, Fort McMurray, Innisfail, and Brooks.[6] Although the years of the UCP regime may be easy to narrate as more of the conservative same by those blinkered by assumptions about conservative unanimity in Alberta, this period also offers ample evidence of the progressive, even radical, potentialities within the province's political culture.

Developments between 2019 and 2021 to which far too little attention has been paid include mobilizations of public sector workers, especially nurses and teachers, against harsh cuts and governmental meddling with pensions, as well as students and faculty who have rallied against post-secondary tuition increases and drastic funding reductions. Despite the challenges posed by the pandemic in 2020 and 2021, Albertans created grassroots movements and communicated their displeasure with the austerity politics of the UCP. Online communities like Albertans Reject Curriculum Draft, a Facebook group of almost fifty thousand Albertans, forcefully opposed the settler-centric and often historically erroneous K-6 curriculum draft proposed by the UCP in spring 2021.[7] There was also significant public support for the Alberta Union of Provincial Employees hospital worker walkouts in October 2020.[8] These and other efforts demonstrate that many Albertans do stand up for education, healthcare, and the public sector more broadly. The fact of the UCP government's existence, and its preference for a reactionary politics of austerity, is not the only fact of Alberta's contemporary political reality. Ongoing and vehement opposition to such politics is not hard to find and is substantial enough to warrant far more acknowledgement, and interprovincial support, than it often gets.

The provincial government has used this rhetoric to its advantage. If Albertans are told—by the premier, MLAs, the media, or the historical literature—that they are alone if they are not conservative, perhaps dissent is less likely. The UCP are banking on this idea and thus are surely happy to encounter and emphasize narratives that imply widespread, unshakeable support for conservative governance. And when opposition to the UCP and other oppressive institutions is not recognized in a meaningful way, the opposition appears even more subdued. Politicians like Kenney, and parties like the UCP, count on people feeling helpless in their situation, reminding them that they cannot make meaningful change until the government changes, which is also considered unlikely. The silencing of dissenting voices in contemporary media and within the historiography, therefore, makes it easier for the UCP to discourage and demean action against their policies.

The myth serves other Canadians and political parties, too, because they can use the explicit shortcomings of Alberta Conservatives to hide their own. In 2016 a popular podcast called *Colour Code* released an episode called "The Angel Complex" to explain how Canadians often "use the United States [as a scapegoat] . . . when we don't want to face our own problems, and that includes the problems that we have with race and racism." As the podcast episode goes on, the hosts ask why some histories—in particular, histories of racism and colonialism—are not included in "how we see ourselves as Canadians."[9] While the episode of *Colour Code* focuses on racism, the angel complex concept can also be applied to topics of misogyny, homophobia, Islamophobia, ableism, and colonialism. The rhetoric of the angel complex is problematic in many ways. It makes systemic oppression invisible by constantly pointing the proverbial finger someplace else. So, interrogating the idea of the Canadian angel complex reveals how often people use problems in other places to avoid addressing the problems in their own backyards, or within their own histories. Importantly, this is a process that plays out *within* Canada as well. The Prairies, and Alberta in particular, are often used as a scapegoat for the oppression and injustice that exists in Canada.

Alberta, colloquially described as "Canada's loud, drunk, obnoxious uncle," has earned its place as the politically conservative stronghold in the country.[10] And while there has been a political legacy of conservative parties in the provincial legislature, the ideological demography of the legislature does not remotely map onto the ideological demography of the province more generally. We believe that the province is more than its reigning political party. By challenging this angel complex, we hope that *Bucking Conservatism* adds to a growing body of literature that reconsiders definitions of activism and conservatism, while drawing out the complexities of systemic oppression. Because, if oppression is understood as following mostly from the actions of a sole individual or community, the systemic ways that it operates within the law, institutions, and day-to-day experiences are made invisible. Using particular peoples or spaces as scapegoats to ignore these larger problems also makes the important work of local activists who are trying to tear down these systems more difficult to appreciate.

Even within the alternative histories of Alberta, some Prairie activists felt their radical efforts were not always recognized during the 1960s and 1970s. During an oral history interview with Rita Moir, for example, she remembered the "Western Express" in the early 1970s. She explained that student journalist activists from across the Prairies gathered on a train to join a large Canadian University Press gathering in Toronto. Moir remembers this trip fondly but shared her feeling that the activists on the Prairies often experienced "western alienation" from student news presses at larger central Canadian schools, like the University of Toronto.[11] In the 1970s, Moir's activism and the important work of her Prairie peers was not always recognized by their central Canadian counterparts. And in ensuing decades, opportunities to explore the history that Moir is a part of have largely not been taken.

Histories of the struggles and triumphs of dissent, activism, and resistance in Alberta confront the angel complex and broaden our definitions of who counts as an activist. Recently, historians have established the importance of recognizing activism beyond marches and sit-ins.[12] While these are important sites of dissent, as Beth Palmer argues, histories outside the highly visible action (specific to abortion in her case) in Vancouver and Toronto provide insight into "a more practical side of abortion activism in the 1970s

that is easily overlooked."[13] These scholars have ignited a historiographical wave that recognizes various activisms, such as letter writing, service
provision, educational and consciousness-raising efforts, and community
building, in the historical narrative. In doing so, they have created more
opportunities to explore a history of activism in spaces rendered "conservative." And there are so many more stories to tell, especially when it comes
to activism in rural places and within immigrant communities, as well as
the experiences and work of Black activists, lesbian activists, and disability
rights activists. The chapters in *Bucking Conservatism* add to this shift and
will hopefully encourage others to look deeper into the history of activism
in the province.

Bucking Conservatism's glance into the activist history of Alberta also
reveals what Grace Ouellette describes as "parallel but separate" streams
between the activisms of Indigenous people and White settlers during the
1960s and 1970s.[14] As Leon Crane Bear, Corinne George, and Tarisa Dawn
Little explain in their essays, Indigenous resistance and community organization existed for decades before the time period covered in this book.
We recognize that the lines between activist issues are not cut and dried.[15]
Indeed, Indigenous people participated in many advocacy initiatives; however, community organizing often centred on the systemic colonialism that
Indigenous people faced daily. There were instances of Indigenous-settler
activist collaboration during the 1960s and 1970s, such as the solidarity
formed between settler and Indigenous activists captured in Tom Radford's
essay "Death of a Delta." Nevertheless, White activists during these decades
fought for reproductive rights, political and ideological shifts in government,
and homes and cities without pollution. Indigenous activists often fought for
the same causes but had the additional burden of fighting to keep their children, retaining rights to their land, maintaining sovereignty, and lobbying for
basic amenities and better living conditions on reserves, as well as fighting
for citizenship and status rights. The systemic colonialism Indigenous people
faced daily, therefore, necessitated additional activist labour not required of
their White counterparts during the 1960s and 1970s.

The recent growth in histories of activism and dissent on the Prairies
is particularly exciting for historians of Alberta. The proliferation of these
kinds of investigations, which can be understood as "counter-histories,"
does more than simply draw attention to political culture(s) beyond the
conservative one that we have been told is firmly entrenched and widely

accepted.[16] These histories prompt a concomitant questioning: If the myth of shared and unanimous conservatism is only just that, a myth, then how should Alberta be understood? The point here is not that it is impossible or wrong to talk about Alberta as a place in which the ideological influence of conservatism is strong. Generalizations about political culture are often useful and necessary. However, too often in the case of Alberta such generalizations are not accompanied by sufficient caution or nuance. This lack of critical engagement routinely causes generalizing to become myth-making. And the myth, once established, is very difficult to dislodge as by force of repetition it takes on the character of fact. De-exceptionalizing the historical political culture of Alberta and moving beyond the myth enables the development of insights relevant for Canadian historiography more broadly and can contribute to the dismantling of a conservative monopoly on the practice of government.

Among the obstacles to a more balanced politico-cultural understanding of Alberta is the tendency to equate provincial electoral results with the actual political outlook of the province, not just in the media, as we've discussed, but in scholarship as well. Clearly, from the mid-1930s, Alberta's electoral history has been dominated by parties on the political right. With the exception of the NDP government of 2015 to 2019, provincial elections have returned majority conservative governments for decades. The Social Credit Party and the Progressive Conservatives carried the banner for nearly eighty uninterrupted years, and the United Conservatives resumed the position in 2019. Conservatism is undeniably a powerful ideological force in Alberta. But scholars have often reproduced this point without identifying precisely, or correctly, how extensive Alberta conservatism has been in areas beyond electoral politics and governance. Prairie historian Gerald Friesen, for example, has described Alberta—"and I do mean all Albertans, not just the government"—as a uniquely entrepreneurial and individualistic province serving nationally in the role of "the tempestuous little brother or sister who is not going to be hushed, thank you very much."[17] In another case, the political scientist Jared Wesley wrote in 2013 that, because of a mechanical process of hegemonic reproduction enabled by the provincial electoral system, "continued rule by the Progressive Conservatives, or some other right-wing party, seems inevitable in Alberta."[18] Conservative rule turned out not to be so inevitable after all, but the more important point is that scholars, like the media, have at times displayed a willingness to discuss Albertan political culture in too-simple, or near-mythical, terms.[19]

The period of conservative electoral dominance in Alberta emerged precisely when Canada and other western democracies were witnessing the normalization of social democracy and Keynesian economic governance in the aftermath of the Second World War. From the late 1930s and throughout the 1940s and beyond, Social Credit premiers William Aberhart and Ernest Manning encountered an exceptional mixture of global, national, and provincial conditions that rendered conservative politics practicable in Alberta just as they were becoming impracticable in much of the rest of Canada. That is, while the interwar crisis of the Canadian state was ameliorated by the emergence of a "national consensus which produced a modified version of the 'welfare state,'" Alberta bucked the trend.[20] The postwar decades in Alberta stand out in comparison because, while Manning governments spent heavily in the areas of health care and education thanks to windfall revenues from the development of the oil industry after 1947, this spending was done in such a way as to minimize its redistributional function.[21] When universal health care appeared on the national political stage in the 1960s, for example, Manning was among its most vociferous critics.

The entrepreneurial themes, free market rhetoric, and elevation of the individual subject that have fuelled conservative politics in Alberta may have looked unique as they emerged in the period after the Second World War, but ideas and practices of this kind have a long history of dominance across Canada, from the nineteenth century to the period of neoliberalism since the 1980s.[22] Stressing the dominance and the uniqueness of conservatism in Alberta can thus be misleading, isolating the province's history within the broader study of Canada's past. Indeed, the ideological and political differences between Alberta and other, ostensibly more progressive places in Canada are almost entirely matters of degree rather than kind. And insofar as Albertan conservatism is not as singular as most discourses suggest, provincial histories of resistance should capture the attention of anyone interested in the history or the present of counterhegemony in Canada. The chapters in this book need not be seen as narrowly provincial. Rather, the dissenters of this volume were participants in historical traditions that are also national and even international. Moreover, the preceding chapters represent only a few of the many activist histories of 1960s and 1970s Alberta. We hope that the essays and reflections gathered in this collection will inspire much more future research on activist stories in the province.

Resisting the myth of a wholly conservative Alberta is important not just for its scholarly and historiographical implications but even more so for its political implications in the present. Especially given the ongoing catastrophe of climate change and the ruthless austerity on display from governments in provinces across the country, interprovincial solidarity is urgently needed but too often, at least with Alberta, difficult to find. Because of the assumption that Albertans are so deeply and so widely conservative, an outlook notably associated with support for expanding the oil industry, people in other provinces disregard the possibility of solidaristic connection. Ongoing instances in the tradition of bucking conservatism thus might not get the recognition or the support they deserve. Such instances today include the work of groups like Idle No More and Sisters in Spirit vigils, both national movements fighting for land and water sovereignty and confronting the epidemic of violence against Indigenous women and girls in Canada, respectively.[23] But there are also local groups such as Neighbourhood Bridges Edmonton, which support community-building and activist initiatives among persons with intellectual disabilities; Climate Justice Edmonton, which have organized opposition to pipeline construction and oil sands expansion; the *Alberta Advantage*, a Calgary-based socialist podcast that offers brilliantly polemical analysis of Alberta's past and present (not to be confused with the Alberta Advantage Party, a group of disgruntled Wild Rose Party members); the Pro-Choice Society of Lethbridge & Southern Alberta, which advocates for safe and judgment-free reproductive and sexual health; the anonymous Handmaids in Lethbridge, who wear red costumes inspired by *The Handmaid's Tale* while silently protesting anti-abortion rhetoric in the city, spurring a province-wide movement; the many local chapters of Black Lives Matter across the province who raise awareness about anti-Black racism in their communities; Defend Alberta Parks which fights proposed provincial legislation that would close over 165 provincial parks in order that the land would be available for future resource extraction; and Indigenous Climate Action, an Indigenous-led climate action group that fights for Indigenous sovereignty, land, and water rights and promotes Indigenous-led climate justice.[24] These groups represent important and effective dissident movements in the country.

We both grew up in Alberta – like many of the contributors in this collection. And living in the province shaped who we are now; it is where our political consciousness – our feminist, socialist, environmentalist, anti-homophobic, anti-racist, anti-fascist, and anti-colonial consciousness – grew and developed under the big prairie skies. As history students, we sought a history that we could identify with and in too many cases we were left wanting. As emerging historians today, we hope that *Bucking Conservatism* disrupts that historiographical tradition. Additionally, we hope it offers a kind of handbook and source of inspiration for activists, and that it might help to establish a sense of belonging in a historical community for those who continue to fight and resist conservatism in the province.

In the days ahead, we hope this collection shows that Albertans can do more than wait for the next election. Resistance, dissent, and activism come in many forms and in many spaces. What is more, we hope that the stories of activism here stress the significance of community building. The conservative voices that the media and the historiography emphasize have found each other, they have organized, and they are loud. They hope to overwhelm the province by their loudness and by the furious pace with which they roll out the conservative political program. But while it is possible to feel overwhelmed individually, through solidarity and community it is possible to fight and win. The activists and other buckers described in this collection made change, sometimes small and sometimes not so small, in their own lives and in the lives of others just by the mere fact that they had other like-minded people around them. Find your people, build your community, and organize in solidarity with others. Continue to break down the myth that living in Alberta means you are resigned to a past and a future of conservatism.

NOTES

1. Alastair Sharp, "'How apropos': Jason Kenney Starts Mandate as Alberta's 18th Premier," *National Observer*, 30 April 2019, https://www.nationalobserver.com/2019/04/30/news/jason-kenney-sworn-albertas-18th-premier.

2. For the official election results, see "Provincial Results: Provincial General Election 16 April 2019," *Elections Alberta*, http://officialresults.elections.ab.ca/orResultsPGE.cfm?EventId=60.

3. Thirty-three of thirty-four Alberta MPs are Conservatives, one is a New Democrat.

4. There are no official statistics about the number of people involved in the convoy, but it is clear that it was far fewer than were involved in the climate strike around the province that day.

5. The UCP, and especially premier Kenney, have repeatedly promoted the idea that political agitation in support of environmentalist goals and against the fossil fuel industry has been the work of "foreign funded radicals." Indeed, the UCP funded a public inquiry into "anti-Alberta energy campaigns" to further investigate the issue. The inquiry was granted four deadline extensions, cost tax-payers approximately $3.5 million, and received substantial criticism. When the report was finally released, it found that only a small fraction of the funds committed to environmental initiatives in Canada were allocated towards protesting and shrinking the Alberta fossil fuel industry. Janet French, "Allan Inquiry Analysis Finds Less Than 5 Per Cent of Foreign Green Funds Targeted Alberta Oilsands," *CBC News*, 31 July 2021, https://www.cbc.ca/news/canada/edmonton/allan-inquiry-analysis-finds-less-than-5-per-cent-of-foreign-green-funds-targeted-alberta-oilsands-1.6125170.

6. Danica Ferris, "Over 1,000 People Gather for Black Lives Matter Protest in Lethbridge," *Global News*, 4 June 2020, https://globalnews.ca/news/7029219/lethbridge-indigenous-black-lives-matter-rally-racism-june/; Christa Doa, "Thousands March in Downtown Calgary as Part of Black Lives Matter Protest," *Global News*, 3 June 2020, https://globalnews.ca/video/7023963/thousands-march-in-downtown-calgary-as-part-of-black-lives-matter-protest; Kaylen Small, "'Cry for Freedom': Black Lives Matter Vigil in Calgary on Saturday," *Global News*, 6 June 2020, https://globalnews.ca/news/7033923/black-lives-matter-protest-calgary-june-6/; Nathalia Cordeau-Hilliard, "Hundreds Pack Jubilee Plaza for Solidarity March," *My McMurray*, 6 June 2020, https://www.mymcmurray.com/2020/06/06/hundreds-pack-jubilee-plaza-for-solidarity-march/; Sarah Rieger, "Small Alberta town's Black Lives Matter Demonstration Draws Hundreds Despite Racist Backlash," *CBC News*, 13 June 2020, https://www.cbc.ca/news/canada/calgary/innisfail-black-lives-matter-1.5611327; Liam Verster, "Black Lives Matter Protest Draws in Massive Crowd of Supporters," *Everything Grande Prairie*, 6 June 2020, https://everythinggp.com/2020/06/06/black-lives-matter-protest-draws-in-massive-crowd-of-supporters/; Josh Hall, "Hundreds Turn Out for Second Anti-Racism Protest in Red Deer,"*rdnewsNOW*, 5 June 2020, https://rdnewsnow.com/2020/06/05/hundreds-turn-out-for-second-anti-racism-protest-in-red-deer/; *Prairie*

Post, "Black Lives Matter March in Brooks," 10 June 2020, https://
www.prairiepost.com/alberta/black-lives-matter-march-in-brooks/
article_0ac6cb18-ab3b-11ea-bf91-8bc04b4b0e4b.html; Caley Ramsay and
Phil Heidenreich, "Over 15,000 People in Edmonton Gather for Equality
Rally at Alberta Legislature Grounds," *Global News*, 5 June 2020, https://
globalnews.ca/news/7030100/edmonton-equality-rally-alberta-legislature/.

7. See Albertans Reject Curriculum Facebook page here: https://www.
facebook.com/groups/353881362641844/. Also see: Allison Bench, "ATA Says
91% of Alberta Teachers Against Draft Curriculum, Doubts UCP Will Listen
to Critics," *Global News*, 9 April 2021, https://globalnews.ca/news/7747838/
ata-ucp-draft-curriculum-survey/; Stephen David Cook, "Teachers Assembly
Votes Non-Confidence in Alberta Education Minister," *CBC News*, 23 May
2021, https://www.cbc.ca/news/canada/edmonton/non-confidence-alberta-
teachers-1.6038125; Michael Franklin, "Alberta's Largest Public School Board
Won't Use Redesigned K-6 Curriculum," *CTV News*, 9 April 2021, https://
calgary.ctvnews.ca/alberta-s-largest-public-school-board-won-t-use-
redesigned-k-6-curriculum-1.5381953; Pamela Fieber, "CBE Will Not Test
Drive Controversial New Alberta Curriculum This Fall," *CBC News*, 10 April
2021, https://www.cbc.ca/news/canada/calgary/calgary-board-of-education-
will-not-participate-alberta-curriculum-1.5982490; Liam Verster, "Petition
for Alberta's Draft Curriculum Be Thrown Out Collects Over 11,700
Signatures," *Everything Grande Prairie*, 28 April 2021, https://everythinggp.
com/2021/04/28/petition-calling-for-albertas-draft-curriculum-be-thrown-
out-collects-over-11700-signatures/.

8. Caley Ramsey, "Health-care Workers Walk Off the Job in Wildcat Strike
Across Alberta: AUPE," *Global News*, 26 October 2020, https://globalnews.
ca/news/7422113/alberta-front-line-hospital-staff-walk-off-aupe/; *CTV News
Edmonton*, "Alberta Hospital Workers Walk Out to Protest Job Cuts Amid
COVID-19, AHS Calls Strike 'Illegal,'" 26 October 2020, https://edmonton.
ctvnews.ca/alberta-hospital-workers-walk-out-to-protest-job-cuts-amid-
covid-19-ahs-calls-strike-illegal-1.5160873; Carrie Tait, "Alberta Union
Leaders Plan Anti-UCP Campaign in Wake of Health Care Workers' Wildcat
Strike," *Globe and Mail*, 27 October 2020, https://www.theglobeandmail.
com/canada/alberta/article-alberta-union-leaders-plan-anti-ucp-campaign-
in-wake-of-health-care/.

9. Denise Balkissoon and Hannah Sung, hosts, "Episode 4: The Angel Complex:
How Canada Compares Itself to the U.S.," *Colour Code* (podcast), 26
September 2016, 0:02:32, https://www.theglobeandmail.com/news/national/
colour-code-podcast-race-in-canada/article31494658/.

10. "Canadians Brutally Roast All of Canada's Provinces and Territories One by One," *Narcity.com*, October 2017, https://www.narcity.com/life/canadians-brutally-roast-all-of-canadas-provinces-and-territories-one-by-one/3.

11. Rita Moir, interviewed by Karissa Patton, 7 October 2014, transcript. Interview housed at the Galt Museum and Archives, Lethbridge, Alberta, 20171019.

12. See Shannon Stettner, ""He Is Still Unwanted:" Women's Assertions of Authority over Abortion in Letters to the Royal Commission on the Status of Women in Canada," *CBMH* 29, no. 1 (2012): 151–71; Beth Palmer, "'Lonely, Tragic, but Legally Necessary Pilgrimages': Transnational Abortion Travel in the 1970s," *Canadian Historical Review* 92, no. 4 (2011): 637–64; Erika Dyck, "Sterilization and Birth Control in the Shadow of Eugenics: Married, Middle-Class Women in Alberta, 1930-1960s," *CBHM /BCHM* 31, no. 1 (2014): 165–87; Lianne McTavish, "Abortion in New Brunswick," *Acadiensis* 44, no. 2 (2015): 107–30; Valerie Korinek, *Prairie Fairies: A History of Queer Communities and People in Western Canada, 1930–1985* (Toronto: University of Toronto Press, 2018); Chris Bobel, "'I'm Not an Activist, Though I've Done a Lot of It': Doing Activism, Being Activist and the 'Perfect Standard' in a Contemporary Movement," *Social Movement Studies* 6, no. 2 (2007): 147–59.

13. Palmer, "'Lonely, Tragic,'" 664.

14. Grace J. M. W. Ouellette, *The Fourth World: An Indigenous Perspective on Feminism and Aboriginal Women's Activism* (Halifax: Fernwood, 2004), 42.

15. See Shannon Stettner, "'We Are Forced to Declare War': Linkages Between the 1970 Abortion Caravan and Women's Anti-Vietnam War Activism," *Social History/Historie Sociale* 46, no. 92 (2013): 423–41.

16. The Marxist historian Domenico Losurdo, thinking with the help of Alexis de Toqueville, describes the concept of counter-history, in simple terms, as history that focuses on developments that have "hitherto been largely and unjustly ignored." See Losurdo, *Liberalism: A Counter-History* (London: Verso, 2014), vii.

17. Gerald Friesen, *The West: Regional Ambitions, National Debates, Global Age* (Toronto: Penguin, 1999), 84, 86. Perhaps Friesen should get the benefit of some doubt, as the book we quote from here was written for a popular press and, presumably, a popular audience. Still, we don't think we can extend as much leeway as these claims need to pass muster.

18. Jared J. Wesley, "Defining Prairie Politics: Campaigns, Codes, and Cultures," in *Place and Replace: Essays on Western Canada*, ed. Adele Perry, Esyllt W. Jones, and Leah Morton (Winnipeg: University of Manitoba Press, 2013), 314.

19. While the emphasis here is on troublesome aspects of this historiography, there are also, of course, excellent histories and historians of Alberta. The

quality and durability of Alvin Finkel's work on the Social Credit period stands out to each of us as exceptional and noteworthy. See Finkel, *The Social Credit Phenomenon in Alberta* (Toronto: University of Toronto Press, 1989).

20. Finkel, *Social Credit Phenomenon*, 4.

21. For more on this issue of government spending and redistribution, see (former Woodsworth-Irvine Socialist Fellowship member) Ed Shaffer, "The Political Economy of Oil in Alberta," in *Essays on the Political Economy of Alberta*, ed. David Leadbeater (Toronto: New Hogtown Press, 1984).

22. See Ian McKay, "The Liberal Order Framework: A Prospectus for a Reconnaissance of Canadian History," *Canadian Historical Review* 81 (2000): 617–45; and Donald Gutstein, *Harperism: How Stephen Harper and His Think Tank Colleagues Have Transformed Canada* (Toronto: Lorimer, 2014).

23. See the Idle No More website, http://www.idlenomore.ca; and "Sisters in Spirit," Alberta.ca, https://www.alberta.ca/sisters-in-spirit.aspx.

24. See the Neighbourhood Bridges website, http://www.neighborhoodbridges. ca/; the Climate Justice Edmonton website, https://climatejusticeedmonton. com/; the Alberta Advantage Podcast website, https://albertaadvantagepod. com; and the Pro-Choice Society of Lethbridge and Southern Alberta website, https://www.prochoiceyql.ca. For more on the Handmaids, see Drew Anderson, "Lethbridge Transit Anti-abortion Ads to be Pulled," *CBC News*, 4 April 2018, https://www.cbc.ca/news/canada/calgary/ lethbridge-abortion-ads-removed-1.4605284; Clair Theobald, "United by Social Media, a Growing Number of Handmaids Emboldened by Recent Abortion Opposition," *The Star*, 10 May 2018; Phil Heidenreich, "Pro-life Rally Attracts Hundreds of People to Alberta Legislature Grounds," *Global News*, 9 May 2018, https://globalnews.ca/news/5260884/march-for-life- alberta-legislature-abortion/; and Sean McIntosh, "Alberta Handmaids in Red Deer," *Red Deer Advocate*, 6 May 2018. See Black Lives Matter Edmonton's website, https://blmyeg.ca/; Black Lives Matter YYC's Facebook page, https://www.facebook.com/BLMYYC; Defend Alberta Parks website, https://defendabparks.ca/; Indigenous Climate Action website, https://www. indigenousclimateaction.com/.

Contributors

Kevin Allen is a fourth-generation Calgarian who has been documenting and profiling queer people and events for more than thirty years. Kevin started the Calgary Gay History Project in 2012 to uncover and preserve stories from Calgary's LGBTQ2 past (www.calgarygayhistory.ca). The project has achieved national recognition and led to the award-winning documentary film *Gross Indecency: The Everett Klippert Story* and the best-selling book *Our Past Matters: Stories of Gay Calgary* (2018).

Leon Crane Bear is Niitsitapi (Blackfoot) from Siksika Nation—one of five First Nations who signed Treaty 7. In 2015, Leon received his master's degree from the University of Lethbridge. He currently resides in Siksika.

Erin Gallagher-Cohoon is a PhD candidate in the Department of History at Queen's University, where she explores the history of queer parenting and queer family formation in Canada. Her master's thesis analyzed the United States Public Health Service's Sexually Transmitted Disease Inoculation Study, a 1940s human experiment that deliberately exposed vulnerable populations, including female sex workers, in Guatemala to syphilis and gonorrhea.

Corinne George is Gidimt'en (Bear) of the Witsuwit'en Nation. She was born and raised in Telkwa and Smithers, BC by her parents Gallahgun (Rita George) and Tsaybesa (the late Andrew George Sr.). She descends from a long line of Witsuwit'en hereditary chiefs and elected leaders. She holds a master's degree in history from the University of Calgary where she completed her thesis: "'If I Didn't Do Something, My Spirit Would Die. . . .': Grassroots Activism of Aboriginal Women in Calgary and Edmonton,

1951–1985." Corinne is the Regional Principal of the College of New Caledonia, Lakes District Campus, in Burns Lake, British Columbia.

Larry Hannant is an adjunct associate professor in the Department of History at the University of Victoria and a writer who specializes in dissent, state repression, and human rights in the twentieth century. His most recent book is *All My Politics Are Poetry* (Yalla Press, 2019).

Nevena Ivanović is a former volunteer researcher at the Calgary Gay History Project. She serves as the public policy coordinator of the Women's Centre of Calgary. Before coming to Calgary from her hometown of Belgrade, Serbia, Nevena worked to support and empower women in politics, build the capacity of other gender equality advocates, and influence public policies to reflect women's needs and experiences. She has a master's degree in public policy and gender and culture and is the co-author of a study on the gender pay gap in three Western Balkan countries.

Tom Langford is professor emeritus of sociology at the University of Calgary and the author of "It Takes A Village. The Case for Universal Daycare," which appeared in *Alberta Views* in October 2016 (https://albertaviews.ca/it-takes-a-village). He welcomes correspondence at langford@ucalgary.ca.

Tarisa Dawn Little is a PhD candidate at the University of Saskatchewan and a White-female settler born and raised in Calgary, Alberta (Treaty 7 Territory and the original territory of the Blackfoot Confederacy). She now lives with her spouse beside the Grasse River, in Canton, New York, an area long occupied by the Iroquois Confederacy.

Ken Novakowski attended the University of Alberta from 1962 to 1967 and in 1965 he joined the Alberta Young New Democrats (AYND) and Alberta NDP. He served as president of the AYND (1965–67), and of the Federal New Democratic Youth (1967–69), was a general vice-president of the Alberta NDP (1967–69), and chaired the left wing Alberta NDP caucus, the Waffle (1969–71). He also chaired the Edmonton Committee to End the War in Vietnam (1967–70). In 1971, he moved to British Columbia where he remained active in the NDP. As a teacher, he was president of the BC Teachers' Federation (1989–92), co-founder of the BC Office of the Canadian Centre for

Policy Alternatives (1997), and executive director of the BCTF from 2000 to 2009. In his retirement, Ken served as the chair of the BC Labour Heritage Centre (2013–19).

Jan Olson is an anthropologist and archaeologist with over thirty years of experience studying Latin America. She teaches anthropology at the University of Alberta and MacEwan University and serves on the board of Alberta Heritage Resources Foundation. More recently, she has worked on oral histories and community development in Edmonton. Her book, *Scona Lives: A History of Riverlots 13, 15, and 17* (2016), focuses on this local history. Jan acts as a land steward in Keepers of the Creek and engages in music and heritage as community building where she lives near Edmonton's Mill Creek Ravine.

Karissa Robyn Patton is a postdoctoral fellow at Vancouver Island University studying histories of gender, health, and activism in mid-twentieth century Canada. She earned her PhD at the University of Saskatchewan, where her dissertation won the 2020–21 University of Saskatchewan Graduate Dissertation Award for Fine Arts and Humanities. Her doctoral research examined reproductive health activism in southern Alberta during the 1970s. A contributor to the volume, *Compelled to Act: Histories of Women's Activism in Western Canada* (edited by Sarah Carter and Nanci Langford), her work can also be found in the *Canadian Bulletin of Medical History*.

Mack Penner, born and raised in Lethbridge, Alberta, is a PhD candidate, Social Sciences and Humanities Research Council Doctoral Fellow, and Dr. Harry Lyman Hooker Senior Doctoral Fellow in the Department of History at McMaster University. His primary research interests include the history of capitalism, neoliberalism, and Canada in the twentieth century. His dissertation work looks at the intellectual history of the Calgary School from a transnational vantage.

Winner of the Queen's Diamond Jubilee Medal and the Billington Award for lifetime contribution to the Alberta film industry, **Tom Radford**'s career spans forty-five years in the Canadian television and film industries as a writer, director, and producer. Born in Edmonton to a Pulitzer Prize–winning newspaper family that came to Alberta in 1905, Tom has carried on a tradition of portraying the distinctive character of the West and North to Canada and the world. He has won the best director prize at the Alberta Film Awards on eight separate occasions, and his films have received ten national and international honours. Tom Radford is a member of the Order of Canada.

Baldwin Reichwein administered provincial social program services in Alberta from 1961 to 1990. His research focus is the history of public welfare and child welfare services in Alberta. He is the recipient of the Canadian Association of Social Workers Distinguished Service Award and co-author (with Gillian Hestad) of *Answering Children's Cries: Child Saving in Lethbridge 1900–1947* (2016).

PearlAnn Reichwein is a professor and historian at the University of Alberta who writes on Canada's western prairie and mountain regions and teaches in the Faculty of Kinesiology, Sport, and Recreation. She is the author of *Climber's Paradise: Making Canada's Mountain Parks, 1906–1974*, which was awarded the Canadian Historical Association's Clio Prize, as well as an IndieFAB Honourable Mention for Environment and Ecology. She is the co-editor (with Karen Fox) of *Mountain Diaries: The Alpine Adventures of Margaret Fleming, 1929–1980* and the co-author (with Karen Wall) of *Uplift: Visual Culture at the Banff School of Fine Arts*, tracing the origins of today's Banff Centre for Arts and Creativity. She has worked in urban parks, national parks, and UNESCO World Heritage Sites. A visiting researcher, she also lectures and teaches in France and Austria. Her leadership for parks and heritage focuses on conservation advocacy.

Jennifer E. Salahub is a professor emerita of art and craft history at the Alberta University of the Arts. Her BFA and MA in Canadian art history were awarded by Concordia University, Montréal, and she received a PhD in the history of design from the Royal College of Art, London. Her long-standing interest in decoration and ornament is reflected in her academic and personal life. In 2018, she was the recipient of the Tom McFall Honour Award in recognition of her "significant contribution to Alberta's Fine Craft culture." She writes and lectures internationally on art, craft, and design.

Louise Swift was born in 1930 in Rossland, British Columbia, and moved to Edmonton in 1960, where she quickly became involved in the activist community. In the fall of 1964, she and her husband moved into a house shared by the Van Alderwegan, the Van Stolk, and the Swift families. Louise became involved in the anti-nuclear movement through her association with Mary Van Stolk and the Canadian Campaign for Nuclear Disarmament. Louise was a member of the Canadian Voice of Women and a founding member of Save Tomorrow, Oppose Pollution (STOP).